D1258943

Tracking Strategies

Tracking Strategies

...Toward a General Theory

Henry Mintzberg

OXFORD
UNIVERSITY PRESS

OXFORD
UNIVERSITY PRESS

Great Clarendon Street, Oxford OX2 6DP

Oxford University Press is a department of the University of Oxford.
It furthers the University's objective of excellence in research, scholarship,
and education by publishing worldwide in

Oxford New York

Auckland Cape Town Dar es Salaam Hong Kong Karachi
Kuala Lumpur Madrid Melbourne Mexico City Nairobi
New Delhi Shanghai Taipei Toronto

With offices in

Argentina Austria Brazil Chile Czech Republic France Greece
Guatemala Hungary Italy Japan Poland Portugal Singapore
South Korea Switzerland Thailand Turkey Ukraine Vietnam

Oxford is a registered trademark of Oxford University Press
in the UK and in certain other countries

Published in the United States
by Oxford University Press Inc., New York

© Oxford University Press 2007

The moral rights of the authors have been asserted
Database right Oxford University Press (maker)

First published 2007

British Library Cataloguing in Publication Data

Data available

Library of Congress Cataloging in Publication Data

Tracking: strategies: toward a general theory of strategy formation / edited by
Henry Mintzberg.
    p. cm.
  Includes bibliographical references and index.
  ISBN-13: 978-0-19-922850-8
  1. Strategic planning. I. Mintzberg, Henry.
  HD30.28.T72 2007

  658.4'012—dc22   2007025756

Typeset by SPI Publisher Services, Pondicherry, India
Printed in Great Britain
on acid-free paper by
Biddles Ltd., King's Lynn, Norfolk

ISBN 978-0-19-922850-8

1 3 5 7 9 10 8 6 4 2

ACKNOWLEDGMENTS

Acknowledgment is made to the following for permission to adapt the following material:

The Institute for Operations Research and the Management Sciences, 7240 Parkway Drive, Suite 310, Hanover, MD 21076 USA (Chapter 2, adapted from *Management Science*, 1978 © 1978).

The Academy of Management (Chapter 3, adapted from *The Academy of Management Journal*, 25:3, 1982 © 1982).

Chapter 4 adapted from 'Strategy Formation in an Adhocracy: The National Film Board of Canada, 1939–1975' by Mintzberg and McHugh published in *Administrative Science Quarterly*, 1985 by permission of Johnson Graduate School of Management, Cornell University, © Johnson Graduate School of Management, Cornell University.

Pearson Education for Chapter 5 adapted from Lamb, R. B, 'Competitive Strategic Management' 1st Edition, © 1984, Pgs. 63–93, and Figure 11.7, originally published in Henry Mintzberg: 'Structuring of Organizations', 1st Edition, © 1979. Reprinted by permission of Pearson Education Inc., Upper Saddle River, NJ.

JAI Press (Chapter 6, adapted from *Advances in Strategic Management*, vol. 4, 1986, Chapter 9, adapted from *Strategic Management Frontiers*, edited by John H. Grant, 1988, and Chapter 11, adapted from *Management Laureates: A Collection of Biographical Essays, Volume II*, edited by S. Bedeian, 1993).

Administrative Sciences Association of Canada (Chapter 7, adapted from 'Tracking Strategies in the Birthplace of Canadian Tycoons: The Sherbrokke Record, 1946–1976' by Henry Mintzberg, William D. Taylor, and James A. Waters, *Canadian Journal of Administrative Sciences*, 1984, Chapter 8, adapted from 'Mirroring Canadian Industrial Policy: Strategy Formation at Dominion Textile, 1873–1990' by Barbara Austin and

Acknowledgments

Henry Mintzberg, *Canadian Journal of Administrative Sciences*, 1996, and Chapter 10, adapted from 'Strategic Management Upside Down: Tracking Strategies at McGill University, 1829–1980' by Henry Mintzberg and Jan Rose, *Canadian Journal of Administrative Sciences*, 2003, all © Administrative Sciences Association of Canada).

The American Accounting Association (Figure 11.6, originally published in *The Nature of Managerial Work* by Frank M. Wolf, 1973). Many AAA articles are available online at http://www.atypon-link.com/action/showPublisherJournals?code=AAA.

There are instances where we have been unable to contact the copyright holder. If notified, the publisher will be pleased to rectify any errors or omissions at the earliest opportunity.

Contents

Contents

List of Figures

List of Figures

List of Strategy Diagrams

List of Tables

1

Of Strategies, Deliberate and Emergent

In the early 1970s, I began a research project that was 'intended to run for another three to five years' (Mintzberg 1972: 1). In fact, it ran into the 1990s, really until now, counting this book. The stimulus was a sentence I read in a book by Herbert Simon, the preeminent thinker in the field of management: 'The series of ... decisions which determines behavior over some stretch of time may be called a *strategy*' (1957: 67; see Barnard, 1938: 231, from which Simon may have developed this idea).

I was intrigued. If strategies could be, not only implemented after being 'formulated', but also be *defined* by behaviors, as they 'form', we would have a way to study the process empirically.

To that point, there had been a good deal of writing about strategy and some rather simple theory about how it was supposed to be formulated, but hardly any systematic investigation about how strategies actually develop in practice. As I wrote back then, 'so long as we viewed strategy as an explicit, a priori set of guidelines, we were restricted to studying strategy-making in abstract, normative terms'—short, of course, of being able to get inside the head of the strategist (something that remains difficult to do). But with Simon's definition, we could study strategies as 'evolved, a posteriori results of decision-making behavior' (1972: 1).

Strategy as Pattern in Actions

The implication of Simon's idea was that strategy is *pattern*: consistency in behavior over time. So what better way to study strategies, and the processes by which they develop, than to uncover patterns in organizations and investigate their origins.

Thus I begin by defining strategy, or at least what came to be called *realized* strategy, as a pattern in a stream of decisions. But as my colleagues and I studied such patterns, we realized that we were not studying streams of decisions at all, but of actions, because those are the traces more clearly left behind in organizations (e.g. stores opened in a supermarket chain, projects worked on in an architectural firm). Decisions were implied by these actions, but these, in and of themselves, proved much more difficult to track down. If a decision is a '*commitment* to action' (Mintzberg, Raisinghani, and Theorêt 1976), the trace it leaves behind can range from a clear statement of intent—as in the recorded minute of a meeting—to nothing.

In using the original definition, we made the implicit assumption that decision inevitably precedes action: if an organization *did* something, it must have previously *decided* to do so. As Barnard (1938: 102–3) suggested, it was just a matter of tracking the decision down. But, on reflection, another interpretation presented itself: the relationship between decision and action can be far more tenuous than almost all the literature of organization theory suggests (Mintzberg and Waters 1990: 1–2; Weick [1979] being one notable exception).

An automobile company introduced a new model. That was clear enough. But when was the decision made: when the board approved it, when the executive committee minuted it, or when the product development team finalized it. One story going around Europe some years ago was that the senior management of a major European automobile company had hired consultants to find out who decided to introduce a particular new model. Evidentially it was not their decision. Did the consultants find out? What if it was no one's decision? What if some stylist was playing with a mock-up of some model; an engineer saw it and started considering the design consequences; others followed, and a few years and thousands of decisions and actions later, the new car appeared?

In other words, must decision always precede action? We answer that question every time we get hit on the knee, just as do the courts of law every time they convict someone of second-degree murder (essentially action with decision, at least prior, explicit decision).

Without, however, needing to answer that question, it became evident that we should have been, and indeed were, studying streams of actions, and then, in investigating their origins, considering the decisions, and a great deal more, that lay behind them.

Figure 1.1a Strategy as plan

Figure 1.1b Strategy as pattern

Strategy as Plan Intended

Look up 'strategy' in any dictionary, or in almost any of the thousands of books and articles on the subject, and you will not find Simon's definition. There is clear consensus on what that word means, and it is not pattern, but *plan*, in one form or another, that is, some intentions for the future. (Figure 1.1 depicts this, compared with strategy as pattern.) As I wrote this, I pulled out my *Paperback Oxford English Dictionary*, prominently marked 'new' (2002), and read as the first definition of strategy: 'A plan designed to achieve a particular long-term aim' (p. 829).

Clear enough. Yet if you ask managers, as I have done many times, to describe not the strategy that their company intends, according to the usual definition, but 'the strategy their company has actually pursued, over the past, say, five years', they respond readily. In fact, I have asked

3

this immediately after requesting them to define the word, which they almost always do as found in the dictionary. In other words, we are perfectly willing to use the word in a way that we do not define it. We may *think* of strategy as plan, but we are perfectly happy to *see* strategy as pattern.

Consider the managers of a company seeking to understand the strategy of a competitor. They may not have access to its thinking, but they can observe its actions. So they infer its strategy from them, as pattern, even if they assume that behind this lies a plan. The press does much the same thing with the 'policies' of a government. To use an example from my initial paper:

When Richard Nixon, early in his term of office, made a number of decisions that appeared to favor the voters of the South (appointment of Supreme Court justices from the South, actions on School integration, etc.), the press coined the term 'Southern Strategy'. What did they mean: simply that, in spite of the fact that Nixon never announced such a strategy, there appeared to be a pattern in his decisions. (p. 1)

Strategies as Deliberate and Emergent

The interesting question, much like that concerning whether decision must lie behind action, is whether plan must lie behind pattern: because there is pattern, must there necessarily have been plan? In other words, must strategies always be *deliberate*? Or can they *emerge*: that is, can patterns just form out of individual actions?

I have investigated these questions too with the managers. After asking them to think about the strategy their company actually pursued over the last five years, I asked them to think back to the strategy their company intended five years ago. Then came the key question: 'Was the strategy the company actually pursued the same as it intended?' I have offered three choices: (1) yes, more or less; (2) no, more or less; (3) something in between. Inevitably there have been a few yes's, usually fewer but some nos, and an overwhelming majority of somethings in between.

Controlling and Learning

What was going on here? Why is such a widely accepted definition, not to mention its pervasive use in the management literature, so casually ignored when people are faced with a few questions about reality?

The answer, I believe, lies in the fact that here, as in so much else in management, we allow the myths to dominate what we know about reality. We know how important is learning in management, but we are mesmerized by the myth of control. That, in fact, is how the word management originated. In its earliest usage, it meant the handling of horses. And once Henri Fayol, the French industrialist, published his book in 1916, management came to mean planning, organizing, coordinating, commanding, and controlling—arguably five words for controlling.

And so too do we prefer to think about strategy in this way. As this word has been so long and so insistently used in the literature, especially that of 'strategic planning', senior managers are supposed to 'formulate' their strategies so that everyone else can 'implement' them. The senior management thinks, the others do (as they are told). But where is learning in all this? Are the others not allowed to learn? Can no one else contribute to strategy? Indeed, is the senior management itself not allowed to learn after it has formulated its strategy?

If deliberate strategy is about control, then emergent strategy is about learning. It suggests that anyone, so-called formulators and implementers alike, can learn their way into strategies—action by action, perhaps also decision by decision. Indeed, strategies can form without people even realizing it, although they may recognize these strategies once they have formed.

It is certainly difficult to imagine an organization where management seeks to exercise no control over the strategy process. But should it be any less difficult to imagine an organization whose people engage in no learning along the way? That is why I get from those managers the answers I do: almost every sensible real-life strategy process combines emergent learning with deliberate control. Purely emergent strategies may be rare—they imply no control. But hardly less rare are purely deliberate strategies—they imply no learning—even though that is what most of the literature prescribes.

So our research set out to study, not just strategy formulation (deliberate), but also strategy formation (also emergent). We did not see the latter not seen as some kind of adjunct to the former, but as an equal partner in the process—as will became evident in this book. Figure 1.2 depicts this, with the basic concepts behind this research. It shows strategies as intended plans, before action, and strategies as realized patterns, out of actions. When the intentions are realized in the actions, more or less, the

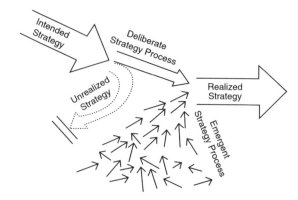

Figure 1.2 Forms of strategy

strategy is shown as deliberate. Intentions not realized are shown as such. And when the pattern realized in actions was not intended, the strategy is shown as emergent.

Strategies along a Continuum

Jim Waters joined me on much of this research, after the early studies. He questioned the label I was using at the time, 'retroactive strategy', and that is how we came to use the word 'emergent'. It is sad that we lost Jim some years ago, and that I cannot be doing this book with him.

In 1985, the two of us published a paper entitled 'Of Strategies, Deliberate and Emergent' (Mintzberg and Waters 1985). It viewed the strategy formation process along a continuum, anchored by deliberate strategies on one end and emergent strategies on the other, with real-world strategies in between. We described perfectly deliberate strategies as having to satisfy these conditions:

First, there must have existed precise intentions in the organization, articulated in a relatively concrete level of detail, so that there can be no doubt about what was desired before any actions were taken. Secondly, because organization means collective action, to dispel any possible doubt about whether or not the intentions were organizational, they must have been common to virtually all the actors: either shared as their own or else accepted from leaders, probably in response to some sort of controls. Thirdly, these collective intentions must have been realized exactly as intended, which means that no external force (market, technological, political, etc.) could have interfered with them. The environment, in other words, must have been either perfectly predictable, totally benign, or else under the full control of the organization. These three conditions constitute a tall order, so that we are unlikely to find any perfectly deliberate strategies in organizations. Nevertheless, some strategies do come rather close, in some dimensions if not all.

As for perfectly emergent strategies:

There must be order—consistently in action over time—in the absence of intention about it. (No consistency means no strategy, or at least unrealized strategy—intentions not met.) It is difficult to imagine action in the *total* absence of intention—in some pocket of the organization if not from the leadership itself—such that we would expect the purely emergent strategy to be as rare as the purely deliberate one. But again, our research suggests that some patterns come rather close, as when an environment directly imposes a pattern of action on an organization.

We then introduced eight 'ideal types' of strategies along this continuum, as follows:

- **Planned Strategies**: originate in formal plans—precise intentions exist, formulated and articulated by central leadership, backed up by formal controls to ensure surprise-free implementation in benign, controllable, or predictable environment; strategies most deliberate

- **Entrepreneurial Strategies**: originate in central vision—intentions exist as personal, unarticulated vision of single leader, and so adaptable to new opportunities; organization under personal control of leader and located in protected niche in environment; strategies relatively deliberate but can emerge

- **Ideological Strategies**: originate in shared beliefs—intentions exist as collective vision of all actors, in inspirational form and relatively immutable, controlled normatively through indoctrination and/or socialization; organization often proactive vis-à-vis environment; strategies rather deliberate

- **Umbrella Strategies**: originate in constraints—leadership, in partial control of organizational actions, defines strategic boundaries or targets within which other actors respond to own forces or to complex, perhaps also unpredictable environment; strategies partly deliberate, partly emergent, and deliberately emergent

- **Process Strategies**: originate in process—leadership controls process aspects of strategy (hiring, structure, etc.), leaving content aspects to other actors; strategies partly deliberate, partly emergent (and, again, deliberately emergent)

- **Unconnected Strategies**: originate in enclaves—actor(s) loosely coupled to rest of organization produce(s) patterns in own actions in absence of, or in direct contradiction to, central or common intentions; strategies organizationally emergent whether or not deliberate for actor(s)

- **Consensus Strategies**: originate in consensus—through mutual adjustment, actors converge on patterns that become pervasive in absence of central or common intentions; strategies rather emergent

- **Imposed Strategies**: originate in environment—environment dictates patterns in actions either through direct imposition or through implicitly preempting or bounding organizational choice; strategies most emergent, although may be internalized by organization and made deliberate

As we go along, we shall see some modification in these types. But for the most part they help to elaborate and enrich the concepts of deliberate and emergent strategies as used in this book.

Strategies as Positions and Perspectives

A paper I published in 1987, entitled 'Five Ps for Strategy' (Mintzberg 1987*b*), extended these first two definitions about process (plan, pattern), to ones about content.

I have asked managers another question: 'Was Egg McMuffin, McDonald's breakfast in a bun, a strategic change for the company?' Almost always, some say yes and others say no. Yes, they say, because it was a new product and new market (breakfasts); no, because it was still the McDonald's way. This suggests that some managers, like Michael Porter (1980), see strategy as *position*, and others, like Peter Drucker ('theory of the business' [1970: 5]), see it as *perspective* (Figure 1.3). Both are right: it is just a matter of definition.

Out of this came what I call 'the Egg McMuffin Syndrome' (Figure 1.4), to compare changing a position with changing a perspective. Changing a position within perspective (Egg McMuffin) is relatively easy: doing new things in the accustomed way. Changing a position together with a perspective is another matter ('McDuckling a l'Orange' anyone?), simply because perspectives are deeply rooted in organizations, in their cultures. Indeed, even having to change a perspective in order to retain a

Figure 1.3a Strategy as position (Michael Porter)

Figure 1.3b Strategy as perspective (Peter Drucker: theory of the business)

position—that is, to keep the same customers in the same markets, as some bookstore chains have had to do to meet the competition from Amazon—can be extremely difficult.

A fifth definition, also in popular usage for strategy, is a *ploy*: a maneuver to confront a competitor or opponent. But this has not figured in our research, because while a ploy may be a strategy of sorts, it is not necessarily *strategic*, in the sense of being of overriding importance.

Four Processes of Strategy Formation

Combing the four basic Ps, as shown in Figure 1.5, reveals the four basic processes of strategy formation that are central to the findings of

Strategy as Perspective

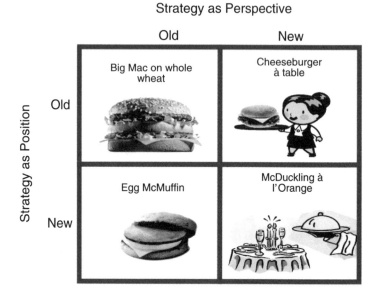

Figure 1.4 The Egg McMuffin syndrome

this book:

- Deliberate plans about tangible positions are closest to the notion of **Strategic Planning**, and most evidentially associated with the writings of Michael Porter.

- Deliberate plans in the form of a broad perspective relate to **Strategic Visioning**, as in Peter Drucker's 'theory of the business' mentioned above.

Strategy Process as

Strategy Content as			Deliberate Plan	Emergent Patterns
	Tangible Positions		Strategic Planning	Strategic Venturing
	Broad Perspective		Strategic Visioning	Strategic Learning

Figure 1.5 Four processes of strategy formation

- Emergent patterns manifested as tangible positions can be called **Strategic Venturing**, as described in the research of Robert Burgelman (e.g. 1983*a*).

- Emergent patterns that result in a broad perspective can be described as **Strategic Learning**, as in the notion of 'sense-making' developed by Karl Weick (1979).

Tracking Strategies

Our definition of strategy as pattern dictated the nature of this research, outlined below and detailed in the Appendix. We tracked strategies in organizations across long periods of time—always decades, usually many, in one case a century and a half.

First we identified key areas of action, for example, the introduction of new products, the building of new facilities, the acquisition of other organizations. Then we identified the actions taken in each area across the whole period, collected into a 'chronology record'. We also developed a chronology of the key events and trends in the environment. In one study—US strategy in Vietnam—these two records together numbered 101 pages. (One page of this is reproduced in Figure 1.6, as an example.) We also collected data on the performance of the organization. From the chronology records of the actions, we inferred patterns, that is consistencies in action, as strategies.

This part of the research was largely archival, making use of annual reports, catalogs, personal records, books and articles about the organization, etc.—virtually any source that revealed its actions.

We then sought to depict these strategies in symbolic form along a timescale (except in the earliest studies), for example as a triangle sloping upward to depict growth in store openings. This enabled us to line up on a big sheet an organization's strategies along a common timescale (see the example in Figure 1.7). By scanning this up and down, we could infer periods in the history of the organization, for example, of continuity, when few strategies were changing, or of global change, when many were doing so. We wrote these up as a strategic history of the organization.

At this point, the nature of the research changed. The history directed us to what seemed to be the key turning points in the organization, and around these, we conducted interviews, where possible, and sought more in-depth materials to help explain what had happened and why.

US DECISIONS & ACTIONS	1965	EXTERNAL EVENTS
At Johns Hopkins, Johnson stresses willingness to negotiate and suggests 1 billion aid program for SE Asia.	4/7	
	4/8	USSR proposes Cambodian neutrality conference.
	4/11	NVN officials denounce Johnson offer.
	4/12	Gordon Walker unsuccessful in UK attempts to meet officials in Hanoi and Peiking.
US urges Hanoi to consider plea of 17 nonaligned nations.	4/14	
Secretary Rusk–Cambodia parley.	4/23	
More troops arrive.	5/3	
	5/3	Cambodia breaks diplomatic relations with US.
Johnson requests 700 million supplemental appropriation.	5/4	
House approves request 408 to 7.	5/5	
SEATO condemns Comm. aggression in SVN.	5/5	
Senate passes appropriation 88 to 3.	5/6	
More troops activated.	5/7	
	5/12	Red China calls for preparation for war (atomic).

Figure 1.6 Example of chronology record in the study of US strategy in Vietnam

Once all this was completed, with the strategies as well as the periods and their explanations written up, we engaged in brainstorming sessions, usually with several members of the research team, sometimes others as well, to explain our findings in conceptual terms, and thereby move toward theories about the strategy formation process. The questions that guided us included:

(a) What are the patterns of strategic change over time (e.g. life cycles)?
(b) What are the relationships between deliberate and emergent strategies?
(c) What is the interplay between the forces of leadership, organization, and environment in the strategy formation process?

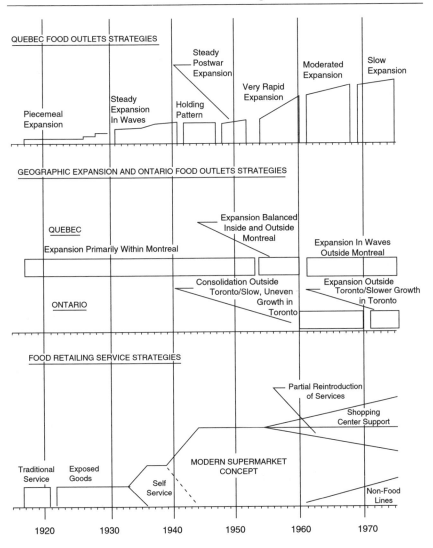

Figure 1.7 Example of strategies depicted

The Studies Reported

Many studies were carried out using this method. A number were small, undertaken as course papers by students, etc., and are not reported in this book. It presents eleven that were more extensive, most under my own supervision, often together with Jim Waters. Many of these were supported by a research grant from the Social Science and Humanities Research Council of Canada. All have been published in one place or another, all but two coauthored or multiple-authored, five of them with Jim Waters, and others who were extensively involved in the research. In two cases (Dominion Textile and the *Sherbrooke Record*), the studies were associated with doctoral dissertations.

These studies are presented here more or less as originally published. This means that the reports sometimes vary in the detail provided and the format of presentation, since the research method was elaborated as we went along, especially after the earliest studies. And in the brainstorming, each study was allowed to speak for itself—we were not testing preconceived hypothesis, but seeking to generate rich theory. The questions addressed may have been common, but the answers sought were not. They allowed for comparison, which provided the basis of the theory developed in the final chapter.

Except for Chapter 2, which presents briefly and compares the first two studies that were done, on Volkswagenwerk, the automobile company, and US strategy in Vietnam (the only study of a political strategy), each chapter presents a single study in considerable detail. These chapters come more or less in the order that they were carried out (but not of the periods of time they covered). They include Steinberg Inc. (a large retail chain), the National Film Board of Canada, Canadian Lady (an undergarment manufacturer), Air Canada, the *Sherbrooke Record* (a small daily newspaper), Dominion Textile (a large producer of textiles), Arcop (a small architectural firm), McGill University, and a professor at McGill University.

The organizations obviously differed significantly—the sample was chosen for this purpose—and so do the conclusions drawn about their strategies and processes. Most notably, as we shall see, is the influence of the form of organization—seen as machine, entrepreneurial, adhocracy, and professional (Mintzberg 1983c, 1989: section II). Yet there proved to be some interesting consistencies among these variations, as we shall see in Chapter 12. Entitled 'Toward General Theory of Strategy Formation', it considers first these differences, especially in terms of the form of organization, onto which map well the four processes introduced earlier (planning, visioning, learning, and venturing). This chapter then considers the similarities, along strategic life cycles in the development of organizations. The book closes with a few words on 'crafting strategy'.

History Lives

One final word. These studies were completed some time ago. While all have been published, they have appeared in many different publications, some not widely distributed. This book brings them together, and addresses their findings together, for the first time. [1]

Does the fact that all these studies ended some time ago—in the 1970s and 1980s, in two cases in the 1990s—negate their usefulness? I believe not. This book is about the personal and social processes of strategy formation. These hardly change over time. While their trappings may be affected by new techniques and fads, the underlying human processes—personal thinking, social interacting, learning from experience, etc.—do not.

Moreover, the findings of this book indicate that long periods of time are needed to understand how strategies form and reform in organizations; not uncommonly did we find several decades of strategic stability. This means that a company today may not have changed its basic strategy—its strategic perspective, if not its various positions—for years (e.g. an IKEA or a Toyota), and may not do so for years hence. So why should the 2000 decade be more important than, say, the 1980s, or the 1890s for that matter? When it comes to trying to understand basic processes of human change, one decade is as good as another. To take a currently pointed example, is US strategy in Vietnam any less important for potential learning than US strategy in Iraq? (Read about the former in Chapter 2, and you may conclude exactly the opposite.) Are the changes in Volkswagenwerk in the 1970s any less revealing because they took place then and not now?

Indeed, the more recent the events, the more likely that researchers have been involved in them, emotionally if not personally, and so the more likely that their findings will be distorted.

We certainly hear a great deal about change these days. Has not, therefore, the pace of strategic change itself changed? Perhaps the facts, which

---

[1] I should add that two books on strategy have come out between this research and this book, *The Rise and Fall of Strategic Planning* (Mintzberg 1994) and *Strategy Safari* (Mintzberg, Alhstrand, and Lampel 1998), both of which made use of the results of some of these studies. But they contain little of the conclusions of this final chapter.

remain to be assessed by historians of a future age, will suggest exactly the opposite: that we make such a fuss about strategic change because there is not all that much of it. (Think of all the companies you know, not just those written up in the press. In any event, there will be more on this in Chapter 12.)

Let us turn now to the stories from history and what they reveal about the strategy formation process today.

2

Patterns in Strategy Formation

Volkswagenwerk, 1937–72, and US Strategy in Vietnam, 1950–73[1]

Henry Mintzberg

The first of published studies, less elaborate in description than those that followed, but backed up by a great deal of data, compares strategies and their formation in two very different contexts: a government that became engaged in a foreign war and an automobile company in a competitive market. Yet some of the conclusions turn out to be remarkably similar: that strategy formation can fruitfully be viewed as the interplay between a dynamic environment and bureaucratic momentum, with leadership mediating between the two; that strategy formation over time appears to follow some important patterns, notably life cycles and distinct change-continuity cycles within these; and that the study of the interplay between intended and realized strategies may lead us to the heart of this complex organizational process.

The first of these studies of strategy formation reported in this book focused on what seemed to be two very different situations: the US becoming involved in, fighting, and retreating from a foreign war, and the history of a major automobile company from its inception well into its maturity. Yet when conclusions were drawn, perhaps due to the large size and machine bureaucratic nature of both organizations, a number of the conclusions drawn from each are remarkably similar.

This report begins with a brief review of the periods of strategy of each, and then presents the conclusions in terms of what became

[1] Originally published in *Management Science* (1978: 934–48), with minor revisions in this volume.

the conceptual focus of all the subsequent studies: the interplay of environment, leadership, and organization; patterns of strategic change; and the relationship between deliberate and emergent strategies.

Periods of Volkswagenwerk

This study is divided into seven distinct periods, as follows:

BEFORE 1948: FLUX

Ferdinand Porsche conceived the idea of a 'people's car' in the 1920s; in 1934, the German Nazi government decided to support the project, and in 1937, with the problems worked out of the design, construction was begun on a large automobile manufacturing plant at Wolfsburg. Just as the plant was to go into full operation, war was declared, and it was immediately converted to production of war vehicles. By 1945 the plant was largely destroyed. The British occupation forces used it to service their vehicles. Later there began some primitive production of Porsche's 'Volkswagen', using in large part East German refugees as the labor force, with many of the raw materials procured by barter. The plant was offered to various Allied interests (including Henry Ford), but all declined, seeing no value in the Volkswagen. In 1948 the British selected Heinrich Nordhoff, a former division chief of Opel, to run the operations.

1948: GLOBAL CHANGE

Nordhoff inherited half an intended strategy—Porsche's design and his concept of the market (an inexpensive automobile for the common man). To this he added the other components of an intended strategy—an emphasis on quality and technical excellence, aggressive exporting, and rigorous service standards, all integrated around the dominant element of the 'people's car'.

1949 TO 1958: CONTINUITY

This intended strategy was ideally suited to the environment of post-war Germany as well as to worldwide export markets. For the next ten years, Nordhoff realized his intended strategy, building up the central organization and expanding manufacturing capacity and distribution channels very rapidly. Two new models were introduced (work on both having begun in 1949), but these were really modifications of the basic Volkswagen. (In 1954 Nordhoff ordered work halted on the design of a completely new model.)

1959: MINOR CHANGE

Increasing competition and changing consumer tastes in Germany and abroad spurred Volkswagen to make some minor modifications in its strategies around 1959. Advertising was introduced in the US in anticipation of the compacts; design of the first really new model, the medium-priced 1500, was pursued; the firm was about to go public and investment was increased sharply in anticipation of a dividend load. But all essential aspects of the original strategy remained unchanged; only some new, essentially peripheral elements, were grafted on to the old strategy.

1960 TO 1964: CONTINUITY

The Volkswagen strategy remained essentially the same in almost all respects, although profits were being squeezed by competitive pressures and increasing costs despite increasing sales. The larger 1500 model was introduced, but it again emphasized durability, economy, and unexcelled appearance.

1965 TO 1970: GROPING

Facing evermore severe pressures, the firm finally reacted in the form of an anxious and disjointed search for new models. Many were introduced in this period, some in contrast to Volkswagen's economy-car image. Some the firm designed itself; others were acquired. Nordhoff died in 1968, and Kurt Lotz became managing director. By 1970, profits were down for the third straight year. The old strategy had clearly disintegrated, but a clear new one had yet to emerge.

1971 TO 1974: GLOBAL CHANGE

An experienced Volkswagen executive, Rudolf Leiding, replaced Lotz in 1971 and immediately began a period of consolidation of the new acquisitions and the development of a new integrated turnaround strategy. The new product strategy was modeled around the successful Audi—stylish, front-wheel drive, water-cooled. Accordingly, a host of existing lines were dropped, a few new ones being concentrated upon to avoid direct competition between models. (Models carried the labels of Golf, Passat, and Beetle.) Complementarity was stressed in their design to assure reliable, economic assembly, and attempts were made to rationalize production on a worldwide basis and to build plants abroad, in low-wage areas where possible. Marketing strategy emphasized performance, reliability, and service. Capital expenditures were very large throughout the period. (These strategies were pursued in what proved to be a period of continuity after 1974, despite Leiding's resignation, with the new products selling well.) After large losses in 1974, Volkswagenwerk became profitable again in the second half of 1975.

At the time of the preparation of this book in 2007, Volkswagen remains a prominent automobile company, the largest in Europe and the fourth largest in the world. Its products still include automobiles called Golf, Passat, and Beetle.

Period of US Strategy in Vietnam

It is impossible, in a short space, to review comprehensively a situation as complex as the US experience in Vietnam from 1950 to 1973. (Our chronology record of decisions, actions, and events numbered 101 pages.) Nevertheless, the central themes can be reviewed briefly, in ten distinct periods, to show the main patterns of change and continuity.

1950: GLOBAL CHANGE

Until 1950, the US government refused requests by France to aid its forces fighting in Indochina. Shortly after Communist forces took over the Chinese government, however, the US changed its strategy and began a program of direct monetary aid to the French.

1950 TO 1953: CONTINUITY

For three and a half years, the US followed a more or less uninterrupted strategy of steadily increasing aid to the French in Indochina. This was accompanied, particularly at the outset, by a strategy of encouraging the French to reduce their colonial ties to the 'Associated States'. Neither strategy accomplished its purpose. By the end of 1953, despite a massive infusion of US aid, the French military position was weaker than in 1950.

1954: FLUX, THEN GLOBAL CHANGE

Late in 1953 the French military position began to disintegrate. Before and during the multination Geneva conference in April, Secretary of State John Foster Dulles negotiated with the allies of the US in order to reach agreement, but his efforts were not successful. The day before the Indochina phase of the conference opened on May 8, the French garrison at Dien Bien Phu fell. At a press conference on June 8, Dulles claimed there was no plan to ask Congress for authorization of the US aid to Indochina, a position confirmed two days later by President Eisenhower. Shortly thereafter the French government fell, and Pierre Mendès-France became premier on a platform of ending the war by July 20. At Geneva a settlement was reached, among other points, dividing Vietnam in two. In the aftermath of Geneva, the French left Vietnam and the US began a program of direct aid to the South Vietnamese, with the intended strategy of democratizing the government of Premier Diem.

1955 TO 1961: CONTINUITY

To the end of the Eisenhower administration, the US pursued an uninterrupted strategy of direct aid to the South Vietnamese, while the intended strategy of democratization was neither realized nor vigorously pursued.

1961: GLOBAL CHANGE

The change in strategy in 1961 was the first time the US government acted in a purely proactive manner, without tangible external stimulus. The new Kennedy team in Washington chose to change the intended strategy from passive aid to active support. On May 11, 1961, a contingent of Special Forces was dispatched to Vietnam to advise and train the Vietnamese. Kennedy also approved the initiation of a covert warfare campaign against North Vietnam. At the end of the year, under pressure from Diem, Kennedy agreed to a buildup of support troops.

1962 TO 1965: INCREMENTAL CHANGE LEADING TO GLOBAL CHANGE

The number of US advisors increased from 948 at the end of November 1961, to 2,646 by January 1962, 5,576 by June 30, and 11,000 by the end of 1962. In 1963, public manifestations began against the Diem government, and the US strategy of support for Diem gradually changed (apparently in contradiction of intentions). First, Washington brought economic pressures to bear on the Diem government, by the deferring of decisions on aid, and eventually, it tacitly supported the coup that overthrew him (after considerable confusion between Washington, the military, and the CIA). With the assassination of Kennedy less than a month later, Lyndon Johnson became president. From the early days of his administration, the debate within the US government over the intended strategy for Vietnam (bombing, escalation, etc.) grew more intense. As the debate went on, the realized strategy began to change to one of escalation of the US war effort. For example, in February 1964, clandestine US attacks began, including patrols and air operations in Laos against the North Vietnamese. Then in August 1964 the first spate of bombings was carried out against the North in reprisal for the attack on US destroyers in the Gulf of Tonkin. And in October 1964 the covert air war in Laos was intensified. Meanwhile, the debate over the official (intended) strategy continued, with various options debated in meeting, memo, and report. Throughout the period, Johnson seemed uncertain how to proceed and reluctant about approving large-scale bombings. But events were dragging him along. Opinion within the government was more and more favoring bombing and escalation; the government crisis in Saigon was worsening; the Viet Cong was stepping up its harassment. On February 6, 1965, after the Viet Cong had attacked the US personnel at Plei Ku, Johnson ordered a major retaliatory strike on the North. On February 11, another similarly justified attack was launched. And on February 13 Johnson ordered sustained bombing on a nonretaliatory basis. Thereafter, with the bombing seeming to prove relatively ineffective, the debate over troop deployment began in earnest. Under pressure from the Pentagon, Johnson approved in April 1964 the first major troop increases and 'a change of mission for all Marine battalions deployed in Vietnam to permit their more active use...'. By June the 'search and destroy' strategy had begun to replace the 'enclave' strategy, and in July Johnson approved General Westmoreland's request for forty-four battalions.

1965 TO 1967: CONTINUITY

Three strategies were pursued in parallel during this period. First, the land war was escalated until the US troop level in Vietnam reached a peak of over half a million in 1967. Second, the bombing campaign was intensified sporadically throughout the period. And third, Johnson put pressure on the North Vietnamese, through periodic variations in the bombing campaign, to come to the negotiating table. Meanwhile, pressures began to build in Washington, notably from McNamara, for a reassessment of the whole strategy. Although this may have constrained the escalation decisions Johnson made, it did not change the basic course of the strategy. By the end of 1967, the ground war was being fought extensively, the air war was being widened slowly, and diplomatic activity went on at a furious pace.

1968: GLOBAL CHANGE

A series of factors apparently stunned Johnson into a major reassessment of the strategy. One was the Tet offensive, begun on January 31, 1968, which for the first time provided tangible evidence of the military reality (a stalemate) in Vietnam. Second was the military request, on February 28, for 206,756 more troops, which according to the *Pentagon Papers* would have meant the call-up of reserve forces. Third, a new Secretary of Defense, Clark Clifford, was working behind the scenes for a bombing halt. And fourth, the New Hampshire presidential primary, and other manifestations of public sentiment, made clear the great resistance to the war effort that was growing among the US population. On March 13, 1968, Johnson decided to deploy 30,000 more troops, but then a few days later a massive change in the strategy was signaled. On March 22, General Westmoreland was recalled to Washington and on March 31 Johnson announced a partial bombing halt, a reduction of the latest deployment to 13,500 troops, and his intention not to seek reelection. Three days later he announced North Vietnam's readiness to meet with the US negotiators.

1968 TO 1969: LIMBO, THEN GLOBAL CHANGE

After a brief period of limbo to the end of 1968, ending the term of the lame-duck president, Richard Nixon took over the presidency and initiated global change in strategy. In effect, Johnson's global change was to halt an old strategy; Nixon's was to replace it with a new one. His was a proactive, integrated strategy—he referred to its goal as 'peace with honor'—consisting of the following elements: 'Vietnamization', which meant the withdrawal of US troops and the equipping of the South Vietnamese to take over the fighting; active peace initiatives to negotiate a settlement, alternated with military pressure (based on air and naval power, to replace the withdrawn land power) to encourage the North Vietnamese to undertake serious negotiations; and 'linkage', the bringing of pressure on the Russians—by threatening a withdrawal of cooperation on other East–West negotiations—to influence the North Vietnamese to reach a settlement.

1970 TO 1973: CONTINUITY

That strategy remained intact into 1973, with only the emphasis of its various components changed from time to time to gain advantage. The US troop withdrawals continued rather steadily throughout the period. So did US military pressure, which consisted primarily of periodic bombing offensives, but also included a ground excursion into Cambodia in mid-1970 and air support for a South Vietnamese one into Laos in early 1971, as well as the mining of North Vietnamese ports in mid-1972. Political pressure was maintained on the Soviet Union during the entire period. And negotiation also continued throughout, although sporadically. An agreement was finally reached in January 1973, at which time the US halted all offensive military activity. (The heaviest bombing of the war took place in North Vietnam just three weeks prior, after an earlier agreement fell apart.) By March 29, 1973, all American combat and support forces had left Vietnam, and effective August 15, all funding for American military activity in or over Indochina was ended. (Fighting, however, continued, the South Vietnamese army and government finally collapsing in April 1975.)

Some General Conclusions about Strategy Formation

Three themes will be pursued in this section. The first is that strategy formation can fruitfully be viewed as the interplay between a dynamic environment and bureaucratic momentum, with leadership mediating between the two. Second, strategy formation over periods of time appears to follow distinct regularities, which may prove vital to understanding the process. And third, the study of the interplay between intended and realized strategies may lead us to the heart of this complex organizational process.

STRATEGY FORMATION AS THE INTERPLAY OF ENVIRONMENT, LEADERSHIP, AND ORGANIZATION

In general terms, strategy formation here can be thought of as revolving around the interplay of three basic forces: (a) an *environment* that changes continuously but irregularly, with frequent discontinuities and wide swings in its rate of change; (b) an organizational operating system, or *bureaucracy*, that above all seeks to stabilize its actions, despite the characteristics of the environment it serves; and (c) a *leadership* whose role is to mediate between these two forces, to maintain the stability of the organization's operating system while at the same time insuring its adaptation to environmental change. Strategy can then be viewed as the set of consistent behaviors by which the organization establishes for a time its place in its environment, and strategic change can be viewed as the organization's response to environmental change, constrained by the momentum of the bureaucracy and accelerated or dampened by the leadership. Both Volkswagen and Vietnam are above all stories of how bureaucratic momentum constrains and conditions strategic change, at least after the initial strategic direction has been set.

Volkswagenwerk

Any large automobile company is mightily constrained by its technical system. Retooling is enormously expensive. This helps to explain Volkswagen's slow response to the environmental changes of the 1960s. But this explanation is not sufficient. Volkswagen was clearly constrained by momentum of a psychological nature as well. The very success of its unique and integrated strategy seemed to reinforce its psychological commitment to it, and to act as a great barrier to the consideration of strategic change.

Even leadership was absent when needed in the 1960s. Nordhoff's period of great leadership began in 1948, when there was little to lose by acting boldly and when little bureaucratic momentum was present. That leadership lasted for the next ten years. But by the early 1960s, when bold action was needed in the face of an increasingly changed environment, the central leadership was not forthcoming. Quite the contrary, instead of pushing the bureaucracy to change, Nordhoff became a force for continuity. When change did come, it was late and it lacked a conceptual focus. The organization groped awkwardly in its new environment, until a new, dynamic leader came on the scene with a fresh strategy in 1971.

Vietnam

Bureaucratic momentum played a major role in the US strategy in Vietnam as well. Earlier in our discussion, the periods 1954, 1961, and 1965 were labeled as global change because various strategies changed quickly and in unison. But in a broader perspective, all these changes were incremental. The precedent of resisting Communist expansion in Southeast Asia—the 'metastrategy' (a strategy of strategies)—was set in 1950. After that, the changes of 1954, 1961, and 1965, while substituting one means for another, simply reinforced the basic direction; they did not change it. Each escalation step seemed to be a natural outgrowth of the last one, one commitment leading to the next. Only in 1968, when the organization was faced with a massive failure, was there a true global change in strategy.

At no time was bureaucratic momentum more evident than during the great debate of 1963–5. The pressures on Johnson to do more of the same—to escalate—became enormous. One could even argue that the creation of the Special Forces by Kennedy became a self-confirming contingency plan. In effect a guerilla fighting force, created in case it might be needed, found a way to make itself needed. It came to be used because it was there. This suggests that strategies can be evoked by available resources (as in the case of the employees, factory, and people's car of Volkswagenwerk of 1948 looking for something to do),[2] and that contingency plans, a favorite prescriptive tool of planning theorists in times of environmental turbulence, may have a habit of making themselves self-confirming, whether they are needed or not.

Of course the environment played a major role in Vietnam too. The US altered its strategy in 1954 and 1965, albeit within the metastrategy, because the changed environment was proving inhospitable to its existing strategy. And the global changes of 1950 and 1968 were certainly evoked by environmental change, in these two cases rather specific events—the fall of the Chinese government and the Tet offensive.

What of leadership? The real tragedy of Vietnam is that, until 1968, the leadership never seemed to mediate appropriately between the bureaucracy and the environment. In 1961, for example, leadership acted proactively in the absence of either significant environmental change or bureaucratic momentum. Kennedy voluntarily escalated the war in a way that made the 1965 escalation all but inevitable. 'All but' because sufficiently strong leadership in 1965 might have been able to resist the environmental and bureaucratic pressures. But the cards were stacked against Johnson. Both the environmental change and the bureaucratic momentum were pulling him in the same direction, each suggesting more

[2] Chandler (1962) made the same point to explain the expansion of the DuPont company after World War I, when it found itself with excess capacity.

of the same (escalation) as the natural next step. It would have taken very powerful leadership indeed to resist these forces, and Johnson did not exhibit it. Only in 1968, facing the most dramatic failure of all and a markedly changed domestic environment, did Johnson finally exert the leadership initiative that reversed the eighteen-year course of the metastrategy.

Thereafter, Nixon exhibited strong leadership too, introducing proactive change in 1969 and pursuing it vigorously to the end. But again, admittedly in retrospect, that proactivity served only to prolong what was inevitably a lost cause. And bureaucratic momentum seemed to play a minor role in the Nixon years, his strong chief advisor Kissinger, standing in place of the policy-making machinery of government. But those two men also fell prey to psychological momentum, pursuing their costly and ultimately futile strategy against public and congressional resistance.

PATTERNS OF STRATEGIC CHANGE

There is no need to dwell on the point that strategy formation is not a regular, nicely sequenced process running on a standard five-year schedule or whatever. An organization may find itself in a stable environment for years, sometimes for decades, with no need to reassess an appropriate strategy. Then, suddenly, the environment can become so turbulent that even the very best planning techniques are of no use because of the impossibility of predicting the kind of stability that will eventually emerge. (What kind of strategic plan was John Foster Dulles to carry in his briefcase to Geneva in 1954?) In response to this kind of inconsistency in the environment, patterns of strategic change are never steady, but rather irregular and ad hoc, with a complex intermingling of periods of continuity, change, flux, limbo, and so on.

But that should not lead to the conclusion that patterns in strategy formation do not exist. Indeed, if we are to make any normative headway in this area, we must find consistencies that will enable organizations to understand better their strategic situations. Thus the prime thrust of our research has been to identify patterns of strategic change.

Waves of Change

Most of our studies show evidence of two main patterns, one superimposed on the other. The first is the life cycle of an overall strategy—its conception, elaboration, decay, and death. The second is the presence of periodic waves of change and continuity within the life cycle. (Longer cycles of this kind could be identified as well, from one life cycle to the next.) What this second pattern suggests is that strategies do not commonly change in continuous incremental fashion; rather, change—even incremental change—takes place in spurts, each followed by a period of continuity. Nowhere is this better demonstrated than in the stepwise escalation of the Vietnam metastrategy in 1950, 1954, 1961, and 1965.

Why do organizations undergo distinct periods of change and continuity? For one thing, such a pattern seems to be consistent with human cognition. We do not react to phenomena continuously, but rather in discreet steps, in response to changes large enough for us to perceive. Likewise, strategic decision processes in organizations are not continuous, but irregular (Mintzberg, Raisinghani, and Theorêt 1976). They must be specifically evoked; they proceed for a time; and then they terminate. Furthermore, consistent with the Cyert and March (1963) notion of sequential attention to goals, the leadership of an organization may choose to deal with the conflicting pressures for change from the environment and continuity from the bureaucracy by first acceding to one and then the other. To most bureaucracies—for example, the automobile assembly line—change is disturbing. So the leadership tries to concentrate that disturbance into a specific period of time, and then to leave the bureaucracy alone for a while to consolidate the change. But of course, while the bureaucracy is being left alone, the environment continues to change, so that no matter how well chosen the strategy, eventually a new cycle of change must be initiated.

Volkswagenwerk

With these two patterns in mind, we can now consider the patterns of strategic change in both studies. Volkswagen began its life (or at least left the incubation stage) in 1948 with what we call a *gestalt* strategy, defined as one that is (a) unique and (b) tightly integrated (in the sense that its elements are mutually complementary, or *synergistic*, in Volkswagen's case fusing around the dominant element of the people's car). The first feature, uniqueness, means that the gestalt strategy deposits the organization in a *niche*, a corner of the environment reserved for itself. If well chosen, therefore, that strategy can protect the organization from attack for a period of time. That is exactly what happened in the case of Volkswagen. But the second feature, tight integration, makes a gestalt strategy difficult to change. The changing of a single dimension may cause *dis*integration of the whole strategy. That also became clear when Volkswagen had to change, when competitors moved into its niche and the market moved away from it. Volkswagenwerk's initial response to the changes in environment was twofold. Before 1959, and after 1959 until 1965, it essentially ignored the changes. And in the 1959 period it resorted to a *grafting* procedure, adding a new piece to its existing gestalt strategy, but avoiding any fundamental change in it. When Volkswagen finally did begin to respond seriously in 1965, that response was an awkward one, a *groping* procedure with no clear focus. After seventeen years with one gestalt strategy, the organization was not accustomed to making major changes in strategy. It was only in the 1970s that Volkswagen was able to develop a clear new strategy, in part, we shall soon argue, a result of its groping procedure.

Gestalt Strategies

A few words on gestalt strategies are in order, since they appear frequently in organizations. First, they seem to develop at one point in time, most frequently when the organization is founded. That is when bureaucratic momentum is weakest, leadership typically strong (entrepreneurial), and environments rather tolerant. In contrast, achieving a gestalt strategy is difficult in an ongoing organization, which has a great deal more bureaucratic momentum. Yet both the Volkswagenwerk of 1971 and the US government of 1969 seemed able to, no doubt because both faced environments beginning to settle down after periods of great turbulence that had severely disrupted their bureaucratic momentum.

Second, gestalt strategies seem to be associated with single, powerful leaders. This is especially true of the two periods mentioned above, as well as that of Volkswagenwerk of 1948. Perhaps the sophisticated integration called for by such strategies can be effected only in one mind. The development of a gestalt strategy requires innovative thinking, rooted in synthesis rather than analysis, based on the 'intuitive' or inexplicit processes that have been associated with the brain's right hemisphere (Ornstein 1972). Thus we are led to hypothesize that gestalt strategies are the products of single individuals, and only appear in organizations with strong leadership, in effect, those that use the entrepreneurial mode. It is difficult to imagine one coming out of a decentralized organization, unless all the decision-makers follow the conceptual lead of one creative individual. Nor can one be imagined resulting from a formal management science or planning process per se, these being essentially analytic rather than synthetic. (That is not to say, of course, that a synthesizer cannot parade under the title of planner or management scientist, or for that matter, advisor, as in the case of Kissinger.) We hypothesize then that planning will normally lead to what can be called *mainline* strategies, typical and obvious ones for the organization to adopt (for example, because the competitors are using them).

Vietnam

Vietnam represents the classic strategic life cycle, although the pattern differs somewhat from that of Volkswagen. The Vietnam metastrategy had a clearly identifiable birthdate, 1950, and unlike that of Volkswagen, which grew rapidly from the outset, this one grew slowly, receiving three distinct boosts, in 1954, 1961, and 1965. It was only after this third boost, however, fifteen years after its birth, that the metastrategy really underwent rapid expansion. Its demise also differed from that of Volkswagen. Whereas the Volkswagen strategy experienced a long, agonizing death, like a developing cancer, the US metastrategy in Vietnam experienced one major setback, like a massive stroke, in 1968, and thereafter remained in a coma until 1973, when it finally expired. (The new gestalt strategy that arose in 1969 served only to bury it. In Volkswagen, of course, only the strategy expired; out of its ashes a new one emerged, and the automobile operations carried on. The Vietnam operations did not.)

The change–continuity cycles were also very marked in the case of Vietnam. Except for the period from 1962 to 1965, when the change was gradual, and largely out of control of the central leadership, periods of change and continuity were always evident. And in the broad perspective, as noted earlier, up to 1968 that change was always incremental. Vietnam in fact represents a classic case of incrementalism, and exhibits profoundly its dangers. Each escalation step was taken without an assessment of what the next step might have entailed, with the result that Lyndon Johnson in 1968 found himself in a situation that Harry Truman, the president under whom the first step was taken in 1950, as well as all the presidents in between (including the Lyndon Johnson of 1965), would have considered inconceivable. Strategy-makers seem prepared to assume positions in incremental steps that they would never begin to entertain in global ones. On the other hand, some of our other studies show that even in simple situations global change is very difficult to conceive and execute successfully. This, perhaps, is the strategy-maker's greatest dilemma—the danger of incremental change versus the difficulty of global change.

DELIBERATE VERSUS EMERGENT STRATEGIES

The Volkswagen strategy of 1948–58 is perhaps the best illustration of a deliberate strategy, both intended and realized. Kennedy's intended strategy of 1961, of advising the Vietnamese, is probably the best example of an unrealized strategy. And the subsequent US strategy of finding itself in a fighting instead of advising role is probably the best example of an emergent strategy, realized despite intentions. (Note the association of these last two with Kennedy's proactive strategy making.)

But practice is always more complicated—and more interesting—than theory, and despite our neat trichotomy, we found a number of other relationships between intended and realized strategies. These include intended strategies that, as they get realized, change their form and become, in part at least, emergent; emergent strategies that get formalized as deliberate ones; and intended strategies that get overrealized.

Formulation Followed by Implementation?

Planning theory postulates that the strategy-maker 'formulates' from on high while the subordinates 'implement' lower down. Unfortunately, however, this neat dichotomy is based on two assumptions which often prove false: that the formulator is fully informed, or at least as well informed as the implementer, and that the environment is sufficiently stable, or at least predictable, to ensure that there will be no need for *re*formulation during implementation. The absence of either condition should lead to a collapse of the formulation–implementation dichotomy, and the use of the adaptive mode instead of the planning one. Strategy formation then becomes a learning process, whereby so-called implementation feeds back to formulation and intentions get modified en route, resulting in an emergent strategy.

The failure to so adapt is dramatically illustrated in a paper by Feld (1959). He describes the problems that arise in military organizations that hold rigidly to this dichotomy, 'The command function of planning and coordination [being] considered to require a sheltered position' despite the fact that 'The conditions of combat are fluid and haphazard in the extreme' (p. 17). Thus, in the infamous battle of World War I, where the British casualties numbered 300,000:

No senior officer from the Operations Branch of the General Headquarters, it was claimed, ever set foot (or eyes) on the Passchendaele battlefield during the four months the battle was in progress. Daily reports on the condition of the battlefield were first ignored, then ordered discontinued. Only after the battle did the Army chief of staff learn that he had been directing men to advance through a sea of mud. (p. 21)

Strategists' Knowledge

The most successful deliberate strategies of our two studies—the gestalt ones of Nordhoff and later Leiding in Volkswagenwerk—were both formulated by men who knew their industry intimately and who were able to predict conditions in environments that were settling down after periods of great turbulence. In sharp contrast is the Vietnam strategy of 1962–5, the most costly emergent strategy of our studies—one realized in a form totally different and far more involving than that intended. Both Kennedy and Johnson had only the most cursory knowledge of the real conditions in Vietnam (Halberstam 1972), and neither was able to predict the conditions of an environment that was becoming increasingly turbulent. As Halberstam noted in his detailed study of the US experience in Vietnam:

[I]t was something they slipped into more than they chose; they thought they were going to have time for clear, well-planned choices, to decide how many men and what type of strategy they would follow, but events got ahead of them. The pressures from Saigon for more and more men would exceed Washington's capacity to slow it down and think coolly, and so the decisions evolved rather than were made, and Washington slipped into a ground combat war. (p. 544)

Emergent Strategy Becoming Deliberate

What can we say then about Johnson's decisions to escalate the war in 1965? Here we have a situation, apparently a common one if our other studies can be used as a guide, where an emergent strategy became a deliberate one. Johnson's decisions of 1965, unlike those of 1968, did not break any pattern. Quite the contrary, they formalized one that was becoming increasingly evident since 1962. The US was fighting a war in 1965, no longer advising an ally. In other words, the strategy-maker perceived an unintended pattern in a stream of decisions and made that pattern the intended one for the future. An emergent strategy, once recognized, became a deliberate strategy. (Thus not only we, but also the leaders we studied, were perceivers of patterns in decision streams.) A similar phenomenon—although less pronounced—seemed to be at play in Volkswagen in the 1970s. Out of the grouping of the 1960s, Leiding perceived an emergent pattern, which we might call the Audi strategy. One car—stylish, front-wheel drive, water-cooled—seemed to be most successful in the new environment. And so he built the new gestalt around it. The general conclusion seems to be that new strategies sometimes have incubation periods. While the old strategy is decaying, one or more emergent strategies are developing peripherally in the organization. Eventually one is selected and formalized as the new, intended strategy. Decisional behavior in effect coalesces around what seems to have worked for the organization—and perhaps also what lends coherence to the frustrating years of failing to realize intentions.

Overrealized Strategies

But the formalization of an emergent strategy is hardly incidental to the organization. As the Vietnam period of 1965–8 shows so clearly, the very act of explicating an implicit strategy—of stating clearly and officially that it is to be the intended strategy—changes profoundly the attitude of the bureaucracy and of the environment to it. Johnson's decisions of 1965 opened the floodgates of escalation. Had he remained in limbo, refusing to make a decision (all the while, the decisions in fact being made for him on the battlefield), it is doubtful that the military bureaucracy could have pursued escalation so vigorously. In effect, the very fact of making a strategy explicit—even an implicit one that is evident to all—provides a clear and formal invitation to the bureaucracy to run with it. (One could of course make the reverse point, that the very fact of his having remained in limbo for two years built up a charge in the military establishment that went off with that much more explosive force when the detonator was finally released.)

To overstate the bureaucracy's position, it says to its management:

> Our business is running the operations; yours is formulating the strategy. But we need a clearly defined, intended strategy to do our job—to buy our machines, hire our workers, standardize our procedures. So please give us such a strategy—any strategy—so long as it is precise and stable [and lets us grow].

The danger in this innocent statement, of course, is that the bureaucracy runs like an elephant. The strategy that gets it moving may be no more consequential than a mouse, but once underway there is no stopping it. As Halberstam noted about Kennedy in 1963 and Johnson after 1965: '[T]he capacity to control a policy involving the military is greatest before the policy is initiated, but once started, no matter how small the initial step, a policy has a life and a thrust of its own, it is an organic thing' (1972, p. 209). Bureaucratic momentum takes over, happy to have a clear strategy, never stopping to question it. The strategy-maker may awake one day—as did Lyndon Johnson in 1968—to find that his intended strategy has somehow been implemented beyond his wildest intentions. It has been *overrealized*. Thus, 'make your strategy explicit' may be a popular prescription of the management consultant (Tilles 1963), but in the light of this research it can sometimes be seen to constitute questionable advice indeed.

QUESTIONING CONVENTIONAL PRESCRIPTIONS ABOUT STRATEGY MAKING

This first article was written with the intention of bringing a new kind of description to the much misunderstood process of strategy formation in organizations. These two studies call into question a number of assumptions about the process, at least in certain contexts. A strategy is not a fixed plan, nor does it change systematically at prearranged times solely at the will of management. The dichotomy between strategy formulation and strategy implementation is a false one under certain common conditions, because it ignores the learning that must often follow the conception of an intended strategy. Indeed the very word 'formulation' is misleading since we commonly refer to as 'strategies' many patterns in organizational decisions that form without conscious or deliberate thought. Even Chandler's (1962) well-known edict of structure follows strategy must be called into question because of the influence of bureaucratic momentum on strategy formation. The aggressive, proactive strategy-maker—the hero of the literature on entrepreneurship—can under some conditions do more harm than the hesitant, reactive one. Contingency planning, a popular prescription in times of environmental turbulence, can be risky because the plans may tend to become actualized, whether needed or not. And so too can it sometimes be risky to make strategy explicit, notably in an uncertain environment with an aggressive bureaucracy.

In general, the contemporary prescriptions and normative techniques of analysis and planning—and the debate that accompanies them—seem unable to address the complex reality of strategy formation. To tell the management to state its goals precisely, assess its strengths and weaknesses, plan systematically on schedule, and make the resulting strategies explicit are at best overly general guidelines, at worst demonstrably misleading precepts to organizations that face a confusing reality.

There is perhaps no process in organizations that is more demanding of human cognition than strategy formation. All strategy-makers face an impossible overload of information (much of it soft); as a result they can have no optimal process to follow. The researcher or management scientist who seeks to understand strategy formation is up against the same cognitive constraints, but with poorer access to the necessary information. Thus he or she faces no easy task. But proceed they must, for the old prescriptions are not working and new ones are badly needed. These will only grow out of a sophisticated understanding of the rich reality of strategy formation, and that will require an open mind, a recognition of how little we really know, and intensive, painstaking research.

3

Tracking Strategies in an Entrepreneurial Firm

Steinberg Inc., 1917–75

Henry Mintzberg and James A. Waters[1]

This study tracks the strategies of a retail chain over sixty years of its history to draw conclusions about strategy formation in an entrepreneurial firm that grew large and formalized its structure. The conclusions focus on the waves of change experienced by the company over the years, its hectic but uneven growth, the infrequency of major strategic reorientations, the strength and weaknesses of the entrepreneurial mode of strategy making, and the entry of the planning mode, but to program more than formulate strategy.

Two themes are pursued in this study. The first is simply to demonstrate how the wide array of strategies used in an organization over the years can be described and analyzed, in both concrete and conceptual terms. In other words, different pictures of that vague concept called strategy are shown—some quantitative, representing specific traces left behind in an organization, and some symbolic, representing possible interpretations of those traces. Second, from the investigation of what is believed to be a classic case of growth, formalization, and diversification of an entrepreneurial firm, some conceptual conclusions about the process of strategy formation under these conditions are drawn. To begin, specific strategies, and related data, of Steinberg Inc. from 1917 to 1975 are presented, and seven distinct periods in the history of the company are inferred.

---

[1] Originally published in the *Academy of Management Journal* (25(3), 1982: 465–99), with minor revisions in this volume.

The study of an entrepreneurial firm, especially one like Steinberg Inc., a retail chain, is a mixed blessing. On the one hand, the company is very open and cooperative, which makes the research a real pleasure. On the other hand, the informality also means a relative absence of formal records. (It is suspected that the study of only organizations with detailed records of their history would bias the conclusions toward bureaucratic-type organizations.) Accordingly, it was difficult to extract the data. Annual reports, which appeared from 1953, helped, and many members of the organization kept their own records of store openings and closings (not always consistent with each other). Beyond that, data collection meant gathering every scrap available—an advertising manager's own list of promotional campaigns, an ad hoc record of private label products, occasional newspaper articles, and so on. These problems, however, were alleviated by the excellent memories of a number of the people we interviewed. Finally, it should be made clear that the approach used produces not so much a full history of a company as one oriented to strategy and major turning points. This means less attention to more regular operating issues and to the rich patterns of human interaction present in any organization.

The Strategies of Steinberg Inc. 1917–74

In the course of this company's sixty-year history, something on the order of fifty distinct strategies were inferred. Some of these were from actual plots of specific decisions and actions, as in the case of expansion strategies based on store openings. Others were inferred from chronological lists in words of decisions and actions, as in the case of service strategies based on descriptions of specific actions. Presented in brief form are these strategies as well as related material on structure, environment, and performance, in symbolic form. (The full report runs some 200 pages.)

QUEBEC FOOD OUTLETS

Strategy Diagram 3A depicts Steinberg Inc.'s food outlet strategies in the Quebec region over the period of the study. (Note that in all the strategy diagrams the vertical dimension has symbolic meaning only.) The strategies were inferred from the pattern of actual openings and closings of food outlets in each (fiscal) year. These are plotted in Figure 3.1.

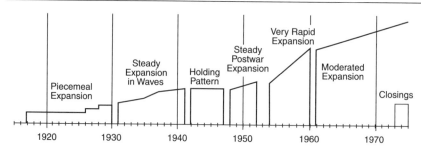

Strategy Diagram 3A Quebec food outlet strategies

The label 'piecemeal expansion' for 1917–1930 is used because only two new stores were opened, one in 1926 and the other in 1928. This pattern changed in 1931 and up to 1941 a net average of 2.2 stores were added per year, the expansion occurring in waves. Following the 'holding pattern' of the war years, the steady expansion resumed, and between 1948 and 1952 the average net addition of stores was 1.8 per year. After 1953, which sits off by itself, there was a very rapid expansion from 1954 to 1960—stores were added at an average of 7.7 per year. From 1961 to 1975, this rate fell to 3.7 stores per year, hence the label 'moderated expansion'.

GEOGRAPHIC EXPANSION

The firm began operations in Montreal and moved into other areas of Quebec and into Ontario later in its history. Strategy Diagram 3B shows

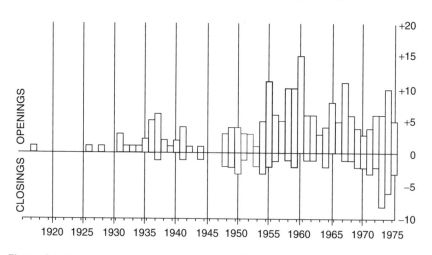

Figure 3.1 Openings and closings of Quebec division food outlets

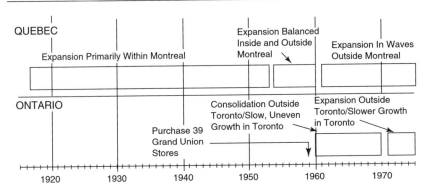

Strategy Diagram 3B Geographic expansion strategies

the strategy followed with respect to food outlet location, both in the Quebec area and in Ontario. These strategies were inferred from the pattern of openings and closings inside and outside the major metropolitan locations in the two areas (later called divisions). In the Quebec division (Figure 3.2), starting with the second store in 1926, expansion took place essentially in Montreal until 1954.

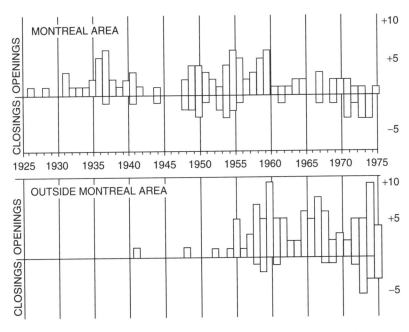

Figure 3.2 Quebec openings and closings inside and outside Montreal area

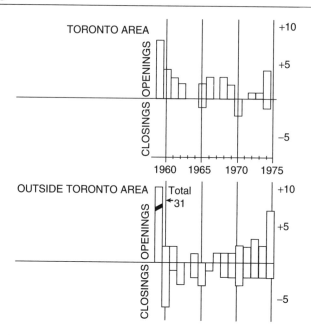

Figure 3.3 Ontario openings and closings inside and outside Toronto area

During the 1954–60 period, expansion was balanced inside (plus twenty-four stores) and outside (plus twenty-nine stores) Montreal. From 1961 to 1975, there was expansion in waves outside Montreal; of the total net addition of fifty-six stores over this latter period, fifty-four were outside Montreal.

An important event in the history of the firm occurred in fiscal 1959— the purchase of thity-nine stores in Ontario from the Grand Union Company. This was the start of the Ontario Division (see Figure 3.3). After this very large addition in 1959, there followed a period from 1960 to 1970 of consolidation outside the Toronto area (minus thirteen stores) and slow uneven growth within the Toronto area (plus sixteen stores). This pattern was somewhat reversed from 1971 to 1975 when there was expansion outside Toronto (plus eight stores) and slower growth in Toronto (plus four stores).

STORE SIZE

Beginning in 1931, the average sales area of both openings and closings increased, although erratically and at different rates. The net effect of these changes was that the average size of operating stores

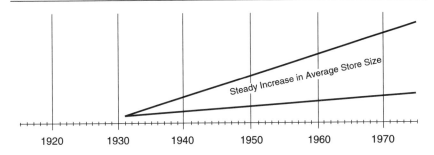

Strategy Diagram 3C Store size strategy

was increased gradually over the study period, as depicted in Strategy Diagram 3C.

MODERNIZATION

In 1963 the firm began a program of upgrading and modernizing existing outlets (changing lighting, fixtures, displays, etc.), as shown in Strategy Diagram 3D.

FOOD RETAILING SERVICE

Strategy Diagram 3E shows the service strategies followed in the food retailing business over the study period. Following the shift in 1922 to taking goods from behind counters and exposing them to customers' view, a major event in 1933 was the conversion of one store to self-service. Between that event and 1936, all stores were converted to self-service, as shown in Strategy Diagram 3E by sloping lines. The next major shift was the addition in 1939 of meat in the stores. During the period 1939–44, stores were gradually converted to include self-service fruits, vegetables, and meat as indicated by the sloping lines; at that point stores resembled smaller versions of a supermarket, as it is known today. In 1954 there began a significant growth in sales of nonfood products and a gradual reintroduction of services in selected areas such as meat,

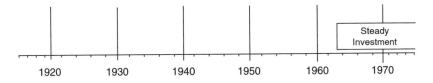

Strategy Diagram 3D Store modernization strategy

41

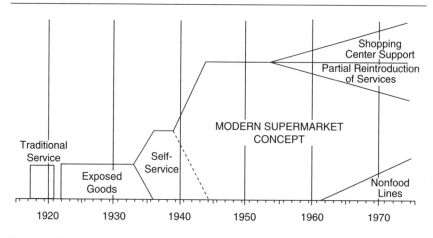

Strategy Diagram 3E Food retailing strategies

cheese, and delicatessen products. The year 1954 also was the start of the move to shopping centers as an enlargement of the one-stop shopping concept.

FOOD PROMOTION

Strategy Diagram 3F shows three related dimensions of the general promotion strategies followed over the study period. In terms of general communications with the public, there was a shift from reliance on

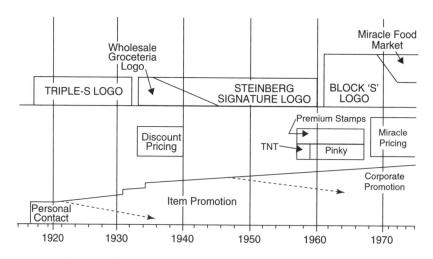

Strategy Diagram 3F Food promotion strategies

personal contact to item promotion (handbills from 1920, first newspaper advertisement in 1931), with the addition of more institutional advertising starting in 1946. The logo used in advertising and on store fronts and private label products also changed four different times as shown. The name 'Miracle Food Market' was employed in Ontario starting in 1969.

The conversion to self-service in 1933 also marked an emphasis on discount pricing, which lasted until the price controls brought on by World War II. From 1957 to 1967, premium stamps, redeemable for merchandise at company-operated redemption centers, were used to build and maintain store traffic. Also during this same period customers could accumulate cash tapes to buy china and tableware at low prices in the store. A major event in 1968 was the introduction of systematic, across-the-board maintenance of discount prices and elimination of special price promotions. The program was called 'miracle pricing'.

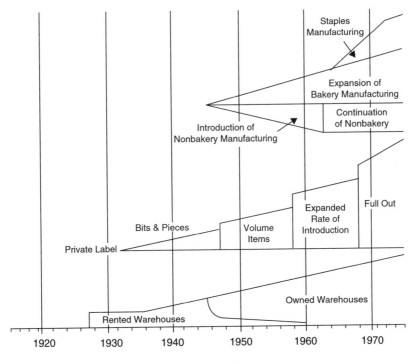

Strategy Diagram 3G Back integration strategies

BACK INTEGRATION

Three related dimensions of back-integration strategies are given in Strategy Diagram 3G. Beginning in 1927, the firm utilized rented warehouse facilities. After the purchase in 1945 of an old aircraft propeller factory, warehousing was done primarily in company-owned facilities.

Manufacturing also began in 1945 in that same building. A small bakery was started and was expanded several times over the study period. Facilities for roasting coffee and nuts and producing meat pies, and so on, were expanded until 1963, from which point capacity remained constant. With initial investments in 1965 in a sugar manufacturer and in 1967 in a flour manufacturer, the company moved into staples manufacturing. Investment in both firms increased until 1972, as indicated in the diagram.

Private label activity began in 1932 with a few products such as coffee and tea. The rate of addition of private label products accelerated over the study period in steps: from approximately 4 or 5 items in 1947, to 50 in 1958, 180 in 1968, and an estimated 600 by 1975.

RETAIL DIVERSIFICATION

Strategy Diagram 3H shows diversification into retail businesses other than food and was inferred from Figure 3.4, a plot of stores in operation over the study period in various business areas. Following forty-five years exclusively in food retailing, from 1962 to 1964 the company followed a steady expansion strategy focused on two new business areas—discount department stores and restaurants in Quebec.

Though not shown in Figure 3.4, in 1965 the company opened (and closed) two gas stations and announced plans to open a furniture store but never did so. Also not shown was a joint venture in large supermarkets

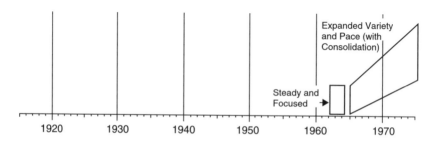

Strategy Diagram 3H Retail diversification strategies

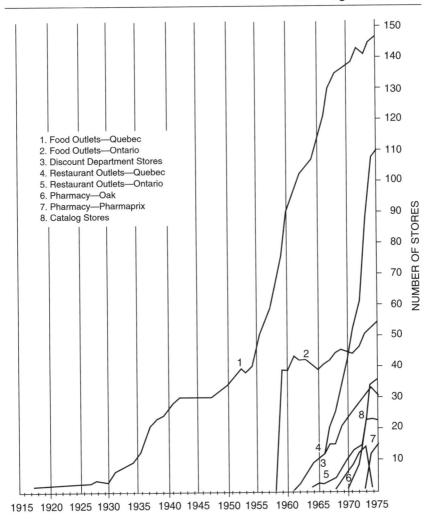

1. Food Outlets—Quebec
2. Food Outlets—Ontario
3. Discount Department Stores
4. Restaurant Outlets—Quebec
5. Restaurant Outlets—Ontario
6. Pharmacy—Oak
7. Pharmacy—Pharmaprix
8. Catalog Stores

NUMBER OF STORES

1915 1920 1925 1930 1935 1940 1945 1950 1955 1960 1965 1970 1975

Figure 3.4 Stores in operation by business area

in France, begun in 1966 and terminated in 1973. Pharmacy outlets in Ontario grew from a start in 1969 until termination in 1974. Restaurant outlets in Ontario began in 1965 and increased steadily through 1974. Catalog stores grew steadily from 1971 through 1974. Beginning in 1974, pharmacy outlets were opened in Quebec (Pharmaprix). Thus, based on these moves, the diversification strategy followed from 1965 to 1974 is described in Strategy Diagram 3H as 'expanded variety and pace (with consolidation)'.

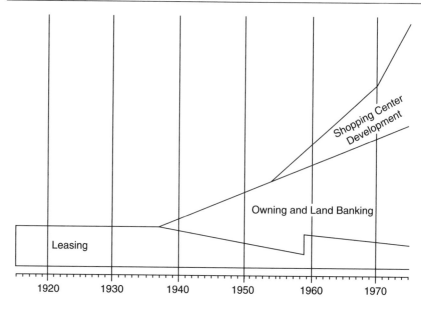

Strategy Diagram 3I Real estate strategies

REAL ESTATE

Until 1937 all store sites were leased (Strategy Diagram 3I). Starting in 1937, an increasing proportion of stores and sites were owned and sites were 'banked' for future development. A discontinuity is shown in 1959 for this strategy to indicate that sites in Ontario (purchased from Grand Union) were largely leased; subsequently, land banking took place very slowly there. The real estate activity in shopping centers showed steady growth with an increased pace starting in 1970, when large regional shopping centers began to be developed.

FINANCE

Strategy Diagram 3J shows the finance strategies employed over the study period. At first, all capital was generated internally from operations. Starting in 1937 with the first owned stores and sites, this source was augmented by mortgage financing in the form of sale–leaseback arrangements.

A major event in 1953 was the first public financing in the form of a $5 million general debenture. The first public sale of preferred stock occurred during fiscal 1954, and until 1965 capital was supplied

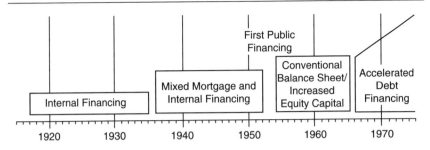

Strategy Diagram 3J Finance strategies

through a balance of equity and debt financing (although all stock sold was nonvoting). Beginning in 1966 and continuing through the period of the study, increasing amounts of debt were undertaken to finance expansions.

ORGANIZATION STRUCTURE

In the evolution of organization structure (Strategy Diagram 3K), underpinning all changes was constant control of all voting stock by Sam Steinberg. From 1917 to 1930, to quote Sam Steinberg, 'everybody

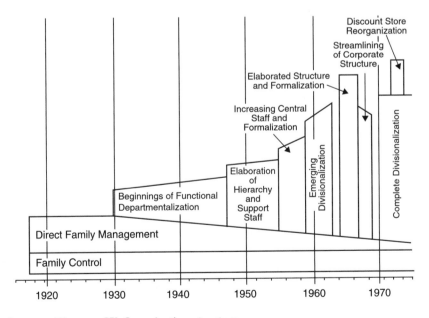

Strategy Diagram 3K Organization structure

did everything'. This fluid approach changed beginning in 1930 with assignment of responsibility for functional areas to specific family members. Starting during this time and continuing through the period of study, nonfamily managers began to assume key positions.

Starting in 1947, the hierarchy became elaborated to the point that store operations were no longer under the direct supervision of Sam Steinberg. This trend accelerated from 1955 to 1959 as more staff groups were created, management training programs were begun, and management budgeting procedures were established.

The period 1959–63 witnessed the gradual emergence of independent Ontario and Quebec operation divisions. As a temporary blip in this trend, between 1964 and 1967 many staff departments were established in the corporate office, and procedures and standards were formalized throughout the firm. With some key personnel changes, this trend was reversed between 1967 and 1969 and many central groups were either cut back or eliminated.

After 1970, divisionalization was extended; prior to this time, a number of business operations reported loosely to Sam Steinberg. From 1970, all operations were run by two executive vice presidents and the president, with Sam Steinberg as chairman. Between 1972 and 1974, reorganizations took place in the discount store operations.

ENVIRONMENT

Some key elements of the environment of Steinberg Inc. may be seen in Strategy Diagram 3L. The period until 1929 saw the establishment of food chains in Quebec and Ontario (though their image, in terms of size of outlets and type of service, was quite similar to the independents). Precipitated by the onset of the depression, the number of chain outlets declined during the 1930s.

Starting in 1941 and accelerating after the war until 1961, chains became increasingly important. In Quebec during this period, their market share rose from 15 percent in 1941 to 35 percent in 1961. The period 1961–8 was a plateau, and chain market share actually declined fractionally during the period. Precipitated by the discount pricing strategy followed by Steinberg Inc., the period 1968–73 involved a price war between the major chains in Quebec and Ontario, which decimated the ranks of the independents. In 1973 and 1974, five major chains controlled 80 percent of the Quebec food market.

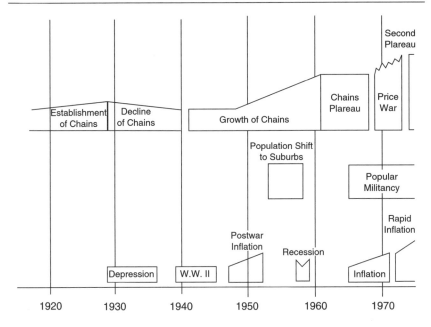

Strategy Diagram 3L The environment

PERFORMANCE

The actual sales and profit data for the firm are shown in Figure 3.5, starting in 1931, the earliest date for which reliable data were available.

As indicated, the only net loss experienced by the firm occurred in 1933, and the only decline in sales volume in the company's history occurred in 1934.

Periods in the History of Steinberg Inc.

All the above strategy diagrams were collected on one large sheet with a common timescale—1917–75. All the strategies were scanned together to identify major turning points and infer key periods in the history of Steinberg Inc. Seven distinct periods were isolated. The interested reader is invited to scan the strategy diagrams to see why those particular years were chosen as the start of new periods. (Space limitations prohibit discussion of this; for a partial rendition, see Figure 1.7 on page 13.)

49

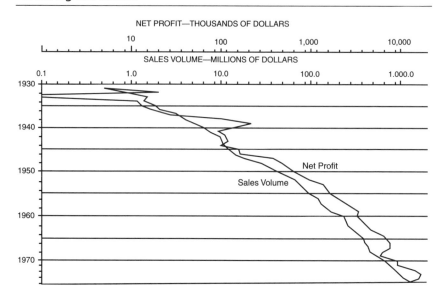

NET PROFIT—THOUSANDS OF DOLLARS

Figure 3.5 Annual sales volume and net profit

1917–30: FORMATION

The years 1917–30 were a period of formation—the traditional family store with seeds of change. The Steinberg store opened in 1917 and in many ways was a typical 'mom and pop' operation, except that it was mom and the kids. It was owned and operated by members of one family, merchandised its goods over the counter, knew its customers well, sold to them on credit, and often delivered its goods to them. Sam Steinberg, the second eldest son, helped his mother out everyday after school from the beginning, and he joined the store on a full-time basis in 1919, at the age of 13.

But in other ways the store was not typical. The children acquired from their mother a strong belief in the quality of the merchandise sold to the customers and a sense of honest dealing with them, beliefs that were to characterize the entire history of the firm. She also taught them a single-minded dedication to the business (e.g. investing in vegetables when 'killings' were being made everyday in the stock market), to which they attributed their subsequent success. Three other changes in the first years signaled strategies that were to come—innovation in service (the exposure of goods) in 1921, expansion of the first store in 1919 (a snap decision by Sam Steinberg, at the age of 13, during a call from the landlord asking him to post a 'for rent' sign on the space next door), the opening of new stores in 1926 and 1928 (the former called, prophetically, 'Number 1'), and the move into bulk purchasing and warehousing in 1927. During the interviews Sam Steinberg recalled images of 'beautiful' competitor stores he wished to emulate, and of other competitors' stores: '[D]ark, dingy . . . Goddamit, after 10 years in business, I'm not going to look like that.'

In Conceptual Terms

This is seen as a period of formation, of the establishment of the basic values or ideology of the company-to-be and the thorough training of the principal actors in the ways of the business. The strategies of the period were tightly integrated and rather stable—this was a period of continuity. The service and control strategies could be characterized as deliberate though implicit, the piecemeal expansion perhaps as deliberate with some emergent characteristics.

1930–41: EVOLVING GLOBAL CHANGE

The period 1930–41 can be called one of evolving global change—perfecting and elaborating a new retailing formula. The advent of the depression notwithstanding, 1930 seemed to usher in a new era of growth for what had just become Steinberg's Service Stores Limited. Three stores were opened in 1931, and not a year would pass until 1943 without a store opening. Success in those years of decline for other larger chains appears to have been based on the reputation the young chain had built up for the quality of its products and services. But until 1933, there was a parochial character to the expansion—new stores were opened to 'take care' of members of the family and to pursue the old customers to new areas of the city of Montreal.

One event in 1933 changed all that. The company 'struck it bad' with one new store, incurring unacceptable losses ($125 per week). And so, over the course of one eventful weekend, its name was changed to 'Wholesale Groceteria', prices were slashed, personal services cut, and full self-service instituted. From there, in the words of Sam Steinberg, 'we grew like topsy'. After suffering a small loss in 1933, profits rose dramatically through to 1939, and sales, after a small dip in 1934, rose to four times their 1933 level by 1940. The company was never again to experience either a loss or a decline in sales. One article decades later claimed that the company assumed in these years a lead in prices that it never relinquished. The other stores were all converted to the same format by 1936, and expansion proceeded in two major waves, the first peaking in 1937 with six stores, the second in 1941 with four. In effect, 1933 ushered in new service and promotion strategies (full self-service and discount pricing), altered the expansion strategy, and eventually led to major changes in other strategies—to one of buying and banking store sites and to mortgage financing—as well as to the continual perfecting of self-service and later the 'supermarket' concept and to a continual elaboration of the structure. The only reversion was the gradual reintroduction of the Steinberg name (in the form of Sam Steinberg's signature) on storefronts.

In Conceptual Terms

Here there was an interruption due to a competitive threat that turned the company around, sooner or later leading to major changes in almost every important strategy. Sooner, the year 1933 saw global change—sudden reversals on a number of important strategies—and later, in exploratory or piecemeal fashion, a number of other strategies were changed in consequence. Throughout this decade, the company moved slowly to a new tightly integrated set of strategies, a new 'gestalt', focused on the dominant element of self-service. These strategies seemed deliberate (after the initial test, a brief emergent phase, as in the converted store of 1933), yet not so much planned as opportunistic. In other words, they were intended, but in no particular way and at no particular time. The approach, above all, was entrepreneurial, centered on the vision of one man who, in his words, made 'all the decisions at all times'. Yet, paradoxically, all this was stimulated by a crisis, albeit one initiated by the company's own expansion. Moreover, the push to serve family needs eventually became a pull to transcend them; one element in the company's success—personal service—became one of the first casualties of that success; and the most hostile of environments became the host for successful innovation. But this major change was not a rethinking of 'what business are we in?' The company well knew what business it was in; indeed, that was the source of its strength. It was a search for 'how are we in our given business?'

1942–7: DELAY AND DIVERSION

This was a period of delay and diversion, a holding pattern from 1942 to 1947. The 1940s brought a prolonged interruption of growth—World War II. Building materials became scarce, labor was in short supply, food rationed, and prices were under government control. Expansion was halted, as was strategic innovation. What does a company with all this energy do when it is held back? First, a great deal of energy had to go into keeping the system going—'begging' for stock, imposing 'rationing on the rationing' to ensure that the scarce goods were distributed fairly among customers, and so on. Second, the delay allowed the company to continue perfecting the new retailing concept. Third, particularly at war end, when building materials remained scarce and the economy uncertain, energies were redirected to new areas that supported the basic operations. A bakery was opened in 1946, other small forms of manufacturing were initiated, and the private labeling program was expanded. But most significantly, the company prepared itself for expansion: it vigorously pursued its strategy of land banking, it engaged an architect to design future stores, it bought an oversized warehouse, it began institutional advertising, and it elaborated its service structure in ways that suggested an intention to expand.

In Conceptual Terms

Never before had this company experienced a period of consolidation; now one was imposed on it, and it reacted in part by coping with the constraints, in part by preparing itself for the expansion that it believed would inevitably come. In other words, this was not contingency planning, planning 'if'. It was planning 'when'. Nor was this planning on paper; this was acting, building the foundation rather than designing the building. One can attribute the long-term perspective, and the confidence in the eventual resumption of expansion, to the presence of an owner who knew that he would be leading the firm in that long term. So the reaction to the interrupt was in some basic sense, again, proactive.

1948–52: RESUMPTION

From 1948 to 1952 was a period of resumption, a return to steady expansion. The economy had begun to change by 1948, and Steinberg Ltd., as it was then called, was all ready to react. Whereas the previous period was characterized by diverted energies and preparation, this one was characterized by a return to one central focus of attention—the expansion in the number of retail outlets. This was the only major change in strategy in this period, but it was one that redirected energies significantly, back to where they were in the 1930s. A new wave of expansion was underway.

In Conceptual Terms

This was a period of resumption, a return to the strategy that most interested this company. But unlike the 1930s, there was less of an exploratory theme. The formula had been worked out. Now it was pursued, deliberately. The years 1948–52 represented a period of continuity.

1952–3: SHIFTING GEARS

The 1952–3 period was one of shifting gears, preparing for the big push. Sam Steinberg emphasized in interviews that waves of expansion were always followed by 'pauses', in order to solidify the changes that had been made, and to bring up the logistical support. But the pause in 1952 was unlike any other, for it led to a fundamental reorientation followed by the most important wave of expansion in the company's history.

The pause at first seemed like the others. In a 1952 article, Sam Steinberg boasted that 'not a cent of any money outside the family is invested in the company' and, asked about future plans, he replied with a 'Who knows? There is so much to do right ahead that it would sound like a wild dream to talk about 10 years from now.... We will try to go everywhere there seems to be a need for us.' Yet a few months later he announced a $15 million five-year expansion program, one new store every sixty days for a total of thirty, the doubling of sales by 1957, new stores to average double the size of existing ones, with parking lots, children's playrooms, and so on.

What caused such a dramatic change in thinking? The industry was perched for its most dramatic expansion ever, with the postwar baby boom and the population shift to the suburbs. Everything was set for a new form of merchandising—the shopping center—and the company most capable of exploiting the trend was the one that had been banking choice land sites for over a decade.

But one component of the strategy had to be changed. Conventional forms of financing were insufficient. The company had to go to public markets for capital. And once that decision was made, things changed permanently for Steinberg's Limited.

After months of searching, Sam Steinberg finally found a financial house that would support a debt issue—allowing him to retain 100 percent control—and $5 million of general debentures were issued in December of 1952. That issue required 'plans'—formal statements of intent. The market would not accept the word of one man; it needed precise descriptions. So the entrepreneur was forced to plan formally, this time on paper, and that drew him, and more importantly his company, partly into a new mode of behavior.

In Conceptual Terms

A pause led to a rethinking, which defined a need, produced a decision, altered in part the mode of strategic behavior, and led (at the start of the next period) to global changes—to a reoriented gestalt. Here can be seen the utility of the externally imposed pause, a time for reflection. Here also it can be seen that a single choice—in this case to go to public financial markets—can have ramifications far beyond its own bounds.

There seems to be a kind of push–pull phenomenon here: an organization is pushed into changing one strategy, and that in turn pulls it into far more consequential changes. The entrepreneur gets drawn by his own successes into a planning mode of strategy making, one less compatible with his own managerial style. Not only does a larger and more formalized organization structure constrain his opportunistic style, but so too does his increasing need to interact with the environment as the leader of an increasingly important organization. (In this case, it was interaction with the financial community; later it was to become interaction with the social community.) Nevertheless, although the initial move may have been reactive, the thrust remained opportunistic—the company *had* to go public but only because it *wished* to expand in a new way. Yet it appears the environment was beginning to close in on an entrepreneur.

1954–60: GLOBAL CHANGE, THEN CONTINUITY

The period 1954–60 was one of global change, then continuity—the big push. According to one long-term Steinberg executive, these were the 'make it or break it' years for supermarket chains, and Steinberg's made it, big. The company's expansion resumed at a rapid pace, most of it in shopping centers and a good deal of it for the first time outside the Montreal area. The strategy of public financing was pursued at an accelerating rate, including the first equity issue in 1955 (but nonvoting), as were the strategies of private labeling and bakery manufacturing. (Voting shares were always held entirely within the family, with 100 percent of them formally voted by Sam Steinberg until the day he passed away in 1978.) The structure became increasingly formalized in those years, with a large addition of central staff in the areas of training, accounting and control, and marketing research.

The company in fact almost did double its sales in five years, from $70 million to $132 million but, instead of the thirty stores it promised, it in fact opened thirty-five (and closed nine), one every forty-seven days. The environment was benevolent in those years, and Steinberg's Ltd., took advantage of that fact.

A new five-year plan announced in the 1958 Annual Report called for a store a month for the next sixty months, and the 1959 report upped the ante, calling for those sixty stores to be built in thirty-six months. But other forces were growing in the firm's environment. In 1957, the start of a brief recession, the company began to redeem its pink cash register slips for gifts, an indication of increasing competition. The hectic expansion of the 1950s had to lead eventually to saturation. By 1959, those slips had become Pinky Stamps, a response, management claimed, to competitive pressures. The competitive war became overt.

More significantly, whereas the company had managed to avoid head-on confrontation with the two other major Canadian chains—the largest a national chain, but a weak second to Steinberg's in Quebec, the other an Ontario-based chain with no Quebec operations—a move it took in 1959 engaged them directly. Up to 1959 every major strategic change Steinberg's made had been one of test-the-water-then-plunge. But a much larger Steinberg's Ltd. of 1959 adopted a different approach in entering the Ontario market: it plunged initially, with the purchase of the thirty-nine-store Grand Union chain there. As one executive noted, 'You can't get into Ontario one store at a time. You need a group of stores.' Its new Ontario competitors reacted strongly, setting off a price war. In 1960, despite an increase in sales of one-third over 1959, profits dipped—for the first time since 1944.

In Conceptual Terms

In the 1950s the organization understood its environment, and took off. Environment and strategy formed a perfect gestalt. The period was one of global strategic change at the start, followed by continuity. Through it all, despite another new orientation, the company remained in the same basic business. It did embark on something new—shopping center development. That, however, was a means to sell food and as such represented a form of vertical integration. Throughout the period, the organization's strategies, as previously, were largely deliberate and proactive, well suited to a benevolent environment, benevolent at least to companies that understood it and could match its rate of change. Steinberg's succeeded because it knew its business well—a condition that dated back to

1917—and because in the 1930s it had the foresight to bank land. 'It', of course, in large part meant Sam Steinberg, but backed up by a larger and larger organization.

1960–74: GLOBAL CHANGE, THEN CONTINUITY

The 1960–74 years were again, a period of global change, then continuity, with a new theme evolving, that of consolidation of traditional business and a search for new related ones. (Data on the company were collected up to the end of its fiscal year 1975, as the strategy diagrams show. But, as they also show, a number of the strategies of this last period seemed to come to a halt, or at least a pause, in the year 1974, notably all those associated with retail diversification. Hence a tentative end of this last period is shown to be in 1974.) The 1960 Annual Report announced 'a year of more conservative achievements', with the emphasis on 'consolidation' of activities, 'improvement' of existing facilities, and 'integration' of the new Ontario operation. A new economic environment faced the company: the supermarket business showed tendencies toward saturation, which were reflected in heavier competition, especially in Ontario where the company found its new acquisition to be in a weak position. Whereas growth in the 1950s could come from finding new places to put stores, in the 1960s it would have to come increasingly from outsmarting the competition and more effectively serving the public. That meant a shift in emphasis from expansion to consolidation, from opening new stores to making the existing ones more efficient and attractive.

Moreover, the social environment was changing too. From a period in which they could do no wrong, in the eyes of the public, the supermarket chains increasingly through the 1960s and 1970s found themselves subjected to all kinds of new social pressures—strikes, consumer protests and boycotts, government investigations. These were the times of the cyclamate scare, California grape boycotts, phosphate pollution from detergents, underweight violations in packages, labeling laws, attacks on excess profits, and on and on. As they grew large, the chains could not maintain a personal touch with their customers. And competition did not help. The whole set of stamp programs, for example, deflected the chains from their basic missions—to deliver food inexpensively. In effect, environments form gestalts too, and that of the 1960s was dramatically different from the one of the 1950s.

And on the eve of this era, Steinberg's had taken its boldest step ever— for the first time a plunge without testing the water. And the water proved cold. In addition to the reaction of the competition, the Grand Union sites themselves proved difficult. Many were inadequate and, in sharp contrast to the Quebec operations, which expanded from a strong base in Montreal, the firm found itself with only eight of its thirty-nine stores in the Toronto area. Consolidation was necessary—eventually, in fact, thirty-four of the thirty-nine stores it bought were closed down. Moreover, the real estate position proved critical in Ontario. Land banking was a key to the company's success in Quebec. But Grand Union had no real estate position in Ontario, and Steinberg's did not begin a strategy of land banking there with its purchase of Grand Union. A number of executives later attributed this to the nonresidence of any member of the family in Ontario until 1970, and to the inability of the managers who were sent there to exercise independent initiative. In Quebec, Sam Steinberg would buy land on instinct, based on his intimate knowledge of the area. That knowledge was lacking in Ontario, and it was not to be developed until much later. And then it was too late; the choice sites were largely gone.

These two points—a changed environment, economically hostile and socially militant, coupled with the difficulty of digesting the company's biggest bite ever—set the stage for a global reorientation of strategy beginning in 1960. The expansion strategy was moderated (and virtually stopped in the Montreal area in terms of net new stores), a new strategy of store modernizations was initiated, there was a surge of centralization and formalization of the structure in the mid-1960s by a new executive vice president (until Sam Steinberg put a stop to it), and attention was increasingly diverted to other spheres of activity. Back-integration and private-labeling strategies were pursued with more vigor. But, more importantly, there arose a strategy of diversification (followed by moves to divisionalize the structure). It began with discount (later to be called 'department') stores; then fast-food restaurants; later, in the mid-1960s, a quickening pace with a sugar refinery and a flour mill (closer to diversification than vertical integration because most of the output was sold on the open market); then pharmacies and catalog stores, as well as other ventures that did not take root (such as gas bars and the joint supermarket venture in France). The results were mixed, with the discount stores especially posing problems shortly after their inception, the catalog chain eventually sold, and the restaurants achieving a good deal of success.

The supermarket business—which continued to dominate, with over 85 percent of the sales by the end of the study period—remained in the doldrums until 1968. Competitive pressures had led to the use of stamps, games, contests, heavy advertising; the Quebec chains actually lost a slight market share to the independents between 1961 and 1969; Steinberg's profit rate leveled out in 1966 and 1967, and dropped in 1968.

And so, in 1968, in contrast to the lingering problems in the new businesses, the company acted dramatically and decisively in the old one, adopting a strategy remarkably similar to the one Sam Steinberg had used on that eventful weekend in 1933, and with the same result in performance. Wholesale Groceteria of 1933 was Miracle Pricing of 1968: significant, permanent, across-the-board price reductions coupled with a complete shift in merchandising philosophy—the elimination of specials, games, and gimmicks (the Pinky stamps had been dropped a year earlier), reduced service levels, advertising budget cut in half. The company in effect returned to what it knew best—basic, no-nonsense retailing, what one executive called 'a pure form of retailing'. And it did so in the old test-the-water-then-plunge way, with a test in one store in a small Quebec city, then implementation in Ottawa, followed quickly by the rest of Ontario and then Quebec. But one important detail differed: Miracle Pricing's champion was not Sam Steinberg, but the head of the Quebec food division, who had to convince not only the chief executive but other officers as well. And in the larger, more formalized Steinberg's Ltd., that took a number of years.

Sales rose sharply in 1969, as the company attracted a significantly greater market share, but profits dropped and then rebounded dramatically in 1970 as the new program took hold. The effect on the Quebec independents, traditionally a strong segment of that market, was 'catastrophic' according to one study of the industry. But, most importantly, Miracle Pricing turned around the Ontario operation and set it on a healthy course for the first time.

Ironically, however, according to the information available, although it probably gave added impetus to the existing strategy of expanding private labeling and to the short-term tendency to streamline the structure, Miracle Pricing seems to have led to no major shifts in strategy outside the sphere of merchandising.

In Conceptual Terms

The period began with a rather sudden, global shift in the environment, to which the company, true to form, reacted early. But that reaction violated what the chief executive himself stressed as the company's key success factor—knowledge of its business. The company was drawn into new businesses, in some sense opportunistically, but without the clear theme or vision that characterized earlier changes. It was a search for 'what business we should be in', but one that could not be undertaken on paper. To discover its strengths and weaknesses, its critical success factors, the firm had to undertake an empirical exploration that spanned decades. A strategic theme of sorts did eventually get established—the 1967 Annual Report called it the 'total marketing package', in effect the offering of a variety of retail services to take advantage of the shopping centers the company owned and/or managed. But, in sharp contrast to earlier changes, this time the strategies were less deliberate, more emergent.

The manner in which the diversification program unfolded is shown in Figure 3.6, starting from the traditional food retailing business at the left, with vertical integration moves above the line and horizontal diversification ones below it, laid out on a timescale. Figure 3.6 shows how the early back-integration moves reinforced each other and later gave rise to ones of diversification. Shopping centers provided the bridge, because what was a means of back integration—to control the sites for stores—became a means for diversification—the mechanism with which to build new kinds of stores. The figure essentially illustrates how vertical integration can lead to diversification, indeed how the same action initiated as one can become the other. Whatever the case, the company was drawn into businesses it knew less about. It was building not on the strength it always had—long-term knowledge of the business—but on its market strength, its control of sites.

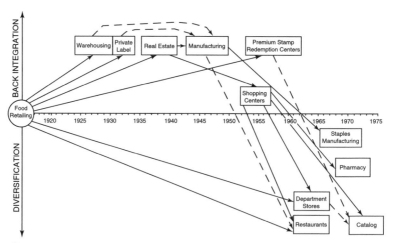

[a] This diagram was inspired by Rumelt (1974), who portrayed the diversification of Carborundum, Inc. in two snapshot views rather than across a continuous timescale.

Figure 3.6 From back integration to diversification

Overall, this period was characterized by dichotomies, the old versus the new, a business based on knowledge versus those based on market strength; having to plunge versus being able to test the water; loose, organic versus tight, formalized structure; intuitive feel versus systematic analyses; the personal touch versus the formal system. Overall, strategies were less deliberate in this period, less explicit, less tightly integrated, and less guided by the vision of one man.

In contrast to the Steinberg's of the 1930s, as the little guy fighting the giants, vulnerable on the economic front but able to move quickly, that of the 1970s was being one of those giants, possessor of a powerful economic position but more vulnerable on the social front. Did Steinberg Inc. of the 1970s in fact have greater control over its own future than did the Steinberg Service Stores of the 1930s?

Strategy Formation in the Entrepreneurial Firm

WAVES OF CHANGE

One theme that emerges from the historical review of strategy in Steinberg Inc. is the presence of waves or cycles. In the largest sense, in this study are seen the classic stages of development cycle as described by a number of management theorists (Chandler 1962; Filley, House, and Kerr 1976; Scott 1973). From the simple structure configuration of the 1920s, the company gradually underwent increasing elaboration and standardization of structure to arrive at a more formalized configuration of the 1970s. (For a more detailed description of these configurations, see Mintzberg 1979b. For a discussion of the concept of the configuration, see Miller and Mintzberg 1983; Mintzberg 1979b.) In essence, as the seemingly inevitable result of growth, the small, personalized, highly flexible (but economically vulnerable) firm transformed itself into the larger, more systematic, more economically powerful (but socially vulnerable) corporation. This transformation will be examined from two perspectives, the entrepreneurial mode and the planning mode. But first, two other themes in the study can be considered: the uneven progress of growth and the infrequency of strategic change.

HECTIC, UNEVEN GROWTH

Within this large, evolutionary cycle, shorter repeating cycles of expansion and consolidation can be detected and referred to as sprints and

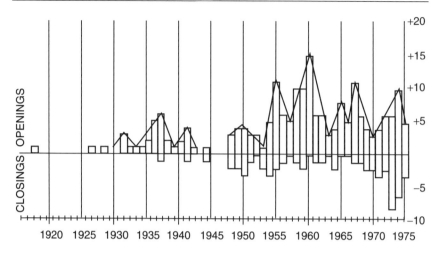

Figure 3.7 Wave pattern of store openings

pauses. As seen in Figure 3.7, an overlay on the plot of Quebec food outlet openings and closings (Figure 3.1), the notion of sprints and pauses is relevant to most of the history of the firm.

The image of sprinting is congruent with conventional notions of entrepreneurial activity as the taking of bold, risky leaps into the future. What is less obvious is that, in the case of Steinberg, these bold leaps or sprints were always accompanied by subsequent periods of pause—times for catching up, consolidating. Sam Steinberg was quite aware of this. In fact it was he who used the word 'pauses':

> I did another thing, and I always did that. After I expanded...then I'd always have a period of pause, pause meaning a year or two to make sure that everything carried and was working out. You are able to cope with the salary, you're able to cope with what you've taken on. I'd always do that. So if you'll study the growth of our company, you'll see that we have a period of expansion and a pause, an expansion and a pause.

This pattern of sprints and pauses suggests an inchworm analogy: an organization leads with some primary strategy, usually related to expansion, then pauses to bring up lagging strategies, for example, logistic support, then leads again, and so on. A number of new stores are opened—perhaps too many, overextending the resources—and then refinancing taken place, warehouses expanded, staff found to man the new operations, and so on. The approach is fundamentally opportunistic as opposed to planned, a probe into the future without full consideration of the consequences.

The result is an unsteady pattern of growth, but one that can generate a great deal of excitement and energy within an organization. Growth becomes the all-out sprint, pause, the time to catch breath, 'to make sure that everything carried and was working out'. The inchworm probes its head into an uncertain future, then brings up its rear—the baggage—to keep pace.

Some definite advantages can be seen in the inchworm form of growth, at least where the organization can absorb the swings. It finds its openings—its short-lived strategic windows—and exploits them to the hilt, damning the consequences, with a faith that other needs—people, money, warehouse capacity—will get straightened out eventually. Sprinting is a way to focus the resources and energy available so that great pressure is brought to bear on opportunities as they present themselves. The organization utilizes its resources fully; were the expansion forced to await a more abstract analysis of the resources available, it might never happen. As one executive noted, 'It took nine months to build a store. When work began, we would ask ourselves who we had to run it. Only bums. But as we got closer to opening, the bums started to look better.'

However, just as the inchworm cannot stretch so far forward that it falls over or is immobilized, so the entrepreneur must know when and how to stop sprinting and start to pause. Some pauses are forced by the environment, as in the World War II period of this study. Others result from a depletion of resources, as in the pause in the early 1950s. But leaders must also sense when 'enough is enough' of sprinting. They may have a personal sense of overextension, may be personally exhausted, or unable to keep up with all the changes. Or they may realize the effects on key managers in terms of long working hours, fatigue, frayed tempers, sagging morale. In any event, the timing of pauses would seem to be critical in order to *sustain* entrepreneurial success.

Finally, sprinting and pausing may be seen as a way for an organization to keep itself energetic. Sprinting provides an inspirational period of change; pausing provides for the maintenance and stability required to renew energies so as to be able to accept once again the challenge of change. Organizations, of course, can plan their expansions systematically and so maintain them at continuous rates. But the cost of this may be reduced emotional involvement and commitment on the part of the employees. Steinberg's discount store operation in fact grew steadily

(Figure 3.4), but that growth seems to have been less inspired and certainly less ambitious and successful.

MAJOR, INFREQUENT STRATEGY REORIENTATIONS

Between the very long cycle of transformation from simple to more formalized structure and the relatively short cycles of sprints and pauses, major reorientations of strategy can be identified. These do not follow any predictable pattern, and in fact seem to occur quite infrequently.

In Steinberg's, a highly adaptive firm, there were shifts in strategic behavior (i.e. a new period in the history), six times in fifty-seven years, or roughly once every ten years. Furthermore, truly major reorientations of strategy seem to have taken place only three times: in the early 1930s, early 1950s, and early 1960s. The first two were key turning points; the first a complete rethinking of strategic orientation—a changed vision by the leader and a gestalt shift in strategy because of a crisis—and the second, the removal of a key constraint, which opened the door to a global reorientation already envisioned by the leader. These were Steinberg's strategic windows to future successes, and the company went through both at the right moment. The third reorientation, in the 1960s—the search for growth in new markets as the old ones became saturated—was less decisive, less focused, and more difficult.

If strategic reorientation really does take place only once every ten or twenty years in the typical firm, it can hardly be a continuous concern of top management, perpetually on their minds. Yet business schools train MBA students by having them analyze several such cases every week, and business management engage in formal strategic planning on the assumption of an annual reassessment of strategy with a rolling five-year time horizon. With these long gaps between necessary reorientations, this annual reassessment can easily become a mechanical extrapolation of information. This kind of exercise, like 'crying wolf too often', may actually *desensitize* top managers to strategic issues, so that the need for substantive change may not be recognized when it does arise. Conversely, it may encourage change when it is unnecessary—a kind of *oversensitivity* to strategic issues. Miller and Friesen (1978), in fact, find evidence of this phenomenon in one of their archetypes of strategic behavior, which they call 'the impulsive firm'.

The essential issue remains unaddressed: how to be ready for a major reorientation when it may be really necessary only once every ten or twenty years? How to avoid atrophy of the capacity to think strategically, while avoiding needless 'tinkering'? Were periods of global reorientation—even every twenty years—surrounded by ones of manifest stability, the problem would be simplified. But they are not. Organizations are always changing, but on different levels of abstraction or inclusiveness. Sam Steinberg's genius seems to have been his ability to shift mental gears from one of these levels to another. After spending years in the 1930s and 1940s worrying about fluorescent lighting and new ways to package meat for self-service, he was able to shift his thoughts in the 1950s to the impact of shopping centers on overall retailing habits.

A striking aspect of Sam Steinberg and many key managers in the firm was their apparent ability to invest themselves in a question about the quality of a shipment of strawberries with the same passion and commitment as in a question about opening a chain of restaurants. The strategy analyst explicitly downgrades the importance of the former questions to focus on the latter, the 'big' questions. Somehow, that distinction seems less clear-cut for the managers of this study. Indeed, their thorough involvement in the day-to-day issues (such as the quality of strawberries) provided the very intimate knowledge that informed their more global vision. That is why analysts may develop plans, but they are unlikely to come up with visions.

THE POWER OF THE ENTREPRENEURIAL MODE

This study highlights the characteristics of the entrepreneurial mode of strategy making in the simple structure. The literature characterizes the entrepreneur as the bold decision-maker, fully in control, who walks confidently into an uncertain future (Mintzberg, 1973a). If anyone fits that description, Sam Steinberg certainly does. That is what gave this organization its spirit, its drive. Even when things looked bleak, the company 'knew'—he knew—that it would bounce back, and that prophecy became self-fulfilling. One is reminded of Starbuck and Hedberg's (1977) description of how Facet turned itself around just because it knew an enthusiastic leadership was taking it over. Mood cannot be discounted as a factor in strategic behavior.

Yet entrepreneurs protect themselves in their bold actions, control them, for successful entrepreneurship is not equivalent to foolhardiness. As noted earlier, periods of pause, followed by periods of sprinting, were used to ensure that the organization remained viable. In addition, with a few exceptions that were to prove significant, Sam Steinberg pursued what can be called a 'test-the-water' approach, always sensing an environment with minor probes before plunging in. In the earlier years at least, Steinberg never undertook a bold move until he had a pretty good idea what the consequences would be. Of course, such an approach was possible in the supermarket business. Such stores are built one by one, as independent units. One does not go to the moon or open an asbestos mine that way. But then, entrepreneurs choose their businesses too.

In addition to the notion of controlled boldness, a major characteristic of the entrepreneurial mode—one repeatedly stressed by Sam Steinberg— is the leader's intimate knowledge of the business. It is intuition that directs the entrepreneur, intuition based on wisdom—detailed, ingrained, personalized knowledge of the world. In discussing the firm's competitive advantage, Sam Steinberg remarked: 'Nobody knew the grocery business like we did. Everything has to do with your knowledge.' He added:

I knew merchandise, I knew cost, I knew selling, I knew customers, I knew everything... and I passed on all my knowledge; I kept teaching my people. That's the advantage we had. They couldn't touch us.

This study shows how effective such knowledge can be when it is concentrated in one individual who (a) is fully in charge (having no need to convince others with different views and different levels of knowledge, neither subordinates below nor superiors at some distant headquarters); (b) retains a strong, long-term commitment to the organization (knowing that, barring a natural disaster, it is he or she who will be there in the long run); and (c) possesses the vision and ability to switch from narrow focus to broad perspective. Under all these conditions—so long as the business is simple and concentrated enough to be comprehended in one brain, and this one was before it diversified—the entrepreneurial mode is powerful, indeed unexcelled. No other mode of strategy making can provide the degree of deliberateness and of integration of strategies with each other and with the environment. None can provide so clear and complete a vision of direction, yet also allow the flexibility to elaborate and rework that vision. The conception of a novel strategy is an exercise in synthesis, which typically is best carried out in a single, informed brain. That is why the entrepreneurial mode is at the center of the most glorious corporate successes.

Embedded in conventional thinking about strategic planning is an implicit image of the strategy-maker sitting on a pedestal, being fed aggregate data that is used to 'formulate' strategies to be 'implemented' by others. But the history of Steinberg's belies that image. It suggests that clear, imaginative, integrated visions depend on an involvement with detail, an intimate knowledge of specifics. As noted earlier, the ability to be passionately involved at all levels of activity in the business was a striking characteristic of Sam Steinberg.

That this remained possible for such a long period of time, even as the company grew very large, likely is a reflection of the simple and repetitive nature of this business. The same simple transaction repeated itself customer after customer, store after store, thousands of times each day. Once the firm shifted from personalized to self-service (i.e. impersonalized service), then 200 stores were not unlike 20 so long as they were concentrated in a geographical area the leader knew well.

THE WEAKNESS OF THE ENTREPRENEURIAL MODE

The personal touch of the entrepreneur was critical to Steinberg's success. The irony was that it was the very success of the entrepreneurial mode that rendered it unsuitable in the longer run. As long as the strategy-maker knew the firm's operations intimately, the entrepreneurial mode was effective. It was when the operations spread beyond the comprehension of one person—first to diversify geographically to regions outside of its leader's personal knowledge, and then horizontally to new kinds of retailing—that a shift in the mode of strategy making became inevitable. No longer could decisions be based on the personalized vision of one individual, because no longer could all the necessary knowledge be focused there.

Growth and diversification (due to saturation of traditional markets) necessitated the building up of a more formalized structure with divided responsibilities and increased distance between Sam Steinberg and the operations. And so the new mode of strategy making was more decentralized, more analytic, in some ways more careful, but less flexible, less integrated, less visionary, and, ironically, less deliberate. The controlled boldness of the test-the-water approach in some cases had to give way to straight plunges (as in the Grand Union purchase), in others to gradual immersion (as in the growth of the discount store chain), although in still others it remained (as in the Miracle Pricing program, so similar to the Wholesale Groceteria changes of the 1930s).

Before the shift, strategy making at Steinberg's could be characterized as the interplay of a leader and an environment, with structure bringing up the rear (to evoke the inchworm analogy once again). Here was a leader very much attuned to the environment, 'reacting' to it 'proactively' with the assumption that the structure was lean and flexible enough to adapt to any change he made (at least given a period of pause). In this entrepreneurial mode, structure clearly followed strategy. But over time, both the environment and the structure became more demanding, until the interplay seemed to be increasingly between a formalized structure and a constraining environment, with leadership caught in between. Eventually strategy, to some extent at least, had to follow structure, as well as environment.

ENTER THE PLANNING MODE, AS PROGRAMMING

Planning seemed to be one element of that new mode of the 1960s and 1970s. The authors feel that the literature on strategy formation is in great need of an operational definition of planning. In other words, a description is needed of what the word actually means in use, not in the abstractions of prescriptive theory. If planning simply means 'future thinking', as implied by some of its most ardent proponents, then all decision making is planning, because a decision is a commitment to action, that is, a commitment to do something in the future. By that token, Sam Steinberg was always a planner. But, also by that token, to quote Wildavsky, 'If planning is everything, maybe it's nothing' (1973). Alternately, if planning is an exercise carried out by people called planners (as opposed to managers), in this study at least, it has little to do with strategy formation. Somewhere in between is the view of planning as the attempt to make and *integrate* a whole set of decisions and to articulate them formally before executing them.

Over time, Steinberg's was drawn into this kind of behavior, not out of choice but out of necessity, because of the demands of the environment. The real turning point was its initial public financing in fiscal 1953. The financial community demands plans for its money; the entrepreneurial mode is unacceptable, at least untempered (on paper at a minimum) by the planning mode. Thereafter, an annual report forces a company at least to go through the motions of planning year after year, and that cannot help but have an influence on strategy-making behavior.

At Steinberg's, planning really was never strategy formulation; it was programming. When Steinberg's developed its first plan in the 1950s, it was not inventing a strategy. Rather it was justifying, elaborating, and making public a strategy it already had, the one based on its leader's vision. That particular strategy was conceived in the entrepreneurial mode, the creativity and synthesis taking place informally and personally. Planning involved the articulation, quantification, and eventual elaboration of the given vision. The first plan took the shift into shopping centers as given, and it figured out how many stores would be built, what logistic support would be necessary, and so on. And, as time went on, the company would be called on increasingly to engage in such planning. For example, the Miracle Pricing program—another vision—required extensive planning in terms of what prices to cut on what products, what shifts to make on the advertising budget, and so on. Such planning-as-programming became increasingly necessary as the company grew. Growth made the company more reliant on public financial offerings, increased the consequences of its strategic moves, and forced it to coordinate more tightly the efforts of more units in its structure.

A tentative conclusion is that companies plan when they *have* intended strategies, not in order to get them. In other words, one plans not a strategy but the consequences of it. Planning gives order to vision, and puts form on it for the sake of formalized structure and environmental expectation. One can say that planning operationalizes strategy. Although such planning-as-programming is not necessary under all conditions, under some it is mandatory. It may be the only way to pull together the diverse decisions of large organizations in stable environments and to handle large and complicated commitments of resources. To draw on another of the authors' studies, one does not invest almost $100 million in a mine in the remotest part of Quebec without a great deal of this kind of programming.

But, as noted, there is an effect of planning on vision, for the inevitable result of programming the entrepreneur's vision is to constrain it. The entrepreneur, by keeping vision personal, is able to adapt it at will to a changing environment. By being forced to articulate and program it, that flexibility is undermined. The danger, ultimately, is that the planning mode forces out the entrepreneurial one; procedure tends to replace vision, so that strategy making becomes more extrapolation than invention. The very fact of programming impedes true formulation, changes in degree drive out changes in kind. In the absence of a vision, planning comes to extrapolate the status quo, leading at best to marginal changes in current practice. It is suspected that these two conclusions—planning-as-programming of a given strategy rather than the formulation of a new one, and planning replacing entrepreneurial initiative as an inevitable result of larger organization and more formalized structure—speak for a good deal of the behavior known as strategic planning.

CONCLUSION

This study shows how the success of the entrepreneurial mode evokes the forces—both in structure and in environment—that weaken it. Steinberg Inc. at the end of the study period remained in some ways in the entrepreneurial mode. But the forces to weaken that orientation were growing stronger. In some ways, society benefits from such a result. It gains a surer, more stable, and systematic service from its enterprises. But it pays a large price too—less color, less innovation, less excitement, less belief in a unique sense of identity. Only by allowing—and these days by actually encouraging—both modes to exist in different organizations can society reap the benefits of both worlds.

Sam Steinberg passed away suddenly in 1978, in fact just after our first interview with him and just before the second one was to take place. His shares passed to his three daughters, the husband of one of whom became CEO of the company. They sold out to a financier in 1989, who attempted to take the company apart. Steinberg Inc. ceased to exist in 1992.

4

Strategy Formation in an Adhocracy
The National Film Board of Canada, 1939–75

Henry Mintzberg and Alexandra McHugh[1]

*Based on the detailed tracking over time of the actions of a single project
organization, strongly resemblant of an ideal type called 'adhocracy', this
chapter shows that strategies can form in a variety of different ways:
from the precedents set by individual actors, from thin streams of activity that eventually pervade an organization, from spontaneous convergence in the behavior of a variety of actors, and so on. These findings
focus on three themes: the emergent nature of the organization's strategies and the difficulties of identifying intention in a collective context;
the cycles of behavior that resulted from attempts to reconcile the concurrent needs for convergence and divergence; and the organization's quest
for adhocracy and the problems this posed for the exercise of formal
leadership. The chapter concludes with a 'grassroots' model of strategy
formation.*

'One best way' thinking has pervaded the field of management since
Frederick W. Taylor (1947) coined the term early in this century. It has
been particularly influential in two spheres—the designing of organizational structures and the making of organizational strategies.

At least until recently, the underlying assumptions of organizational
design have been that organizations require articulated objectives,
sharp divisions of labor; clearly defined tasks, well-developed hierar-
chies, and formalized systems of control. In fact, this configuration of
elements—close to the ideal-type, machine-like bureaucracy Weber (1958)

[1] Originally published in *Administration Science Quarterly* (1985: 160–97), with minor revisions in this volume.

first described—appears to remain the predominant conception among practitioners in government, mass production, and the consulting profession: to many of them, 'machine bureaucracy' is not just one alternate form of structure, it *is* structure.

Correspondingly, strategy making still tends to be equated with planning—with the systematic 'formulation' and articulation of deliberate, premeditated strategies, which are then 'implemented'. This, however, is inconsistent with more contemporary forms of structure and sometimes with the conventional forms as well.

One important contemporary form is project structure, or 'adhocracy' (Bennis and Slater 1964; Toffler 1970). As described by Mintzberg (1979*b*), this configuration includes the following elements:

1. The organization operates in an environment that is both dynamic and complex, demanding innovation of a fairly sophisticated nature. Each output tends to be unique (e.g. a film, the prototype for a new product).

2. The production of complex, unique outputs forces the organization to engage highly trained experts and to combine their talents in multidisciplinary teams.

3. These experts are housed in specialized units, for administrative and housekeeping purposes, but are deployed in temporary teams to work on their projects; the structure thus takes on the form of a matrix.

4. Because of the complex and unpredictable nature of its work, the organization relies largely on mutual adjustment for coordination, which is encouraged by semiformal structural parameters such as liaison personnel and standing committees. Coordination by direct supervision and standardization are discouraged, as are the more formalized aspects of structure that support them, such as hierarchy, performance controls, and rules.

5. The organization is decentralized 'selectively': power over different decisions is diffused in uneven ways, subject to the availability of information and expertise needed to deal with the issue at hand. Consistent with Stinchcombe's (1963) proposition that structures tend to reflect the age of founding of their industry, adhocracy seems to be common in industries that have developed in the last sixty years or so: they seem to be the structure of our age.

This chapter presents an in-depth study of strategy in one such project organization, to suggest a very different view of the strategy formation process, which seems to be associated especially, but not exclusively with the configuration called adhocracy.

The National Film Board of Canada as an Adhocracy

The National Film Board of Canada (NFB) was founded in 1939 as an agency of the federal government of Canada to produce and distribute films that would interpret Canada to Canadians and to people abroad. It has since developed an international reputation for the quality of its documentary filmmaking and for its innovations in film content, process, and technology. In 1975, the NFB had a permanent staff of approximately 950 people, with an annual budget of CAN$23.5 million. The NFB was an organization quite unlike any other: a film company with full production and marketing functions, concentrating on short, documentary films aimed at predominantly nontheatrical markets, that fell under full state ownership.

The NFB also seemed to fit the description of an adhocracy quite well. Each of its films was unique, and many were distinguished for their sophistication and innovation. Each required a distinct but temporary project, which drew together experts from a variety of functional departments. This suggests matrix structure, as is indicated in Figure 4.1, the NFB's organigram (c.1975), in which the filmmakers were shown suspended under a structure of studios and specialized functions, as well as regions. In fact, the absence of connections between the filmmakers and the structure indicates the relative weakness of authority and hierarchy in the organization. Controls existed in the NFB and attempts were made at formal planning, but most of the real coordination had to be achieved through mutual adjustment. Selective decentralization is perhaps best illustrated by the process surrounding the approval and funding of film projects.

On average, the NFB made about seventy-five films per year. Had it been structured as a machine bureaucracy, word would presumably have come down from high, dictating subject matter, length, style, etc., resulting in a stable and rather deliberate film-content strategy. The facts reported here are rather different. Aside from the specific films commissioned, or 'sponsored', by other government departments, all the others drew on

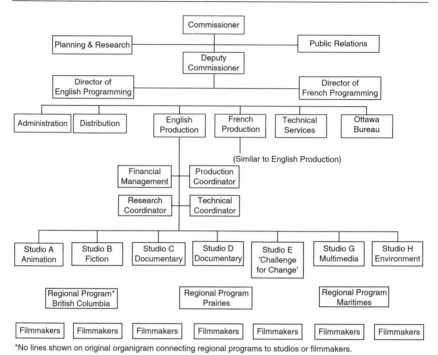

Figure 4.1 Organigram of the National Film Board of Canada (*c*.1975)

the general budget of the organization, supplied by the government and supplemented by revenues from the sale and rental of films. Film ideas generally originated with a filmmaker in consultation with an executive producer and were eventually proposed to a standing committee—the Program Committee—which consists of representatives elected by the filmmakers, appointees of the Distribution Branch (marketing), the Director of Production, and the Director of Programming. As chief executive officer, the Film Commissioner had to approve this committee's choices, and almost inevitably did. Thus, control over film choices was distributed across all levels of the organization and among various functions.

On first impression, then, this project-by-project working rhythm would seem to epitomize adhocracy. As we probe more deeply into NFB history, we shall elaborate on this conclusion, showing how its structure was in fact an evolved compromise, a balancing act worked out in response to the demands of the individual project, on the one hand, and the need for a certain order, on the other. As in the other studies reported in this book, the research proceeded as follows:

Step 1: Collection of basic data. The study began in the archives, with the search for traces of decisions and actions taken by the organization, sorted into various strategy areas, as well as traces of external trends and events in the environment and indicators of performance. Sources for this data included film catalogs, annual reports, in-house documents, and books and articles on the organization, all supplemented by interviews to fill in the gaps.

Step 2: Inference of strategies and periods. The data on decisions and actions were arranged in chronological order, when possible plotted on common timescales, and analyzed to infer patterns or consistencies over time, i.e. strategies, which were represented in symbolic form, lined up on a common timescale, and scanned to infer distinct overall periods in the history of the organization.

Step 3: Analyses of each period. At this point, the character of the research changed, from the systematic collection of 'hard' data to the more intensive investigation of more qualitative data. Interviews were conducted with key people who were present, and reports of the period were studied to explain the major changes in strategies. A number of 30–40-year-old NFB veterans were accessible, as were several reports, books, and theses on or related to the organization, including the Massey Commission Report (1951), McKay (1965), James (1968), Gray (1973), McInnes (1974), Jones (1976), and Hardy (1979). Posing very specific questions in the interviews, based on the data gathered, aided recall and helped to avoid distortion.

Step 4: Theoretical analyses. The researchers then brainstormed around a number of theoretical questions to try to interpret each historical period, as well as the entire study, in conceptual terms: the patterns of strategic change, the relationships between deliberate and emergent strategies, the interplay of environment, leadership, and organization, and the relationship between strategy and structure.

The study of the NFB from 1939 to 1975 took place on-site over a number of years and eventually resulted in a 383-page document based on an extensive amount of data. In particular, each of the 2,839 original films completed between 1939 and 1975 were categorized along a number of dimensions and then were plotted and analyzed in various ways.

The first section describes the various *realized* strategies that were inferred in the behavior of this organization across thirty-seven years. Each period is then described in the second section. The final section develops a conceptual interpretation of the entire study.

Strategies of the NFB, 1939–75

The NFB, of necessity, took a large number of actions over the course of thirty-seven years. Discussion with its members, as well as our own overall assessment of its activities, suggested the following areas to be of central importance: first, the films produced, which could be analyzed in terms of various characteristics—the number made, their duration in minutes, the content, the original language of production (English or French), whether sponsored by other government agencies or not, produced in black and white or color, and in 16 or 35 mm—and then financing, staffing, distribution (marketing), and the internal structure.

A full presentation of all the strategies identified, together with the data and text that support their inference, is well beyond our space limitations here. We therefore present only those strategies most revealing of the course of the organization over time and related material, in graphic and symbolic form, with a minimal amount of textual material, except for the area of film content (because of its importance and what it reveals about our method of inferring strategies).

FINANCE

Since most of the NFB's financing arrived as direct grants from the government, the area of finance is not only one of strategy (internal actions) but also of environment and performance. Figure 4.2 shows the total annual revenues of the NFB, by source. Of particular importance were the sudden, temporary dips in appropriations (notably in 1947–9, 1958, 1970–1), known to employees as periods of 'austerity'.

STAFFING

Figure 4.3 shows the number of persons on regular staff since 1945, as well as temporary employees ('on contract') since 1957. The strategies inferred (for the most part, directly from these data) are represented symbolically in Strategy Diagram 4A. In this representation of strategies, and all that

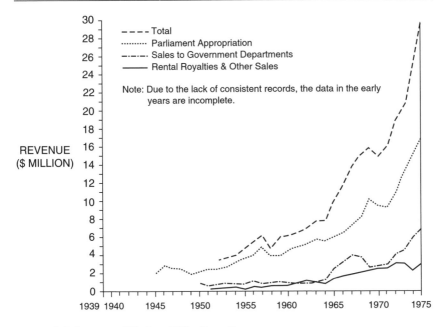

Figure 4.2 Sources of National Film Board's revenues

follow, the vertical dimension is used to symbolize certain characteristics of strategies but does not represent any specific scale.

DISTRIBUTION

Distribution, the NFB's name for marketing, can be divided into three main channels: theatrical, nontheatrical (e.g. schools, church groups), and television. A variety of distribution strategies were inferred from a

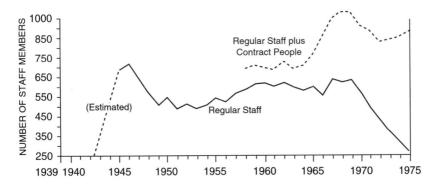

Figure 4.3 Staffing levels

STAFFING

Strategy Diagram 4A Staffing

DISTRIBUTION

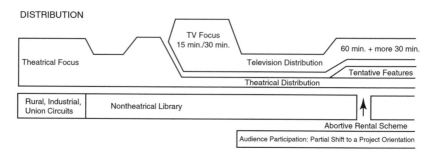

Strategy Diagram 4B Distribution

PRODUCTION STRUCTURE

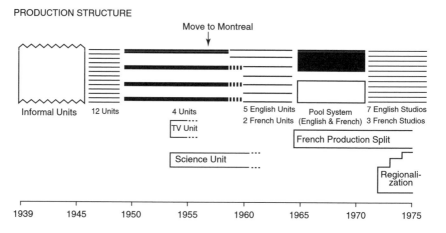

Strategy Diagram 4C Production structure

FILM NUMBER AND LENGTH

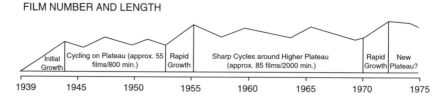

Strategy Diagram 4D Film number and length

number of sources, notably archival records on the media employed in different periods and a statistical analysis of the duration of films by year. The latter, for example, revealed a heavy emphasis on films for television from 1953 to 1957 (sharp rise of films in the 12–15-minute and then 26–30-minute range to fill slots in the newly created Canadian Broadcasting Corporation network), and the beginnings of a feature film strategy in the mid-1960s (first significant appearance of films longer than 60 minutes). These two strategies, as well as a number of others inferred (to be discussed later), are shown symbolically in Strategy Diagram 4B.

STRUCTURE

Of particular interest in the structuring of this organization are the forms of departmentalization used in the production function over the years, as well as the separation of French and English filmmaking (always a contentious issue). The various forms of structure are shown symbolically in Strategy Diagram 4C.

NUMBER AND LENGTH OF FILMS

An analysis and comparison of several types of records in the NFB archives uncovered 2,839 original films completed between 1939 and 1975. A plot of their number per year, as well as of their average duration in minutes, led to the inference of the strategies shown in Strategy Diagram 4D.

LANGUAGE OF FILMS

Plots of the number and duration of films in the French and English languages revealed sharply different patterns for each, as shown in Strategy Diagram 4E and 4F.

SPONSORSHIP OF FILMS

Films made by the NFB under direct contract to other government departments (e.g. training films for the RCMP) accounted for exactly one-quarter of the total over the years, and 21 percent of all minutes of films produced. Figure 4.4, which shows the proportion of minutes of sponsored films by year, reveals one strong surge after World War II, which is depicted in Strategy Diagram 4G.

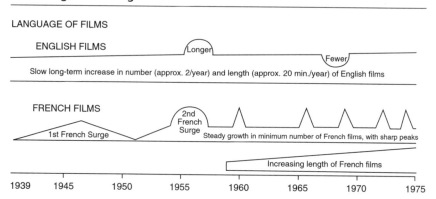

Strategy Diagram 4E and 4F English and French Films

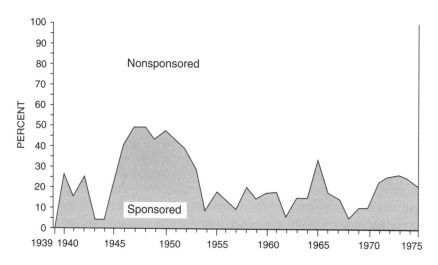

Figure 4.4 Proportion of minutes of sponsored films

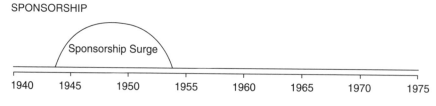

Strategy Diagram 4G Sponsorship

CONTENT OF FILMS

Finally, and perhaps most importantly, is the actual content of the films made by the NFB. The 2,839 films were each assigned to one of thirty-seven content or related categories, chosen partly with regard to the categories actually used in NFB film catalogs. The data for three years in the 1970s was coded by two people independently, with almost complete agreement. We found it most useful to analyze each of the thirty-seven categories over time in terms of three basic flows:

- *trickle*—defined as a stream of five or fewer films per year.
- *blip*—defined as one or two years in which production increased by an increment of five, from a trickle before and after.
- *focused strategy*—defined as five or more films in a category for at least three consecutive years.

The apparent ambiguities that arose from these definitions (e.g. a sequence of 0-6-3 films, not quite a blip, or one of 2-6-4-7-3 films, not quite a focused strategy) were few and minor and were dealt with on an exception basis; no sequence occurred of 5-5-5, which could technically be defined as either a trickle or a focused strategy.

The content categories fell into a number of distinct patterns. Nine of them revealed only trickles, whether steady or sporadic (accounting for 10 percent of all films made). In effect, attention to each of these categories was always marginal, even if sometimes steady, as shown in the example in Figure 4.5a. A further thirteen categories contained trickles with a blip or two, while four more had recurring blips (accounting in all for 38 percent of all films produced). Many of these blips represented sponsored series, as in Figure 4.5b, of films in the 'educational practice' category. Finally, there were the categories that contained focused strategies, in five cases (and 21 percent of films) trickles and/or blips that

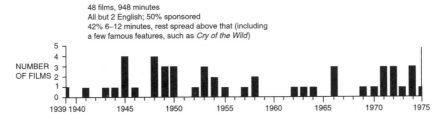

48 films, 948 minutes
All but 2 English; 50% sponsored
42% 6–12 minutes, rest spread above that (including a few famous features, such as *Cry of the Wild*)

Figure 4.5a Natural environment category. Example of steady trickle

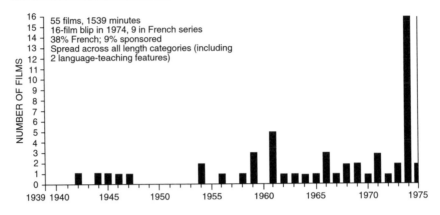

Figure 4.5b Educational practice category example of trickle with blip

grew into centers of focus (e.g. Figures 4.6a, 4.6b, 4.6c), in three cases (11 percent of films) centers of focus that reduced to trickles (possibly with recurring blips, e.g. Figure 4.6d). In only one category (7 percent of films) did recurring focused strategies appear. In another important case (12 percent of all films), a single focused strategy disappeared after two blips (Figure 4.6e). And finally there was one case of a small, isolated focused strategy at the end of the study period. Figures 4.6a–4.6e show some of the more important content categories that will be discussed below.

What seems to stand out in this analysis is the great diversity of activity: with one possible exception, no content category sustained the attention of the organization. Some did so temporarily, in waves or single surges,

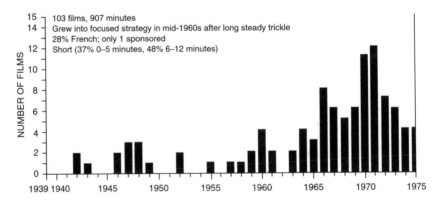

Figure 4.6a Experimental films trickle growing into focused strategy

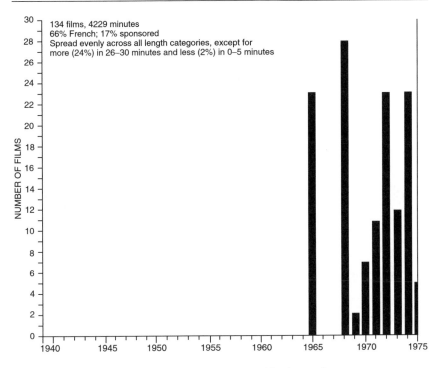

Figure 4.6b 'Challenge for change' blips followed by focused strategy

and a remarkable number received steady or recurring marginal attention (i.e. trickles). But, overall, films ranged widely across these content areas. Indeed, further analysis revealed that in every year but three since 1947, more than half the thirty-seven content categories were represented.

Yet diversity does not tell the whole story; indeed, it does not correctly capture the reality of these data. It is when the trickles, blips, and focused strategies are each combined that the most revealing picture emerges. Figure 4.7 shows the cumulative number of films that fell into the trickle, blip, and focused strategy categories per year. The number of trickles climbed sharply to a peak at the end of the 1940s, declined for several years, and then grew again periodically. Blips seemed to be cumulatively what they were individually: they tended to occur in clusters but irregularly (except for the early 1960s). Likewise, focused strategies seemed to be cumulatively what they were individually. In other words, the organization seemed to focus on focused strategies for certain periods, notably during the war around defense and then industry themes, the mid-1950s around general series for television, and the mid-1960s

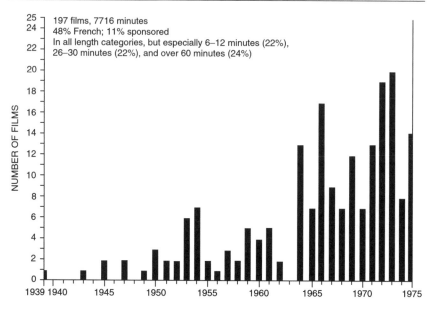

Figure 4.6c Sociology films trickle growing into focused strategy

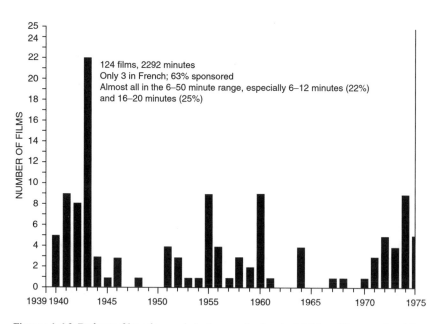

Figure 4.6d Defense films focused strategy reducing to trickle with recurring blips

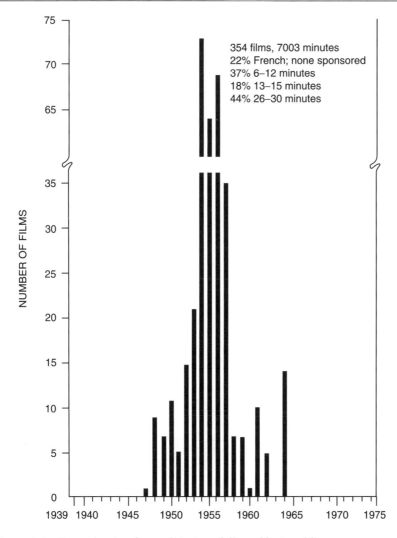

354 films, 7003 minutes
22% French; none sponsored
37% 6–12 minutes
18% 13–15 minutes
44% 26–30 minutes

Figure 4.6e General series, focused strategy followed by two blips

and then the 1970s around experimental, social, and sociological themes.

These patterns are more clearly illustrated in Figure 4.8, which shows the percentage of trickles, blips, and focused strategies per year. One message seems evident: this was an organization that cycled into and out of focus, at least partially. Several periods of focus stand out: the early 1940s, the mid-1950s, the mid-1960s, and the 1970s. It would be equally accurate to conclude that periods of pervasive diversity stand out

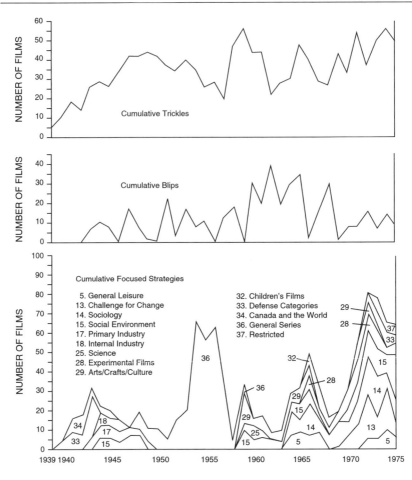

Figure 4.7 Cumulative trickle, blip, and focused strategy films

as well—one largely of trickles in the late 1940s and early 1950s, a second of mixed trickles and blips in the late 1950s and early 1960s, as well as a brief period of trickles and some blips in the late 1960s. Of course, this organization could never be characterized as highly focused, since at least half of its output was almost always in trickles and blips. Nevertheless, given the substantial diversity among the various film-content categories themselves, the cycling between periods of focus and diversity seems to be remarkably regular (six, six, five, six, four, and two years, as well as at least six years in the last cycle). This suggests some intriguing order in diversity, with perhaps some fundamental forces at play.

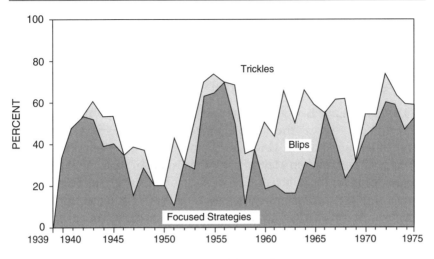

Figure 4.8 Proportion of trickles, blips, and focused strategies

Shown symbolically in Strategy Diagram 4H are these periods of focus and diversity in film content. Because of the importance of film content itself in this organization, as well as the fact that many other important strategies changed in accordance with these periods (e.g. the sponsorship surge in the first period of divergence, the initial rise and decline in hiring in the first two periods), we used these periods of forward diversity primarily to identify the major periods in the history of the NFB.

Periods in the NFB History

While the previous section introduced the skeleton of this organization's history, in the form of its realized strategies, this one adds some flesh,

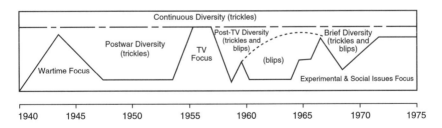

Strategy Diagram 4H Focus and diversity in film content

describing its story across six periods to explain how these strategies developed.

1939–45, WARTIME FOCUS: BUILDING THE FOUNDATION

In 1938, the Canadian government invited John Grierson, a Scot with a missionary zeal for the making of documentary films, to report on government filmmaking. Grierson recommended the establishment of a strong film unit, and on May 2, 1939, the Canadian Parliament passed an act providing for the establishment of a National Film Board. Four months later, war broke out, and several weeks after that, sensing an opportunity to pursue his belief that the documentary films should serve a positive propaganda function in a democracy,[2] Grierson accepted an invitation to head the new organization. He hired creative and energetic but inexperienced Canadians and began to train them under a trio of trusted colleagues he brought over from England. Organic in the extreme—in its on-the-spot hiring practices, rapid job shifts, and deliberate and gleeful flaunting of civil service procedures—the organization was dominated by a sense of excitement and mission. By the end of the war, the NFB contained over 700 people.

Under Grierson's dictum, 'Bang'em out and no misses', production rose to about sixty films per year by 1943 and stabilized there. About half of the films were made under the Wartime Information Program, with others on subjects such as Canadian agriculture, cultural activities, and industry. A fair proportion of films in 1940–2 was sponsored by government departments (notably the armed forces), with Grierson the master salesman.

Thanks to special wartime government allotments, important newsreel series were developed for distribution in commercial theaters. This was part of a four-pronged, intended (and subsequently realized) strategy of distribution, announced in 1940: to reach urban audiences through theaters and special screenings (e.g. in factories), to make films and projectors available for private screenings, and to reach, through traveling NFB projectionists, the rural half of the Canadian population that could not get to theaters.

---

[2] There is a touch of irony in this, given the controversy that erupted in early 1983 when the US government insisted that three films marketed by the NFB in USA, including one on nuclear warfare, be formally labeled 'propaganda'. This latter film subsequently won an Oscar.

In Conceptual Terms

This was a period of formation, of the establishment of a basic, tightly integrated ('gestalt') set of strategies which created a strong foundation that sustained the organization for decades. Although specific strategies changed, the fundamental norms established in this period did not—a concentration on documentary-style filmmaking, a concern for the social impact of films, grassroots distribution, and high standards of excellence and innovation. A confluence of three situational factors gave rise to the gestalt strategy: (*a*) the newness of the organization, which allowed for organic structure and the enthusiasm associated with creation; (*b*) the outbreak of war, which provided an unexpected but compelling sense of mission; (*c*) and the naming of a highly charismatic leader, who could resist bureaucratic pressures and exploit the first two factors to drive the organization on a course of excitement and excellence.

A number of strategies, notably growth in staff and number of films and the favored channels of distribution, were clearly intended by the leader and so can be called deliberate. The film-content strategies, however, were largely imposed by the circumstances of the environment and so were more emergent (while an intended strategy of attention to French production was partially unrealized). For the most part, the strategies were bold and proactive, in part a consequence of the vision of the leader. Thus, the mode of strategy making can be characterized as entrepreneurial, and the organization structure rather simple and leader-led, although it exhibited clear indications of the coming characteristics of adhocracy.

1946–53, POSTWAR DIVERSITY: A PERIOD OF GROPING

In 1945, World War II ended, and on October 31 of that year John Grierson resigned his post and left Canada. The NFB had suddenly lost both its charismatic leader and much of its early purpose. But signs of change had preceded these two key events. Toward the end of the war, the structure began to consolidate: in 1944, a personnel office was established and the first organigram issued, production was divided into twelve units, and the accounting function was strengthened, as were government controls over the NFB. Before he departed, Grierson issued a memo in an attempt to define a postwar mission for the NFB—'a living and growing educational service'. Unfortunately, however, these new intentions lacked the definition, appeal, and sense of urgency of the previous mission, and without Grierson's presence, they were not to be realized so easily.

Many of the NFB's realized strategies changed shortly after the war. Affected by government austerity, staff levels dropped, as some filmmakers quit and others were let go, and the rural circuits were replaced by film libraries; the focus on theatrical distribution declined and, most notably, the overall content focus disappeared: first defense and then industry strategies faded, with only a small content strategy, in social environment, continuing until 1948.

Grierson left behind a well-trained staff at the NFB, all ready to go but not sure where. And so they went everywhere. In 1948, twenty-seven of the thirty-seven film-content categories were represented; during the next two years trickles peaked at over 80 percent of all films produced, and the year after that, films in focused strategy categories reached an all-time low of 10 percent.

The NFB, without focus or purpose, let the market define purpose. Filmmakers became particularly responsive to the numerous film ideas suggested by the Canadian public. Moreover, the proportion of sponsored films rose, as attention turned from war themes to government department priorities.

Helping to explain this responsive posture were the pressures exerted on the NFB in the late 1940s. Vociferous complaints from the private film industry of unfair competition led the NFB to avoid films on specific subjects in favor of more general ones. Moreover, fueled by anticommunist feeling in the US as well as the NFB's own reputation for unorthodox behavior, the 'NFB Red Scare' erupted. The RCMP issued a questionnaire requesting information about fellow employees and eventually produced a list of about twenty suspects, people who had been 'outspoken'. Some were fired and others resigned, with 'disastrous' effects on the filmmakers' willingness to take risks (Salutin 1978: 20).

Ross McLean, who had lured Grierson to Canada to do the original study and who joined the NFB in its early years, had become its second commissioner in 1945. As an insider, McLean was well liked by the staff, but he did not try to impose his own ideas, and power naturally diffused down the hierarchy, at least to managers at middle levels. In 1949, the Board of Governors replaced McLean with Arthur Irwin, a former magazine editor with no film or government experience. The appointment caused a furor among the staff, which viewed him as a hatchet man. Nevertheless, as Grierson remarked in later years, 'Irwin saved the [NFB]. No one else could have done it' (quoted in McKay 1965: 89).

As Irwin arrived on the scene, a management consulting firm was completing a study of the NFB's finances, and a government royal commission—Massey Commission—was gearing up to study cultural agencies in Canada. The former made constructive recommendations for reorganization (which led to the consolidation of filmmaking into four units), while the latter drew out strong testimonials of grassroots support for the NFB and concluded that it had provided pride and satisfaction to Canadians, helping to protect 'the nation from excessive commercialization and Americanization' (Massey Commission 1951: 58). The result was a new film act in 1950, drafted by Arthur Irwin in consultation with governmental officials, and the end of austerity: new growth began in both government appropriations and staff levels. Thus, Irwin had well managed the 'boundary conditions' of the organization, although he was frustrated in his personal desire to become involved with filmmaking. Like his successors, Irwin had little influence over the actual content of films. The NFB was moving closer to the adhocracy form.

In Conceptual Terms

This period began with global, or 'quantum' change (Miller and Friesen 1980, 1984), as the important strategies suddenly reversed themselves. Strategy-making behavior changed just as dramatically—from integrated, visionary, proactive, and somewhat deliberate and centralized, to diverse and disjointed, lacking in direction, emergent, reactive, and more decentralized. All these reflected quantum change in situation too—in leadership, purpose, financing, and external pressure.

That the NFB survived at all must be explained in good part by Grierson's legacy—the establishment of a firm foundation, built of competent staff; an ideology that stressed excellence and service; and the grassroots support this engendered. In its time of crisis, the NFB fell back on the seeds of strategies that developed during the war, notably sponsorship and the film libraries. These sustained it until new leadership brought a new consolidation and renewed growth. But that leadership brought no new strategic purpose or focus. This was clearly a period of groping.

1954–7, TELEVISION FOCUS: A PERIOD OF CONCENTRATION

The first television station in Canada, government-owned, opened in September 1952. The new medium provided a purpose for the NFB, and its effect was dramatic, if ultimately mixed, in consequence.

The advent of television, which was to alter distribution channels permanently, forced the NFB to rethink its entire role. The internal debate centered on the NFB's position vis-à-vis the government-owned Canadian Broadcasting Corporation (CBC). One group of filmmakers wanted nothing to do with the new medium, which it considered a rather debased form of film, while another not only pushed for an active strategy of supplying films to the CBC but also was ready to revolt over delays in pursuing it. The director of production was caught in the middle, while the commissioner 'did not want to jump into television. He doubted that the Production units were strong enough to undertake the volume required and maintain quality' (McKay 1965: 100).

A single decision was, however, made to adapt existing NFB films for a television series, and then one filmmaker's proposal for a '15-minute (weekly) series of location films in the documentary tradition to be shot very quickly on locations across the country' was accepted and rushed into production (McKay 1965: 97). A script would be written one day and shot the next, sometimes with no editing and with most of the commentary ad-libbed. With that precedent established, other filmmakers leaped in, and the organization focused its attentions as never before or since, in terms of style of production, channel of distribution, and content of films.[3] At the limit, 'General Series' accounted for 70 percent of all films produced in 1956 and 64 percent in total from 1954 to 1957. In consequence, trickles dropped to their lowest levels ever, only three blips appeared in the four-year period, and the number of content categories dropped in 1956 to fourteen, its lowest point of the study period, excluding the first four years.

Strategies in areas other than content and distribution also changed as a result of the television focus. The number of films increased rapidly, and French production experienced a surge. The French filmmakers, lacking the grassroots distribution channels so well established in English Canada, seized on the new medium to reach their audiences (and were encouraged by the transfer of NFB offices from Ottawa to Montreal).

---

[3] While the general series category, which alone dominated in this period, was technically not one of content, the fact that the films were related and were the only ones not individually titled (named by series and number) supports this conclusion.

They consequently formed a missionary pocket within the organization, reflecting the atmosphere in English production during the Grierson years. The sponsorship strategy also came to an abrupt end, dropping to about 7 percent of films produced in 1954. In 1955, theatrical bookings began a dramatic decline, as commercial cinemas felt the impact of television, although nontheatrical audiences were less affected, with school bookings in particular rising significantly. Circumstances were thus vindicating Grierson's departing vision for the NFB, although without him, the educational orientation appeared to emerge from forces in the environment rather than being deliberately imposed by the leadership.

Once again, things seemed to be working for the NFB—in a sense, a new gestalt strategy seems to have been achieved. But this was not quite right. During this period, by producing films designed for regular spots on television, the NFB was forced to tailor material to a series of thirteen or twenty-six films, each a uniform fifteen and, later, thirty minutes. This encouraged formula work instead of innovation. The filmmakers thus discovered that their organization was rather specialized, that creative excellence produced on an ad hoc basis could not easily be converted into a film every Tuesday at eight. Routine proved to be anathema to this emerging adhocracy.

The result was that by 1958 the NFB had dropped the television focus as fast as it had picked it up. It would, in fact, continue to produce films for television and promote that channel of distribution vigorously, but on the NFB's own terms: the length of films might be controlled, but not the regularity or the content. Ad hoc films for television could thus reflect the NFB's intrinsic strengths.

This return to ad hoc excellence was perhaps signaled by the emerging role of production Unit B, one of four, which relied on the general budget to make nonsponsored films. A loose grouping of several highly creative filmmakers, Unit B produced several internationally acclaimed films, winning major awards at the festivals of Cannes and Venice. But Unit B was a unique group producing unique films, and its orientation was not easily copied. Thus, while one focus was dissipating, no overall new one was yet emerging.

In Conceptual Terms

This was a period of sharp focus, of unprecedented concentration of resources, built around a new channel of distribution. Yet this focus did not reflect any deliberate strategy emanating from central intentions. Quite the contrary, the film-content strategy emerged as one decision set a precedent that stimulated a pattern of actions by many people at the base of the organization. This was, in other words, a pattern in contradiction to the intentions of the senior management. Remarkably, the pattern formed quickly: the strategy was literally spontaneous. One gets a sense of how quickly (and thoroughly) a project organization can change direction of its own accord, independent of its formal leadership. With little standardization, patterns can shift, virtually as quickly as the various projects terminate. And ironically, because the NFB's new strategies were bold and aggressive in response to environmental change, we can characterize them as proactive, emergent, and aggressive, even though adaptive.

Was this reorientation good for the NFB? In terms of providing a focus and a shot in the arm, the answer must be 'yes'. It gave French production a real start, and for English production formed a bridge from the groping of the postwar years to a renewed concentration. But the answer must be 'no' in terms of the NFB's particular demands. In retrospect, the television focus seemed to be an aberration, unsuited to the distinctive competences of the NFB. On the surface, the television medium looked so appropriate—after all, film was film, a screen was a screen. But a seemingly insignificant difference—the need to produce regularly, on schedule—proved significant, at least for an NFB intent on retaining its standards of excellence and its character of adhocracy. This organization, like others we have studied (e.g. Steinberg's), proved to be a highly specific instrument, restricted in its ability to exploit its strengths through diversification.

As the television focus came undone, new precedents were being established in the more flexible, creative filmmaking of Unit B, but these were not to spread nearly so fast or pervasively. The NFB had discovered its weaknesses rather quickly; it would take longer to know its strengths. Structure may have followed strategy in this period, as Chandler (1962) prescribed; in subsequent periods, the reverse would prove the case.

1958–64, Post-Television Diversity: Experimentation and Evolution

History repeated itself. With the television focus gone and with the coming of a brief period of austerity, staff levels stabilized; trickles increased sharply and then were partly displaced by a surge of blips (themselves widely diverse); only a few small focused-content strategies appeared; and the diversity of content categories reached its highest levels (in 1958–60). This time, however, sponsorship was not the response, although it did rise temporarily, perhaps tentatively. The NFB was now a more established and secure organization. Because its old strategies seldom disappeared, but instead remained in the system at lower levels of attention, the existing orientations could take up the slack left by the loss of focus. Instead of focusing on a single strategy, therefore, the NFB pursued a portfolio of its existing ones.

This was perhaps clearest in distribution. Television bookings continued to be pursued and, after dropping sharply in 1960, began pronounced growth again to 1963. Theatrical bookings continued to decline but, after some concerted promotion, also began to recover to previous levels in the early 1960s, with a sharp rise provided in 1965 by the first feature films. Nontheatrical bookings, through the NFB's unique grassroots distribution channel, continued to rise, as a diversity of audiences—e.g. schools, colleges, exhibitions, national parks—was tapped.

While there was no clear focus in film content, a number of tendencies were manifesting themselves. The year 1960 heralded what could be called a series strategy, reflected in the increase in blips. Several were dramatic; writers, directors, and actors were honing the skills necessary for making dramatic feature films. The first of these, in 1963 and 1964, emerged not from any managerial intentions, nor even from the filmmakers' own initial intentions, but from films approved in shorter lengths, which ended up long (suggesting that 'decisions', like strategies, can emerge).

Unit B continued to experiment, coming up with a classic called *Lonely Boy* (about singer Paul Anka) in 1962; its actions were to affect the rest of the NFB deeply, as Jones (1976: 124–5) noted, although 'the beginning [of this iconoclastic orientation] does not seem to have been a planned or a conscious one'. For example, the climate of experimentation was encouraged by technological developments: as sound and camera departments reduced their equipment to about 15 pounds by 1963, more candid shooting styles could be developed.

Unit B's days were numbered, however. Near the end of this period, a poll of English filmmakers found almost universal dissatisfaction with the unit system—the barriers it imposed on communication and the impediments engendered by the position of executive producer, the middle manager who headed each of the units—and those polled urged decentralization to the level of film director. Thus, as the period ended, a new structure was created: the pool system. The units were disbanded and the members of each language group combined in a large pool, free to float from project to project.

In Conceptual Terms

For the second time there was a sudden shift from focus to diversity. Yet this did not give rise to another period of groping, partly because the organization was now more secure and partly because it had inherited a legacy of leftover strategies that provided it with several established orientations. Thus we characterize this as a period of experimentation and evolution.

Ironically, the NFB in this period of diversity appears to have been rather successful, building on strengths rather than succumbing to weaknesses. (While there are no obvious measures of performance in such an organization, the response to its films—awards won, critical reviews, number of bookings, and sizes of audiences—give some indication of the perceived quality and acceptance of the films.)

In fact, the environment was now benign (the austerity being at least brief), and so encouraged experimentation, as did the absence of focus itself. In effect, in contradiction to the prescriptions of strategic management, here was an organization experiencing some of its most successful years with neither clearly articulated strategies nor well-defined target markets. Diversity, emergent strategy, a virtual absence of planning, and a steady weakening of direct managerial authority over operations were all associated with excellence and creativity.

In an odd way, there was integration in the diversity, in that the three major elements of the period all combined neatly: diversity in film content, diversity in distribution, and diversity in structure (an increasing structural orientation toward adhocracy). Diversity in content encouraged innovation, much of it in categories that had received little attention in the past. In effect, strategies were growing where seeds had been sown years earlier. Concurrent with the range of content and the experimentation, a variety of distribution channels were promoted. And since the distribution branch responded to production, increasingly tailoring its efforts to individual films (as opposed, for example, to premarketing series to television), it, too, inevitably approached an adhocracy orientation. Production, meanwhile, was not only removing the last blocks to filmmaker control over films, but was doing away with departmentalization altogether. Yet there was to be a limit to adhocracy, too.

1965–8, FOCUSED EXPERIMENTATION AND SELF-EXPRESSION: A PERIOD OF CONVERGENCES

The NFB was at this point poised for a change, and a radical shift in the environment in the mid-1960s provided the impetus. In part, there was opportunity: preparations for Canada's Centenary of 1967, accompanied by the international fair, Expo 67, in Montreal. As a result, appropriations, after falling slightly in 1963, began to grow rapidly. So, too, did contract personnel. There was also social upheaval, which the earlier wartime experience showed to be a means for defining purpose at the NFB. The 'Quiet Revolution' was changing the nature of Quebec and its relationship with the rest of Canada. Canadians were feeling the impact of the Kennedy assassination of 1963 and observing with dismay the intensification of the war in Vietnam. Popular music was revolutionized by the arrival of the Beatles, while directors such as Godard and Richard Lester were creating new styles in filmmaking. A revolution in cultural and social norms was thus in progress, to culminate in the upheaval at the end of the 1960s. And what better organization to interpret such upheaval than a creative, nonprofit filmmaking agency specializing in documentaries? And so the NFB entered a third cycle of relative focus, though it was not to concentrate its efforts as it had previously.

In film content, two small focused strategies carried through from the previous period, while two others began in 1964, including a major one in sociology that was to be sustained to the end of the study period. Two others arose in 1966, including one to be sustained in experimental films, which is of particular interest.

Up to 1960, every single film but one in the trickle we call experimental films was made by Norman McLaren, the NFB's most celebrated filmmaker. For years he was almost a unit unto himself, allocated an annual budget for his own use. But in the 1960s, experimentation in film content began to pervade the organization, culminating in Unit B's lavish production for Expo 67 of *Labyrinth*, hailed by *American Cinematographer* as 'the most ambitious film project in Canadian film history' (quoted in the NFB's *Annual Report*, 1968).

The proportion of trickles remained rather steady at about 40 percent throughout these years, and blips were erratic, while focused-content categories grew sharply, peaking in 1966 at 55 percent of production before declining sharply for the next two years (perhaps a reflection of the passing of Expo 67 and the Canadian Centenary). Overall we identified a focus across content categories on experimentation and self-expression of various kinds, a convergence of trends that had begun in previous periods. (A future Commissioner defined the filmmakers' philosophy as *'Je veux faire mon film'*—I want to make my film.)

Much the same was true in distribution. The traditional channels remained strong. Theatrical bookings rose dramatically in 1965, as a result of new 'art theaters' and a new contract with Columbia Pictures. Telecasts continued to grow, while nontheatrical bookings experienced some increased growth and then more than doubled at the end of the period. This last form of 'custom distribution' continued to receive considerable attention: NFB distribution officers across Canada and abroad assisted local libraries and film councils and sold prints to a wide variety of audiences.

Meanwhile in production, the 'radical restructuring—or destructuring' (Jones 1976: 200)—into pools was manifesting itself, putting the onus on filmmakers to initiate projects and culminating almost thirty years of progressive decentralization: as Jones (1976: 199) noted, from Grierson as the first commissioner, who brought autonomy within the NFB, to the director of production, next to the executive producers, and finally to the filmmakers themselves.

In Conceptual Terms

This was a period of convergences—first of a variety of external factors and then a variety of internal ones. The social environment seemed to undergo a kind of gestalt shift around 1963, perhaps triggered by the dramatic political events of that year in the US, but encouraged, too, by accelerating change in Canadian politics and Anglo-Saxon culture. Whatever their effect on society at large, all these served to define purpose for the NFB. Thus, for a third time the NFB found focus, not in any intended strategies of its own managers but in the conditions of its environment.

This time, however, the focus reflected certain tendencies in the previous period, namely the budding experimentation complemented by the decentralization associated with the pool system. The variety of strategic changes initiated by the NFB may appear to have been rather diverse and disjointed, but they, too, converged on the themes of experimentation and self-expression, natural responses to the new environment. The filmmakers were certainly making their own films, but they did so together, and with a certain consistency.

Supporting these themes, and being supported by them, the structure of the NFB shifted closer to pure adhocracy, in both production and distribution (and in staffing, with the emphasis on contract hiring).

Strategy-making behavior reflected this, too. Many of the key strategies continued to be emergent, more the result of mutual adjustment among operating personnel than imposition by a central management. Yet, here again, the strategies, even when emergent, comprised elements that were bold and proactive, more than ever.

1969–75, RETHINKING AND PARTIAL RENEWAL: A PERIOD OF DICHOTOMIES AND STRUGGLE

In 1968, the dip in focused strategies reached its low point and in the next year began a sharp rise again, to a new peak in 1972. Because that dip was briefer and less extreme than the ones of the earlier periods labeled diversity (never reaching the low proportions of focused films of the others, and sustaining throughout two important focused strategies, on sociology and experimental films), we did not identify it as a distinct period of diversity. But neither was it a continuation of the last period, because the dip and the subsequent severe budget cuts announced by the government seem to have caused more than an interruption in strategies. Rather they appear to have evoked a kind of pause within the NFB, which led to a partial shift in orientation.

Government austerity hit the NFB's appropriations especially in 1970 and slightly in 1971, but perhaps did more damage through its effects on other departments of the government, whose purchases from the NFB dropped by 34 percent in 1969. As a consequence, staff levels began to fall after 1969, by 18 percent up to 1972, before beginning to recover, in the form of contract hiring.[4]

The austerity measures, although severe in production, proved traumatic in distribution. While production could delay work during austerity, distribution was forced to make permanent changes, especially in the nontheatrical area. It virtually dismantled its dispersed system of traveling representatives and customized services, and consolidated its activities into twenty-nine regional offices. And in 1970, it introduced for the first time a rental fee for the loan of films. That strategy lasted only nine weeks, however, until the public outcry forced the government to insist that it be terminated. Nevertheless, the damage was done: between this and the consolidation of offices, nontheatrical bookings plummeted to half their 1969 level in two years. Theatrical bookings, however, grew significantly

---

[4] The permanent staff continued to decline to the end of the study period, from 654 in 1969 to 272 in 1976, after which the government agreed to put many contract people on permanent staff.

in this period, due to feature films (notably, *Cry of the Wild*), the growth of film societies, and a few particularly successful shorts. Television bookings, after peaking in 1970, declined somewhat toward the end of the study period due to shifts by the CBC.

Not all the NFB's problems of these years were externally created, however. An internal report in 1968, four years after the pool-structure reorganization, recommended a vastly expanded administrative component—planning office, management committee, training program, more thorough accounting procedures, etc. Most of these recommendations were adopted, as a direct result, Jones (1976: 234) argued, of the 'anti-routinizing character of the pool system' and became

the means of coping with the uncontrollability of the organization. To a large extent, the purpose of the measures was not to exercise prior control but to 'pick up the pieces', to rationalize, after the fact, the irrational character of the operation so that it would appear to conform to government operational norms. (p. 234)

But conventional bureaucracy had never served the needs of the NFB either:

By 1970...the authority of the individual filmmaker had been severely diminished. A growth of committees had sapped a portion of the productive energy of the filmmakers, who increasingly had more hurdles to jump before being able to start a film. (p. 240)

The pool system had thus backfired, producing the opposite effect intended: it was so unstructured that it evoked new, dysfunctional structures.

Thus, in 1971, the NFB reverted partly to the unit system, now called studios, 'voluntary associations of filmmakers, from 5 to 15 per studio, dealing with areas of common concern' (*Crisis Committee Report*, as quoted in Jones, 1976: 241). Moreover, in one of the rare instances of the realization of explicit managerial intentions (outlined in the 1966 NFB *Annual Report*), a strategy of regionalizing production began in earnest in 1971, with the opening of a filmmaking office in Vancouver, followed by those in Halifax, Winnipeg, and Toronto.

Overall, by the early 1970s, the NFB began to settle down once again. Austerity ended, the crisis in distribution was over, and the structure was moving back into a natural balance. Film content, too, was coming back into focus, or at least multiple foci, after the sharp dip in focused-content categories in 1967–8. The rapid rise in the focused-content categories during the early 1970s was spread across a number of content areas, with seven appearing in parallel after 1972. Only experimental and, more significantly, sociology films remained in focused categories throughout the dip and austerity years, while new categories appeared in the early 1970s, the most important being 'Challenge for Change'.

In a way, Challenge for Change was to the making of films what the pool system had been to the organization of filmmaking—a natural experiment for the NFB and probably doomed from the outset. Conceived in 1967 as a radical reaction against 'mainstream' cinema and the 'glorification' of the filmmaker, it was designed to involve in the making of films the subjects of the films, particularly disadvantaged people who were to speak out on social issues. Thus, power over production, which had over the lifetime of the NFB moved down the hierarchy in steps, was now to take the ultimate step and go to the people, beyond the formal organization altogether.

Challenge for Change appears in our statistics as two giant blips (the result of two forerunner series in 1965 and 1968) before sustaining itself as a major focused strategy beginning in 1970. It was stimulated by the development of the handheld video camera, a light, flexible unit that provided the important feature of instant playback. Challenge for Change also evoked a proliferation of discussion groups, workshops, and new methods of distribution, well integrated with production. In 1972, a videotape center was established in downtown Montreal (and later in federal penitentiaries), where groups whose proposals were accepted were taught the skills of filmmaking and loaned the equipment. As in a number of the NFB's earlier experimental initiatives, this one gained worldwide attention and left its mark on the organization as well as on filmmakers around the world. By 1980, however, it had disappeared, like the pool system, perhaps valid in principle but difficult to sustain in practice.

In Conceptual Terms

The clearest characteristic of this period is its confusion. For over three decades, the NFB, while cycling into and out of focus on a surprisingly regular basis, also had been gradually blurring the distinction between focus and diversity. As strategies tended to cumulate over time, remaining in the system at least as echoes of earlier foci, there was a continuing trend toward greater diffusion. Moreover, experimentation reached its ultimate and futile peak in this period, both in organization (the pool system) and in filmmaking (Challenge for Change).

Thus, we label this a period of dichotomies and struggle, with the organization exhibiting focus and yet, at the same time, groping. The pause provoked a reoriented focus, with elements of old strategies combined with certain new ones around the themes of experimentation and social involvement. Film content focused, not in a few but in several categories, while filmmakers moved across the land, temporarily (for Challenge for Change) or permanently (through regionalization). Challenge for Change in particular represented a move toward greater diversity and eclecticism—particularly in where films were made, how, and by whom. In effect, to be experimental in the NFB of this last period was not to experiment in films themselves so much as in the social process of making films. The NFB, while perhaps more deliberate in some of its strategies during this period, remained (after austerity) bold and proactive.

These same dichotomies appeared in other areas as well. Distribution, which had gradually been diffusing power, adopting more of a project orientation, and becoming somewhat more emergent in its own strategy-making behavior, suddenly became more centralized, more rationalized, and more deliberate. Yet, while this was happening, the filmmakers themselves were evolving newer and more eclectic methods of film distribution too.

The dichotomies in structure were even more interesting. The limits to adhocracy had become apparent. The ideals of freely floating filmmakers, of delegating production to the people in the film, and of merging distribution with production on a film-by-film basis, all helped to identify the need for structure. An organization can diffuse power and deny procedure only to a point before it ceases to have meaning as an organization. Coordination, departmentalization, and expertise proved to have some function, no matter how limited, even in the NFB. Thus it reverted toward adhocracy.

We leave the NFB in 1975 in a somewhat confusing state. It knew itself to be a high-quality innovator—that had always been its unique niche—but having pushed the limits of innovation past the point of feasibility, it was not clear how it would be able to use that distinctive competence. It had also learned, again by exceeding the bounds of feasibility, how it had to structure itself. But for what? At the end of the study period, the NFB had competence and it had structure; all it needed was purpose.

A Conceptual Interpretation of Strategy Formation at the NFB

THE ORIGIN OF STRATEGIES

In an organization in which all things—actions, decisions, projects, and especially the basic outputs, the films themselves—are so loosely coupled, in which management, hierarchy, and systems of control are so weak, it becomes fair to ask why patterning of behavior, namely strategy, appears at all. Yet patterns are evident throughout the NFB's history and across all its activities. Why should an organization with such an overwhelming need for uniqueness in its outputs also exhibit a need for consistency?

Perhaps the strongest force for consistency is the intrinsic need to take advantage of established skills and knowledge. Once a technical problem is solved (e.g. filming in northern climates), or an external constraint removed (e.g. breaching the television medium), there is a natural tendency to exploit the situation.

A second force for consistency is fashion. Fashionable preferences about subject matter (sociology after the mid-1960s), channels of distribution (television in the mid-1950s), even methods of making films (experimentation in the 1970s) can be no less stringent at the cutting edge of an art than in its mainstream. In effect, any artist who holds his or her finger in the wind before deciding which way to turn encourages the prevalence of strategies.

There are, of course, also administrative needs for consistency, usually related to efficiency or economy, and mostly encouraged by the central management. In fact, a few of the strategies that appeared at the NFB came in the conventional, top-down way, deliberately imposed by management in response to such needs: staff cuts, for example, had to be imposed pervasively in response to budget reductions. Even some of the changes that grew out of grassroots consensus had to be agreed upon formally and implemented deliberately from one center (as in the pool system, or regionalization).

But this process of formulation followed by implementation was hardly pervasive in the NFB, especially in the important area of film content. Patterns formed aside from, or sometimes even despite, managerial intentions, often by the actions of a variety of people in the organization, as well as from forces in the environment.

In a number of important cases, a single, seemingly inconsequential decision, meant to be ad hoc, established a precedent that evoked a pattern (e.g. television series). In some others, a pattern formed without even that single decision (e.g. feature films). Some strategies took longer to appear, although the process was similar. A thin stream of activity (a trickle) eventually took hold and began to pervade the organization (e.g. the experimental focus that grew out of McLaren's 'personal' strategy).

This process of a peripheral strategy spreading to become a central focus is probably more common and important in organizations than is realized. Especially when casting about for new directions—perhaps the result of a crisis—an organization may seize on some long-established but peripheral pattern inside itself and make it pervasive. In effect, the trickle can serve as a bellwether that suggests a new direction, based on skills already established in the organization. Organizations that fail to recognize this phenomenon likely end up discouraging those very initiatives that can be the source of new strategies.

Can we call 'emergent' the process by which a single precedent or trickle becomes a focused strategy? Consider the sharpest example of it in this study, the spontaneous convergence on the television focus of the mid-1950s. This had all the common ingredients—a single filmmaker acting in his own interests, the reaction to his precedent by a number of colleagues, and an environment ripe for these initiatives. This seems to be a perfect example of an emergent strategy. Not only did the pattern not reflect managerial intentions, it positively violated them. Yet the pattern did reflect a certain consensus of intentions among filmmakers themselves, even if these were not formally articulated. Is that deliberate for them, even for the 'organization', if emergent for the management?

Likewise, the feature film strategy seemed to reflect filmmakers' wishes. Getting prime time in a theater is, after all, the dream of most people in this business. But what if, as in this case, the pattern came to be because one film happened to run long? Does this make it emergent all around? Emergent strategy means *unintended order*. (Brian King, a doctoral student at McGill, defined it in a 2006 paper as 'when preparation meets opportunism'.) Did the 'organization' intend the pattern? How do we read the collective mind?

Our point is not that these strategies should be labeled deliberate or emergent, but that the determination of intentions in a collective context such as this is complex and interesting, worthy of much more attention. This matter goes to the heart of the very meaning of 'organization' itself, by which we mean collective action in the pursuit of a common mission.

CONVERGENCE IN STRATEGIES THEMSELVES

Not only did this loosely coupled organization achieve patterns, namely in its behavior, it also regularly achieved patterning among these patterns, that is, focus around clear periods of strategic perspective in its various positional strategies.

A number of forces drove this organization toward convergence. Probably paramount was the simple need for a sense of definition. In a way, if an organization does not stand for something, does not represent some comprehensible theme or orientation, it lacks definition in the minds of its public as well as in the minds of its own members, and this can undermine it externally and internally. Another force for convergence was the periodic presence of strong environmental influences—the war, television, shifts in culture. As noted earlier, the NFB tended to find its own definition in social disruption—in society's loss of definition. A third force for convergence, as Miller and Friesen (1980, 1984) and Miller and Mintzberg (1983) have pointed out, is that organizations often find it convenient to converge around certain themes, achieving stable and harmonious gestalts or configurations for certain periods of time before allowing themselves to undergo the disruption of periodic revolutions. This may help to explain why the television focus was maintained so clearly for four years and then was dropped so suddenly.

Leadership, a force for convergence in many organizations, was not a major factor here, at least after Grierson's formative years. Planning—a formal means to achieve convergence—also seemed to play virtually no role in this organization, although other common bureaucratic pressures did: rules and procedures emanating from the government as well as the natural drive to rationalize, standardize, and formalize.

Alongside the forces for convergence in this organization were also those for divergence, or variety. Prime among these was the obsession with innovation. Above all, no two films must ever be alike; artists must not get into a rut. Filmmaking is a fashionable business and while fashion is certainly a force for conformity, among its users, among fashion *designers* it is a force for individuality. Thus, even while it was encouraging patterning, fashion was also acting to break down established patterns.

Moreover, the members of the NFB could not help but realize that the only way to maintain the creative and flexible character of the organization was to shake it up periodically, to change not only the content of its films, but also the channels of distribution, procedures, structures, even people. Change for its own sake becomes a logical activity in such an organization. Without change, adhocracies die (i.e. become bureaucracies). The television focus forced the organization into regularity, which encouraged bureaucracy, so it had to end.

Likewise, much of the later pressure to bureaucratize was deflected by the variability of the organization, its refusal to settle down. People came and went on contract, activities escaped rules under the guise of being experimental (even when they were not), structures were shifted frequently, and rules flaunted for the sake of freedom, if not art. It seemed that every time the NFB was in danger of sinking into a comfortable regularity, a Unit B or a *Labyrinth* film or a Challenge for Change program would shake it back into diversity. Thus, the NFB never stayed still long enough for anyone to pin any effective performance measure on it (although government technocrats continually tried).

Of course, the environment contributed to divergence too. When an organization must be particularly responsive to its environment, as is typical of adhocracy, change in the environment becomes a force for divergence. And, as we saw, the environment of the NFB underwent a number of gestalt shifts.

CYCLES OF STRATEGIC CHANGE

How did the NFB reconcile the conflicting needs for convergence and divergence, for focus on strategic perspective on one hand and on variety in its strategic positions and over individual films on the other? It gave sequential attention to each (Cyert and March 1963), at remarkably regular intervals. No sooner did the NFB have definition for a few years than suddenly everything went off in all directions. The system seemed likewise to tolerate divergence for only so long before the need for a new definition was felt. Thus the NFB cycled into and out of focus.

This pattern of strategic change is quite unlike the ones we found in the bureaucratic and entrepreneurial organizations that were studied. There, the periods of convergence around given strategic orientations were typically much longer (a decade or two), while those of divergence were very brief. In effect, those organizations could not tolerate much divergence, and so had to leap from one strategic focus to another, through some sort of strategic revolution. The NFB, in contrast, could tolerate such periods for a time—a characteristic probably typical of adhocracies. It could function without focus; indeed, at times it thrived on divergence.

DRIFT TO DIVERSITY

Superimposed on these regular cycles of convergence and divergence there seemed to be a long-term trend toward greater diversity, blurring strategic definition. There always was considerable diversity at the NFB, always, for example, a significant proportion of trickles in film content as well as attention to several channels of distribution. Compare this with a Volkswagenwerk that could focus almost all its attention on one automobile model for a long period of time. In the case of the NFB, that diversity seemed to increase significantly over the years.

The explanation for this seems to lie in another characteristic of the NFB: it tended to retain its old position strategies, albeit at reduced levels. For example, hardly any film-content category disappeared after being the center of attention; likewise, new channels of distribution, after being the center of attention for a time, reverted to more modest places alongside existing ones. Each strategy too seemed to have its time of focus, perhaps because this organization, ever oriented to what was fashionable, tended to overdo ('overrealize') its new strategies before finding appropriate places for them. This meant that the NFB tended to accumulate its strategies in much the same way a library accumulates its volumes. Over time it became the agglomeration of all its past and present patterns.

This accumulation of strategies would appear to have its positive side, as noted earlier, enabling an organization to maintain multiple capabilities and so to have several options whenever reorientation of attention becomes necessary. But the price can be a loss in the capacity to focus, to achieve definition. As the organization ages, it becomes increasingly diffuse, more and more difficult to understand, and direct, whether through leadership or the consensus of many people. Not only did the NFB lack definition in its later years, but there was room for serious doubt about whether it would ever again be able to achieve truly focused definition, at least in the absence of major crisis.

THE QUEST FOR ADHOCRACY

Of course, the reason for the diversity was the tolerance of the organization: there was plenty of room to hide in a pocket and experiment, as did the unknown Arthur Lipsett when, working as an assistant, he produced his award-winning film *Very Nice, Very Nice* from unwanted outtakes of other films.

Machine bureaucracies, top-down and obsessed with rationalization, tend to sweep clean after strategic revolutions. The new regime focuses on its target markets and chosen products, integrates production around these, and works to rid the organization of the vestiges of any leftover strategies. Adhocracies, in contrast, cater to impulse, sometimes based on peripheral patterns tolerated or simply lost within the system. That provides their great strength—their ability to innovate—but it also gives rise to the problem of achieving focused direction.

In fact, the NFB was not created with an adhocracy structure. That too emerged; indeed, the organization had to exceed the bounds of adhocracy in order to find a workable balance. The charismatic leadership under which the NFB was created established an internal ideology that laid the groundwork for the coming adhocracy. The NFB moved toward this structure in steps, as it developed internally, and as changing external norms made the various elements of this structure more acceptable (e.g. matrix form, decentralization to experts, an emphasis on multidisciplinary teamwork, continuous innovation). This happened in distribution, with customization, as well as in production, where power moved down the hierarchy to the filmmakers. But then, with the pool system in which filmmakers floated freely and with Challenge for Change, which sought to send power outside the organization, the NFB discovered that there were limits to how far even adhocracy could go.

The strength of adhocracy, in contrast to machine bureaucracy that seeks to control its environments in order to support its standardized system of mass production (Woodward 1965; Galbraith 1967), would seem to be its rapid and continuous responsiveness to the environment, with minimal organizational interference.

In this regard, the NFB had a curious relationship with its environment. In one sense, it was highly responsive—to social trends, new fashions, new media, and social turmoil. Ultimately, the NFB found its purpose— when it did—in the world around it, not in itself: it truly was a mirror of its society, and, in terms of the quality of so many of its films, it performed its mission brilliantly. Yet in another sense, this was truly an organization that 'did its own thing'. Except during the war years, the NFB as a whole catered largely to its own needs, by selecting those parts of the environment to which it cared to respond. It was, in other words, far quicker to pick up the opportunities that pleased its insiders than to help resolve the problems that plagued its external stakeholders. That is why the organization could be so proactive while so much of its behavior was at the same time emergent. And that also helped to make it so creative.

A government intent on bringing such an organization under control could have done so—at the expense of the quality of its work. Or the government could have cut it off to fend for itself in the marketplace— probably with the same result. The fact is that the NFB served a particular and valuable role as it was, providing at the time a Canadian presence in the film industry that would not likely have existed without government support, and, in the world at large, sometimes setting standards of quality and innovation met by no other organization in the industry.

LEADERSHIP IN ADHOCRACY

The dilemma of leadership in managing adhocracy lies in trying to exercise influence without being able to rely on formal controls. NFB managers had their hands on some levers of decision, such as staffing levels and the design of the structure itself, but not on others, notably the content of specific films. Trying to manage such a situation is a little like trying to drive an automobile without controlling the steering wheel. You can accelerate and brake, but not set direction. As noted in the Arcop study (ahead), when a creative organization develops strategies for design, it cannot easily design strategies.

The NFB did have strong leadership at various times, interestingly enough particularly during periods of little order: the chaos of the founding years, the groping after the war, and the diversity following the television focus. Moreover, the organization also sustained strong grassroots leadership through people who, despite their lack of formal authority, established the tone and set the precedents for others to follow.

The effective leaders at the helm of an organization such as this were the ones who managed well the 'boundary condition'—Grierson, who kept government bureaucrats at bay (a role he explicitly reserved for himself), and Irwin, who dealt with scandal and negotiated favorable legislation. Creativity is inherently controversial; it can flourish only if the artists are well protected from public attack. And much of the responsibility for that protection falls on the formal leadership of the organization.

Another aspect of central leadership here, given that the content of some key strategies cannot be managed, is ensuring that the right kind of people are hired and that they are protected by the appropriate structures. A film can be no better than the capabilities of the people who get to make it. That is why conventional administration—which assumes that outputs can be determined by rules, standards, and plans—is so fruitless in an organization of experts. Such devices can never improve the poor performers, only impede the good ones. Hence, management has to ensure that the organization is staffed with the best possible people, that hiring mistakes are corrected quickly (so that resources are not wasted in the form of dead weight that sinks the enterprise), and that structures are established to leave the capable people largely free to work as they know how. Some controls are obviously necessary—just to keep the lid on spending, for example—but the obsession with control found in machine bureaucracy is anathema to the exercise of expertise.

Its inability to dictate fundamental strategic direction (establish target markets, select products or services) does not, of course, preclude management from trying to influence it. Managers can, for example, seek to define broad boundaries around what is done, developing 'umbrella strategies'. They can also exercise their influence on the emerging patterns, encouraging or discouraging those they find promising or dangerous. In effect, the managers of adhocracies must do what we do as researchers—look for patterns in streams of actions—but in their case, in order to act on them.

Of course, this can only be done by leaders who have vision (or can find it in others and borrow it). And this brings us to a final aspect of leadership in adhocracy, perhaps the most critical one—the creation of mission, vision, culture, in Selznick's (1957) terms, 'the embodiment of purpose', 'the infusion with value'. That was what made Grierson such a great leader: he defined the organization in a way that people could understand and rally around. Adhocracy provides only the structure; vision infuses the purpose that produces inspired innovation. The NFB sustained itself on Grierson's vision for decades and would likely have blown apart without it.

But that vision had to fade eventually, as that great enthusiasm sustained itself only in pockets of the organization. The NFB found new areas of focus, but aside from these pockets, it never seemed to develop a new surge of purpose. Without this, and with increasing diffusion of its energies, one ends up wondering how much longer this organization of paradoxes—of developing pattern amid uniqueness, of cycling between convergence and divergence, of achieving direction without being directed, of strategies that emerge while being proactive, of finding its order in disorder—can survive.

Conclusion: A Grassroots Model of Strategy Formation

The findings of this study put into question virtually every conventional belief about how strategies are supposed to be created in organizations.

Is the reader to conclude, therefore, that the NFB was some kind of aberration—a government agency with a quasi-market function, lacking the discipline of the bottom line and operating in the never-never land of cinema, to boot. Can its experiences be generalized to other organizations, even profit-making adhocracies, let alone more conventional bureaucracies? Such a conclusion would be too easy, in our opinion. The NFB may be an extreme case, but as such it can highlight behaviors that we believe are to be found, in muted form, in all kinds of organizations. It is expressed below as a grassroots model of strategy making, in six points.

1. *Strategies grow initially like weeds in a garden; they are not cultivated like tomatoes in a hothouse.* In other words, the process of strategy formation can be overmanaged; sometimes it is more important to let patterns emerge than to force an artificial consistency upon an organization prematurely. The hothouse, if needed, can come later.

2. *Strategies can take root in all kinds of strange places, virtually wherever people have the capacity to learn and the resources to support that capacity.* Sometimes an individual actor or subunit in touch with a particular market niche creates his, her, or its own pattern. This may not even happen consciously as the external environment imposes a pattern on an unsuspecting organization. Other times many different actors converge around a theme, perhaps gradually, perhaps spontaneously. Senior managers can also fumble into strategies; these, in some cases, developing gradually in their minds to emerge in a form that can give the impression they were designed quickly and deliberately. The point is that organizations cannot always plan where their strategies will emerge, let alone plan the strategies themselves.

3. *Such strategies become organizational when they become collective, that is, when the patterns proliferate, to pervade the behavior of the organization at large.* Weeds can proliferate and encompass a whole garden; then the conventional plants may look out of place. The same holds true for emergent strategies. But, of course, what's a weed but a plant that was not expected. With a change of perspective, the emergent strategy, like the weed, can become what is valued (just as Europeans enjoy salads of the leaves of America's most notorious weed, the dandelion).

4. *That process of proliferation may be conscious but need not be; likewise, it can be managed but need not be.* The process by which these initial patterns work their way through the organization need not be

consciously intended, by formal leaders or informal ones. Patterns may just spread by collective action, much as plants proliferate themselves. Of course, once the strategies are recognized as valuable, the process of proliferation can be managed, just as plants are selectively propagated.

5. *The pervasion of new strategies, which themselves may be emerging continuously, tends to occur during distinct periods of divergence that punctuate distinct periods of the convergence of established, prevalent strategies.* Organizations, in simpler words, like gardens, appear to accept the biblical maxim of a time to sow and a time to reap (even though they can sometimes reap what they did not mean to sow). Periods of integrated continuity tend to be interspersed with periods of quantum change, in clear cycles (for reasons cited in Miller and Friesen 1980, 1984; and Miller and Mintzberg 1983). Sometimes these cycles are of short duration and are balanced between convergence and divergence, which seems to happen in adhocracies. They appear to require distinct periods of experimentation and renewal to work out new strategic themes, although at the risk of excessive confusion. Other times, these periods are of longer duration, with an emphasis on continuity, which is interrupted by occasional, brief, and highly disruptive strategic revolutions. This seems to happen in machine bureaucracies (as we saw in the Vietnam and the Volkswagenwerk studies). Such organizations appear to require these long stretches of continuity to ensure efficiency in their operations, although at the risk of inflexibility. Either way, the blurring of the distinction between periods of change and continuity would seem to indicate organizational dysfunction (if this study is any guide), just as mixing up sowing and reaping would destroy the productivity of a garden.

6. *To manage this process is not to preconceive strategies but to recognize their emergence and intervene when appropriate.* A destructive weed, once noticed, is best uprooted immediately. But one that seems capable of bearing fruit is worth watching, perhaps cultivating, even building a hothouse around. To manage in this context is thus to create the climate within which a wide variety of strategies can grow (to establish a flexible structure and supportive culture, plus to define guiding 'umbrella' strategies), and then to watch what does in fact come up—and not be too quick to cut off the unexpected. While keeping one eye on this process of emergence (the results of which must sometimes be made deliberately), managers must keep the

other eye on the cycling convergence and divergence, knowing when to promote change for the sake of external adaptation and when to resist it for the sake of internal efficiency. Most important is to avoid the excesses of each—failure to focus, or else capture by bureaucratic (or psychological) momentum. In other words, managers have to be able to sense when to exploit an established crop of strategies, and when to encourage new strains to displace it.

This grassroots model of strategy formation is false, as anyone who seeks to test it in a broader context will quickly find out. But it is no more false than the widely accepted conventional model—the 'deliberate' (or 'hothouse') view of strategy formulation—which no one has bothered to test. A viable theory of strategy making must encompass both models. No organization can function with strategies that are always and purely emergent: that would amount to a complete abdication of will and leadership, not to mention conscious thought. But none can likewise function with strategies that are always and purely deliberate: that would amount to an unwillingness to learn, a blindness to whatever is unexpected. We believe that there has to be a little bit of the NFB—a few strategic weeds at least—in every organization.

The NFB continues to exist as an agency of the government of Canada, still producing many documentary films. In 2007 there remain, however, few filmmakers on permanent staff. Most films are now being done on a freelance basis or as coproductions with other organizations. This year NFB received its twelfth Academy Award, for the animated short *The Danish Poet*, coproduced with Norway's Mikrofilm AS.

5

Into the Mind of the Strategist
Canadian Lady, 1939–76

Henry Mintzberg and James A. Waters[1]

This study tracks the strategies of an undergarment manufacturer, from its inception through three major shifts in its strategic behavior. The involvement in our brainstorming sessions of one of the chief protagonists enabled us to enter somewhat into the mind of the strategist. Conclusions are drawn about strategic reorientation as a process of unfreezing, changing, and refreezing.

Canadian Lady Inc. (later renamed Canadelle Inc.), founded in 1939, was primarily a manufacturer of women's undergarments, notably brassieres, in Canada. To infer its strategies since its inception, we divided its decisions into seven functional areas: product lines, facilities (plants, warehouses, office), marketing, manufacturing technology, licensing, finance, and organizational structure. The strategies inferred, over thirty in number, were then combined to describe four major periods in the company's history. (Note that the history of the company is discussed up to 1976, although the strategy diagrams are shown till 1978.)

One unique feature of this particular study is that the individual who was the president of the firm for the last seven years of our study period joined the team for the brainstorming sessions. As a practitioner with strong conceptual interests—he holds an MBA from Harvard and taught part-time at the McGill Faculty of Management for a number of years—his presence was most worthwhile. We begin with the strategies and then discuss the periods before drawing overall conclusions.

---

[1] Originally published in *Competitive Strategic Management* (R. B. Lamb, ed., Prentice-Hall, 1984), with minor revisions in this volume.

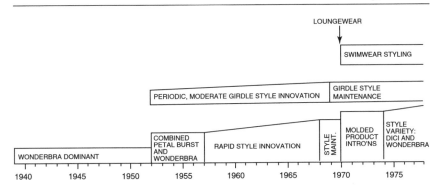

Strategy Diagram 5A Product lines

The Strategies of Canadian Lady

PRODUCT LINES

The company's products included brassieres, girdles, and swimwear, with minor sales of such items as lingerie sets including panties, combination bra-slips, and shampoo for elastic products. Three major product strategies are described. With respect to brassieres, six different strategies were inferred:

1939–52: Wonderbra Dominant

The company began in 1939 with licenses to produce Lovable and Wonderbra brassieres in Canada. Lovable was a low-end brand, which was not very successful, and that license was dropped around 1941. Wonderbra was a trademark for a brassiere product employing a diagonal slash strap, which provided more comfort and freedom of movement for the user.

1952–7: Combined Petal Burst and Wonderbra

In anticipation of expiration of the Wonderbra patent and forthcoming negotiations with the US patent owner, and in response to a new fashion trend—the pointed-bust look—the company launched Petal Burst. This product, employing a spoke-stitched cup in combination with the diagonal slash strap, became an important part of the line, reaching 50 percent of its brassiere sales by 1957.

1957–68: Rapid Style Innovation

The year 1957 marked the introduction of the first product design not covered by the diagonal slash patent. Over the next twelve years, a variety

115

of new styles were introduced almost every year, under new brand names such as Risque, Curve-V, Fleur de Lis, Petal Teen, Scandale, Young Wonder, and Wonder Bare. Also during this period, size ranges were extended for many lines and additional colors were introduced.

1969–70: Style Maintenance

During these two years, the company engaged in extensive product and manufacturing work to produce a brassiere with a molded cup (discussed under 'Manufacturing Technology'). While this experimentation was going on, very few style innovations were introduced (see also 'Organization Structure'). Hence the strategy is labeled 'Style Maintenance'.

1970–3: Molded Product Introduction

Molded bras, with molding done by subcontractors, began to reach the market in 1970 under the Wonderbra brand name. Two styles were introduced, but while response was favorable, production difficulties prevented sales from becoming significant. In addition, the difficulty of working through outside subcontractors impeded design innovation (see 'Manufacturing Technology'), and no new styles were introduced in 1971.

The first in-house molded brassiere was introduced in 1972. The company also began to experiment with in-house production of the two styles that had been introduced earlier. During 1973 substantial improvement in the molding process was achieved, but no new products were introduced to the market. During this transition period, similar garments were imported from France under the brand name Pomone.

1974–8+: Style Variety—Dici and Wonderbra

In 1974 a new product line aimed at the younger consumer was introduced under the brand name of Dici. Younger people wanted a more natural, 'less-bra' look. In keeping with this demand, Dici styles were all seamless and included both molded and nonmolded stretch fabric designs. The brand name grew out of a packaging innovation (a cube, like dice, with holes in it so the customer could see and feel the product).

The brassiere business was thus consolidated into two major segments, Dici and Wonderbra. A variety of Dici styles were introduced with regularity, as the product line came to represent a substantial portion of the business. At the same time, regular style innovation resumed in the

Wonderbra line, in both sewn styles and molded heavier fabrics. Regular style innovation continued through the end of the study period for both major lines.

(In 1978, after the study period, Dici Nova was introduced as a natural-look product for the woman interested in high fashion. The line was expensive and appealed more to the Wonderbra-age customer. It was also in response to the fact that the original Dici customers were now four years older.)

Over the study period, girdles represented a variable portion of the firm's business: at the high point, 1966, one-third of the overall volume; at the end of the study period, only about 5 percent. With respect to girdles, two strategies were inferred.

1952–68: Periodic, Moderate Style Innovation in Girdles

The first girdle product, called 'Winkie', was copied from a US product. This was followed by 'Scandale' in 1957 (a French design licensed from the USA), and 'Oblique' in 1961 (also licensed from the USA). In 1964, all brands were consolidated under the umbrella brand of Wonderbra (e.g. 'Oblique by Wonderbra'). 'Secret Service' by Wonderbra was introduced later in the year. Over this period, the firm also made moderate style innovations, but at a considerably slower pace than it did with brassieres.

1969–78+: Style Maintenance in Girdles

With the advent of miniskirts and panty hose, the market for girdles dropped at the rate of approximately 30 percent per year, beginning in 1969. The firm serviced the existing market but introduced few new styles.

Following the introduction of 'loungewear' in 1970, which met with a poor response, the company introduced a line of swimwear to use the leftover material. One strategy is identified for the swimwear business, as follows:

> **1970–8+: Swimwear Styling.** The line of swimwear was marketed on the basis of fit—brassiere was sized and sold through corset departments where clerks were trained to fit the customer. Once introduced, the firm followed industry practice of annual styling changes in color, fabric, and/or style. By the end of the study period, swimwear represented approximately 12 percent of total sales volume.

PLANT, WAREHOUSE, AND OFFICE FACILITIES

Decisions with respect to the establishment and consolidation of plant, warehouse, and office facilities appear as events in the history of the firm. The overall strategy in this area might be described as 'sporadic expansion in blocks', although we prefer to show specific detail. Strategy Diagram 5B depicts the expansion moves as follows:

- 1939: Total operations located at 4475 St. Lawrence Street, Montreal.

- 1945: Sewing and cutting operations moved to 9500 St. Lawrence, while the office and finished-goods warehouse remained at 4475 St. Lawrence; the move resulted in a net expansion of capacity.

- 1952: Additional sewing capacity in Quebec City, 248 km from Montreal, because of labor scarcity and high costs in Montreal. During the same year, warehouse moved from 4475 to 9500 St. Lawrence.

- 1964: 4475 St. Lawrence closed; offices and warehouse moved to Cremazie Boulevard, resulting in a net expansion. Operations (and some warehouse) continued at 9500 St. Lawrence.

- 1966: Purchase of bankrupt lingerie plant in Lac Megantic, 193 km from Montreal. Expansion was partly an opportunistic move in response to the availability of a plant all set up for sewing and the opportunity to get training grants and tax holiday of three years. Most importantly, this location permitted the hiring of locally available skilled workers, already trained to sew.

- 1972: Expansion by purchasing a plant in Hawkesbury, Ontario, 96 km from Montreal. As with Lac Megantic, labor availability and government training grants were important considerations. Swimwear was produced here because labor regulations were more flexible regarding working hours and conditions than in Quebec. This different classification would otherwise have required different

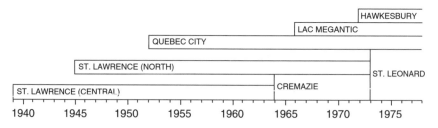

Strategy Diagram 5B Facilities

working conditions in the same plant, causing confusion in operating practices.

- 1973: All Montreal operations consolidated in the suburb of St. Leonard. This was not only a consolidation aimed at eliminating communication problems arising from fragmented locations, but also an expansion of total operating space.

MARKETING

Three dimensions of marketing strategy are described. With respect to sales force, two strategies were employed.

1939–49: Mixed Agents and Direct Salespeople

After starting with sales agents, the firm gradually switched to direct salespeople. One agent was retained in Ontario until his death in 1949.

1949–79: Direct Salespeople

Since 1949, all selling was done by company salespeople.

With respect to the content of advertising, three different strategies were employed:

1939–65: Product Feature—Bras and Girdles

Emphasis was on specific products and their features (e.g. Dream Lift, Oblique, Petal Burst).

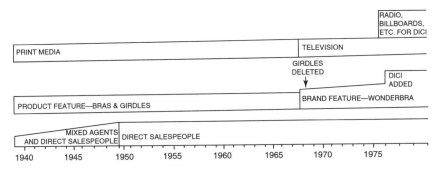

Strategy Diagram 5C Marketing

1966–74: Brand Feature—Wonderbra

After a complete shift to television advertising (discussed below), the company switched from a product emphasis to a brand emphasis. Advertisements attempted to build consumer awareness of the one brand name—Wonderbra. It was quickly discovered through marketing research that women did not want to see girdles advertised on television; they were seen as armor against sex, while the reverse was true for bras. Thus, beginning in 1967, the content of advertising was focused exclusively on Wonderbra brand brassieres. The advertisements were based on fashion and emotional appeal (see discussion of 'Product Lines'), included a male in the picture, and the theme—'We care about the shape you're in'—was used in one form or another from 1967 through the end of the study period.

1974–8+: Brand Feature—Wonderbra and Dici

With the addition of the Dici line, both brands were featured, but always in separate advertisements. Dici was aimed at a different market segment (see discussion of 'Product Lines') and advertisements made a distinctly different appeal—no males—'It's like wearing no bra at all' or 'Dici or nothing'.

With respect to advertising media decisions, three strategies were inferred:

> **1939–66: Print Media.** All advertising took place in newspapers and magazines.

> **1966–74: Television.** After a change of advertising agency in 1966, the first TV commercials were shown in 1966. Following their success, most of the advertising budget was put into TV applications.

> **1974–8+: Television and Radio, Billboards, Subway Cars.** Advertising for the mobile Dici consumer was on radio, billboards, and subway cars. Budget restrictions did not initially allow TV advertising of Dici; moreover, there was some question about whether it would be as cost-effective for this market. Most of Wonderbra advertising continued on TV.

MANUFACTURING TECHNOLOGY

Canadian Lady had never undertaken the production of basic textiles, so the basic manufacturing technology dealt with the cutting, shaping,

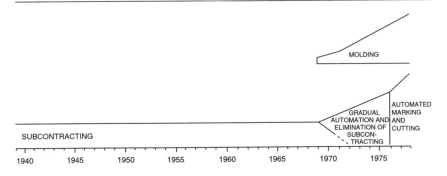

Strategy Diagram 5D Manufacturing

and sewing of yard goods. The manufacturing technology strategies are described as follows.

1939–69: Subcontracting

In these years, substantial portions of the manufacturing process were contracted out to suppliers and subcontractors. Laminations (i.e. combinations of fabrics) were done by the textile manufacturers. Textiles were pre-slit by these manufacturers for binding tapes and straps. In addition, shoulder and hook-and-eye straps were obtained through subcontractors, which employed homeworkers to sew these subassemblies. The final sewing, assembly, and packaging were done in-house.

1969–76: Gradual Automation and Elimination of Subcontracting

Following a study in 1969 of opportunities for vertical integration, an increasing portion of the manufacturing process was brought in-house and automated. The first step for the company was to purchase basic yard goods and do its own laminating and slitting. Research was undertaken, and machines were developed to make hook-and-eye tapes and to produce shoulder straps. By the end of the period, all this work was done in-house.

1976–8+: Automated Marking and Cutting

A major increase in automation took place with the introduction in 1976 of the Camsco computer-assisted marker and the Gerber automated cutting machinery. Both these machines produced substantial increases in textile usage, efficiency, quality, reliability, and speed of production.

1969–78+: Molding

This period covered the emergence of molding technology as an important element of manufacturing. At first this work was done by subcontractors. Because of high costs, quality-control problems, difficulties in introducing new designs, excessive lead-time requirements for the manufacture of new products, and inability to control material waste, a program was undertaken to develop an in-house molding capability. After a two-year lead-in period (1969–70), during which new fabric specifications were developed, proprietary molding machines were manufactured, and a mold-making shop was established, all molding was done in-house. This was the final step in eliminating reliance on subcontracting. Upward of 50 percent of brassiere production became molded.

LICENSING

Licensing involved the selling, on a royalty basis, to other manufacturers technological know-how, brand use, promotional aids (posters, ad copy, etc.), and, where applicable, patent rights.

Generally, a future licensee would import products from Canada for a few years and then begin domestic manufacturing. In a few cases, the period of importation was extended; in some cases, notably Switzerland, the 'licensee' was primarily an importer and only engaged in limited manufacturing. While exact data are not available, exports independent of license arrangements were always a negligible portion of total sales. From 1963 to the end of the study period, net income from licensing represented between 2 and 6 percent of the company's total profits.

Three different strategies were identified over the study period, as follows.

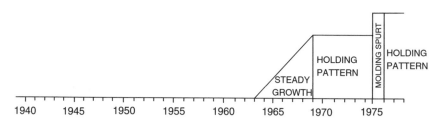

Strategy Diagram 5E Licensing

1963–9: Steady Growth

A new license arrangement was established in each year of this period except 1968. The licensees were in most of the major developed countries of Europe (England, Germany, Switzerland, Sweden, Italy, and the Benelux countries) and in South Africa. Two licensees were established in 1969, but one of these was minor and expired within a few years.

1969–74: Holding Pattern

Over the next five years, only one license was established (Australia in 1971). This was a minor arrangement and expired within a few years. The license/export arrangements established in the previous period were maintained, though royalties began tapering off because no new-product innovations were made available to licensees.

1975: Molding License Spurt

In 1975, three licensees were established for the transfer of molding technology know-how. Two of these were for new countries (Mexico and the USA) and one was an addition to an existing license arrangement.

1976–8+: Holding Pattern

Following the spurt in 1975, no subsequent licenses were established in the next few years, suggesting the start of a holding pattern.

FINANCING

1939–78+: Internal Financing

A constant strategy of internal financing was pursued over the study period. Only short-term borrowing was employed, and this never exceeded $1 million. Neither the formation of Reldan in 1947 nor the acquisition of the company in 1969 by Consolidated Foods resulted in long-term capital additions to the firm.

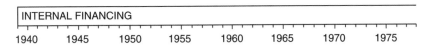

INTERNAL FINANCING

| 1940 | 1945 | 1950 | 1955 | 1960 | 1965 | 1970 | 1975 |

Strategy Diagram 5F Financing

ORGANIZATION STRUCTURE

Three periods were identified in the evolution of organization structure over the study period.

1939–61: Simple Structure

From 1939 to 1952, the firm was almost literally a one-man show. M. Nadler founded the firm, owned all the stock, and supervised all the details. However, his brother, D. Nadler, operated as an executive in the areas of advertising and sales.

In 1947 a new corporate unit called Reldan (Nadler spelled backwards) was created to provide a specific equity interest for D. Nadler after the war. Reldan was owned 50/50 by the Nadler brothers and was not completely separate from Canadian Lady. M. Nadler was president of both operations and made all the major decisions. From 1947 to 1952, sales of certain products (e.g. garter belts, strapless bras) were reported through Reldan, even though the two companies shared the same facilities (offices, manufacturing plant, warehouses, etc.). Beginning with the Winkie girdle in 1952, all girdle products were reported through Reldan.

L. Nadler, M. Nalder's son, joined the firm in 1955, working in various positions in sales and quality control. He went to Harvard Business School in 1959 but continued to take an active interest in the firm (e.g. with a classmate, he studied the firm as part of a course assignment).

1961–9: Increasing Formalization

After graduating from Harvard, L. Nadler rejoined full time in 1961 as secretary–treasurer. At his urging, the two firms were merged; D. Nadler

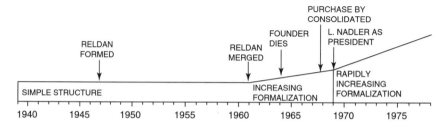

Strategy Diagram 5G Organization structure

received 25 percent of the resultant company, L. Nadler 10 percent, with M. Nadler retaining 65 percent.

L. Nadler brought with him many other ideas and desires for change. The firm began to hire MBA graduates in various positions as well as computer specialists, mathematicians, and accountants. Various clerical functions were automated during this period, including accounting and marketing reports, as well as routine credit decisions and product allocations among customers in times of shortage.

Upon the death of M. Nadler in 1964, D. Nadler became president and L. Nadler assumed the post of executive vice-president. The firm was sold to Consolidated Foods Inc., a US-based conglomerate, in March 1968.

1969–78+: Rapidly Increasing Formalization

In July 1969, L. Nadler became president of the company. Although he had been pushing for some time for a formalized long-range planning process for the company, the acquisition by Consolidated forced the development of this process.

A key change was the imposition of formal decision rules ensuring that new products would meet established profitability criteria. This was followed by the institution of a rule that a new stockkeeping unit (SKU— a specific product size, color, package, etc.) be introduced only if an old SKU was dropped—to arrest the proliferation of SKUs in brassieres. Extensive budgets, market and environmental analyses, and capital investment plans began to be produced annually. An incentive compensation system for key executives was established. The formalization of work procedures and job specialization begun in the previous period continued but at a more rapid pace.

PERFORMANCE

Figure 5.1 presents combined annual net sales for Canadian Lady and Reldan over the study period. Missing data are represented by straight-line extrapolation between the years for which sales figures were available.

From 1939 through 1963, sales volume grew slowly, with an average increase of approximately $160,000 per year over the period. From 1963 through 1978, sales volume grew much more rapidly, with an average increase of approximately $1.6 million per year over the period. For the

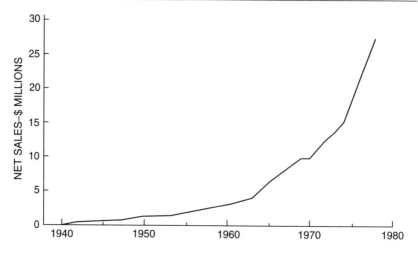

Figure 5.1 Annual net sales

three years from 1975 to 1978, the average sales growth was $3.2 million per year. Table 5.1 shows additional details of performance that were available. Beyond the rapid sales growth, these data reveal the rapidly increasing share of the undergarment market. Over this six-year period, roughly three-quarters of sales volume was to customers in Quebec, Ontario, and the Maritime Provinces of Canada, the balance to those in Western provinces, with minor exports.

Periods in the History of Canadian Lady

We combined all the graphical representations of the strategies on a single sheet with a common horizontal timescale, and then scanned the

Table 5.1 Performance of Canadian Lady

Year	Sales ($ million)	Pretax operating profit %	Canadian market share %
1972	12.614	14.3	20.6
1973	13.422	15.3	19.1
1974	15.011	13.7	19.7
1975	18.039	14.6	21.6
1976	21.261	14.0	24.2
1977	24.900	12.3	26.8

sheet to infer distinct periods in the history of strategy formation in the organization. Figure 5.2 reproduces this sheet, and indicates four periods for Canadian Lady.

From its inception, we could see no reason to introduce a new period until 1952. The figure shows only two seemingly minor changes before that year. In 1952, however, major changes occurred in product lines, and the Quebec City plant was opened. While a number of changes occurred in subsequent years, prior to 1968 these were spread out and none, in our view, signaled any major reorientation of the company. Thus we treat 1952–68 as one consistent period. As is evident in Figure 5.2, this is clearly not true subsequently: the years 1968–70 stand out for a number of major changes, notably in product line, but also in manufacturing technology and some other areas. Subsequently, to the end of the study period, there was a steady stream of changes. But these, as we shall see, were manifestations of the reorientation of 1968–70, and so we treat 1970–6 as a single period. Each of these periods is described in turn.

1939–52: SMALL, SIMPLE, FOCUSED OPERATIONS—PERIOD OF MAKING A GIVEN STRATEGY WORK

Canadian Lady was started in 1939 when M. Nadler, sensing an opportunity in a business he knew a little about, obtained an exclusive license from New York to manufacture and market Wonderbra brassieres in Canada. Despite his lack of knowledge (he had been in dress retailing), Nadler entered the business because, in the words of his son, 'brassieres were stable' and they made money. The license covered patent rights to a unique shoulder strap design—diagonal slash—which permitted greater movement and comfort for the garment wearer. The license agreement also covered manufacturing know-how and marketing and promotional aids, including use of the Wonderbra trademark, with resulting benefits from the advertising in the US.

Throughout this period the company remained small, with annual sales volume eventually reaching $1 million. The product line was primarily based on the diagonal slash feature brassiere in a variety of sizes, materials, and colors.

All internal operations were located at first in a 4,200-square-foot factory/warehouse at 4475 St. Lawrence Street in Montreal. In part because of its own size and partly because of limitations imposed by the war, the firm subcontracted the work of sewing the shoulder strap assemblies to

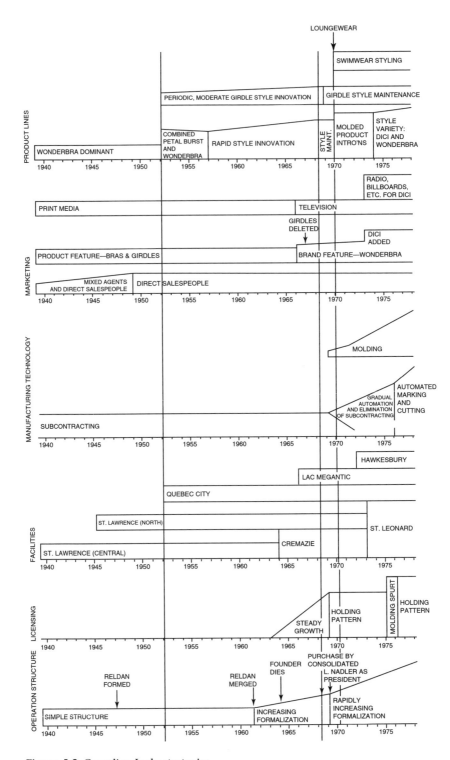

Figure 5.2 Canadian Lady strategies

women who worked in their own homes. Increasing volume and the release of some of the wartime constraints brought on an expansion of operations facilities, and additional factory/warehouse space was leased at 9500 St. Lawrence Street in 1945.

In 1947 a new corporate unit was formed called Reldan, to provide M. Nadler's brother D. Nadler with a specific equity interest in the firm. It was differentiated from Canadian Lady only in terms of accounting records.

Thus the period was spent in establishing the firm, via the entry route of licensing. Toward the end of the period, however, the role of single-product licensee, dependent on an unresponsive licensor for product and marketing innovation, was beginning to chafe M. Nadler. He clearly had intentions for growth and, as discussed below, was engaged in the design work that would facilitate his gaining of independence from the original licensor.

In Conceptual Terms

Our conceptual interpretation of this period is shown in Figure 5.3, with environmental factors on the left (in parallelograms), organizational and leadership factors on the right (in rounded rectangles and diamond shapes, respectively), and the strategies down the middle (in rectangles). What we have here is a fairly typical entrepreneurial beginning, with its resource limitations, giving rise to focus on a single product, limited financing, constrained operations, and simple structure. Atypical, perhaps, was the entrepreneur's lack of knowledge of the business, encouraging the licensing arrangement, and a wartime economy that imposed stringent resource constraints.

In terms of the strategies pursued, this was a period of stability, with signs of the changes to come appearing at the end. These strategies appear to be deliberate for the most part, although not particularly formalized (except, of course, for the licensing). They reflected the stability of the industry environment, the stage of development of the firm, and what we were told was an absence of stringent competition. The strategies were not particularly bold or unique (not what was earlier called 'gestalt strategy'), although they did seem to be integrated around the basic status of the firm in these early years.

Thus we characterize the period as one of getting established—simply surviving, learning the business, building a base in it—and then beginning to consider how to become free of the initial constraints. The object of the company in these early years was to make a given strategy

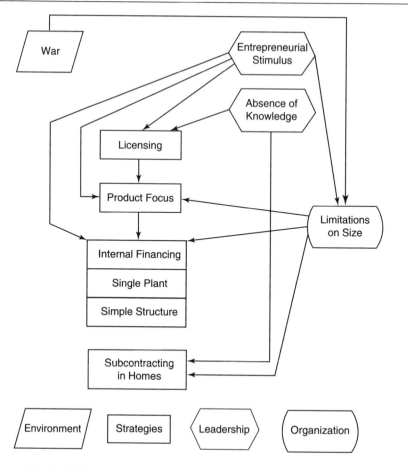

Figure 5.3 Establishment

work. The energies for most of the period were on operating matters, not strategic ones.

1952–68: BECOMING AN INDEPENDENT, BROAD-LINE WOMEN'S UNDERGARMENT MANUFACTURER—PERIOD OF CHANGE IN THRUST FOLLOWED BY GROWTH

The Wonderbra patent was due to expire in 1952. In anticipation of this, and because of M. Nadler's concern that the New York designer was not responding to a new-product trend—the pointed-bust look introduced by Dior—the firm began to design a new brassiere that would not use the Wonderbra technology. Maidenform, a major competitor in Canada, had a pointed-bra product that was selling well, and Canadian Lady wanted a design with which it could compete.

As a result, a number of major shifts took place in Canadian Lady in 1952, all of which were to initiate a period that can be characterized as the flowering of an independent, broad-line women's undergarment manufacturer. With respect to the mainline brassiere business, the Petal Burst line, designed in-house, was launched in 1952 and was a major success. Petal Burst received a major advertising and promotional effort at the expense of Wonderbra, and by 1957, it represented 50 percent of brassiere sales volume.

The Winkie girdle line was also introduced in 1952. It was copied from a US product and was the firm's initial entry into the sizable girdle market, which was roughly the same size as the brassiere market. Girdle sales increased steadily until, by 1966, they represented approximately one-third of the firm's total volume. Girdle sales were reported through Reldan until 1962 when the accounting distinction was eliminated by merging the two companies. Also in 1952, sewing operations were established in Quebec City, increasing total plant area by 10,000 square feet.

After all this, no shifts in strategy occurred until 1957. During the five-year period of 1952–7, negotiations continued with the Wonderbra licensor, the success of the Petal Burst line greatly strengthening the company's bargaining position. In 1957, these negotiations were concluded with Canadian Lady obtaining world rights to the Wonderbra know-how and name, except for the US, Africa, and Latin America.

Ironically the conclusion of these negotiations coincided with a decision not to limit product designs to the type covered by the diagonal slash patent. The firm had hired its first full-time designer in the early 1950s, and design innovation became a major route to growth. From 1957 to 1968 the product strategy was characterized by steady style innovation, with new products and names introduced almost every year.

With new products, new style variety, and new manufacturing capacity, annual sales volume grew from $1 million in 1952 to approximately $8.8 million in 1968. Significantly, the firm had established its independence from the original licensing arrangement.

Increasing task specialization and formalization of procedures began to take place in the early 1960s, following the return of M. Nadler's son Larry to the company after completion of his MBA at Harvard. The resulting structure had sufficient vitality so that the death of M. Nadler in 1964 caused no immediate changes in the directions being pursued.

Production capacity was expanded twice, in 1964 and in 1966, to support the strong growth in business. Other evidence of the continuing transition to independence was the beginning of a foreign licensing program in 1963, which grew steadily till the end of the period. The original licensee was now the licensor of its own products and technology. The advent of the overseas licensing program was stimulated by the strong success of a new product, known internally as Wonderbra 1350, one of the first lace brassieres that emphasized fashion and sex appeal. On the domestic front, the success of this product and similar others helped to increase the rate of sales growth over the period.

Perhaps the clearest symbol of the full transformation to independent status was the shift in 1966 in the advertising and promotional effort, from a focus on product features to one on brand awareness. The company thus began to promote itself as a company, rather than promoting individual products.

A related change, the result of which gives a hint of the next period in the firm, was the move to television advertising in 1967. One-half of the 1967 television budget was allocated to Wonderbra girdles, but in the words of L. Nadler, 'It was a big mistake.' It was discovered that women did not like to see girdles on television, so the television budget was switched exclusively to brassieres six months into the year. Girdle sales continued at the same pace as before, and the company in fact introduced a new design in 1967. But the social reactions to the advertisement were a harbinger of changes to come.

In Conceptual Terms

As shown in Figure 5.4, what particularly characterizes this period is a confluence of a few major changes in the environment—the running out of the patent coinciding with the appearance of Dior's pointed look, and the resultant rise of competition. All this occurred together with the maturation of the firm and the owners' push for growth. In effect, conditions around and inside an organization can shift in global or 'gestalt' ways too—that is, all at once, even suggesting their own form of integration (later we shall see a much clearer example of such a shift). In this case, as implied in Figure 5.4, external changes and threats, internal developments, and managerial values all pointed in the same direction. Often, no matter how complementary, such changes require a tangible stimulus to evoke action. In this case, that stimulus was provided by the expiration of the patent—ostensibly a problem.

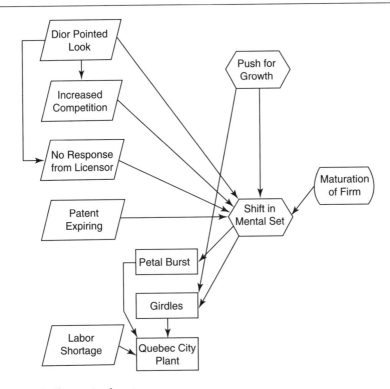

Figure 5.4 Change in thrust

Such a gestalt shift can stimulate a change in the mental set (or world-view, *Weltanschauung*) on the part of responsive managers. That is what seems to have happened in this firm. From operating within a given strategy, the managers began to put that strategy itself into question—to rethink their concept of the business. This led to two major changes: (1) in the traditional product—their own brassiere, and (2) in the market—the introduction of girdles. A third change resulted immediately—in plant capacity and location. And from all this, quite suddenly followed extensive and sustained growth of the firm, with the managers reverting to pursue set strategies, the company thereby experiencing a long period of stability.

Again strategies of the period appeared to be deliberate—in part, a kind of battle plan to deal with the licensor—but this time they were more original to the firm, although not particularly unique. They did, however, represent an opening up, a breaking away from earlier constraints, presumably associated with a sense of excitement. The stimulus, a problem—how to deal with loss of patent protection—was turned into an opportunity. In these regards, strategic behavior of this period, compared with the last, can be described as more proactive.

1968–9: RETHINKING THE BUSINESS—PERIOD OF RECONCEPTION

A great deal changed, beginning in 1968. For one thing, the head designer quit and product-style innovation in conventional lines dropped dramatically. New styles of sewn brassieres were introduced, but these were the results of previous work, and no new styles were introduced in 1969. The growth of licensing also came to an end in 1969, and in that year the firm was sold to a US conglomerate, Consolidated Foods. This was done in order to convert the assets to cash value so that they could be divided between M. Nadler's brother and son.

But the real changes were taking place in the environment. A sexual revolution of sorts was brewing. In sharp contrast to Dior's pointed look, women wished to appear more natural. 'Bra burning' was a major symbol of the social upheaval of the times, and for a manufacturer of brassieres, the threat was obvious. The miniskirt dominated the fashion scene, which led to the development of panty hose, which challenged use of the girdle. Moreover, the girdle itself was threatened by the same social trend that was demanding increased freedom, comfort, and naturalness. As the executives of Canadian Lady put it, '[T]he bottom fell out of the girdle business.' Sales dropped by 30 percent per year, eventually stabilizing at about 5 percent of the firm's total business. Essentially, the whole environment that for years had been so receptive to the company's strategies suddenly seemed to become rejective.

But in crisis loomed opportunity, new trends were emerging which offered hope for a management sensitive enough to perceive them and intuitive enough to appreciate them. As L. Nadler, who became president in 1969, described it, this was a time of confusion and groping, in which two key events led to a sudden crystallization of ideas, which gave birth to a major reconception of strategy.

At this time a French company was promoting a light, sexy, molded garment called 'Huit', with the theme 'Just like not wearing a bra'. Its target market was 15–20-year-olds. Though expensive when it landed in Quebec, and not well fitting, the product sold well. L. Nadler flew to France in an attempt to license the product for manufacture in Canada. The French firm refused, but Nadler claimed that what he learned in 'that one hour in their offices made the trip worthwhile'. He learned that the no-bra movement was going to manifest itself primarily as a less-bra movement. What women seemed to want was a more natural look. He also found that the French product was being target-marketed to younger people.

The second event, shortly after, was a trip to a sister firm in the Consolidated Foods group. There L. Nadler realized the importance of market segmentation by age and lifestyle so the company sponsored market research to better understand what women wanted from a brassiere. The results indicated that for the more mature customer, the brassiere was a cosmetic, which she wore to look and feel more attractive. The product had an important sex appeal dimension for these customers (see 'Marketing'). Moreover, it was found that the Wonderbra brand had high recognition among these consumers. In contrast, the younger customer wanted to look and feel natural. The sex appeal dimension was considerably less important. Also, in the minds of these consumers, the Wonderbra brand name was associated with older women. Based on these distinctions, L. Nadler became convinced that some major product line differentiation was required.

These two events led to major shift in strategy. L. Nadler describes it as a kind of revelation—the confluence of different ideas to create a new mental set. In his words, 'All of a sudden the idea forms.' His groping had led to two new major concepts in the firm's strategy. On the marketing side was market segmentation, specifically the division of the market into older and younger customers, and on the technology and manufacturing side was the use of molding.

Canadian Lady initiated an intensive technology development program to produce its own molded brassiere, stimulated by the recent introduction of new fabrics. The firm introduced a molded garment made out of tricot under the Wonderbra name for older customers and a stretch garment of Lycra for the younger ones. It should be noted that Canadian Lady was able to proceed with its development work without having to seek budget approval from its new parent firm. Canadian Lady was profitable, and the Consolidated Foods executive to whom it reported was occupied with other, less successful, divisions.

Another major change during the period was the development of a line of swimwear. This product was born from the ashes of a mistake. In late 1969, the company introduced a line of loungewear that 'was a complete disaster'; nobody placed orders. Substantial amounts of specialized fabrics (colors and prints) had been purchased, and the company was faced with the prospect of a large write-off. It was decided to experiment with the fabric to produce a line of bikini swimwear. The product was introduced in early 1970, and was greeted with success in the marketplace.

Finally, this period saw the start and acceleration of work to automate the manufacturing processes. A study of opportunities for vertical integration was completed in 1969, which led to an ongoing strategy of more and more in-house manufacturing.

In Conceptual Terms

This was clearly a period of global change for the firm, of 'organizational revolution', in which almost all its strategies changed at once. (Remaining ones changed subsequently as a result, as we shall see.) In the short space of two to three years, the company changed ownership and top management, saw the permanent downturn of one of its major product lines (girdles), began the experimentation required to respond to a major threat to its mainline business (brassieres), experienced a major product introduction failure (loungewear), successfully introduced another product as a result (swimwear), and established new strategies for automation and vertical integration.

Of particular interest here is the fact that the environment changed in global fashion, or perhaps more to the point, in gestalt fashion as well, as shown in Figure 5.5. Everything seemed to change all at once. It was as if the rug had been pulled out from under the firm.

How does an organization respond to such a gestalt shift in the environment? The pattern here is probably typical of effective management. A gestalt shift in situation elicits a gestalt shift in strategy. But not immediately. Managers used to a given conception of their world cannot just change overnight. As the chief executive of this organization described so clearly, the initial feeling was one of confusion, which stimulated a vigorous search for information, for every available scrap that might help explain what was happening, what opportunities might be available. Much as gestalt psychologists and scientists themselves have described the creative process, the chief executive went through a period of *preparation* (informing himself), followed by *incubation* (the uncomfortable, subconscious process of trying to put the disparate pieces together), to one of *illumination* (the sudden discovery—in this case, two of them). The fourth stage, of *verification*, had its equivalent here too, as we shall see in the next period.

The illumination was the shift in mind-set and worldview, as we noted, involving a reconception of the firm's markets and production technology. Segmenting the market in two may not seem like a great

136

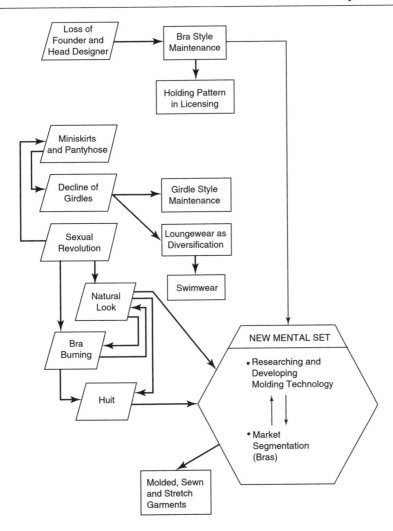

Figure 5.5 Reconceptualization

innovation in retrospect; but to a firm used to thinking in one way for decades, the change must have been dramatic—it certainly had significant strategic consequences.

And once the reconception had taken place, the object was to follow its dictates—to work out the new technology (which was to take some time), and reach the new segments. In L. Nadler's words, 'Once the insight is there—once you understand it—you know what to do about it and you go.' In other words, the notion of reconception implies a high degree of deliberateness, a thought more in a general than a specific sense. The thrust was deliberate, but the details of it—the specific strategies—by having to be worked out, had an emergent quality to them. One could describe a deliberate umbrella under which specific orientations emerged. In fact the one move outside the umbrella—the diversification into loungewear—proved ineffective, and that was quickly pulled back in.

There is at least one major, if implicit, assumption in such an approach to strategy making—that the environment, no matter how sudden and dramatic its change, has become firmly established in a new direction. Much as an automobile turns from one highway on to another, so Canadian Lady proceeded as if its business environment was once again on a steady course. That proved to be a good assumption; had it not, the reconception could have proved dysfunctional, compared with a more adaptive mode of strategy making, with no deliberate thrust encompassing specific strategies.

The approach was largely entrepreneurial, in the sense that both the strategy-making process and the strategies themselves were very personalized, centering on one individual whose behavior seemed to be as much intuitive (as we are describing the processes of synthesis and illumination) as they were systematic or analytic. But once attention turned to developing the insight, and once the takeover by the parent firm was consolidated, the analytic component was to become more significant.

In the study of Steinberg's (see Chapter 3), we discussed the 'proactive reaction'—the turning of problems or crises into opportunities, oversolving them if you like. Here, again under entrepreneurial conditions, we see this phenomenon. Bra burning became, not a cause for panic and diversification (as in the case of some competitors), but an opportunity to serve old markets in new ways. What in strategic management might have been categorized as a 'dog' was going to perform like a 'star' (Henderson 1979).

1970–6: GETTING SETTLED IN NEW DIRECTIONS—PERIOD OF ELABORATING THE NEW CONCEPTS

Although the new directions were more or less identified during the 1968–70 period, much more time would be required to establish them in an integrated way. For example, because some senior people in the company resisted the new concepts, the president formed two task forces of younger ones, bypassing the usual chain of command. Starting in 1970, one task force worked on molding technology and the other on marketing a new 'young' brand.

As the task forces pushed their mandates, molded brassiere products, produced by subcontractors, began to hit the market under the Wonderbra name. Quality-control problems existed (fit, durability), but good product acceptance encouraged continued effort. Some molded brassieres were imported from France to supplement the subcontracted production.

Meanwhile, the marketing task force was being sabotaged by the regular organization. In order to minimize conflict and consolidate the innovations of the task forces, both were eventually merged into the organization as their work continued.

Eventually, out of this development effort came Dici, the new line for younger women, as well as molded Wonderbra products. Internal production began in 1973, although production problems continued as the Dici brand hit the market in 1974. These problems were eventually worked through, and by 1974 the firm was able to introduce a variety of styles, once again in both molded and sewn brassieres. Success with Dici also stimulated a short burst of licensing activity in 1975.

During this settling-in period, the firm nurtured the fledgling swimwear line. In 1972 a plant was purchased in Ontario, and the swimwear was produced there. By the end of the study period, this line grew to account for about 12 percent of total company sales volume.

As part of this settling-in, in 1973 all the Montreal operations—plant, warehouse, and office—were consolidated at modern facilities in the suburb of St. Leonard. The plant incorporated the technological developments of the previous years and was highly automated. This automation reached its peak in 1975 with the installation of new marking and cutting machinery, the first of its kind in the garment industry in Canada and the first in the world in the brassiere business.

Finally, the company was also getting used to operating as a division of another company. This period saw the installation of annual budgets and business plans. Long-range plans for automation and market penetration were prepared, and small amounts of short-term funds were advanced by Consolidated. The increase in automation permitted increased sophistication in purchasing, production planning, and manufacturing, and led to increases in the hiring of technical specialists and to the formalization of work procedures.

In summary, a great deal of energy went into the development of molded brassieres and into a marketing effort tailored to various segments. As these developments were successful, the technology and facilities fell into place, so that, by the end of the period, the company had emerged as a solidly established division of a major corporation. Sales for 1976 were $21 million, almost double what they had been at the start of the period, and the company seemed poised for a period of continuing growth.

In Conceptual Terms

This period is very different from the last. It cannot be characterized as one of stability in strategy—as Figure 5.2 shows, there were changes in strategy throughout it, in parallel and on a piecemeal basis. Yet there was not the same groping. The general thrust had been determined: this was a period of elaboration, of pursuing the consequences of the new concepts. As noted earlier, the thrust was deliberate, with some specific strategies partially emergent, although once these were established, they became firmly deliberate as well. In simpler terms, once the firm had resolved certain specific problems—both technical and organizational—it then pursued the resulting strategies in explicit ways.

One can imagine the mood in the firm—of being up to date, if not on the cutting edge, of knowing what it wished to do, and of moving full-steam ahead to do it. The approach was clearly proactive. The concerns, however, were not conceptual, as in the previous period, but operational: how to solve technical problems, how to organize around a new strategic thrust. As the company's president remarked, 'We were pushing the strength we had for all it was worth.' As can be seen by comparing Figure 5.6 with Figure 5.5, whereas the previous period was driven by the environment, this period was driven by the concepts—by the results of the previous period. Note that in Figure 5.6, the conceptual diagram for the period developed by L. Nadler and the authors, no major environmental shifts appear. The environment naturally remained important, but all its major dimensions were moving in a constant direction. The challenge was to operationalize efficiently what was proving to be the right concept.

Commensurate with greater attention to operating issues within this given strategic thrust, behavior became much more analytic and decentralized, with more planning, the use of task forces, and so on. In effect, as the needs changed, so did the mode of behavior.

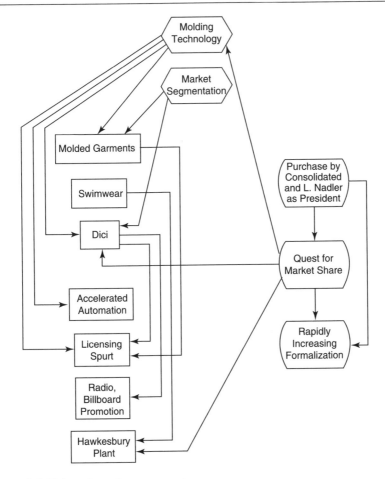

Figure 5.6 Elaboration of new concepts

Some Conclusions about Strategy Formation

INFREQUENT STRATEGIC REVOLUTIONS

One conclusion in our other studies is reinforced here. Major shifts in strategic thrust happen only rarely, and they tend to be revolutionary rather than evolutionary. Only two major shifts in thirty-seven years is not unusual. The implications of this for strategic management are, we believe, important (and evident), and we shall return to them shortly.

Of special interest in this study is one particular pattern by which such shifts occur. Canadian Lady was, of course, the classic entrepreneurial firm in the process of formalizing and adopting more of what is called a 'professional' style of management. Many firms subsequently undergo another transition, involving diversification followed by divisionalization (Scott 1973). But Canadian Lady did not. In fact, its president referred to the firm's good fortune in having its loungewear sortie nipped in the bud, thereby maintaining the focus of the management on its basic business.

DELIBERATE ENTREPRENEURIAL STRATEGIES

Commensurate with the entrepreneurial mode of strategy making that dominated during this study, we see an inclination toward the formation of deliberate strategies, or at least the quick perception of emergent patterns to make them deliberate, in the form of what we called the 'proactive reaction'—turning problems and crises into opportunities.

The shifts we see in this firm were, we believe, characteristic of its entrepreneurial foundation, as well as of the fashion nature of its business. Twice in its history the firm introduced sudden and major changes in its strategic thrust, in both cases in response to rather sudden and global shifts in its environment. The two changes were similar in nature, but because the second was more pronounced on all counts and because we had access to its key actors, we concentrate our discussion on it.

The pattern seems clear enough. Coming out of a long period of stability in strategy, with an environment that has long been, if not munificent, then at least acquiescent, the firm finds that many of the important parameters have suddenly changed, all at once. Initially it is stunned, like the boxer who never saw the punch coming. But in time it adapts. Drawing on Lewin's (1951) notions, we can describe this adaptation in three stages: unfreezing, changing, and refreezing.

UNFREEZING

The process of unfreezing is essentially one of overcoming the natural defense mechanisms to realize that the environment has changed. Effective managers are supposed to scan their environments continually; indeed effective *strategic* managers are supposed to be especially in touch with changing trends.

One danger of strategic management is that it may encourage managers to be *too* much in touch. Managers may be so busy managing strategic change—the big issues—that they may fail to do well what matters most of the time, namely to operate effectively with a given strategy. (Remember that Canadian Lady was not abnormal in experiencing only two brief periods of major strategic change in thirty-seven years.) Or, equally dangerous, and perhaps more likely, is that the firm gives so much attention to strategic monitoring when nothing important is changing that when something finally does happen, the firm does not even notice it. The trick, of course, is to pick out the discontinuities that count. Many changes are temporary or simply unimportant. Some are consequential and a few, revolutionary. For Canadian Lady, the changes in 1968 were of the latter category.

CHANGING

The second step is to be willing to step into the void, so to speak, in order to shed one's conventional notions of how the business is supposed to function (the 'industry recipe', as Grinyer and Spender [1979] have termed it), and really open one's mind to what is happening. Critical is the avoidance of premature closure—not to seize on a new thrust before it is clear what the signals really mean. This takes a special kind of management, one able to live with a good deal of uncertainty and discomfort. L. Nadler was able to articulate his feelings at the time, as president: 'There is a period of confusion before you know what to do about it.... You sleep on it . . . start looking for patterns . . . become an information hound, searching for [explanations] everywhere.' This stage may be painful, but in our view it is critical to successful resolution.

Strategic change of this magnitude seems to involve mind-set before strategy and to be essentially conceptual in nature. In other words, the concepts of the strategy-maker(s)—his or her *Weltanschauung*—must change before anything else can change. If this study gives any indication, while problems and threats in the environment may provoke the unfreezing, it is opportunities that stimulate the changing. With some idea of what *can* be done, the strategy-maker(s) will begin to converge on a new concept of the business—a new strategic thrust. Our guess is that the experience here—of one or two basic driving ideas—is typical: change in mind-set is stimulated by a small number of key events, probably one critical incident in most cases. Continuous bombardment of facts, opinions, problems, and so on, may have had to prepare the mind for the change, but one simple insight probably creates the synthesis—brings all the disparate data together in one sudden 'eureka' flash, like a supersaturated liquid that immediately freezes when disturbed slightly.

REFREEZING

Once the mind is set, assuming it has read the new environment correctly and has not seized prematurely on trends that have not themselves stabilized, then the refreezing stage begins. Earlier it was the managerial mind-set that refroze; now it was the turn of the organization. Here the object is not to read the environment, at least not in a global sense, but, in effect, to block it out. This is not the time for the monitoring precepts of strategic management or for questioning things. It is time to work out the consequences of the new strategic thrust. It has been claimed that obsession is an ingredient in effective organizations (Peters 1980), For this period of refreezing (not unfreezing or changing), we would certainly agree. This is thus the time for pursuing the new orientation—the new mind-set—with full vigor. When we asked L. Nadler how the post-1970 period differed from that of the two previous years, he commented: 'Any idea is acceptable so long as it's . . . .' He motioned with his hands in two parallel lines to indicate that so long as it is strictly within the bounds of the new concept. A management that was open and divergent in its thinking must now become convergent. We wonder how many executives fail in one or the other—remaining convergent when divergence becomes necessary, or failing to settle down to a convergent pattern after a period of divergence.

While unfreezing was a time of great discomfort, refreezing is probably one of great excitement (at least for those who accept the reorientation). The organization now knows where it is going; the object of the exercise is to use all the skills at its command to get there. That is not to say that all is creative. Refreezing is characterized by an analytic mode of behavior, with heavy emphasis on formal evaluation, planning in the form of programming, and so on. Of course, not everyone accepts the reorientation; for them, the discomfort now begins, and this can spill over to the strategy-maker(s) if considerable resistance arises. (At this point, it helps if the organization is small, as was Canadian Lady.)

SYNTHESIS APART

The pattern we have been describing is one among a number that appears to be common, given the other studies in this book. Yet it is an important one for the organization that experiences a sudden but a permanent shift in its environment, as opposed to a gradual one, or is exposed to a more generally turbulent environment (i.e. one that does not stabilize).

The process of adaptation that we have been describing is strongly intuitive and personal, at least in its early stages, in the sense that it depends on the synthesis created by a single mind (or a few that can work in concert). It is also a process characterized by design, the achievement of a unique strategy to cope with a new environment.

This intuitive synthesis does not preclude analytical techniques, which certainly play a role in preparing for such processes and in pursuing their outcomes. However, the synthesis, the attainment of a new concept of the business, stands apart from those techniques. This process of adaptation by design stands in sharp contrast to approaches favored in the field of strategic management, which tend to emphasize selection from a portfolio of generic strategies based on formal analysis of specific parameters in the environment.

Larry Nadler left Canadian Lady in 1980. Its operations were subsequently folded by its parent company into HanesBrands Inc., which was sold in 2006. The Wonderbra label, developed in Canada, gained worldwide prominence in the 1990s (see Wikipedia), and in 2007 is the property of Canadelle Limited partnership of Canada, a wholly owned subsidiary of HanesBrands Inc.

6

Does Planning Impede Strategic Thinking?
Air Canada, 1937–76

Henry Mintzberg, J. Pierre Brunet, and James A. Waters[1]

What is the relationship between formal planning and strategy formation? Despite a vast literature on planning, very little is known about how it influences the creation of strategy. This chapter tracks the strategies of a large airline across forty years of its history, finding that the organization was set on a clear strategic course rather early in its history and remained there. The high degree of planning that arose after that impeded strategic change. Specifically, operational planning discouraged strategic thinking. Other issues that came out of this study include the strong convergence of strategies over time, and the rise of leadership to buffer political influence while the organization fell increasingly under the influence of its industry environment.

Air Canada was the state-owned airline of Canada and the seventh largest airline in the International Air Transport Association (IATA) group in terms of passenger-kilometers (*c*.1973). It flew an all-jet fleet to virtually every large population center in Canada, as well as to a number of major airports in the US, Europe, and the Caribbean. We traced its strategies from its founding in 1937 until 1976, when the then chief executive took office.

This chapter begins with a recounting of the strategies inferred over this time. This is followed by a discussion of the history of the airline in

---

[1] Originally published in *Advances in Strategic Management* (Volume 4, JAI Press, 1986), with minor revisions in this volume.

three periods. A full presentation of both strategies and historical periods is necessary to appreciate the patterns of behavior that evolved in this organization (particularly the strong convergent trends over time), the reasons why they evolved, and the effect this had on, as well as the messages it contains for, the practice of strategic management.

Strategies of Air Canada, 1937–76

The strategy areas identified in Air Canada are the purchase of flight equipment, the introduction of new destinations, the relationship with the government, the provision of flight services (including mail, regular passengers, charter, cargo, and special services), as well as financing, diversification, and organizational structure. (Pricing was examined as well, but is not discussed in this report.) Of particular interest in this study was the wealth of quantitative data available in many of these areas. This enabled us to track most of the strategies in quantitative terms and to display our results graphically, to better understand how we inferred strategies.

FLIGHT EQUIPMENT STRATEGIES

Figure 6.1 shows a plot of the actual number of aircraft in the Air Canada fleet over the study period, categorized by type. It reveals a number of interesting patterns. The purchase of the different types of aircraft looks rather regularly staggered throughout, for the most part appearing in sequenced pairs of two: 14-Hs and Lodestars (which we call the early small planes), DC-3s and DC-4s (the early workhorses), Viscounts and Vanguards (the prop jets), DC-8s and DC-9s (the jets, the former appearing earlier in the sequence but falling back into the pattern due to a slower rate of acquisition), and the 747s and L1011s (the wide-bodies). While each block on Figure 6.1 can be viewed as a cycle of strategy in its own right—that is, a phased pattern of purchase, use, and disposal of each type of aircraft—we have instead chosen to show the pairs as the flight equipment strategies, depicted symbolically in Strategy Diagram 6A.

Of particular interest in Figure 6.1 is the fact that all the individual aircraft blocks before 1954 show sharp, stepped increases (especially for the arrival of DC-3s in 1946 and DC-4s in 1948), while none of the blocks after 1954 do, with the exception of the arrival of seventeen Vanguards in 1961 (but at this point a much smaller percentage of the total fleet). This

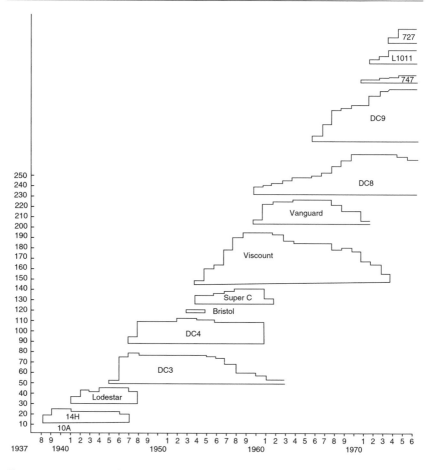

Figure 6.1 Number of aircraft in the fleet by type

suggests a much more regular sequencing of specific additions of aircraft after 1954, implying a more planned, less entrepreneurial approach.

A plot of the total number of aircraft in the fleet (Figure 6.2) indicates a series of rather well-defined cycles along a path of steady growth, while a plot of total available seats (Figure 6.3)—a more accurate indicator of resources devoted to flight equipment—appears to be much smoother. After an initial step in 1938, the latter graph shows a fairly steady level of seats until 1945, followed by a sharp rise for three years, and then relative stability until 1953. Thereafter, the available seats grew rather quickly and regularly to almost the end of the study period, except for a sharp increase in 1960 which was followed by five years of slower growth. These patterns are shown in Strategy Diagram 6B.

148

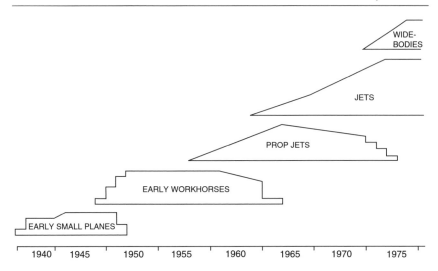

Strategy Diagram 6A Flight equipment strategies

New Destination Strategies

Figure 6.4 plots additions and deletions of flight destinations over the study period, broken down to broad markets—Canada, Europe, the Sun Belt (Miami, Tampa, the Caribbean, Bermuda, and Mexico City), and the rest of the US. Figure 6.5 plots these same data cumulatively to highlight

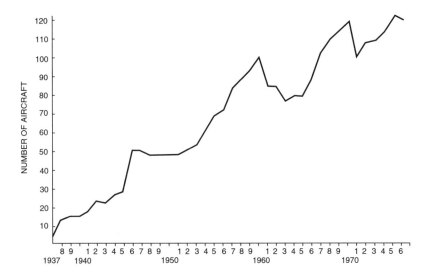

Figure 6.2 Total aircraft in the fleet

149

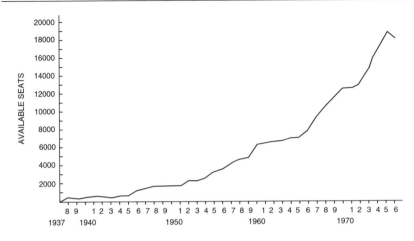

Figure 6.3 Total capacity of the fleet

the relative attention given by the airline to these different markets over time.

In Canada, the data show a good deal of activity up to 1955, in three surges with particularly strong steps in 1938, 1947, and 1955 (eight, six, and seven new destinations). In the twenty-one years that followed, only one new destination was added in Canada, while eleven were dropped. (In most cases, these were fueling stops required before the introduction of jet aircraft, or else small centers ceded to regional airlines). Activity began in earnest outside Canada in 1946. In three years from that date, eleven destinations were added, after which only one new destination appeared in each of the next six years (up to 1954). Following a hiatus of three years, additions of new destinations outside Canada were made sporadically, producing an overall pattern of gradual expansion in

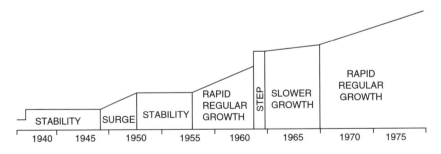

Strategy Diagram 6B Passenger capacity strategies

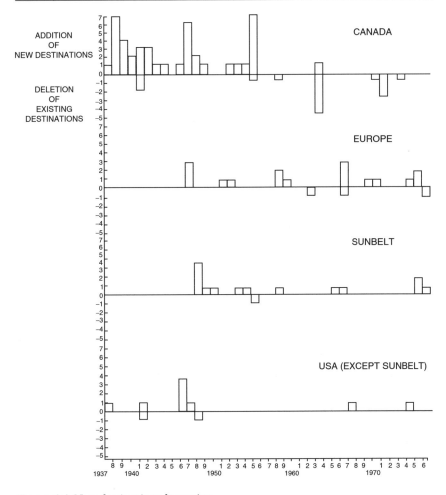

Figure 6.4 New destinations by region

waves. The patterns represented by these data—labeled the destination strategies—are depicted in Strategy Diagram 6C.

Service to destinations can also be considered in terms of total route miles, shown in Figure 6.6, perhaps a more reliable indicator of total activity because it accounts for various connections between given destinations (e.g. the additional distance covered when Toronto–New York was added after Montreal–New York). The curve shows a fairly steadily increasing level of total route miles to 1965, interrupted by a major surge,

151

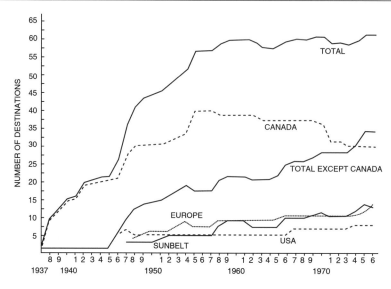

Figure 6.5 Cumulative destinations served

in 1947–8. After a major jump in 1966 (distorted by the addition of a long but infrequent service to Moscow), the total grew somewhat more erratically. The difference between the stability in total destinations and the continued growth in total route miles suggests a strategy of rounding out service to existing destinations (i.e. connecting previously unconnected cities, but both already served by Air Canada). Those patterns are shown in Strategy Diagram 6D.

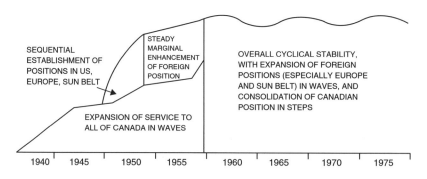

Strategy Diagram 6C Destination strategies

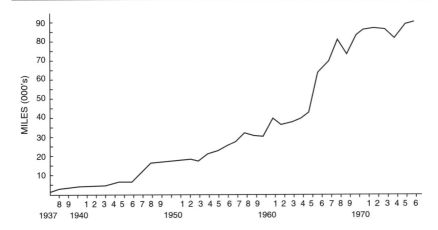

Figure 6.6 Total distance covered by flight schedules

Government Relations Strategies

Since its inception Air Canada had been a government 'crown corporation', technically a wholly owned subsidiary of Canadian National (CN), the government railway. The history of the corporation suggests three overall patterns of relationship with the government.

During the first ten years of its existence, Trans-Canada Air Lines (TCA, as it was then known) was a 'truncated' organization, in that its employees had responsibility only for its operations, while government or CN officials made major decisions. Its presidents, until 1947, were, in fact, the presidents or directors of the already large CN, with only limited time available for the small, fledgling airline. The CN also provided many of the airline's corporate functions in these years.

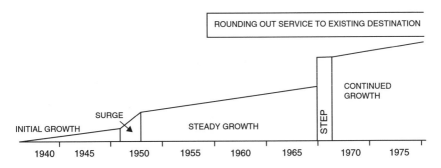

Strategy Diagram 6D Flight activity strategies

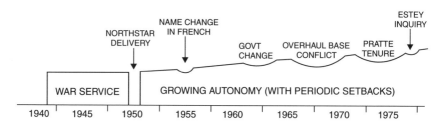

Strategy Diagram 6E Government relation strategies

C. D. Howe, the federal government minister responsible for Air Canada from 1935 to 1957, was the driving force behind the airline. He had it established in the first place, hired its first managers, and figured prominently in its major decisions until 1957. To quote one senior executive of the airline, 'What Howe said, went' in those years.

From 1939 to 1947, the airline is shown in Strategy Diagram 6E as pursuing a 'war service' strategy, since it contributed to the war efforts in a number of ways, notably by carrying out maintenance and overhaul work for the Royal Canadian Air Force, and, from 1943, by transporting mail, cargo, and officials to and from the UK under the noncommercial 'Canadian Government Trans-Atlantic Air Service' (CGTAS).

A single event just after the war is indicative of the state of the airline at that time, and probably colored the thinking of its managers for many years to come. The government purchased a number of DC-4 aircraft, modified them to suit Canadian conditions (labeling them 'Northstars'), and then, on the orders of Howe, had twenty-three of them delivered to TCA, which had in fact ordered only twelve. The result was that, through no intention of its own, the airline suddenly found its seating capacity increased by 61 percent in two years.

When G. R. McGregor, a decorated World War II pilot who joined the airline as traffic manager in 1945, became its first full-time president in 1948, a strategy began which was never to abate, although it suffered periodic setbacks: growing autonomy from the government.[2]

Whereas earlier, strategies tended to be imposed and/or emergent, this one reflected clear intention on the part of the managers of the organization and so was strongly deliberate. Early in the McGregor tenure, for example, many of the corporate services were brought in-house, and the head office was moved from Winnipeg to Montreal.

[2] See Hafsi (1981) for a detailed discussion of Air Canada's autonomy strategy, and Sexty (1980) for a discussion of the autonomy strategies of Canadian government-owned business corporations in general.

154

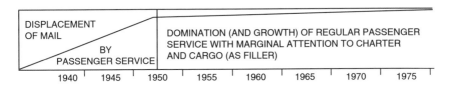

Strategy Diagram 6F Flight service strategies

The setbacks occurred as the federal government occasionally sought to impose specific strategies or decisions on its airline. But the outcomes of most of the ensuing struggles serve to illustrate the long-term trend, most notably the government's attempt to stop the transfer to Montreal the work done at the Winnipeg overhaul base. There was a good deal of conflict, and the transfer was delayed for many years, but it eventually took place.

Other setbacks in the achievement of autonomy (shown as dips in Strategy Diagram 6F) included a request in 1953 for a change of name that was approved by the government in French only; a change of government in 1957 which replaced Howe and the Liberals with a more hostile Conservative government; the appointment of Yves Pratte, an outsider, as chief executive in 1969 over the favored inside candidate; and the Estey Parliamentary Inquiry of 1975 into management practices in the airline.

FLIGHT SERVICE STRATEGIES

Air Canada's airplanes provided four basic services over the years: they flew passengers on regular and charter flights; carried mail; and delivered cargo. Figure 6.7 shows the annual revenue for each of these services over the study period.

More revealing is Figure 6.8, which plots these same data on a percentage basis. Mail revenues, which accounted for two-thirds of the total at the outset, steadily gave way to passenger revenues. By 1948, when the curve changes shape, mail revenues were down to 18%, and dropped to 2.4% by the end of the study period. Once established, passenger services always dominated. The proportion of cargo revenues grew in three waves (that peaked in 1943, 1955, and 1970), but barely climbed over 10%, and ended the study period at 9%. Charter revenues, aside from a single blip of 7.1% in 1948 (the result of a special airlift to bring European refugees to Canada), never reached 4% and ended the study period at 2.7%.

The message is clear (and will be further supported later in the text): from the mid-1940s, this was a regular passenger airline. Interviews

155

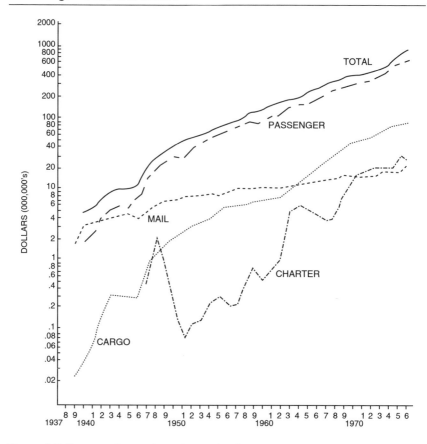

Figure 6.7 Revenues by service category total

confirmed the observation that cargo and charter received only marginal attention from the senior management, even though each had its own champions within the system. For example, regular passenger traffic estimates were always used for scheduling aircraft. 'At that time, after the passenger schedules had been completed, cargo was given a copy and told what space they would have, on what routes', according to one interviewee. Likewise, except for the purchase of a few Bristol Freighters in the early 1950s (as a defensive move against rival Canadian Pacific Airlines—CP Air), cargo needs always received low priority in aircraft purchase decisions.

The performance data of Figures 6.7 and 6.8 suggest, therefore, two clear patterns in the actions of the system, which are depicted in Strategy Diagram 6G: displacement of mail by passenger revenue before 1948, and

156

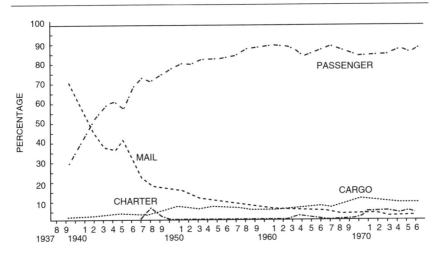

Figure 6.8 Proportion of revenue by service category

domination of passenger revenue with marginal attention to cargo and charter thereafter.

Two other intended strategies can be mentioned, although they are not shown in Strategy Diagram 6G because we view one as unrealized, the other as incidental. In 1972, Air Canada initiated a 'Rapidair' service between Montreal and Toronto. Intended as a kind of commuter or shuttle service modeled after the US ones, Rapidair ended up, after only a few days, being little more than a convenient form of check-in. In 1974, Air Canada provided the manpower and management for a federal government-sponsored short takeoff and landing (STOL) service between downtown Montreal and Ottawa. The service was only experimental, however, and was terminated in 1978.

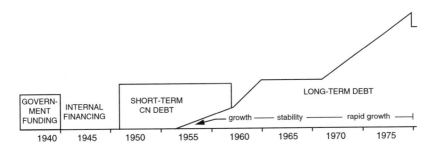

Strategy Diagram 6G Financing strategies

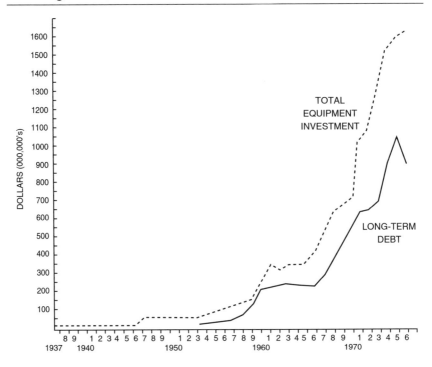

Figure 6.9 Outstanding long-term debt and total equipment investment

FINANCING STRATEGIES

Figure 6.9 depicts the annual total of outstanding long-term debt as well as the total equipment investment. Strategy Diagram 6G depicts the inferred financing strategies over the study period. From 1937 to 1940, the airline received direct government funding in the form of an initial capitalization of $5,000,000 and subsidization of losses. From 1940 to 1945, the airline was able to finance itself internally from its profits (net income is shown in Figure 6.10). Losses beginning in 1946 forced it to borrow from CN in the form of short-term renewable notes, and despite profitable operations from 1949 to 1959, this borrowing continued until 1957. Long-term debt began in 1953 and grew slowly until 1958 after which it increased rapidly (due to commitments for prop jets and DC-8s). Debt then remained relatively steady until 1967, from which point it grew rapidly as investments in the jet fleet increased significantly, due to the need to purchase expensive wide-body aircraft. Servicing the debt then became a major pre-occupation.

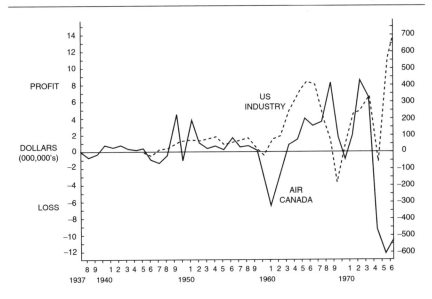

Figure 6.10 Net income

DIVERSIFICATION STRATEGIES

Figure 6.11 shows Air Canada's annual non-air transport revenue both as a percentage of total revenue and in absolute dollars. Clearly, after the war years, this revenue remained a minor part of the total, typically less than 3%. During the war, the small airline provided maintenance services to military aircraft, a reflection of the expertise it had already developed. These services continued, but diminished in importance. Diversification income only began to grow again in the mid-1960s, from three sources: expansion of outside maintenance revenues; the offering of transportation consulting services (after 1971, particularly related to the company's innovative computer reservation system); and minority equity investments (in an innkeeping company in Bermuda in 1972, a freight movement company, a cargo facility, and 25 percent of Air Jamaica, all in 1975, and an air charter operator in 1976). Although these moves were few and cautious, they do suggest a minor strategy of support for the airline's Sunbelt operations, which is shown together with the other patterns inferred in Strategy Diagram 6H.

ORGANIZATION STRUCTURE

Finally, Strategy Diagram 6I depicts the development of the organizational structure of Air Canada over the study period. As noted earlier, until 1948

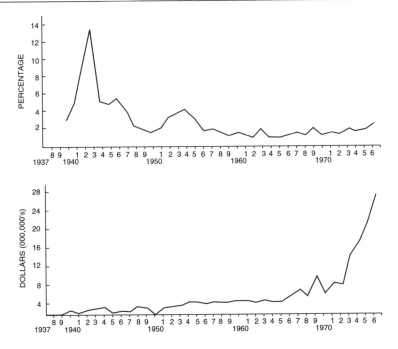

Figure 6.11 Non-air transport revenue

we depict Air Canada as a 'truncated' organization. The CN provided its chief executive officer, secretary treasurer, comptroller, legal council, medical officer, architectural group, and purchasing, insurance, advertising, and public relations functions. With the appointment of McGregor as president in 1948, the airline immediately gained control of a number of corporate functions, and more were taken over in subsequent years, so that by 1952 most were under its control (although not until after 1967 was the transition complete, when medical and legal services were brought into the airline).

There also began with the McGregor tenure a gradual formalization of structure, and, notably, the introduction of more systematic operations

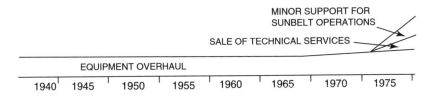

Strategy Diagram 6H Diversification strategies

160

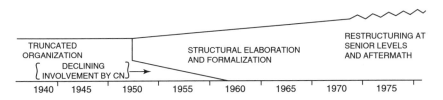

Strategy Diagram 6I Organization structure

planning (of schedules, staffing, maintenance, purchasing, and the like). One interviewee noted that by 1955, most of the present rather detailed planning procedures were already in place.

In late 1968, shortly after he was appointed chairman, Yves Pratte commissioned a study of Air Canada's corporate structure. After a year of analysis by McKinsey & Co., it was decided to make significant changes to the airline's management structure, particularly involving marketing and the institution of regional operating groups.

But the reorganization was remembered less for any specific changes than for the ways in which they came to be. More than a decade later, opinions remained very divided on this restructuring: while most interviewees accepted that there was a need for change, many viewed the means by which they were instituted as irresponsible. Some were surprised, not by the commissioning of the study, but by Pratte's acceptance of virtually all its recommendations. Others simply believe he lost control to outsiders. Pratte himself resigned at the end of 1975, and was replaced on an interim basis by Pierre Taschereau, chairman of the CN. But in the view of most of the people interviewed, while the operations of the airline kept functioning throughout these years in their (by then) highly structured way, the senior management levels did not really settle down again until 1976, when Claude Taylor, a long-term and popular insider, was named chief executive officer.

THREE POLES OF STRATEGY

To conclude this discussion of Air Canada's strategies, we highlight three areas in particular. Flight equipment and destination (or route) development seem clearly to have been the driving forces of this system, with government relations as the third pole of a triangle from which all the other strategies flowed. In other words, as depicted in Figure 6.12, the attention of the senior management seemed always to have been firmly riveted on the purchase of aircraft, the introduction of routes,

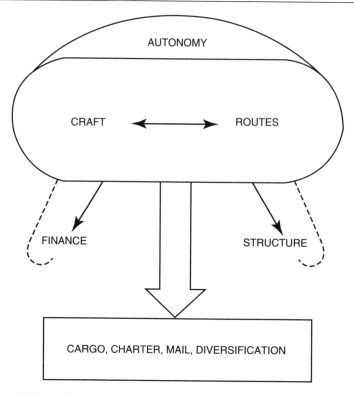

Figure 6.12 Interplay of strategies in Air Canada

and, perhaps as the means of protecting these two, the attainment of autonomy from the government. All other strategies were treated, in our opinion, as secondary.

Some of these other strategies were simply derivative, in the sense that they just followed leading strategies (e.g. financing that adapted to equipment purchases or structure that responded to growth of passenger services—note that despite the traumatic nature of the 1970 reorganization, no changes in strategy seemed to result from it). Other strategies appeared to be no more than peripheral, perhaps championed by some unit within the organization, but never receiving much of the attention of senior management. These include cargo, charter, mail, and diversification.

Essentially, this organization focused on the mission of moving people on a scheduled basis—specifically of transporting Canadians through their country and to key centers in the US, Europe, and the Atlantic Sunbelt. The airline's most important concerns were, therefore, first to

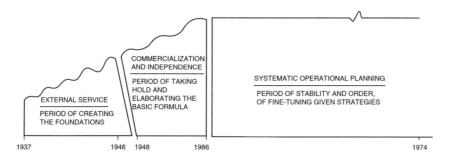

Figure 6.13 Periods in the history of Air Canada

establish these services, and second to provide them on a reliable and efficient basis, with a minimum of governmental interference and at the lowest fares and rates consistent with the maintenance of a sound financial position.

Strategic Periods in the History of Air Canada

Reviewing and comparing the different strategies inferred, with a particular focus on key strategic changes, enabled us to infer distinct periods in the history of an organization. In Air Canada, two points of change stand out in the forty years of its history—one shortly after World War II and the other in the mid-1950s. These suggest three distinct periods in the history of this organization, around which we find strong convergence. These are shown symbolically in Figure 6.13 and listed below:

- 1937 to war end: External service, a period of creating the foundations
- Postwar to 1955: Commercialization and independence, a period of taking hold and elaborating the basic formula
- 1955 to end of study period: Systematic operational planning, a period of stability and order, of fine-tuning given strategies

In delineating these periods, we find convergence not only around the two main points of change, but also in the progression of the periods themselves. From loosely organized beginnings, Air Canada matured into a highly stable organization in two basic steps, the first creating the essential foundations and the second enabling it to break free of direct external control and consolidate its basic strategic direction.

In describing these periods below, we continue to build up the arguments that will underlie the conclusions drawn about strategy formation and strategic thinking in the final section of the chapter.

1937 TO WAR END: EXTERNAL SERVICE—A PERIOD OF CREATING THE FOUNDATIONS

From its founding in 1937 until the end of World War II, the airline was a small organization seeking to get on its feet by the addition of new destinations within Canada. The war interrupted that process early, and diverted attention to war service, notably in the strategies of providing equipment overhaul services and in running the Canadian Government Trans-Atlantic Air Service. But in a sense, these strategies served to continue, indeed to accelerate, the process of organization development.

Air Canada remained a truncated organization throughout this period, lacking a full-fledged management structure, let alone a full-time chief executive. It was controlled externally, especially by Howe in the federal cabinet. The company flew small passenger aircraft, with unpressurized cabins, forcing the pilots to make their way through mountain passes to reach Canada's west coast. Stories circulated of pilots having to land at emergency fields and accepting the hospitality of local farmers for days on end because of bad weather. But this did not make much difference, since Air Canada remained largely a mail carrier in this period (passenger revenue only surpassing that of mail in 1945).

The flavor one gets in this regard is of an incomplete organization, an appendage of a larger system, that responded to external needs rather than its own needs as a system. In a sense, TCA was a function of the federal government—its flying arm—rather than an organization in its own right. Yet by serving in this capacity, it took the steps that allowed it to emerge eventually as a complete organization.

Most organizations appear to be founded by entrepreneurial initiative or at least to exhibit it in their formative years through the strong leaders that are attracted to their helms. A curiosity of this organization is that such initiative was not contained within its structure, but rather emanated from the federal cabinet. That might have had an influence on the airline's willingness to take risks in the future. Indeed, the final major event of this period, Howe's imposition of the Northstars on the airline, was perhaps the only real shock in the whole study period, and perhaps the last really high-risk strategic initiative.

Thus we call this period 'external service', one of 'creating the foundations'. These foundations included the skills the airline would need throughout its history as well as the essential skeleton of its domestic route structure. This was, therefore, a period of learning: about aircraft maintenance, new ports of call, and dealing with the problems of Canada's weather and its geography, not to mention its government. This was not, however, a period of learning how to make strategy. External forces drove the airline, the weather being the most literal but not the most important of these: they included the government that controlled the airline formally and the events in the world at large (especially World War II).

As a result, the airline's strategies were not so much integrated as disjointed. Yet in some small, sometimes almost inadvertent ways, the organization did manage to create a strategic foundation on which it would later be able to build. It was the airline, for example, that volunteered to run the CGTAS in the hope of developing its overseas expertise. Because its role was dictated largely by outside forces, its strategies were largely explicit, in a sense, public. They were also deliberate, but not by the organization, since the intentions behind most of them were those of the government, not the airline's own executives. 'Deliberately imposed' would be a more accurate expression. Likewise, while there was proactive behavior due to external entrepreneurship, the organization itself was largely reactive, both to that entrepreneurship and to environmental events.

POSTWAR TO 1955: COMMERCIALIZATION AND INDEPENDENCE—A PERIOD OF TAKING HOLD AND ELABORATING THE BASIC FORMULA

It was not until the war was over for a time that significant strategic changes began to occur. But then they came quickly, so that in the space of two years (1946–8) the airline underwent *global* strategic change— of many strategies in a brief space of time. And these basic changes continued to manifest themselves through to the mid-1950s, but in a more incremental fashion.

In the years 1946–8, the airline was given its own chief executive; it began to take over its own corporate functions and to gain autonomy from the government; it underwent its second surge of expansion in Canadian destinations and moved in a significant way into the US, then Europe (beginning with the takeover of the transatlantic service), followed by the Caribbean; its available seats increased dramatically (as the early workhorses arrived in large numbers) as did its total route miles; and it began to establish (and later, in the 1950s, to elaborate and formalize) its planning systems. After 1948, many of these trends continued, but at a slower pace, until 1955.

The flavor of the organization was now totally different. Coming out of years of response to external influence, culminating in Howe's imposition of the additional Northstars, the corporation was now taking hold of its own destiny and settling down, commercializing itself, and shaping its structures accordingly. The war had ended, domestic demand for passenger services was developing, and the organization was staffed with 'Young Turks', eager to provide these services (and to challenge any federal officials who impeded these efforts).

Whereas earlier, mail delivery and service to the war effort (which included a form of diversification—the selling of maintenance services), figured prominently in its strategies, now the organization focused on one task: the comprehensive provision of regular passenger services to Canadians. That became, and was to remain, the dominant element of the strategy. Hence, in contrast to the earlier disjointed strategies, in this period we find tightly integrated ones, built on the three poles discussed earlier—the elaboration of routes, the purchase of passenger aircraft, and the steady gain of autonomy from the government. Howe accordingly became less a controller, more a protector. As he told McGregor soon after he became the airline's first president, 'Keep your hands out of the taxpayer's pocket, and I'll keep the politicians off your back.'

In contrast to the last, this period finds the system manager driven, within a rather benign environment. Except perhaps for the move into the Caribbean (to make use of the unexpected Northstars), the strategies again seemed largely deliberate, but this time in response to the initiatives of the corporation's own management, although increasingly influenced by industry forces. The organization's moves can be called expansionary and proactive without being labeled bold. After global change at the outset of the period, which established the basic formula, the airline settled down to pursue rather steady incremental change in response to steadily developing market demand.

1955 TO END OF STUDY PERIOD: SYSTEMATIC OPERATIONAL PLANNING—A PERIOD OF STABILITY AND ORDER, OF FINE TUNING GIVEN STRATEGIES

Since we are describing Air Canada as being on a convergent path to a stable, systematic mode of operating, it may seem arbitrary to pinpoint one year for a change of period. The fact is that 1955 stands out strongly as the year when considerable change did take place; some strategies exhibited a final surge; others ended, to be replaced by new ones after 1955.

The year 1955 saw a final surge in new Canadian destinations (seven in all) after nineteen years of steady growth; thereafter only one new destination was added while eleven were eliminated, suggesting a new strategy of consolidation within Canada. Outside Canada, after somewhat steady growth since 1946, new destinations began to increase only in cyclical fashion after 1955. (The federal government had run out of desirable domestic destinations to trade for foreign ones in bilateral negotiations.) Also, a strategy of rounding out service to existing destinations appeared to gain importance from 1955. Moreover, whereas new airplanes had all arrived in blocks, or steps (in effect, suddenly) up to this time, after 1955 (except for the Vanguards of 1961) none did; they arrived instead in somewhat steady progressions, carefully sequenced.

One strategy not fully developed by 1955 was that of gaining autonomy from the government, since the takeover in corporate functions continued for several years, and new conflicts arose. But in some sense, these were temporary setbacks in a strategy that was by 1955 well established.

No less surprising than the appearance of all these shifts around 1955 was the relative absence of strategic change in the two decades that followed. Jet aircraft did, of course, begin to arrive in 1960, and widebodies in 1971, these had a profound effect on the airline, but not on its basic posture. The jets caused the airline to do things better, and so to attract many more passengers, but not to do different things. These aircraft simply created new ways to serve existing markets.

The areas of organizational strategy can be described in generic terms as follows:

- Mission (products and services as well as markets)
- Means to perform the mission (facilities, machinery, etc.)
- Supplying the mission (raw materials, finance, manpower, etc.)
- Marketing the mission (pricing, promotion, distribution)
- Supporting the mission (external relations, etc.)
- Extending the mission (vertical integration and diversification)

In Air Canada from 1955 to 1976, the only really significant change appeared to be in the means to perform the mission (i.e. in-flight equipment). Strategies associated with all the others remained remarkably stable for the twenty-one years. Equally surprising, a number of means of extending the mission that some US airlines were pursuing vigorously—such as charter, cargo, and diversification into tourist ventures—received scant attention in Air Canada. To the extent that these strategies were pursued at all, Air Canada followed broad industry patterns.

The arrival of Yves Pratte as chief executive officer in 1969—an outsider appointed over McGregor's handpicked successor—is most interesting in this regard.

Pratte and Yves Ménard, his associate, conceived an intended strategy of diversification for the airline, to serve customers through minority interests in travel agencies, hotels, and so on. But the energy invested in pursuing those intentions declined significantly after Ménard left, so that the strategy actually realized was only a shadow of what was intended. (One senior executive asked, if the company had diversified, responded that it 'tried to'.)

Of greater impact was the McKinsey reorganization initiated by Pratte. The McKinsey reorganization certainly did shake up the management structure. But, as noted earlier, it seemed to lead to no major change in strategy. Indeed, it may have impeded or delayed rather than encouraged strategic change. After the reorganization, the senior executives apparently consumed so much energy adapting to the shifts in structure and personnel, and protecting themselves politically, that they seemed to lack the time to initiate any significant change in the basic direction of the airline. As one executive commented, this was 'a time when everybody looked after themselves'. Moreover, the McKinsey reorganization may simply have reinforced at the executive levels the analytic mode of operating that had long since pervaded the operating levels. And this mode, we shall argue, may have discouraged strategic change. Perhaps most indicative of this period was the comment of one planning executive, '[D]uring the McKinsey crisis, the detailed plans, implemented faithfully by the operations people, saved the day. Management did not know which way to turn for a time but the planes kept on flying.'

It is in these comments that we find the characteristics of this final period. This was a period driven by the desire for stability and order, the airline having already gained control of its political destiny as well as its technical and market operations. Its strategies appeared to be deliberate, yet, paradoxically, they also seemed implicit—so deeply established that they were internalized in the system. These strategies were also tightly integrated, the result of the orientation to planning and the focus on

168

regular passenger operations. Thus, we have a period dominated by systematic operational planning, in other words, refining or fine-tuning a given and successful set of strategies.

The planning process itself solidified at the start of this period. Although there had been budgets from the beginning (and one-year operating plans after World War II), solidification of the process reached its final stage in 1955 when J. J. Smith, a member of the finance group, developed the 'blackboard exercise'. Used prior to the introduction of summer and winter schedules, this process divided the airline into five operating sectors, called 'five little airlines'—transcontinental routes, transatlantic routes, thin southern routes, short-haul routes, and other small North American routes. A pro forma income statement was used by the executives to establish fares and schedules, and also to try to control the level of profitability, at least during the years when costs and revenues could more easily be managed. This planning system, with modifications made in 1965 to separate the long-range plans, was used till the end of the study period.

Whether long range or short, however, the system was clearly focused on operations, not strategy—the object was to program what was, not to create what had not been. Indeed, the very definition of the 'five little airlines' implied a stable route strategy, or at least encouraged the stabilization of it (e.g. *thin* southern routes). Also significant was the time and attention operational planning received from the very top levels of management.

Thus the dominant culture was oriented to the highly managed operations, specifically to moving regular passengers on established routes (and, when necessary, engaging in marketing to attract sufficient numbers of those passengers). While it would perhaps not be accurate to describe Air Canada as reactive—since it was responding more to its own needs for planning and order than to external pressures—it could not be characterized as highly proactive either. The major exception to this was, of course, the continuing strategy of gaining autonomy from the government. But, interestingly enough, that strategy seemed to have been designed to protect the planning process—to seal the organization off from unexpected demands of the environment so that the operations could be managed tightly from within. Pratte tried to be proactive in other spheres, notably with respect to diversification, but a combination of factors—some, but not all, beyond the control of the organization itself—stopped him. His proactive, intended strategies never became organizational, and thus were never really realized.

In another sense, however, Air Canada was reactive. It followed industry trends. It had become a large, world-class airline, in many ways undifferentiated from the others, especially some of its US counterparts. Once the Vickers airplanes were phased out, Air Canada flew the same airplanes as they did; attended to demands for charter services in accordance with changes in IATA rules and the corresponding moves of its competitors; supplied cargo services in accordance with its available aircraft and industry trends; and flew mostly to large, established urban centers in Canada and abroad. Even its diversification strategies, such as they existed, were not for the most part unusual. Where Air Canada did excel, in computer systems and maintenance, for example, was a reflection of its orientation to operating efficiency, not strategic innovation.

In a sense then, the more Air Canada was drawn into the mainstream of its industry, the less control it had over its own strategies. How could a world-class airline, for example, refuse to fly wide-bodied jets or to offer charter services across the Atlantic? Ironically, Air Canada traded the imposition of strategies by the government for that by the industry.

This 'nesting' within the industry is perhaps best indicated by a comparison of Air Canada's results with those of the US airline industry. As shown in Figure 6.14, the smooth exponential growth of Air Canada's revenue since the late 1940s followed closely that of the US airlines. Air Canada's passenger load factor changed much more erratically over the years with swings of ten percentage points from one year to the next. Yet when these figures are compared with those of the US industry, as can be seen in Figure 6.15, the similarity is striking (even though Air Canada's load factor tended to remain higher, presumably due to less competition on some key Canadian routes).

A Conceptual Interpretation of Strategy Formation at Air Canada

In seeking to interpret forty years of Air Canada's history in conceptual terms, we focus first on the pattern of change in strategy formation over these years as a function of the interplay of environment, leadership, and organization, and second on the nature of the planning orientation that developed in Air Canada and its effect on the propensity of the airline, or at least its executives, to think strategically.

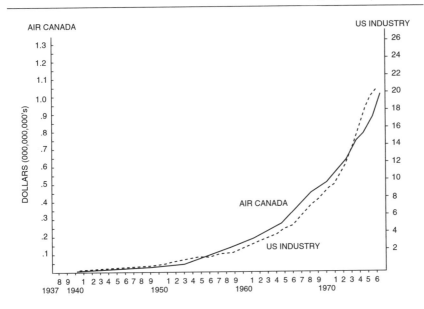

Figure 6.14 Total revenue

PATTERN OF STRATEGIC CHANGE AS A FUNCTION OF ENVIRONMENT, LEADERSHIP, AND ORGANIZATION

The three periods we have identified differentiate themselves clearly in terms of the interplay of three forces: an environment demanding certain kinds of adaptation, an organization seeking to protect and elaborate itself as a formalized system, and a leadership sitting between these two sets of forces. Figure 6.16 summarizes the discussion that follows.

Briefly, the environment—in the form of government—clearly dominated the first period; the second period saw the rise of leadership, which served gradually to buffer the organization from that environment as well as to draw power into the formal organization; and the organization (in an implicit alliance with its industry in the environment) dominated the third period, despite periodic attempts by both government and externally imposed leadership to influence it.

First Period: Environment

As noted earlier, a unique feature of Air Canada was the absence of internal entrepreneurship at its outset, or indeed, of internal leadership in general for the first decade of its existence. It did have its entrepreneur, after a fashion, but that individual was a minister of the government,

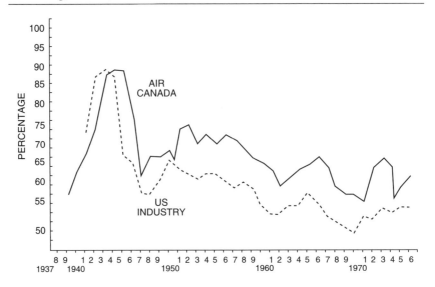

Figure 6.15 Passenger load factor

not a manager of the airline. He was able to impose major decisions on the new airline because the organization was small and malleable; it did not even provide many of its own regular services. Thus, in its earliest period, Air Canada was controlled by an important element in the political environment.

Second Period: Leadership

What really established the second period were the actions of the airline's first full-time chief executive, a strong-willed leader who worked on two concurrent fronts: inside to build up the organization and its given mission, and outside to protect it from the political environment. In effect, the second period is characterized by strong leadership, but serving to strengthen the organization.

Note that this leadership, perhaps because it came from within the organization, perhaps because of the previous history, was not really entrepreneurial. The airline did not innovate in any dramatic way, by inventing new markets or establishing new ways of doing things. Rather, it was oriented to the elaboration of its given direction, dedicating its real skills to doing that well. And, as the period progressed, the leadership seemed to become less a separate component than a natural and intrinsic part of the organization.

172

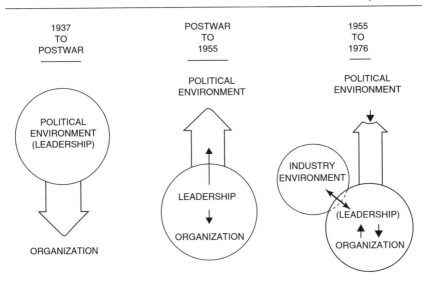

Figure 6.16 Interplay of environment, leadership, and organization in the three periods

Third Period: Organization

Thus, by the start of the third period, it was the organization as a system—firmly and formally established—that seemed to have become clearly dominant, but in a kind of implicit coalition with another element of the environment, the industry. Gradually over the years (but long before the establishment of formal airline alliances), Air Canada had grown into a complementary and supportive relationship with other world-class airlines, in a kind of exclusive club. They exchanged ideas and copied each other's changes in services. This, of course, helped to avoid strong competition (indeed, Air Canada shared some routes, such as to Moscow and Prague, alternating flights on different days of the week with its foreign counterpart). All the while, on its domestic routes, Air Canada experienced strong, sustained demand for passenger services, and faced limited competition from other Canadian carriers.

The political environment in this third period cannot, however, be called passive. It would be more accurate to say that it flared up occasionally, seeking to impose its imperatives on the organization. But for the most part it failed, appearing more as an impediment than a real force for change. The organization was simply too strong and established, too set in its procedures (Hafsi 1981). Moreover, the airline was sometimes able to evoke its industry relationships to protect itself from government influence.

The Pratte appointment was perhaps most indicative of the forces at play in this period. Imposed on the airline against the wishes of some senior managers, Pratte tried to effect strategic change and failed. Even his use of the McKinsey people to reorganize the management structure seemed to have no effect on the strategies pursued, since the operations continued to function smoothly despite the disruptions at senior levels. As noted, Pratte tried to effect this strategic change, not in the central mission—in routes and crafts—but through diversification, that is, extension of the mission. Here, ostensibly at least, he could act alone, negotiating joint ventures with outsiders with a minimum of involvement of other executives, who knew the airline industry a lot better than he did. But even in these peripheral areas, he did not succeed. Then surprisingly, in his letter of resignation, Pratte praised the airline and its staff but had harsh words for the government's attitude toward the organization: what had been designed as a force for the political environment ended up being one for the organization!

Except for an occasional conflict in the political sphere, the overall environment of this period of twenty-one years can be characterized as remarkably stable and supportive. It was largely predictable, contained few discontinuities, and little in the way of severe competition, while the hostilities that did arise proved largely manageable. Aspects of the environment may have seemed complex, for example, by imposing the need to schedule services and to coordinate the introduction of new aircraft. But the planning system that developed proved adept at rationalizing, and also simplifying, that complexity. This left the organization as the dominant force of the period.

A Steady, Stable Progression

These three distinct periods in fact seem to represent a single steady progression, or convergence, similar to one we have seen in a number of our studies (at least for machine-like organizations that provide mass-manufactured products or services). Even organizations that are created and built by their own entrepreneurs tend eventually to formalize their structures, as they develop and grow large, so that systems eventually come to dominate leadership. Strategies that may have been bold and innovative at the outset (as a means to find and develop a niche) tend to become incremental and conservative in the mature years (to protect the niche).

When the market environment does undergo major change, as we saw in our study of Volkswagenwerk, the organization tends to be highly resistant to strategic change and to experience a difficult period of groping before settling into a new strategic direction. Air Canada faced no such shift in its environment (deregulation started much later in Canada), and so continued to pursue its given and successful strategies to the end of the study period.

Our study of 'Steinberg's', the supermarket chain that grew large over the course of almost sixty years under its entrepreneur, exhibits certain similarities with Air Canada but with some interesting differences, which we attribute to entrepreneurship and the nature of the business. In Steinberg's, the organization and its planning system eventually displaced entrepreneurial vision. But that shift took half a century. And before it did, the organization voluntarily and proactively undertook two major strategic reorientations, in our opinion for two reasons: a supermarket chain is intrinsically more flexible than an airline, and this one was led by an owner with considerable entrepreneurial vision, as well as the power to act unilaterally.

PLANNING ORIENTATION AND STRATEGIC THINKING

Of particular interest in the last half of the Air Canada study is the prevalence of planning and the absence of strategic reorientation. We believe that there is a relationship between these two.

When asked why the McKinsey reorganization seemed to have so little effect on the basic strategy of the airline, one senior executive commented with an expletive that management means nothing in the operation of this business. What he must have had in mind was strategic management, or perhaps senior managers, certainly not management systems, because this airline was dependent on such systems during a good part of its history. (As noted, it was sustained by such systems through the management crisis that followed this reorganization, in the opinion of this particular executive among others.) From at least the mid-1950s, Air Canada used planning, budgeting, and scheduling procedures of various kinds to manage its operations—notably to schedule its flight activities and to coordinate the purchase of aircraft with the provision of services on different routes, even to control its revenues. The organization was run as a highly interdependent system, tightly and formally controlled by its planning procedures.

175

Forces for Planning

The fact is that a planning orientation especially suited Air Canada's particular needs. Indeed, a whole set of forces drove it to this reorientation:

(1) First, long lead times were inherent in its key decisions. In its earlier years, Air Canada could buy new aircraft and incorporate them into its operations rather quickly (the Northstar deliveries suggest just how quickly). Likewise, at least within Canada, it could introduce new routes just by informing the government of its intentions. But in later years, Air Canada typically had to order its new airplanes three to six years in advance. As for new routes, international ones required two to five years of complex bilateral negotiations conducted on the airline's behalf by the Canadian Department of External Affairs, while after 1955, even new domestic routes required lengthy negotiations with the federal government. Thinking far ahead about these decisions therefore became mandatory.

(2) Planning does not mean just thinking ahead about single decisions; it presumably also implies some kind of attempt to interrelate different decisions. Thus, perhaps an even stronger force for planning was needed to coordinate the different activities of this organization—the aircraft available, not only the routes but also the specific timetable for the aircraft to be flown, the scheduling of maintenance and flight crews, and so on. All of these activities had to be coordinated in one tightly integrated system with machine-like precision. And that system stretched beyond a single airline. As Newman, Summer, and Warren have noted,

> Preparation of tickets in Vienna that will be understood in Nairobi and Seattle, that can be reissued in Baghdad and cancelled in Tahiti, and that provide the basis for allocating the fare, collected among a dozen different airlines, requires an impressive use of standard operating procedures. (1972: 693)

Likewise the arrival of new aircraft had to be tightly coordinated with the introduction of new routes or the expansion of existing ones. One need only imagine a conversation in a hanger: 'Hey Fred, there's a guy here who says he has three 747's for us; who ordered them?' While the introduction of new routes may have driven the acquisition of new aircraft in the early years, when aircraft were small and few and the airline was rounding out its Canadian services (except for the Northstar deliveries, when the opposite happened), in later years the two were tightly coordinated through planning.

(3) Of course, the story of Fred is amusing because of the cost of modern jet airplanes. If Air Canada could have bought its equipment the way Steinberg's bought its produce, there would not have been the same need for planning. The coupling of activities could have been loosened by the purchase of redundant equipment. Thus, a third factor that encouraged planning was the capital intensity of the decisions the airline had to make (at the rates at that time, $36 million for a single Boeing 747 in 1976). This encouraged a third element of the planning process, beyond future thinking and integration—the reliance on an analytic mode of decision making. Costs and benefits had to be carefully analyzed before new aircraft were bought, also before new routes were introduced. And the data to do so, as we found out in our archival investigation, were abundant.

(4) Size was also a factor. As the airline grew, it moved into the mainstream of its industry. Unlike a small airline, which might be able to find a few aircraft quickly to satisfy its needs (say from a bankrupt competitor), a large airline requires many aircraft (and, to keep maintenance expenses in line, of limited variety). Also, to maintain its world-class status, Air Canada had no choice but to follow certain industry trends (such as flying 747s). Thus, to acquire aircraft, it was forced into the long industry queues, and therefore had to plan.

(5) Safety is another factor, which cannot be underestimated. Steinberg's could afford a few weak stores, Volkswagen even some weak automobile models. But Air Canada was an organization that could not afford mistakes, at least in the air. And the mentality that dominates an organization's operations tends to pervade its administration. Safety in the operations meant, among other things, the careful programming of contingencies (what to do in the event of a snowstorm, or an engine failure, or a hijacking); in the administration, this doubtlessly encouraged the planning orientation, to avoid surprises in the broader sense—with regard to basic strategic direction.

(6) Another contributing factor was the airline's status as a government organization. When Howe asked the airline to stay out of the taxpayers' pocket, he meant, 'stay out of the politicians' minds'. A secret to success within the government—one Air Canada learned the hard way—is to avoid the attention of the politicians. And

one way to do this is to avoid surprises and bad publicity, which encourages the planning of things as carefully as possible. Moreover direct external control tends to drive organizations to a highly analytic mode of functioning—never to act impulsively, to justify all of its moves with hard data, in general to be systematic and orderly (Mintzberg 1978a: 288–91). Last and not the least of the factors was the airline's influence in its own markets. As Canada's flag carrier, Air Canada had, at least until the end of the study period, a favored competitive position in many of its key markets. For example, it always dominated the Montreal–Toronto corridor, the heaviest by far in the country. Moreover, demand for air passenger services grew steadily throughout the study period. Air Canada was, in other words, usually in a demand-driven situation (except for brief periods after the arrival of new aircraft), and so seldom had to scramble for markets. As one executive commented, 'We could forecast the future very accurately.' Predictability and control are, of course, prime prerequisites for successful planning.

Strategic Thinking?

All of these factors point in one direction—to systematic, formalized planning. They formed a consistent 'gestalt' that would have driven any organization toward a highly systematic, precise mode of administration. Air Canada was so drawn. And it executed that orientation effectively: this was a well-run, highly efficient airline. But the price of its planning orientation, in our view, was a lack of attention to strategic thinking.

What do we mean by strategic thinking? In some sense, we mean conceptual thinking, about the organization as a whole—about its basic missions:[3] new ways to conceive them, elaborate them, extend them. Strategic thinking is to operational thinking what the first derivative in calculus is to the given formula, a step up, if you like, from the basic relationship.

The lack of attention to strategic thinking in the last half of our study period is indicated by a number of factors. One is specific evidence, not just of the absence of significant strategic change, but of the repeated discouragement of such change. The Rapidair experience is perhaps most indicative. Air Canada embarked on a shuttle experiment already proven on certain US routes, and withdrew (in all but name) after only a few days,

[3] In his study of Fortune 500 manufacturing firms, Rumelt (1974) noted the relative absence of diversification in what he called the 'heavies' of US industry, the large, capital-intensive, mass-producers such as steel and aluminum firms.

during which the executives saw no change in reservation patterns. The attitude was not one of 'let's make this thing work', but rather, 'oh, well, we gave it a try'. Ambitious changes are sustained by inspiration; this one was subverted by calculation.

This is not to argue that the airline housed no individuals who thought about broad strategic changes. Cargo, charter, presumably even Rapidair had their champions, people who may have thought they would help to remake the airline. Indeed, Pratte showed indications of this in his intentions for diversification. But the *organization* did not exhibit these intentions. In other words, strategic thinking seems not to have been part of the dominant culture, notwithstanding the wishes even of the organization's formal leader. As one executive noted, 'We weren't too preoccupied with strategies. We just did the job as we saw it.'

In our opinion, all the forces that encouraged planning in Air Canada discouraged strategic thinking. The long lead times, the size of the organization and of its capital expenditures, and above all, the interrelatedness of its activities focused attention on operational planning and drew attention away from major change. The concern for safety, the fact of government ownership, perhaps also the absence of entrepreneurial origins, made the airline sensitive to what statisticians call 'type two errors'. In other words, Air Canada seemed to prefer avoiding risks, even when that meant foregoing opportunities. As time went on, most of these factors increased in importance, gradually locking the organization into a tighter set of constraints—in effect, into its existing strategies. The domestic route system became saturated; foreign routes became increasingly difficult to secure; lead times on the ordering of new aircraft increased significantly; the organization became larger and its capital expenditures grew exponentially; the increasing size of aircraft made safety more of a concern; and occasional conflicts with the government drove home the desire for more autonomy.

Locking into Industry

Ironically, as it grew more independent of its government owner, and while it seemed to develop enviable control of its own markets, Air Canada became increasingly locked into its industry structure as well. That was the price of its growth, its market influence, and its success. Joining the 'club' of world-class airlines provided it with both protection and limitations: it became the 'defender' of its own territory within that club.

In our view, not only did a common set of forces both encourage planning and discourage strategic thinking, but planning itself reinforced this latter tendency. The more the organization relied on detailed, systematic, routine specification of its existing procedures, the less its people were encouraged to think beyond those procedures to new orientations (perhaps best indicated by the example used earlier of 'thin' southern routes). Moreover, the analytical orientation inherent in formal planning is more conducive to marginal change or adaptation than to significant reorientation. In essence, then, planning meant the programming of a given orientation, and that focused attention on elements of what was, rather than on images of what could be (Mintzberg 1994).

The argument could, of course, be made that Air Canada had little need for strategic thinking. It was highly successful as it was. With steady market growth and new aircraft coming on stream periodically, its executives had plenty to think about.

Two main factors seem to stimulate strategic change. One is external shock, as noted in the studies of Volkswagenwerk and US strategy in Vietnam. Another is slack resources, as well as boredom in traditional markets, which seem to evoke additions to existing strategies (e.g. diversification) rather than shifts in these per se. But a growing Air Canada in relatively stable and protected markets may have experienced neither. So long as there was much to worry about running an airline and little in the way of excess resources, and so long as the economic environment underwent no major change—such as a significant shift in customer demand or deregulation—concentrating on excellence in operations, within a given strategic context, seemed to be perfectly appropriate.

But, as we saw in the case of Volkswagenwerk, the danger of this is that such a change can catch the organization off guard, unable to respond, and so ultimately vulnerable. Moreover, we have also seen examples of organizations (e.g. Steinberg's) that, at critical moments in their history undertook major strategic change as a result of managerial initiative, and so enhanced their market positions and sustained their performance.

As noted earlier, the one internal shock—the McKinsey reorganization—although perhaps intended to encourage strategic change, in fact, probably discouraged it, by creating a political situation that depleted the energies of the senior management, and thus made it more rather than less risk averse. Moreover, the effect of the reorganization was to increase the organization's analytical orientation (e.g. by moving a number of operations research people into positions of senior management; Davidson [1981] discussed the particular influence these people had in

Air Canada). Strategic thinking would, however, seem to require a good deal of intuition and inspiration, at least in advance of formal analysis. An overemphasis on analysis, or at least premature analysis, may have had the effect of impeding inspirational type change.[4]

Thus we conclude that the very forces that encourage formal planning, as well as such planning itself, tend to drive out strategic thinking. More precisely, the more an organization relies on planning in the formal sense, the less likely its people are to think strategically, and the less inclined it will be to undergo strategic change (as opposed to elaboration or extrapolation of given strategic direction). We argued a related conclusion in the Steinberg study, for the company's later years—that planning is essentially the programming of a given strategy rather than the creation of a new one—and we believe it is reinforced in this study. Formal planning, and the associated forces that encourage it, may discourage the very mental state required to conceive new strategies—a state of openness and easy flexibility that encourages people to step back from operating reality and question accepted beliefs. In short, formal strategic management may prove incompatible with real strategic thinking.

Air Canada was privatized by the Canadian government in 1989. It later declared bankruptcy, as did so many other North American airlines. It still continues to fly as Canada's major carrier, although beset by competition from discount carriers. In 2007, it is the world's twelfth largest airline.

---

[4] See Mintzberg (1979a: 133–9, 147–8) for an elaboration on this point.

7

Tracking Strategies in the Birthplace of Canadian Tycoons

The *Sherbrooke Record*, 1946–76

Henry Mintzberg, William D. Taylor, and James A. Waters[1]

The strategies of the Sherbrooke Record, *a small English-language daily newspaper in Quebec's Eastern Townships, are tracked across three decades, as it functioned under the control of two of Canada's most prominent businessmen, John Bassett Jr. and later Conrad Black. The newspaper experienced a long period of stable strategy in the face of accelerating change in its environment under one leader, and then was turned around financially at the expense of its quality by the other leader.*

The *Sherbrooke Record* is a small, English-language daily newspaper in the Eastern Townships of Quebec. This chapter tracks its strategies over a thirty-year period with two sets of intentions. One is to contribute to our understanding of how strategies form in organizations. The other is to document the history of an organization that can be viewed as something of a Canadian institution, since two of the country's most prominent businessmen virtually began their careers there. John Bassett Jr., former owner of the *Toronto Telegram* and a major influence in the Canadian broadcasting industry, joined the *Sherbrooke Record*, which was owned by his father, upon his return from the European theater of World War II. He sold it in 1968. One year later, a young Conrad Black, who was to rise to the apex of Canadian business at age 34 with his unexpected takeover of

---

[1] Originally published in the *Canadian Journal of Administrative Sciences* (June 1984: 1–28), with minor revisions in this volume.

182

Argus Corporation, purchased the newspaper together with two partners and held it until 1976.

A prime source of data in this study was issues of the newspaper itself, 2,500 of which were scanned over the thirty-year study period. Similar chronologies were built up of performance information (e.g. circulation, profits) and of trends and events in the organization's environment (Eastern Townships demographics, changes in postal rates, newsprint prices, etc.).

This report begins with a brief review, largely in diagrammatic form, of the strategies, environmental trends and events, and performance outcomes identified from 1946 to 1976. This is followed by a description of the roles that John Bassett Jr. and Conrad Black played in the evolution of this newspaper over that time. The final section interprets this description in conceptual terms and presents some observations about strategy formation in general and the behavior seen early in the careers of these two Canadian 'tycoons' in particular.

Strategies of the *Sherbrooke Record*

Figure 7.1 provides a summary description of all the strategies inferred as having been pursued by the *Sherbrooke Record* over the thirty-year study period. All are shown on a common timescale, divided into major strategy areas. The findings of these studies are summarized below.

NEWS COVERAGE

Over the years 1946–69, the newspaper maintained a sufficient number of staff reporters (three to four) to cover the courts, hospitals, police activities, and local meetings. This local news was presented together with world news from the wire services, major league sports, and one syndicated Hollywood gossip column. In 1969–70, staff was reduced, and from then to the end of the study period, local coverage was limited; the rule of thumb was 'if in doubt, leave it out'.

LOCAL EMPHASIS IN EDITORIALS

A sample of issues from the months of October over the study period indicated that the number of editorials per month on local topics trended

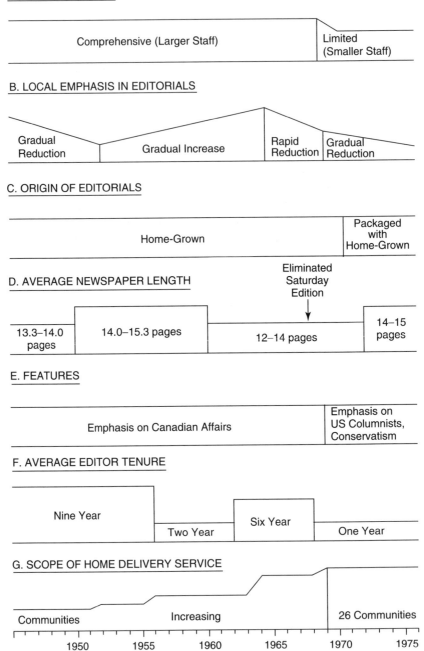

A. NEWS COVERAGE

Comprehensive (Larger Staff) — Limited (Smaller Staff)

B. LOCAL EMPHASIS IN EDITORIALS

Gradual Reduction — Gradual Increase — Rapid Reduction — Gradual Reduction

C. ORIGIN OF EDITORIALS

Home-Grown — Packaged with Home-Grown

D. AVERAGE NEWSPAPER LENGTH

Eliminated Saturday Edition

13.3–14.0 pages — 14.0–15.3 pages — 12–14 pages — 14–15 pages

E. FEATURES

Emphasis on Canadian Affairs — Emphasis on US Columnists, Conservatism

F. AVERAGE EDITOR TENURE

Nine Year — Two Year — Six Year — One Year

G. SCOPE OF HOME DELIVERY SERVICE

Communities — Increasing — 26 Communities

1950   1955   1960   1965   1970   1975

Figure 7.1 Strategies of the *Sherbrooke Record*

184

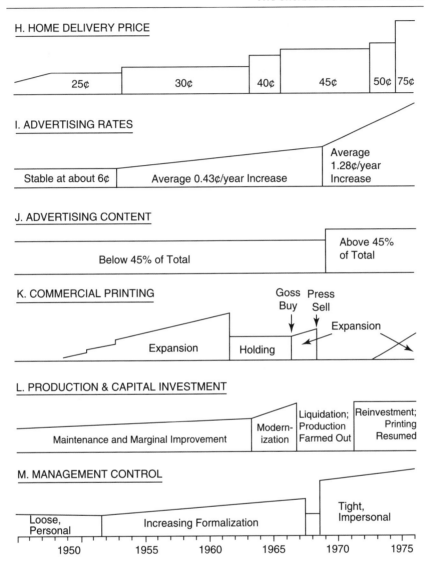

Figure 7.1 (*continued*)

downward until 1952 (generally remaining over five), trended upward until 1966 (with a peak of sixteen), dropped rapidly over the years 1967–9 (to four), and then declined until there was only one editorial with local emphasis in the month of October for the three years 1974–6.

ORIGIN OF EDITORIALS

Prior to mid-1971, almost all editorials were written by *Record* staff. After that time, packaged editorials (from places such as the *Winnipeg Free Press* and *Calgary Herald*) were in the majority.

AVERAGE NEWSPAPER LENGTH

Again sampling from the month of October, the average length of the newspaper was below fourteen pages from 1946 to 1950 and from 1961 to 1972. In the 1950s and later 1970s, it averaged above this figure. The Saturday edition was eliminated in 1968.

FEATURES

From 1946 to 1969, features appearing in the *Record* changed only moderately and can be characterized as focusing on Canadian politics. After 1969, there was an increased use of conservative columnists and an increased emphasis on US political activity.

AVERAGE EDITOR TENURE

Prior to 1969, there was relative stability in the position of the editor, except for 1956 to 1962, when three different editors were employed. After 1969, the editorship became a 'passing-through' position, with a new person hired each year (an apparent reflection of compensation limitations).

SCOPE OF HOME DELIVERY SERVICE

From 1946 to 1951, carrier delivery service was available in nine communities. This service was extended by 1952 to another three communities and continued to expand until 1969: 1956 (+ three), 1964 (+ nine), and 1969 (+ two). After 1969 it remained stable at twenty-six communities.

HOME DELIVERY PRICE

Prices rose gradually in stepwise fashion over the study period, and only on two occasions, 1964 and 1976, was the weekly rate raised more than 5 cents. Newsstand and mail subscription rates increased roughly in parallel with home delivery rates.

ADVERTISING RATE

The flat per-line rate remained around 6 cents until 1953, rose gradually in steps between 1954 and 1969 (average 0.43 cents per year increase), and then jumped dramatically after 1969 in steps through 1976 (average increase of 1.28 cents per year).

ADVERTISING CONTENT

As a percentage of total newspaper content, advertising remained slightly below 45 percent until 1969, and ranged between 45 percent and 50 percent thereafter to the end of the study period.

COMMERCIAL PRINTING

Starting in 1949, the *Record* pursued an expanding strategy of commercial printing, using its excess capacity until 1962, when two major customers were lost because of a strike. The purchase of a new press in 1967 spurred renewed growth until the printing operations were sold in 1969. With the purchase of a new press in 1973, the commercial printing strategy was resumed, but the scope and volume of business during 1973–6 did not reach the levels of the early 1960s.

PRODUCTION AND CAPITAL INVESTMENT

From 1946 to 1967, production facilities were slowly modernized. The purchase of the press and a building in 1967 signaled a spurt of modern-ization, which lasted until 1969. From 1969 to 1973, the press and other facilities were sold off and production was contracted out. The purchase of the new press in 1973 stimulated a new phase of facilities improvement and in-house production.

MANAGEMENT CONTROL

Until 1952, control was loose and personal, with day-to-day operations and personnel decisions left to local management. From 1952 to 1968, there was increasing formalization and major decisions were reviewed by staff people at the *Toronto Telegram*. Sale of the paper in 1968 to local people marked a return to the earlier control style for one year. After 1969, when the newspaper was sold to nonlocal people, control became very tight and impersonal.

Environment and Results of the *Sherbrooke Record*

Some of the major environmental trends and performance results are presented in Figure 7.2, and are described briefly as follows.

ENGLISH-SPEAKING POPULATION

While the absolute English-speaking population in the Eastern Townships remained stable or declined very slightly over the study period, its relative importance (as a percentage of total population) declined from around 18 percent of the total in 1941 to around 11 percent of the total in 1976 (Caldwell 1974; *Census of Canada* 1976).

POSTAL COSTS

The postal cost for mail subscription jumped 29 percent in 1952 and then remained stable until 1968 when new postal rates effectively increased mailing costs by over 400 percent to $6.81 per subscription.

NEWSPRINT COSTS

After a period of fairly rapid increases (averaging $10 per year) to 1952, the price per ton of newsprint rose gradually (average increase of $1.20 per year) until 1969. From 1969 to 1973, price increases averaged $6 per year and after 1973 averaged around $37 per year.

RETAILER ADVERTISING

Because of pressure to charge lower local advertising rates, emergence of new television competition, and the shift of increasing portions of national advertising budgets to French-language media, revenue from national advertisers declined over most of the study period. Following a period of depressed advertising, as a result of uncertainty surrounding the opening of a new shopping mall in Sherbrooke, local advertising increased steadily after the Carrefour de l'Estrie opened in 1973.

LABOR RELATIONS

After 1960, approximately one-third of employees were unionized. An eleven-day strike occurred in 1962. The union dissolved when the *Record*'s press was sold in 1969.

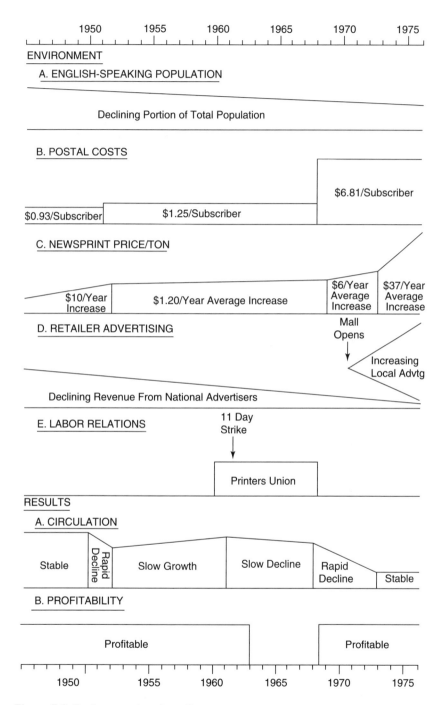

Figure 7.2 Environment and results

CIRCULATION

As shown in Figure 7.3, audited paid circulation averaged about 9,350 through 1951. Following a precipitous drop in 1952 (to about 8,100), it gradually increased to about 9,200 in 1961 and declined slowly in 1968 to about 8,900. From 1969 to 1973, circulation fell rapidly to around 6,300 and remained at that level until 1976 when it rose to about 6,650.

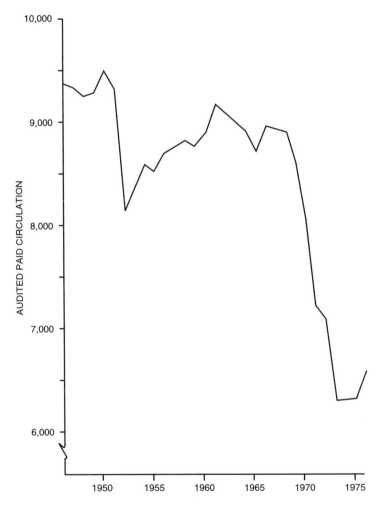

Figure 7.3 Audited paid circulation, the *Sherbrooke Record*, 1946–76

PROFITS

Although actual data were not accessible, informed sources indicated that the only period in which the newspaper did not show a profit was 1964 to 1968, when small losses were incurred followed by a substantial one in 1968.

The History of the *Sherbrooke Record*

Using these inferences of strategy as well as other material gleaned from documents and interviews, we can now review the history of the *Sherbrooke Record* in terms of two major eras, separated by a brief period of transition.

THE BASSETT ERA: ACCELERATING DETERIORATION IN CONDITION

The Bassett era really began in October 1936, when John Bassett Sr. of Montreal, president of the *Montreal Gazette*, purchased the *Sherbrooke Record*. In that same year, his son, John Bassett Jr., graduated from Bishop's University (in Lennoxville, close to Sherbrooke) and went to Toronto, and the *Globe and Mail*.

During the war years, while Bassett Jr. was in the army, the *Record* continued to be operated by individuals appointed by Bassett Sr. In 1945, Bassett Jr. bought the newspaper from his father. Although he spent 1945–8 in Sherbrooke, he did not appear to spend an inordinate amount of time on the day-to-day operations. 'I will give the orders, and you carry them to the troops', is the way the manager at the time described Bassett's approach.

The *Record* had a very 'folksy' work environment during this period. Bassett always tried to retain the older employees, even when they were not very productive, including a number of veterans, whom Bassett insisted the newspaper had a responsibility to keep employed. Bassett also tended to offer positions on the newspaper to people he had met during the war.

In the fall of 1948, Bassett left for Toronto, and left the newspaper in the hands of Ivan Saunders, who became managing editor, and Doug Amaron, editor. Although Bassett maintained his interest, both financial and otherwise, the day-to-day administration of the paper remained in the hands of his managers in Sherbrooke. After he purchased the *Toronto*

Telegram in 1952, the *Sherbrooke Record* could no longer occupy the same level of importance to him.

The *Record* thus fell under the control of the Telegram Publishing Company and its more sophisticated management staff, including accountants who put increasing pressure on Bassett to reconsider his ownership of the *Record*. He, nonetheless, remained committed to quality news coverage at the newspaper and insisted that the courts, the hospitals, police activities, and local council meetings be properly covered. Bassett's wife was from the area, and he retained personal ties to it. This meant that the newspaper always had an adequate number of staff reporters, usually three or four.

In addition, until about 1962, the *Record* was able to employ editors of a quality beyond what might have been expected for its size. In 1956, Amaron left for a higher salary and for the next six years or so, Bassett filled the editor position by sending three different editors from Toronto. The Telegram Publishing Company subsidized their salaries. In many ways, the ambition of these editors was a luxury for the *Record*. One young editor, for example, always insisted on substantial, and costly, photo coverage.

With a strike in 1962 by twenty of the *Record*'s employees seeking higher wages, a reduced work week, and other concessions, John Bassett's interests with the affairs of the *Record* began to decline more quickly.

Unfortunately, the major effects of the strike were not limited to higher labor costs; the *Record* lost two major clients for its printing services and took many years to recover. From 1964 to 1968, the *Record* lost money, apparently for the first time.

These years were also notable for the lack of evidence of major actions taken to recapture the *Record*'s former financial health. When advised by Saunders that the newspaper did not have a bright financial future and should be sold, Bassett's reply was that the *Sherbrooke Record* would go on forever. Yet he made no observable effort to ensure that future.

This recommendation was likely based on the realization that the future for an English-language newspaper in Sherbrooke was at best uncertain. Many of the environment forces that affected the *Record* in these years were not, in fact, new, but were rather a continuation, and intensification, of the problems of the 1950s. The anglophone market in the Sherbrooke area continued to grow at a very slow rate and the structure of national advertising continued to shift power to large retailers and national agencies, and to favor the electronic media increasingly.

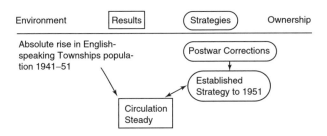

Figure 7.4 Period of stable strategy

The Quiet Revolution also brought a certain pessimism to the English-speaking population of Quebec.

In 1967, a decision was taken by Bassett and the *Telegram* board to purchase a new Goss offset press. On the surface, this decision seemed to break the ongoing pattern of declining interest. But the details suggest another interpretation—that the decision, which seemed to have no economic justification, was made only because Bassett was unwilling to give the newspaper any serious attention. The new press was designed with the possibility of an eventual transfer to Toronto: it was built to meet both Ontario and Quebec wiring regulations.

In any event, the day this decision was announced, Bassett also announced that he was divorcing his wife, to marry another woman. This broke an important connection for him to the area as Saunders put it, 'His interest was finished. . . . He only came down once after that. . . .'

Less than a year and a half later (as the *Telegram* itself began to lose money—it closed in September 1971), Bassett and the Telegram Publishing Company abruptly sold the *Record*.

In Conceptual Terms

As shown in Figure 7.4, from the end of World War II, after a few corrections to the long-established strategy, there followed a period of relative stability till 1951. This is the first part of the Bassett era. It was integrated around a traditional set of values—small community, local orientation, personal involvement, and so on. The different strategies pursued by the organization appear to be rather deliberate, although probably implicit, and they were generally conservative in nature.

Figure 7.5 indicates the increase in postal rates of 1951 as the signal of change—the first clear sign of an environment that was to deteriorate at an accelerating rate. This deterioration manifested itself in

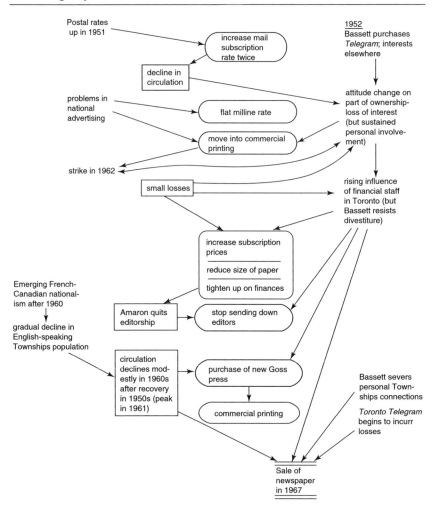

Figure 7.5 Period of accelerating deterioration in condition

two ways. One was as a series of shocks, the other steadily worsening trends. As can be seen in Figure 7.5, and especially in Figure 7.6, these shocks were few at first but became more frequent and severe: the postal rate increase in 1951, the strike of 1962, the sharper increases in postal rates, newsprint, etc. in the late 1960s, and the problems created by the development of the Sherbrooke mall. The trends included the decline of the anglophone population of the Townships together with the rise of the Quiet Revolution and the problems associated with national advertising.

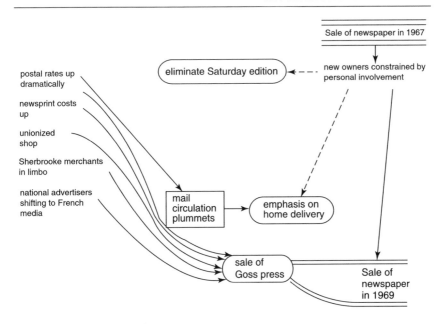

Figure 7.6 Interim period

For sixteen years, however, the firm made few strategic changes, instead reacting in an occasional ad hoc manner to specific stimuli (such as increasing mail subscription rates in response to the postal increase). Essentially, the strategies in 1967 were much like those in 1951—traditional, conservative, and largely implicit—although the environment had changed significantly.

Hence we view the years 1951–67 as a period of 'accelerating deterioration in condition'—a period characterized more by what happened in the environment than in the organization. Three interacting factors seem to explain the lack of response to the deterioration in condition. First, traditional strategies that have long been successful have a habit of perpetuating themselves, even after conditions change (as we saw in the Vietnam and Volkswagenwerk studies). People get used to doing things in a certain way, feel comfortable with the old patterns (strategies).

Second, the environment did not change suddenly so much as gradually—the deterioration, in other words, was characterized more by trends than by events, at least for most of the period. Yet events did occur—the postal rate increase of 1951 and especially the strike of 1962—and the trends, as already noted, were accelerating.

But here the third factor comes in. Bassett retained a personal link to the organization, yet lost interest in the administration of it. And that had the effect of locking in the existing strategies. A little like the spoiled rich child, this organization was looked after materially but ignored emotionally, and so it lost touch with its environment. A kind of dry rot set in. Even in the face of the losses—although small—the situation did not change. Only when Bassett's personal situation changed—when he finally severed his personal links with the Townships—did he finally act. And then, rather than changing its strategies, he sold the organization.

TRANSITION: INTERIM PERIOD

The *Sherbrooke Record* was sold in August 1968 to Saunders, its president at the time, and R. Stafford, a local chartered accountant. Consistent with the loyalty he had always exhibited to the *Record* staff, Bassett gave his employees first opportunity to purchase the newspaper, at a price close to the cost of the physical assets. This new ownership inaugurated a brief transition period and represented a return to local ownership and direct management.

Faced with rising costs and declining revenues, the new owners eliminated the Saturday edition of the paper. Then came the huge jump in postal rates at the beginning of 1969, which forced a large increase in mail subscription rates, which in turn led to a drop in circulation. Moreover, uncertainty about the new mall in Sherbrooke depressed the advertising budgets of local merchants, and, with increasing competition from French-language media, advertising revenue declined too.

Saunders and Stafford realized that they did not have the resources necessary to carry on, and, in March 1969, sold the new Goss press back to the Goss Company. This reduced their investment, and also made the *Record* itself more marketable. Saunders and Stafford were aware at this time of the interest of Black and his associates in the newspaper.

In Conceptual Terms

The new owners of 1967 did not make any major changes in strategy. Their one immediate change, piecemeal in nature, was the dropping of the Saturday edition. They were also personally involved with the traditional strategy, and so apparently unable to make the type of changes necessary. And then, just as they settled in, the environment underwent what might be called quantum change—dramatic and pervasive, as shown in Figure 7.6. The newspaper was hit with a number of sharp and concurrent price increases, notably a fourfold rise in postal rates, together with a drop in advertising due to the problems of the Sherbrooke mall. Whether because of commitment to the traditional strategies or simply because they lacked resources, their responses were only marginal—emphasizing home delivery, selling the Goss press. Finally, they were forced to sell the newspaper.

Because these few months represent renewed owner interest in the newspaper without any real strategic change, we view this not so much as a period in its own right but rather as an 'interim' period, an *indication* of transition without the manifestation of it. Piecemeal changes were made, but the overall traditional strategy did not change. Piecemeal changes to an integrated strategy, however, signal *dis*integration.

THE BLACK ERA; GLOBAL CHANGE

At this point, the continued survival of the *Record* was at best uncertain, and in June 1969, it was sold to a group headed by Black; all were under 30 (Black was only 24). His partners included Peter White and David Radler.

Eventually the group ended up buying twenty-one small newspapers in Canada under the banner of the Sterling Group. The *Record* was the first daily added to this group, and in many ways represented an experiment for them. This sale marked the beginning of radical change for the *Sherbrooke Record*. Starting in June 1969, the newspaper was completely transformed. Coming to Sherbrooke a few hours a day, the new owners took turns creating new controls, which would transform the newspaper into the type of organization they wanted it to be. Tight financial controls, lean budgets, low-cost labor, and the dominance of advertising over editorial content were the cornerstones of the system they installed. Profitability was the paramount goal. Black himself characterized these actions as an attempt to rebuild the financial strength of the enterprise, and suggested that in such a policy, there is no place for sentiment (personal correspondence from Black).

Thus, while the newspaper remained relatively small, the 'folksy' operating atmosphere was eliminated. As Saunders described it:

Bassett's theory was that if you have people with an organization for a number of years you have to keep these people...keep them until death. Younger people like Black had no mercy for these people—they just came in and wiped them out...J—,D—, the part-time truck driver since 1937, and they chopped others.

At one time, I had 12 'vets' who came back from the war... some were not all that productive, but we carried them. One... is a bit of a mental case. We carried him; they let him go the next day. It is not that we were after brownie points but it was just the decent thing to do.

The three young owners had bragged when they purchased the newspaper that they would make money out of Sherbrooke, but they would never live there. Their approach after the first few months of their ownership was to take turns coming to Sherbrooke from Montreal. Later, important instructions were telephoned in, mainly from Black, as was the occasional editorial piece. These calls, twice monthly on average, seemed to terrify the employees on the receiving end.

A young reporter recalled that seldom, if ever, did he receive any real training to become a reporter—the reason he had taken the position at such a low salary. The *Record* was too understaffed. Budgets were extremely tight; reporters were discouraged from taking taxis, even making long-distance telephone calls, and internal disputes between editorial and advertising were consistently settled on the basis of the effects on advertising revenue.

This new orientation had a marked effect on quality. Young, inexperienced editors were hired and once they gained sufficient experience, left—about one each year. Fewer staff reporters were allowed, thus reducing local coverage. National and international coverage was reduced, while packaged editorials were used in increasing numbers. In contradiction to its self-proclaimed role, the *Record* ceased to be 'the voice of the Eastern Townships'. The average daily size of the newspaper was small, but the proportion of advertising was up.

Circulation dropped from 8,633 in 1969 to 8,063 in 1970, 7,240 in 1971, and 6,327 in 1973; more than the decline of the English-speaking population. No concerted effort seems to have been made to reverse the decline, suggesting that the Black group was consciously prepared to trade off quality and circulation for profits. The organization marketed its advertising space more aggressively, and benefited from the contacts the new owners (Black in particular) had in Toronto and Montreal. The *Record* also began to benefit from the increased advertising activity of both the provincial and federal governments. Within a few months of the purchase, the *Sherbrooke Record* returned to profitability.

In late 1972, a new press was purchased, both to reduce the expense and inconvenience of printing the newspaper outside of Sherbrooke and to supply outside printing revenue. By this time, the Black group had acquired a number of local weekly newspapers, which could be printed in their press.

By 1973, the Sherbrooke retail market had improved considerably, mainly because of the long-awaited opening of the Carrefour de l'Estrie—a 110-store mall. Other retail establishments also opened around this time. Profits at the *Record*, reportedly rose to the tune of $100,000 per year late in the period. Yet, as indicated by interviews with *Record* employees and even by the editorials of departing editors, the *Record* lost, to a considerable degree, the confidence of the English-speaking population of the region.

In 1979, Black and his associates sold the *Sherbrooke Record* to George MacLaren, a Sherbrooke lawyer, for a price approximately forty times what they had initially paid for it.

In Conceptual Terms

It was in 1969 that a new period is clearly indicated, one of *global* change, when almost all the strategies changed suddenly. A glance down the 1969 column of Figure 7.1, which depicts all the strategies, gives some idea of the pervasiveness of the change. Likewise, our flow diagram shown for this period in Figure 7.7 indicates for the first time a large number of concurrent strategic changes. Yet, ironically, also for the first time, there were relatively few environmental changes, and these tended to be favorable (the return of national advertising and the opening of the shopping mall), although the unfavorable demographic trends did continue. Was the Black group simply lucky, or was its timing good?

An interesting characteristic of the deliberate changes was that they focused on administrative matters, not on the content of the newspaper itself. We have referred to this as a 'process strategy'—the management of the processes by which things happen in an organization (hiring, structure, etc.), but not of those things themselves. Such a strategy is partly deliberate and partly emergent, or, if you will, deliberately emergent; process matters are dictated deliberately while content ones are allowed to emerge. The new owners imposed severe financial constraints, cut the number of staff, lowered salaries, favored the advertising department over editorial, and increased the proportion of advertising. (This last strategy was of a content nature but did not apply to editorial content per se.)

The overall result was a sharp decline in quality, which was certainly a realized strategy (a clear pattern in the organization's actions), although probably not a deliberate one. In other words, we cannot conclude that the Black group intended to reduce quality; only that this was the natural

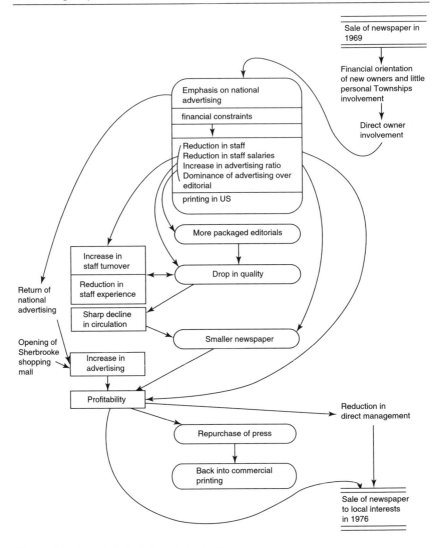

Figure 7.7 A period of global strategic change

consequence of the other strategies they pursued (in contrast, say, to a newspaper owner who deliberately turns a quality publication into a 'yellow' journal to gain market share). On the other hand, the Black group certainly made little effort to maintain quality; they seemed to have little concern about it.

In any event, the new overall strategy—tightening the administration to squeeze whatever profit potential remained in the newspaper—worked.

Enough of a market remained to make money, even after the circulation dropped significantly. At least for a time. But once the new owners turned the organization around, they promptly sold it.

Thus, we see this as a period of global or quantum change—a kind of strategic revolution (Miller and Friesen 1980)—with deliberate strategies in process and emergent ones in content (at least editorial content). The dominant element in the new set of strategies was cost reduction, supported by an emphasis on advertising. The new strategies were aggressive and tightly integrated. But they were not innovative. These were the most conventional of strategies, available to anyone with the requisite financial and administrative knowledge, not to mention the hardness to see them through. The new owners simply imported their strategies into the organization, 'readymade', what the Boston Consulting Group (1972) has called 'harvesting' or 'milking'.

The consequent quality reductions do not show up on income statements quite so fast as cost reductions, and so the approach has often proved viable in the short run. But the long run has often proved otherwise.

The strategies can be questioned from a social perspective, since they encourage a certain economic one-dimensionality at the expense of quality, craft, and commitment. Quality does not lend itself to measurement (Mintzberg 1982), and so tends to be forgotten by a calculating management. But those who make and consume the product do feel the difference, as did the anglophones of the Eastern Townships. Of course, continued losses would have meant no newspaper. So Black and his associates must be given credit for salvaging the paper.

A Conceptual Interpretation of Strategy Formation at the *Sherbrooke Record*

We focus on three themes—the pattern of strategic change over time; the contrast between deliberate and emergent strategies; and the interplay of environment, leadership, and organization in the process of strategy formation.

PATTERNS OF STRATEGIC CHANGE

Judging from some of our other studies, the pattern of change that occurred at the *Sherbrooke Record* appears to be common: long-term

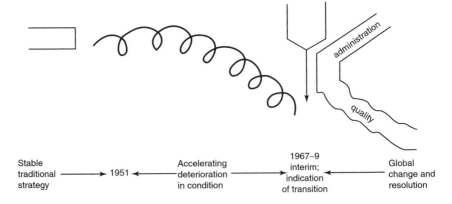

| Stable traditional strategy | | Accelerating deterioration in condition | 1967–9 interim; indication of transition | Global change and resolution |

Figure 7.8 Pattern of strategic change in the *Sherbrooke Record*

deterioration of a situation with little or only piecemeal response ('grafting'), followed by crisis, and then global change in strategy. This is shown symbolically in Figure 7.8 and is captured well by Miller and Friesen (1980) in their 'quantum theory' of organizational change—long periods of evolution, of steady incremental change in traditional directions (more of the same), punctuated occasionally by brief periods of revolution, of sudden, dramatic, and pervasive shifts in direction.

The fact that we found only major realignment of strategy in (at least) thirty years of the history of the *Sherbrooke Record* is also not uncommon. We saw only two such realignments in sixty years of history at Steinberg Inc. and only one in Volkswagen across almost the same years as the *Sherbrooke Record*. Five-year planning prescriptions notwithstanding, organizations (even ones with active owners) seem to realign their strategies only very rarely. (In fact, as we argue in forthcoming work, formal planning seems to be a force for extrapolation of given strategies, not realignment.)

What distinguishes this study from our others is the nature of the revolutionary change in strategy. In the other studies, that change came from within, and entailed the design of new strategies, notably the creation of new products, new ways to manufacture products, and new ways to serve customers. The management had to comprehend new or changed environments and to create new strategies that would use their organizations' distinctive competencies in those environments.

The *Sherbrooke Record*, in contrast, presumably because it was small and lacked the capacity to correct itself, required outside help after Bassett's departure. Thus, its strategic revolution was imported, so to speak, but at a price, not only of its independence, but also of its integrity. And so too were its new strategies imported, readymade. Far from taking into consideration the *Record*'s distinctive competencies, these strategies tended to destroy them. Thus, the *Record*'s strategic revolution—unlike the others we have studied—required no period of groping, learning, or testing. It happened almost instantly.

DELIBERATE AND EMERGENT STRATEGIES

Another way to put the same conclusion is that the Black group came into the organization with a set of clearly specified intended strategies and then realized them as such. The strategies pursued by this organization in this last period were, in other words, deliberate. To take the clearest example of this, Radler gave the advertising person at the *Record* a chart to determine the number of newspaper pages as a function of the number of lines of advertising.

Strategy is usually defined in terms of intention and thought to be made correctly only when it is deliberate. Yet even when the *Record* was being turned around, there were also clear examples of emergent strategy— namely those related to the editorial function. In other words, the pattern or consistency in the behavior of the organization with respect to editorial content, news gathering, and reporting appeared without the apparent intervention of the leadership; it was just the natural consequence of other intentions of that leadership, namely with respect to budgets, advertising policy, and personnel. To generalize, deliberate strategies can produce emergent ones, inadvertently.

Our research has indicated that some organizations (such as a Steinberg or a Volkswagenwerk or an Air Canada) appropriately pursue mostly deliberate strategies, while others (such as a National Film Board or an Arcop) appropriately pursue mostly emergent ones. The *Record* is much closer to the former group. Even before the Black era, most of its strategies were rather deliberate. Some were necessitated by the phenomena in question: for example, the use of syndicated columnists or the setting of advertising rates requires the making of specific decisions to establish patterns of activity. (Advertising prices can hardly be negotiated each time someone wishes to buy space in a newspaper.) Likewise, the commercial printing strategy had to be deliberate because of the financial commitments involved. When an organization makes a major capital investment, it must usually make conscious decisions—that is, assess the consequences and plan for them—before it acts. Hence its strategies tend to be deliberate.

Other, more general factors also contributed to the deliberate nature of the strategies. Our studies indicate that strategies sometimes go through an emergent phase before becoming deliberate. As in the case of the first expansion in new stores at Steinberg, this sometimes reflects the need for experimentation—for learning. It may also reflect the fact that once emergent patterns clearly establish themselves, they become recognized, then accepted as such, and so become deliberate. Because up to 1967 many of the *Record*'s strategies were long established (before the beginning of the study period), they had become deliberate (even if they may have once been emergent). And as noted earlier, the strategies brought in by the Black group were readymade—pretested elsewhere, a 'business model', if you like—and so deliberate at the *Sherbrooke Record*.

The nature of the organization itself also contributed to the deliberateness of the strategies. When the power for making important decisions must be shared—as in an organization such as the National Film Board, in need of technical expertise and creativity—then the central management cannot impose specific intentions, and strategies therefore tend to emerge. The fact that the *Sherbrooke Record* was a small, simple, and integrated organization meant that its management could maintain central control, and so impose its intentions (when it had them), particularly in the functions of administration, advertising, and printing.

The editorial function is somewhat different, and so it is not surprising that here is where the clearest example of emergent strategy was found. No expensive technology drives this function, and no a priori decisions are necessarily required to guide a subsequent pattern of action (as in the setting of advertising rates). Indeed, the very nature of this function—deciding which unpredictable news breaks to report on, and how—encourages ad hoc response to external events; this in turn favors the emergence rather than the imposition of strategies.

Of course, personal values are very much wrapped up in the editorial function, and these can encourage a management to try to impose its intentions on the editorial staff, say support for a certain political philosophy. But realizing these intentions is another matter, not only because of the unpredictable nature of the news, but also because staff members inevitably have considerable discretion in interpreting news events, and they have values of their own. Thus, nothing can be given to a reporter to control his or her stories equivalent to the chart that was given to the advertising person to calculate the size of the newspaper. All management can really do is appoint editorial staff with the values it favors, and thereby indirectly encourage pursuit of its intentions. In other words, it must revert to managing the process of strategy formation, not the content of the strategies themselves. There is no evidence in this study that the Black group wanted to control the content of the newspaper per se, but we did see editorial strategies emerging as a consequence of the management of process, notably in the reduction of quality as a result of the tight management of the bottom line (to take a specific example, in the reduction of local editorials as a result of reducing the discretionary time of the editorial staff).

There seems to be an important message here for any country whose newspapers are largely subjected to chain ownership. When the owners of such chains respond to public concerns about the editorial function by claiming that they do not seek to control the content of their newspapers, their reply may be correct, but it misses a key point: they influence the content, often for the worse, by virtue of their control of the administration.

INTERPLAY OF ENVIRONMENT, LEADERSHIP, AND ORGANIZATION

The analysis of the interplay of environment and organization, with leadership designed to serve in a mediating role between the two, can also reveal a good deal about strategy-making behavior. Sometimes, organization plays the dominant role, capturing the leadership (and sometimes even the environment as well for a time), as we saw in our studies of the US strategy in Vietnam, from 1965 to 1968, and Volkswagenwerk, in the 1960s. Sometimes environment dictates strategies to the organization and its leadership, as in Arcop with respect to its 'choices' of markets and locations. And sometimes leadership can be preeminent, dictating to a malleable organization and carrying it to a safe niche in the environment, as in Steinberg until the organization grew large and the environment more demanding.

The *Sherbrooke Record* is the story of a small and malleable organization, but with its own traditions; an environment that gnawed away at the organization, at first slowly and imperceptibly but later much more overtly; and three leaderships, one that could have acted but did not, a second that could not act, and a third that did, with a vengeance.

If ever there was an organization in which leadership could have acted, this was it. The organization was small and easy to change, while the environment, for all but a few years in the later 1960s, was not imposing even though it seemed to be deteriorating. Indeed a study of this organization, together with three other small anglophone ones in the Eastern Townships (Taylor 1983), found that the quality of the leadership and the attitudes of the employees (the organizational culture) explained success and failure far more than did deterioration in demographic conditions (namely decline of the anglophone community). In other words, each organization could find a relevant niche, and make it work, so long as it possessed enthusiasm and energy.

Unfortunately, until the late 1960s, the *Sherbrooke Record* was saddled with a leadership that was detached administratively even if it was involved sentimentally. That leadership would not act, but neither would it let go. So long as an organization's strategy is appropriate, that is not a bad kind of leadership to have: the organization is protected, yet not bothered; the employees can get on with pursuing the given strategy. But a time always comes when strategic change is necessary, and then that kind of leadership stymies it: those who can take the initiative would not, while those who may want to cannot. Thus, despite its small size and malleable nature, in the absence of leadership during these years of environmental change, the *Record* exhibited a surprising amount of strategic inertia.

The leadership did change in the late 1960s, to one that was involved both administratively and sentimentally. But by this time the environment had emerged as the dominant force, and proved too much for that leadership. So it gave way to a more powerful leadership, but one less personally involved and smart or lucky enough to have entered the scene just as the environment settled down somewhat. Thus, while the forces of organization dominated (passively) in the 1951–67 period (in the face of disinterested leadership and a gradually deteriorating environment), and those of the environment dominated in the 1967–9 period (in the face of a vulnerable organization and its leadership), those of leadership dominated in the 1969–76 period, resisted neither by environment nor by organization. Even sharp declines in the circulation did not deter the new leadership in pursuing its given strategies. And other aspects of the environment became more supportive—the worst postal-rate increases had passed, and the new shopping center was finally opening. Although demographic trends continued to deteriorate, enough of a market remained to be exploited profitably.

The organization was now more malleable than ever, ripe for the picking, or—in the metaphor of strategic management—harvesting. The new 'external' management, free of sentimental involvement, could make the internal changes necessary to exploit the market that remained and render the organization profitable. The existing organization was in fact reduced to almost nothing. It was truncated at the top (with management becoming external) and at the bottom (with its printing contracted out), while its editorial function in between was curtailed substantially. The *Sherbrooke Record* was almost literally harvested!

Thus our tale of two Canadian tycoons is one of sharp contrasts in leadership. One was detached administratively but involved sentimentally; the other was detached sentimentally but involved administratively. One served the organization well so long as it did not have to adapt; the other served it well only while it was forced to adapt. The failings of the first brought in the second. In that sense they complemented each other, at least over time. But we are left wondering, in conclusion, if either (or both, in sequence) is what we really want in our society. Perhaps the message of the *Sherbrooke Record* is that healthy organizations and healthy societies need leaders who both act and care.

An executive closely associated with Hollinger Corporation, which grew out of the Black, White, and Radler initial foray into the *Sherbrooke Record*, wrote to the first author in 2006, after reading this study, that 'time has proven that the intended and realized strategies you identified in the Sherbrooke case became the modus operandi for Hollinger to this present day.' At present, Black is being tried on criminal charges in a US court; Radler has pleaded guilty and is testifying against Black. Hollinger earlier removed both from office and sold all its Canadian newspapers, and was forced to sell the *Telegraph* in the UK as well. It actually re-aquired the *Sherbrooke Record* in 1999—'Was Black getting sentimental like John Bassett?' wrote co-author Bill Taylor in an e-mail on 14 March 2007—but was forced to sell it along side the others in 2006.

Taylor added: Black's 'delibrate actions of controlling his empire through Rovelstone (another company) as a personal asset eventually produced a context in which a pattern of questionable expenditures emerged, even if he did not deliberately try to defraud. Too bad you can't argue emergent behaviors in the courts!'.

As for the *Sherbrooke Record*, however small it remains in such a tiny market, it continues to publish daily, with a circulation in 2007 of about 5,000.

8

Mirroring Canadian Industrial Policy
Dominion Textile, 1873–1990

Barbara Austin and Henry Mintzberg[1]

This chapter tracks the strategies of a 'quintessentially Canadian company', Dominion Textile Inc., through most of its history, from 1873 to 1990. Created entrepreneurially, but soon consolidated politically, it became the dominant player in an important industry in Canada, faltering bureaucratically before renewing itself competitively. As discussed in the conclusions, the company always mirrored Canadian industrial policy closely, through the states of 'getting there' politically, 'staying there' positionally, and 'keeping there' competitively. Overall, it was remarkably deliberate in its strategic behavior, yet that deliberateness exhibited emergent consequences, much as a slinky toy placed on a top step walks its way down the stairs.

This study tracks the strategies of Dominion Textile Inc. in order to tell the history and infer lessons for strategic management of what, in many ways, is the quintessential Canadian company. Dominion Textile has figured prominently in the history of Canadian industry, much as General Motors and DuPont, as described by Alfred Chandler (1962), figured prominently in the history of US industry. Indeed, following the evolution of this company is much like following the evolution of Canadian business in general, since not only

[1] Originally published in the *Canadian Journal of Administrative Sciences* (1996: 46–64), with minor revisions in this volume.

did its business strategies mirror Canadian industrial strategy over the years, but even its evolving management style reflected what was often considered the stereotypical Canadian management style, including dramatic shifts in the later years. Thus, what follows is almost as much of a history of Canadian business as a history of a Canadian company.

This story of Dominion Textile is told from 1873 until 1990, drawing on the first author's (Austin 1985) study of the company in her doctoral dissertation, using the methodology that has been applied to the other studies in this book.

The study of Dominion Textile was based on an examination of shareholders, directors, and executive committee *Minute Books* in the company's possession, including the associated companies. The firm began in 1873 as the Hudon Cotton Company, became Hochelaga Cotton following a merger in 1885, and the Dominion Cotton Company in 1890, in a consolidation with six small firms. Dominion Textile itself was created in 1905 by the consolidation of four cotton textile companies. Included in the company's collection of *Minute Books* are those of companies acquired by Dominion Textile, including Montreal Cotton (1873–1948) and Merchants Cotton (1880–1905). This information was augmented by newspaper articles (from the 1870s onward), and information in *The Canadian Textile Journal* since 1883 (Austin 1983). Many interviews were held with retired and current company executives. E. F. King, who joined the company in 1920, was particularly helpful in explaining company policies for over fifty years. In addition, a thorough examination was made of several rival companies, including Wabasso (Austin 1993) and Hamilton Cotton (Austin 1992). Joining the authors in the brainstorming session were William Taylor, a Canadian academic who has conducted similar studies, and Deborah Dougherty, a US academic, then at McGill, known for her work on new product development.

The first section summarizes the company's strategies as inferred from the data in six areas (materials, fabrics, and processes [considered together], product markets, geographic markets and competition, marketing, mill expansion, and organization structure), as well as a review of labor policies. The second section reviews the company's history in terms of seven distinct periods inferred from the strategies, and the third section presents a conceptual interpretation of the study.

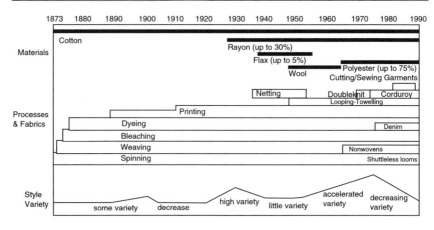

Strategy Diagram 8A Materials, fabrics, processes, styles

Strategies of Dominion Textile

MATERIALS, FABRICS, AND PROCESSES

Strategy Diagram 8A shows the various materials, fabrics, and processes found at Dominion Textile over the years. For the first fifty years, the company processed cotton through the basic methods of spinning, weaving, bleaching, and dyeing or printing. Printing was expanded in the 1920s when fabric finishing became important. Rayon fiber was first used in 1926, followed for a time by flax and wool, until polyester became important in the 1960s.

From 1963 to 1980, Dominion Textile expanded into a wide range of fabrics, including double-knits, corduroy, carpet yarns, and nonwovens, integrating forward into garment manufacturing in 1981. The 1975 acquisition of DHJ (Dubin Haskell Jacobson) expanded the firm's expertise into denim and interlinings.

PRODUCT MARKETS

Initially, the company sold coarse cotton fabric as a finished good to households and to industry, particularly for bags used to transport commodities (Strategy Diagram 8B). Sales to garment manufacturers, first for men's shirts in the 1890s, and in the 1920s for women's and children's clothing, and sheets and towels, became the most important product use. During both wars, 1914–18 and 1939–45, military uses dominated production. In the late 1920s, the firm became the major Canadian supplier

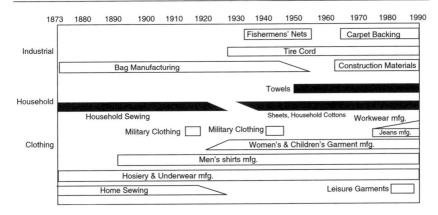

Strategy Diagram 8B Product markets

of tire cord and rayon fabric. Between 1953 and 1975, the company's products expanded into most areas available in textiles, including carpet backing and construction materials. After 1975, Dominion Textile selectively served niches it developed in denim, industrial engineering fabrics, work wear, interlining, and carpets.

GEOGRAPHIC MARKETS AND COMPETITION

In the early years, Dominion Textile sold its goods exclusively in Quebec and Ontario, expanding sales in 1890 to the Maritimes and Western Canada (Strategy Diagram 8C). Periodic markets were developed in China and Australia in the 1890s, in the UK during both world wars, and in the US during World War I. Beginning in 1955, UK sales were again developed,

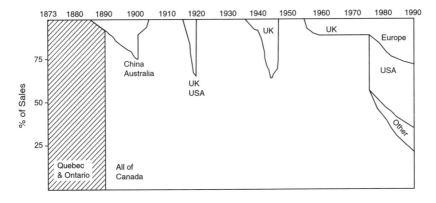

Strategy Diagram 8C Geographic markets

211

and after 1975, markets in the US, Europe, and China were expanded. By 1990, three-quarters of the company's sales were outside of Canada.

Competition in the Canadian market was dominated by UK firms until the 1879 Protective Tariff created, within a few years, a market for Canadian-made goods. Domestic producers sought to control domestic competition in the 1880s with cartels to limit production, and in the 1890s by mergers. Following the creation of Dominion Textile in 1905, until 1939 Canadian producers, protected by tariffs, stayed within agreed-upon niches. World War II cut off virtually all foreign competition. After the war, the market share of Canadian producers dropped to 40 percent in 1956, and was then stabilized through tariffs to around 50 percent in the 1970s. In 1989, when the Free Trade Pact with the US began, Canadian firms had one-third of the domestic market share.

MARKETING

Strategy Diagram 8D symbolically represents changes in marketing chan-nels, the vertical scale indicating growth and decline. Initially, goods were sold to dry goods wholesalers through a single commission agent, saving the company the expense of a selling unit. In 1897, the company formed its own small internal Selling Department to sell directly to wholesalers, converters, and department stores. After 1920, the rapid growth of the ready-to-wear clothing industry forced Dominion Textile to adopt a mar-keting view and to inventory its own goods, enlarging the merchandising function into warehousing, repacking, and credit.

Wartime restrictions (1940–7) diminished the Sales Department's func-tion to the allocation of rationed goods. In 1953, the firm returned to marketing rather than selling, developing a grassroots sales force to inter-pret customer demands. The use of trademarks, brand names, and large advertising campaigns, as well as an extensive warehouse and trucking

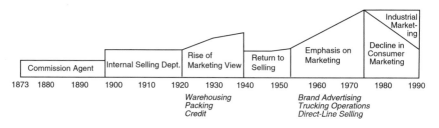

Strategy Diagram 8D Marketing

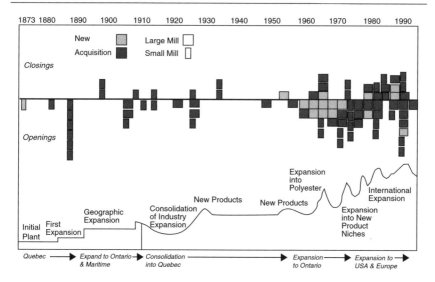

Figure 8.1 Mill development

operations, centered on direct-line merchandising and selling based on the end use of the product. In the 1980s, the firm returned to being a middleman, thus reducing inventory, closeout, and consumer advertising costs.

MILL DEVELOPMENT

Figure 8.1 and Strategy Diagram 8D show mill openings and closings and the strategies inferred from the data. The company began with one mill in Montreal and acquired two mills in Quebec in the 1880s. Acquisitions in 1890 in Quebec, Ontario, and the Maritimes, made Dominion Cotton the largest textile company in Canada. In 1905, the company merged with three Quebec companies to form Dominion Textile. Production was consolidated in the large Quebec mills, while small mills in Ontario and the Maritimes were closed.

After 1945, Dominion Textile periodically expanded in waves, followed by shakeouts. Acquisitions in the late 1940s and 1950s expanded the product line into terry toweling and cotton blankets. In the 1960s, the company constructed seven mills, the first new mills since 1873, to the tight controls required to produce polyester. In an expansion wave in the early 1970s, Dominion Textile acquired several small entrepreneurial firms in new niches (double-knits, carpet backing, corduroy, and industrial fabrics).

213

Another wave of international expansion began in 1975 with the acquisition of DHJ, a US firm two-thirds the size of Dominion Textile, with mills specializing in denim, interlining, and double-knits. In the early 1980s, the company closed many Canadian mills because some plants were inefficient, or market tastes had changed, or in order to leave behind unionized labor problems. International expansion was renewed in the mid-1980s, following the company's takeover bid of Burlington, when it acquired several of Burlington's US and European specialty mills.

STRUCTURE/MANAGEMENT STYLE

Strategy Diagram 8E presents the periods in the firm's structure, which reflect historical changes in management style. Changes in structure signal a shift in the 'dominant management logic' (Prahalad and Bettis 1986: 489) of the succession of executives, who over 117 years changed from being entrepreneurs (1873–81), to a partnership of merchants (1882–1904), to that of an asset managed by financiers (1905–53), to professional management executives espousing the marketing view (1953–80), to an organization with increasingly international perspectives.

The founding entrepreneur acted as both the president and mill manager. His successor, a dry-goods wholesaler, managed the company like a partnership, with the Montreal merchants, the major shareholders, taking executive functions.

Following the merger organized by financiers in 1905 to form Dominion Textile, the firm was structured as a holding company while it was centralized financially. By 1909 it was operated as a simple machine-like organization. The president in the period 1909–39, Sir Charles Gordon (who became president of the Bank of Montreal), and vice president Sir Herbert Holt (president of the Royal Bank of Canada) were leading Canadian financiers in the 1920s and 1930s. Their management style was remote, bureaucratic, and conservative.

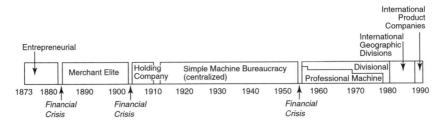

Strategy Diagram 8E Structure/management style

Sir Charles's son, Blair, president from 1939 to 1962, maintained the same management style. The only anomaly was in the rayon subsidiary, a joint venture with Burlington (1945–52), where its president, King, became familiar with the divisional structure and the US market-driven management style. New products, such as rayon, were managed in subsidiaries, termed sideshows, so as not to disturb the core operation.

Management style changed sharply in 1953 when Blair Gordon, facing a financial crisis, reluctantly made King vice president of sales and a director. King introduced basic changes in values, beliefs, and attitudes, especially in response to the environment. Between 1953 and 1977, the structure was divisionalized in a deliberate set of steps: first, product divisions (1953); then sales divisions (1955); then two major divisions (1970); then four (1974); and finally full divisionalization of all the functions (1977). In the process, about thirty subsidiaries were absorbed as the decentralized structure could now accommodate the increased variety in processes, products, and markets, as illustrated in Figure 8.1. The executives were determined to rework the company to reflect their personal goals of expansion, which they saw limited by the declining market in Canada for domestic textiles.

By 1980, reflecting the international acquisition of DHJ, Dominion Textile was divided into three geographic companies (Canada, the US, and International), directed by the Montreal headquarters. In 1988, the structure was changed to a matrix form, with six international product companies based on specialized products: Dominion Yarn Group (US and Canada); Swift Denim (US, Canada, and Europe); Apparel Fabrics (Canada, Italy, and Ireland); Consumer Products and Industrial Products (both US and Canada); and Technical Fabrics (worldwide).

LABOR

The early mill hands, often entire families together, were former farm workers. Technicians were hired in Britain. To retain experienced workers, management built cottages and recreational facilities. The paternalistic attitude reached its peak in the 1930s, with efforts to keep all the mills operating, even at a loss, to reduce social distress in the mill towns.

A crippling strike in 1947 marked the increasing power of unions, as well as growing tension between French-speaking workers and English-speaking managers and the beginning of the dissolution of paternalism. A bitter strike in 1966 influenced management's decision to expand, when

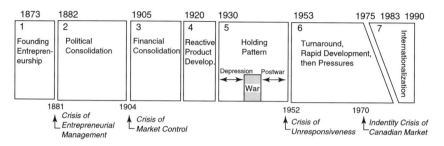

Figure 8.2 Periods in the development of Dominion Textile

possible, to the US, where the majority of textile workers were nonunionized. By 1990, the majority of the 13,000 employees were outside Canada and nonunionized.

Periods in the History of Dominion Textile

The strategies shown in Strategy Diagrams 8A to 8E were aligned for analysis in a brainstorming session. Joined by other academics, we debated the various changes, and identified seven basic periods in the 117-year history, which are shown in Figure 8.2 and discussed in turn below. Single critical changes, or several important ones that together suggested significant shifts in the direction of the company, were examined. For example, a single event, the management change in 1882, from entrepreneurial leadership to that of large shareholders of the Montreal business elite, allowed the firm to expand to dominate the Canadian market, culminating with the Dominion Textile consolidation in 1905. The period is termed Political Consolidation, because the shareholders used their considerable political influence to lobby for the maintenance of tariffs to sustain production.

1873–81: FOUNDING ENTREPRENEURSHIP

The origin of Dominion Textile was from the Hudon Cotton Company, a small cotton-spinning operation started by Victor Hudon, an entrepreneurial Montreal dry-goods wholesaler. The Montreal mill used British machinery, while the layout followed the US model of integrated operations, which soon included weaving, bleaching, dyeing, and printing. The goods were consigned to a single commission agent who handled merchandising and selling.

In 1879, the government's 25 percent tariff on imported textiles attracted new entrants to the industry. Between 1879 and 1883, the number of Canadian cotton mills rose from four to twenty-three. The tariff initially brought enormous profits to the company, but as new mills came into production, the Canadian market was soon saturated, leading to keen price competition. The founder, Hudon, was ousted by the directors in 1881 and replaced with a professional mill manager, and Andrew Gault as president.

1882–1904: POLITICAL CONSOLIDATION

Conflict of interest between business and government is a twentieth-century concept. In this period, the new president, Gault, used political leverage (his brother was a member of the federal parliament, and senators were executives) to lobby to maintain high tariffs. Multiple directorships in competing firms were another feature of nineteenth-century business practices. Gault became president of four leading textile companies.

In the 1890s, a period of cyclical downturn in the industrialized world, these informal connections could no longer control the textile market. With the support of Montreal merchants and bankers, the firm, already the largest in Canada, expanded geographically, acquiring six mills in Ontario and the Maritimes, to control 25 percent of the market. Agents sent to China, Australia, and British colonies in Africa developed an export market (see Strategy Diagram 8C).

In 1897, a new Liberal government reduced tariffs, resulting in an increase of UK and US imports. To become more competitive, the company dismissed its commission agent, formed a small Selling Department, and introduced branding and promotion. In the early 1900s, most firms in the Canadian textile industry faced bankruptcy because of overproduction and severe price competition. The death of Gault in 1903 ended his multiple presidencies of firms, resulting in unrestrained competition. A financial crisis followed which threatened the stability of the entire Montreal business community. A syndicate of leading financiers organized a merger of four firms in order to protect their mutual interests.

1905–19: FINANCIAL CONSOLIDATION

The directors of the new company, Dominion Textile, were no longer merchants, but financiers with no direct experience in managing firms. For the next thirty years, the president, Charles Gordon, and vice president,

Herbert Holt, managed the firm to make it a major player in the Canadian business establishment. Technology, market size, and fashion demands were slow to change. Tariff increases in 1907 and 1911 protected the industry from severe foreign competition, allowing informal agreements among competitors.

Just as financial assets were consolidated, the administration was gradually centralized and bureaucratized. The volume of output was controlled to match the cyclical demand for goods. The Selling Department took orders from jobbers twice a year. Wage rates were tied to the selling price, raised when the mills were running at full capacity, lowered when orders fell off.

During World War I the company could sell all it could produce, including to the UK and US armed services. Profits accumulated in the Surplus Fund, invested in the stock market by Holt, which was used in the 1930s and later in the 1950s to ward off financial failure.

1920–9: REACTIVE PRODUCT DEVELOPMENT

Once it had consolidated politically and financially, Dominion Textile defined its market position by emphasizing manufacturing efficiency while entering into promising new product areas. A mature industry, textiles did not share the 1920s boom in new consumer products. Preferential tariffs determined that the UK was still the main competitor. Technology evolved slowly. The mills were kept in good repair, but were not expanded. Rather than compete directly, the company preferred to control the market through agreements with other textile firms, and specialized in certain lines to gain economies through manufacturing efficiencies.

But a shift to readymade clothing after 1920 soon made garment manufacturers the company's largest customer group. To meet their demands for a wider variety in styling, in part the result of the spillover effect of the US magazine advertising, Dominion Textile was forced to increase its inventory of goods and shorten the time between production and delivery. The Selling Department, influenced by the rise of the marketing view in the US, persuaded the company to increase the range of styles offered to respond to customer demands.

1930–52: HOLDING PATTERN

The company's strategies in its products, processes, and structures changed little during this period, despite the radical shifts in the environment—the Depression in the 1930s and World War II, followed by a business boom. Dominion Textile continued to dominate the industry, producing about half of all Canadian textile output.

During the Depression, despite a loss in sales, management kept all mills operating, motivated by a social conscience to maintain jobs in its mill towns. Selling prices in many lines were so low that goods were sold at manufacturing cost with no profit margin. Dominion Textile incurred losses from 1930 to 1936, but survived. Managers proudly told the authors during interviews in the 1980s that the company had never missed a dividend. When this story was checked back to 1905 with the financial records, it proved correct. From 1930 to 1936, the company sold securities in the World War I Surplus Fund when necessary.

World War II brought a complete turnaround, from underuse (with imports amounting to 30 percent of the market) to guaranteed sales of all products. Textile industry production and prices were placed under control of the government Wartime Prices and Trade Board. The function of the Selling Department became allocation—rationing supplies to customers while production for national war supplies received management's complete attention. By 1943, the plants, having operated continuously at full capacity, were run down and production figures began to fall.

The boom conditions continued until 1948, when the removal of federal price supports brought sudden and severe competition from virtually tariff-free imports. International competition in the Canadian market—first US, then Japanese—forced the domestic market share to fall from nearly 100 percent in 1947 to 45 percent in 1957. Dominion Textile survived by gradually replacing its equipment and emphasizing productivity. While the productivity drive doubled output in the late 1940s, it created clashes with increasingly militant unions. During several bitter strikes between 1948 and 1952, the company executives gradually lost their sense of social responsibility to the workers.

The long production runs of wartime had left operations inflexible. The Manufacturing Department had difficulty returning to smaller batches and styling variety. Marketing skills, which had withered away during the war were needed after 1948, but only remained in the rayon subsidiary under King. Dominion–Burlington, a joint venture from 1945 to 1952 with the US textile giant, gave Dominion Textile expertise in synthetics technology, and Burlington access to Canadian consumers. The freer management style, emphasizing individual initiative, that King developed in the rayon subsidiary contrasted with the bureaucratic style at headquarters, where senior managers were remote figures to the rest of the company, committed to their own financial interests and personal careers.

After 1948, Canadian textile manufacturers could not meet the low prices and diversification of styles and fabrics of US textile imports. Several large domestic companies closed, and it seemed likely that Dominion Textile would soon have to follow. To hold market share, it operated at a loss between 1950 and 1955, using the last of the World War I Surplus Account to survive.

1953–74: TURNAROUND, RAPID DEVELOPMENT, THEN PRESSURES

The period 1953–61 saw Dominion Textile develop into a modern corporation by adopting a new management style, which broke away from the protective style of the past. The success of the company involved a combination of new marketing concepts leading to good manufacturing management. In 1953, Blair Gordon brought King back into the parent organization from the rayon subsidiary, marking the company's reluctant acceptance of postwar conditions. Since the 1920s, King had been an enthusiastic practitioner of aggressive marketing. The old guard was admitting the conservative manufacturing orientation no longer worked, a signal that the company would make a radical break from a top-down manufacturing orientation to a consumer-driven strategy.

King became vice president, Marketing, and a director, to counterbalance the influence of the Manufacturing Department. Structure became a tool of the marketing strategy. Product units, defined by customers served—a concept familiar to King from his contacts with Burlington in the rayon joint venture—were gradually introduced into the Marketing Department in 1955. The product line was redesigned with greater attention to quality, reflecting New York style trends. The company launched an intensive national advertising campaign aimed at the end user of the product, emphasizing trademarks and brand names, stressing Tex-made on its sheets.

The international textile industry underwent broad changes after 1960, a result of major technological breakthroughs in equipment and processes, particularly with the introduction of polyester, a substitute for cotton for many purposes. Starting polyester/blend operations was considered risky because it radically changed textile manufacturing, requiring new machinery, buildings, and production techniques to meet strict tolerances for temperature and humidity. In the early 1960s, the company built three new polyester/blend mills, and by 1975, polyester accounted for 75 percent of production. The new plants were built in Ontario, still in Canada but remote from the perceived labor and political tensions of Quebec. As these new mills came into production, plants too old to renovate were closed, including the original 1873 mill.

The new synthetics had provided opportunities for entrepreneurs to form companies to produce new specialty products, making innovative use of the fibers. This fragmented group of companies went through a shakeout in the early 1970s. Dominion Textile acquired some of them, in a wide variety of processes—corduroy, double-knits, and industrial fabrics—widening the already considerable product line.

As its less adaptive domestic competitors failed, Dominion Textile entered into some of the newly vacated niches. It had always been the company with the broadest product line, but now it produced an ever-increasing variety of fabrics, colors, and designs. International competition, including from Asian and Communist-block countries, tended to specialize in long-run lines at low cost. When Dominion Textile could not match these imports on cost, it expanded its style range, further fragmentizing operations. The broader product base included goods manufactured directly for the consumer market.

Reaching new customers in the Canadian market meant a large increase in the number of small orders. Eventually the diversification of styles got out of hand, leading to inventory and control problems. This diversification was not consistent with the company's product policy of low cost, which required concentration on long runs. But by being flexible and responsive in reacting to changing consumer tastes, Dominion Textile was able to expand its share of the declining domestic market.

External pressures increased enormously as a result of international GATT (General Agreements on Tariffs and Trade) agreements, Canadian government legislation on environmental, health, and safety routines, and nationalistic social legislation of the Quebec government. In 1970, a federal-government policy statement on textiles called for stabilized protective tariffs in some lines but designated Canadian textiles a sunset industry (see Mahon 1984).

On the surface, in 1975, Dominion Textile appeared to be a mature firm, overwhelmingly dominant in an otherwise declining industry. Underneath, new configurations, a capital-intensive rather than labor-intensive technology, and a structure of four operating divisions was evolving. The senior executives were predisposed to confound government experts by acting when an opportunity was perceived for international expansion.

1975–90: INTERNATIONALIZATION

Activity in this period was dominated by the realization that, in order to grow in textiles, the company would have to expand outside Canada, particularly to the US, which offered a larger, more protected market, lower wage structures, and building and operating costs. In 1975, eager to try their skills in the US market, the executive team, headed by the new president, Tom Bell, bought DHJ, a company with two-thirds of Dominion Textile's annual sales, the fourth largest North American denim producer, as well as an international marketer of interlinings. DHJ became a bridgehead, awakening the company to opportunities in international markets.

In the early 1980s, following further US acquisitions, Dominion Textile redefined itself as a North American company producing goods with a strong market position in both the US and Canada. The divisions were made into separate companies on a geographic basis, with Montreal the holding company headquarters. The US operations became Dominion Textile (USA) Inc.

In 1984, the company faced a flood of imports and was forced to admit that Canadian sales would continue to decline, especially as a free-trade pact between Canada and the US seemed inevitable before 1990. Manufacturing operations in Canada were further reduced. Executives blamed the downsizing of their Canadian operations on the federal government for allowing more duty-free imports from low-wage countries. But the declining domestic market reflected the policies of international cotton regulatory groups, such as GATT and the Multi-Fiber Agreement (MFA). Government actions and international trade agreements affected Dominion Textile more than any other Canadian textile firm because it was the overwhelming industry leader, while in the US, Dominion Textile was one of many players.

The company gradually moved from producing a wide product line to a selective one, especially when it could be a specialty producer in both the US and Canada. For example, in 1979, it started production of denim in Canada and soon dominated the field. The policy of geographic and product balance meant the number of styles, which had risen to around 800 in 1970, gradually cut back to around 100 in the early 1980s. Marginal Canadian lines were dropped. Between 1982 and 1988, fifteen of the thirty-one Canadian plants, those not competitive or with severe labor problems, were closed, and the remainder realigned and consolidated.

Pressured by the increased globalization of trade, the impending Canadian free-trade pact with the US, and the prospects of more open markets in Europe in 1992, the company shifted its focus from the Canadian to the US market. In 1987, Dominion Textile failed in a takeover bid for Burlington Industries, the largest US textile company. To finance its leveraged buyout, Burlington executives were forced to sell to Dominion Textile their largest denim operation, making it the leading denim manufacturer in the world. The acquisition of Burlington's European plants gave the company European leadership in work wear, while another acquisition made it the US leader in carpet backing, further strengthening its world product mandate in selected niches.

In 1988, Charles Hantho, former president of CIL (Canadian Industries Limited), Canada, the ICI (Imperial Chemical Industries) subsidiary, was named president, the first external appointment in the firm's history. The structure was changed to a matrix basis to reflect the new acquisitions and the global product focus of six major lines—denim, industrial products, yarn, consumer products, apparel fabrics, and interlining. Each line was represented by a separate company, to coordinate management of these global products.

An important aspect of Dominion Textile going international was its pride in its long history. Executives saw it as their responsibility to pass on the successful record. In 1983, senior management of the company was wholly Canadian, not the result of a deliberate policy, but because of difficulties recruiting US managers to live in Quebec.

Initially, the international operations used Canadians, but by 1990, 75 percent of the managers were not Canadian and had been with the company for less than two years. The corporate history and traditions that had developed over a century were quickly lost.

The company had survived by becoming international, but this success brought dangers. As a survivor in the Canadian textile industry, Dominion had learned to be flexible. But by 1990, in place of its self-perception as the Canadian industry leader was one of being a firm 'caught-in-the-middle' internationally.

Conceptual Interpretation of Dominion Textile's History

POLITICAL, POSITIONAL, COMPETITIVE ERAS

In essence, these seven periods can be described as constituting three strategic eras, as shown in Figure 8.3. Each was interrupted by a crisis

223

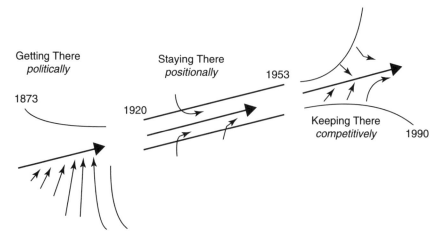

Figure 8.3 Three eras in Dominion Textile's history

that bumped the company up to a faster pace of evolution when its management realized that their view of the environment was historical and not current (Kiesler and Sproul 1982: 557). In the upheavals of the 1920s and 1950s, conditions had radically changed. Survival was dependent on management finding a new 'dominant logic' (Prahalad and Bettis 1986: 498). Figure 8.3 shows our conceptual depiction of the company in terms of these three eras.

We call the first 'Getting There', the building up of the company, first entrepreneurially, but soon politically and financially, into the dominant and highly protected player in Canadian textiles. That proceeded from the 1873 founding to about 1920.

Then followed the era of 'Staying There', sustaining and exploiting the established position with the necessary moves, without inspiration, which lasted for over thirty years.

The third era, following the shock of the early 1950s, and continuing to the end of our study period in 1990, we call 'Keeping There', the by-now necessarily aggressive and competitive actions to try to sustain the historical position of the company. That shock, followed by the gradual removal of other protective coverings, allowed a new style of manager to take over, de facto before de jure. In order to 'keep there', the company had to 'go elsewhere', literally in terms of expansion abroad, but also figuratively in terms of consolidation around new product lines and even more direct involvement in technological change.

DOMINION TEXTILE AS THE QUINTESSENTIAL CANADIAN COMPANY

Dominion Textile achieved industry dominance in 1890, and maintained that by its leadership in technology, products, and marketing. It was the firm others followed, historically in terms of cartels, and later during competition. In the 1980s the company became a major international textile firm and an exemplary Canadian company by going abroad when the national policy tariffs changed.

Dominion Textile may not have been the typical Canadian company—the country obviously supported all kinds of firms of every conceivable size and performance—but if DuPont and General Motors represented the quintessentially US corporate success stories, as described by Chandler (1962), then Dominion Textile must be the Canadian equivalent. The stories are different, but in the same way that the national industrial policies of the two countries have been different.

Of particular interest is the way the evolution of this company so closely mirrored Canadian industrial policy over the past century.

The Canadian textile industry was influenced by tariffs, which gave Dominion Textile a momentum it maintained for 110 years. What is remarkable about the company is how it emerged as a major international player in a very old industry, and how it kept there when the national economic policies changed and removed all its props.

In the First Era

Bliss (1987) has commented on the 1879 National Policy that:

Its advent was a spectacular demonstration of the influence that this new manufacturing 'class' was able to wield in the developing country. Although it neither created nor sustained Canadian manufacturing in any general way, the National Policy molded both the structure of the Canadian economy and the course of debate about the society's future for many generations. (1987: 227)

Within the context of this industrial policy, in the first era, 'Getting There', Dominion Textile grew rapidly after the 1879 tariff, consolidating itself politically after 1881 and financially into the ruling cartel after the crisis of market control in 1904. The industry survived lower tariffs under a Liberal government (1897–1911), mainly through the 1905 Dominion Textile merger. Conservative governments from 1911 to 1921 again rewarded their supporters in the Montreal business community with higher tariffs.

Textiles, traditionally the first manufacturing industry of any industrializing country, had been a major player in the government's industrial policy until the end of World War I. But by 1920 the industry was mature, and was gradually superseded in importance by other industries, such as pulp and paper, and automobiles. Government tariffs sustained employment in the industry from 1920 to 1939, but did not encourage its growth.

In the Second Era

'Staying There', was the company's stance by the early 1920s, as the dominant player in Canada, not unresponsive to market forces, but hardly leading them aggressively either. Having gradually evolved its products, markets, and plants, it settled into its managed environment, sufficiently protected to respond to changing market tastes at its leisure.

Gradually, however, through decades of what amounted to a strategic holding pattern, led by an elite and detached management, the company became increasingly moribund (as, some might argue, did Canadian industry in general). It was sustained, remarkably, by World War I profits for three decades after that war ended.

Dominion Textile was certainly a proactive company—the aggressive first mover in its industry in Canada (and, of course, the reason why it became the subject of this study, being the most visible survivor)—but on the world stage it was reactive, the acquirer of established technologies and product ideas, even if often the most aggressive promoter of these within Canada. Indeed that attitude of acquisition pervaded the company, for even at home, Dominion Textile was far more inclined to purchase its plants for expansion than to build them from scratch.

That could not, of course, continue forever, and by the late 1940s, the company was stunned into reality by sudden tariff cuts. This was, perhaps, the first real shock from an environment that had hitherto always been at least acquiescent, but it was certainly a harbinger of things to come.

The environment changed dramatically in 1948, when tariffs were effectively removed and the domestic market share plummeted. The company faced probable bankruptcy when the last of the World War I fund was gone. Reluctantly, its president, Blair Gordon, the son of the knighted president from 1909 to 1939, relinquished formal power to the young Turks, led by King. Outside the elite establishment, but inside the operation of the company, King began taking over direction of the company in the early 1950s.

In the Third Era

In this era, King was determined that the company would 'do all things ourselves that we could control before we would go to the government and ask for help to protect the industry' (personal communication 1983).

The Canadian government provided piecemeal tariffs from 1956 to 1989, subject to the dictates of the GATT and the MFA regulations. By expanding its products into most niches, building new mills to produce polyester, developing a divisional structure, all aimed at selling customers what they wanted, Dominion Textile overwhelmingly dominated the industry in Canada. It no longer coexisted with competitors, but acquired the promising ones and created competition that other domestic firms could not match.

The Liberal government's 1970 Textile Policy made it clear that it saw textiles as a sunset industry. Dominion Textile executives accepted the fact that growth was no longer possible in Canada, and began in 1975 to reposition its operations in the US and later Europe. When the Progressive Conservative government's Free Trade Pact with the US in 1989 eliminated textile tariffs in ten steps over ten years, Dominion Textile was deliberately repositioned to survive the end of government support for the industry.

Thus when the Canadian government recognized the futility of protecting its manufacturing sector for domestic production, there stood a newly energized Dominion Textile, poised to move aggressively on the international scene, virtually the dream of the Progressive Conservative government elected in 1984. (Who in Ottawa would ever have imagined that stodgy old Dominion Textile would march alongside Northern Telecom with its high technology?)

Why, indeed, would a textile company, of all things, with so much of a domestic orientation, so long protected and then suddenly buffeted by severe foreign competition, be the one to make the big moves abroad? Perhaps the events were idiosyncratic, reflecting the leadership that happened to be present. But our suspicion is that it was the long-standing establishment mentality that provided the base from which the new wave of leadership, developed in the peripheries of the organization (as we shall discuss), could act. Perhaps that did not seem like going for broke to people who, however marginal they may have been within the company, were still themselves members of that dominant and secure establishment company called Dominion Textile.

A HISTORY OF DELIBERATE EMERGENCE

To ask whether this company tended to develop its strategies deliberately or in a more emergent fashion would almost seem rhetorical. What conceivable organization could ever have acted more deliberately, whether it was the early establishment of the cartel, the later exploitation of it, or the final break with it in the form of aggressive expansion abroad? Yet, curiously, one dimension that never seemed to figure in any of the studied history was the set of procedures of formal planning. To understand why, we need to consider both the nature of the industry and its relationship between environment, leadership, and organization.

Sideshows

Textiles always tend to be a focused industry. At least before synthetics, companies tended to be dedicated to it. In other words, they knew what business they were in (even if, as Perrow [1970: 161–5] described, some were more dedicated to specific fibers than to textiles in general). But industry focus did not necessarily mean tight integration. This was never the equivalent of, say, the automobile industry, with a tightly integrated value chain from design through fabrication and assembly to distribution (even if the technological changes brought in by synthetics did increase mechanization significantly [Sabourin 1992]). Theme visions always held the pieces together more than tight gestalts or precise plans.

The pieces could thus be disconnected, or assembled in various ways, with other pieces added peripherally (say rayon production alongside cotton, printing added to weaving, sheets for beds produced alongside bags for bulk goods). Companies could, in other words, move sidestream as well as upstream or downstream more easily than in many other industries, which are impeded as much by mental predispositions as by actual technological differences (see Galbraith 1983).

This did not, perhaps, breed opportunism per se, but rather an easy responsiveness. In some ways, we can think of this as a dabbling industry, one that facilitated trying new things within the overall theme, whether new fabrics, new processes, new locations in the stream, or new markets. Bear in mind that this was a company whose core competencies were not unique. Their people were skilled at what they did, but what they did was done elsewhere, whether technical or political. Indeed, Dominion Textile until late in its history hired virtually all its skilled technicians from the UK.

It is perhaps most telling that the company itself referred to its additional activities in areas such as new product development (e.g. rayon alongside cotton) as its 'sideshows'. The implication, of course, was that the focus was elsewhere, on a center stage, in fact, the source of the funds that supported the sideshows. What Dominion Textile did centrally—cotton, then polyester, for garment manufacturers and later as household fabrics—constituted its cash cow.

One key consequence of these easily engaged-in sideshows was that periodically one of them could draw off sufficient attention so that it quietly took over center stage. Indeed, we can see this repeatedly during the history of the company, for example from the home sewing market to the one for garment manufacturers in the 1920s, from cotton to polyester (via rayon as the initial sideshow) in the 1960s, from Canada to the US in the 1970s, even from elite management to the young Turks in the 1950s, as these peripheral players (King himself having developed in the rayon operation) displaced the traditional ones at the center of the business.

The Emergent Quality of the Sideshow

The implication of this is that while sideshows reflected deliberate efforts to experiment and elaborate, their eventual encompassing of the main show had an emergent quality to it. Each sideshow may have been developed through conscious intention—indeed, perhaps the very idea of supporting sideshows was consciously intended. But that any sideshow should take over center stage, let alone which it would be, would hardly seem to have reflected conscious intention. Even the single most important acquisition, of DHJ (the US denim company) in 1975, was described by the chairman in a 1982 interview as 'a bite we think we can handle without sapping the core of our operation'. A decade later, producing denim internationally was the core business.

Leadership Taking the Lead

Another characteristic of this particular company, perhaps again a reflection of the dabbling quality of the industry plus its dominant position in it, is that in the interplay of environment, leadership, and organizational factors, the latter seemed to be surprisingly weak compared to the other two. We get no sense of bureaucratic momentum here, notwithstanding the company's size and the machine-like nature of its technology. There was a clear period of management momentum in the 1930s and 1940s, to be sure, but with that management so removed from the operations (geographically as well as in status), that too seemed almost independent of organizational forces. Indeed, when change did finally come, it came from within the operations at the expense of its senior management.

And so the play seemed to be between leadership and environment, with leadership almost always taking a proactive stance vis-à-vis the environment, even if in response to environmental pressures. In other words, when problems had to be solved and crises arose, the leadership moved aggressively, whether it was the political establishment of a cartel in response to competitive pressures a century ago, or the competitive move into the US in response to declining protection in the Canadian market much later. At almost all stages of the company's history, whether its posture was political or competitive, a proactive management positively attacked the environment. Even the two World Wars caused more temporary deflections than permanent changes; shifting markets and depleting competencies for a time, until things got back on track.

'Slinky' Strategy

To express this in conceptual terms, we think of this company as having pursued a kind of 'slinky' process of strategy formation, the reference here to the children's toy rather than any pejorative tone of the word. A child puts the slinky on a step, deliberately guides it to the next step, and then watches it 'walk' down the stairs by itself. Leadership is the key, and proaction is necessary, but once started, the process leads to actions of its own. So it has been at various stages of the history of Dominion Textile.

This can be seen even in management itself. Just as the move into rayon could not have been foreseen as the facilitator of the move into polyester, even more so could these sideshows not have been foreseen as the source of the managerial talent that would eventually turn the company around. King was, in a sense, weaned on the new synthetics; a sideshow that provided a place where he could escape the deadening effect of the central management. When crisis struck, there was a manager with a proven track record of aggressive action. King's protégé, Tom Bell, was president of the company during its most aggressive years (1974–89), and was mentored by King in the rayon subsidiary in those earlier times. (In 1946, Bell, then in his early twenties, was selected by King from the headquarters' Personnel Department to be a sales liaison with Burlington Industries in North Carolina for the Dominion–Burlington joint venture. In 1987, as president of Dominion Textile, Bell led the takeover bid for Burlington!) And in perhaps the final irony, King told us during interviews that he did not agree with the Bell team's latest moves abroad, but as he was about to retire and since this was to be their company, he let them get started under his chairmanship.[2] In effect, he put the slinky of Tom Bell's team on the next step and then had to watch it proceed from there.

Such has been the history of Dominion Textile, the quintessentially Canadian success story, with leadership driving environment but surprised by the consequences of the actions it itself began, much as the slinky goes down the stairs. Of course, a slinky stops when there are no more stairs. Or else it falls over the edge and collapses when the next step is too high.

Dominion Textile continued downsizing during the 1990s. In 1997 there were only two remaining factories and four lines—notably denim and nonwovens. The company's shares were acquired in 1997 by Polymer Group Inc., which kept the nonwoven operations but sold the denim mills, abruptly ending a firm that had been a Canadian institution for 124 years.

[2] Bell believed that King agreed with the move internationally, but questioned the plan to help Bell and his team closely examine possible problems. (Interview, T. Bell, President Dominion Textile, March 1982).

9

Strategy of Design

'Architects in Copartnership', 1953–78

Henry Mintzberg, Suzanne Otis, Jamal Shamsie
and James A. Waters[1]

> *This is the story of strategy and structure in a distinguished organization of*
> *architects across almost thirty years of its history. In fact, it is really a story*
> *of avoiding the making of strategies and resisting the forces of organization,*
> *in order to sustain creative excellence in craft. As such, the story contains*
> *some interesting messages for a society that experiences the imperatives of*
> *administration.*

Arcop ('Architects in Copartnership'), which evolved from a working relationship of three architects in a basement in Montreal in 1953, became a
renowned designer of major buildings in Canada. As can be seen in Figure
9.1, the firm peaked with billings of over $3 million and a staff of almost
150 people in early 1966 before it fell back to under $1 million and 30
people in 1970. It then began a more moderate cycle of growth, which
peaked, with almost $2 million in billings and seventy people in 1975.
Much of the success of Arcop can be attributed to its basic adherence to
the principles of fine design. It has been said that being inside an Arcop
building is a celebration.

In this study, the primary sources of archival data were the records on
jobs and billings, payroll files, financial reports, memos, circulars, and
some personal files of the partners. Interviews were held with nineteen
people, including five of the partners and two former ones (out of nine

---

[1] Originally published in *Strategic Management Frontiers* (John H. Grant, ed., JAI Press, 1988),
with minor revisions in this volume.

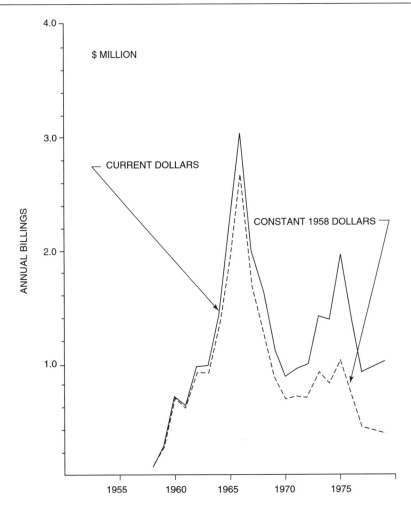

Figure 9.1 Annual billings of Arcop

in all), four associates and three former associates, one secretary, and four other former employees, one in drafting, the rest in various administrative positions.

Our report begins with an accounting of the organization's strategies, as inferred from its streams of actions, divided into two broad groupings: job strategies—the nature of the architectural work done by the firm—and organizational strategies—the manner in which the firm pursued its work. Following the description of these strategies, the performance of the firm (revenue, profits, prizes, and awards) is discussed and, together with selected job strategies, compared with general industry trends. This is followed by a narrative history of the firm, divided into four basic periods. The report concludes with a conceptual interpretation of the study under two themes: first, cycles of change within a strategic umbrella and, second, adhocracy and the reluctant organization.

Job Strategies at Arcop

The architectural work of Arcop can be broken down into two major categories. *Design and construction work* constituted the core service of the firm and includes initial conceptual design, final design, work drawings, and the supervision of construction; it can also include auxiliary services such as interior design or landscaping work. This can be distinguished from *study and planning work*, which involves land-use planning for individual sites or large urban areas as well as general research on the feasibility of potential building designs. Furthermore, most work occurs in stages and can extend over several years. Jobs can also remain inactive between stages if the client does not authorize work on the next stage right away. Arcop was frequently contracted to work on certain stages or even specific physical portions of a larger piece of work.

For the purposes of this study, a job is defined as architectural work on a single building or a specifically delineated geographical area. Work that was resumed after being terminated for at least eighteen months was registered as a new job. Jobs that generated less than $5,000 in revenue were not included in the study; in total, they represented less than 2 percent of total revenue in any year. Using the criteria specified above, 267 separate jobs were identified over the study period. This, however, includes only three significant jobs between 1953 and 1958 when the partnership was just forming. (Owing to a lack of data, figures for these years are not plotted.) Annual work volumes were estimated from the periodic billings on various jobs. As such, all billings were adjusted to derive annual figures. In practice, the billings occurred erratically, commencing long after a job had been started and continuing past the termination of actual work. Finally, total cumulative billings were used to classify jobs by size.

In the remaining part of this section, annual dollar volumes are broken down by the size, the type, and the location of the jobs.

Table 9.1 Overview of 267 jobs at Arcop, 1953–79

Type of work	Job size					
	500 M	100 to 500 M	40 to 100 M	15 to 40 M	5 to 15 M	Total
Design and Construction						
Residential	—	1	5	11	23	40
Commercial	$5^1/_2$*	0	6	16	21	$56^1/_2$
Leisure	$2^1/_2$*	6	3	6	11	$28^1/_2$
Industrial	—	—	—	1	7	8
Institutional	1	4	9	6	8	28
Governmental	1	4	4	6	5	20
Subtotal	10	23	27	46	75	181
Study and Planning						
Site development	—	2	5	17	22	46
Urban development	—	4	10	9	17	40
Subtotal	0	6	15	26	39	86
Total	10	29	42	72	114	267

* Two jobs, Onandaga Auditorium (half leisure, half governmental) and Le Chaudrierre (half commercial, half governmental) are each split between two categories.

Table 9.1 provides an overview of some of the breakdowns in terms of the number of jobs across the entire study period.

SIZE OF JOBS

As indicated in Table 9.1, the 267 jobs were classified into five different size categories:

(1) Very large: total billings of $500,000 or more (10 jobs; 4 percent of total jobs).

(2) Large: total billings between $100,000 and $500,000 (29 jobs; 11 percent).

(3) Intermediate: total billings between $40,000 and $100,000 (42 jobs; 16 percent).

(4) Small: total billings between $15,000 and $40,000 (72 jobs; 27 percent).

(5) Very small: billings between $5,000 and $15,000 (114 jobs; 42 percent).

Figure 9.2 shows the percentage distribution of the annual work volume by job size. It indicates an almost total dominance of the larger jobs up to 1966, and then a gradual decline till about 1970, after which a steady level

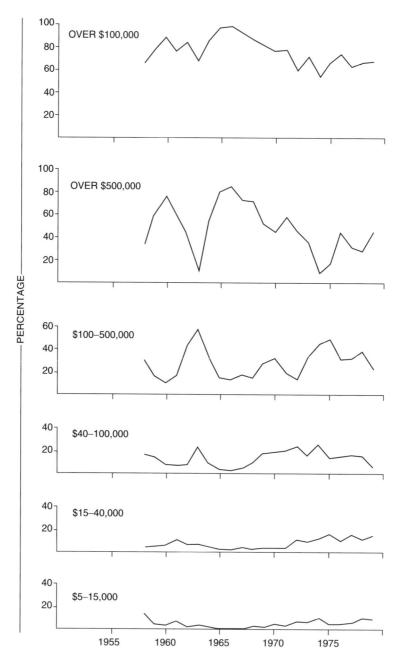

Figure 9.2 Percentage distribution of annual volume by size of jobs

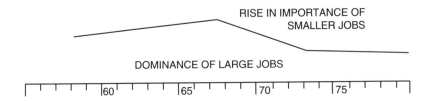

Strategy Diagram 9A Job size strategies

of about two-thirds of the volume in these larger jobs was maintained. These interpretations are depicted as strategies in Strategy Diagram 9A. In addition, it could be argued that each very large job was a strategy unto itself, in the sense that it set off a significant pattern of actions in the organization over a considerable period of time. The ten very large jobs, with total billings of over $500,000 each, have been separately identified in Figure 9.3. These jobs are depicted as strategies in their own right in Strategy Diagram 9B.

TYPES OF JOBS

Arcop's jobs involved (see Table 9.1): (*a*) design and construction work: 181 jobs, including all 10 of the very large jobs and 23 of the 29 large ones; (*b*) study and planning work: 86 jobs, including 6 of the 29 large ones.

Figure 9.4 shows the percentage breakdown of annual volume between these two categories. The former was always dominant, although the latter rose to a level of about 25 percent in the late 1960s and remained rather steady through to 1977. The resulting strategies are depicted in Strategy Diagram 9C.

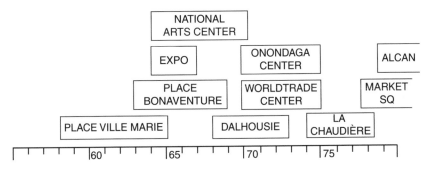

Strategy Diagram 9B Very large jobs as strategies

237

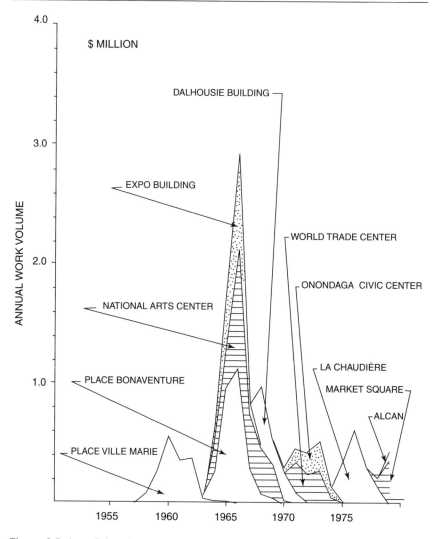

Figure 9.3 Actual distribution of work volume in jobs over $500,000

Furthermore, the study and planning work has been divided into (*a*) site development: focusing on a single plot of land involving single building or connected set—forty-six of the eighty-six jobs; (*b*) urban development: encompassing a larger area of a city or suburb including, many buildings—forty of the eighty-six jobs.

Figure 9.5 shows the percentage distribution of the annual volume of study and planning work, divided into its two major categories.

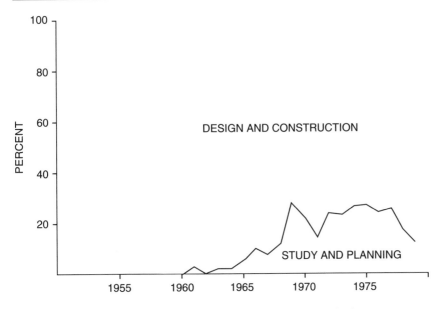

Figure 9.4 Percentage distribution of annual volume by type of jobs

Essentially urban development work seems to have displaced site development in the late 1960s and continued to account for about two-thirds of the study and planning work, as depicted in Strategy Diagram 9D.

Similarly, design and construction, the dominant work, has been broken down into six categories: (*a*) residential: buildings to provide private accommodations; e.g. houses, apartment buildings; forty jobs, referring to Table 9.1, none very large and only one in the large category; (*b*) commercial: buildings to accommodate business or trade; e.g. offices, hotels, restaurants, shops; fifty-six jobs, five very large and eight large; (*c*) leisure: buildings used primarily for recreation and entertainment; e.g. auditoriums, museums, resorts, exhibition halls; twenty-eight jobs, eight very large and six large; (*d*) industrial: buildings used in

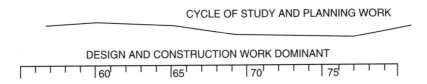

Strategy Diagram 9C Job type strategies

239

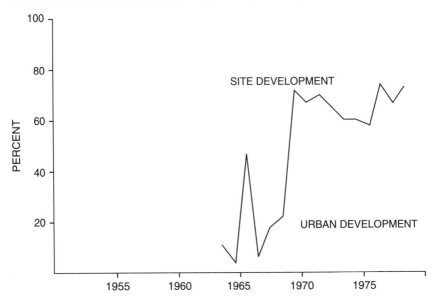

Figure 9.5 Percentage distribution of study and planning work

connection with industrial operations; e.g. plants and warehouses; eight jobs, none in the very large or large categories; (*e*) institutional: buildings to provide services to the community; e.g. schools, hospitals, churches, social service centers: twenty-eight jobs, one very large and four large; (*f*) governmental: federal, provincial, or municipal buildings providing administrative space or buildings for public use; e.g. town halls, fire stations, subway stations, public offices; twenty jobs, two very large and four large.

Figure 9.6 plots the percentage distribution of annual volume in each of these categories. Most striking in these data is the peak-and-valley character, with different markets rising and falling in no evident pattern.

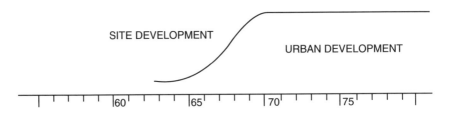

Strategy Diagram 9D Study and planning job strategies

240

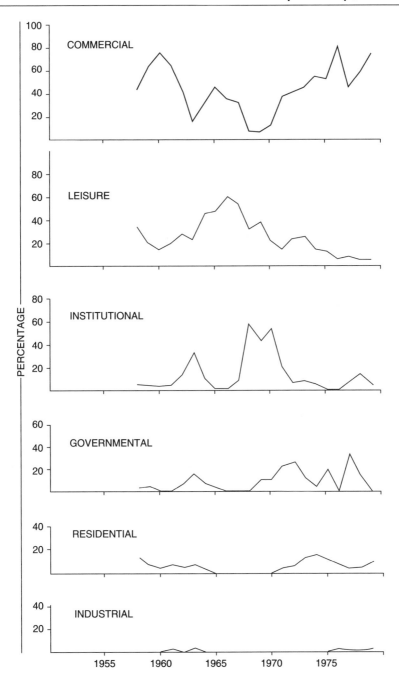

Figure 9.6 Percentage distribution of design and construction work

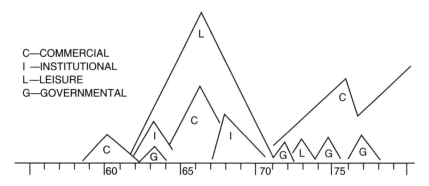

Strategy Diagram 9E Design and construction job strategies

We show the strategies in Strategy Diagram 9E as a series of cycles, each representing a major but temporary focus of activity.

LOCATION OF JOBS

The jobs were categorized according to six different locations: Quebec, Ontario, Eastern Canada, Western Canada, the US, and Overseas. Table 9.2 shows the number of jobs in each area by size for the entire study period. Figure 9.7 shows the percentage distribution of annual volume over time by location. Quebec—Arcop's home base and only office site up to 1973— provided much more work than any other location. In fact, Quebec dominated until the late 1960s. Strikingly, a peak-and-valley character is evident for all locations, including Quebec (at least after the early 1960s). In general, job locations are more diversified in the latter half of the study period. The more important cycles are depicted as strategies in Strategy Diagram 9F.

Table 9.2 Job location by size

Location	Job size					
	500 M	100 to 500 M	40 to 100 M	15 to 40 M	5 to 15 M	Total
Quebec	5	13	25	34	46	123
Ontario	1	3	3	17	31	55
Eastern Canada	2	5	3	5	11	26
Western Canada	—	3	1	1	3	8
US	2	3	9	8	18	40
Overseas	—	2	1	7	5	15
Total	10	29	42	72	114	267

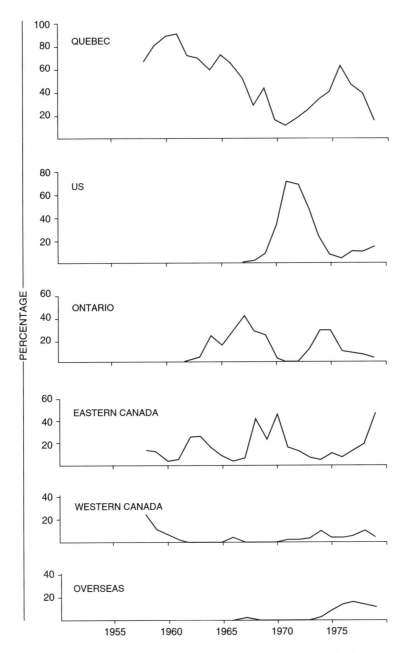

Figure 9.7 Percentage distribution of annual volume by location of jobs

243

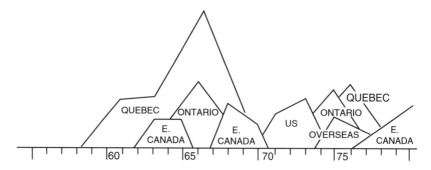

Strategy Diagram 9F Job location strategies

Organization Strategies at Arcop

Whereas the preceding section dealt with the nature of the firm's architectural work, this section deals with the strategies involved in acquiring and conducting the various jobs. These 'organization' strategies are discussed in the following categories: partnership, staffing, offices, affiliations with other architects, marketing, and structure. Data in some of these categories have again been restricted to the period starting in 1958 because of a relative lack of data from 1953 to 1958.

PARTNERSHIP

Architects must be registered by provincial boards to be able to practice on their own in Canada, although they can work in firms under registered architects without obtaining registration. Most Canadian architectural firms existed as individual proprietorships or partnerships because most provinces did not allow incorporation. Some firms, however, incorporated service companies that employed nonregistered architects. The majority of staff in architectural firms were architects and drafting or technical people, with a smaller number of people employed to carry out administrative and office tasks.

The nature of the partnership at Arcop changed over the study period; Figure 9.8 depicts the tenure of the various partners over the study period, while Strategy Diagram 9G characterizes these data in terms of four partnership strategies over the years.

Essentially, before 1958 the six architects who were to form Arcop each solicited and carried out their own work, although a single large job in Vancouver served to unify them into a partnership. There was

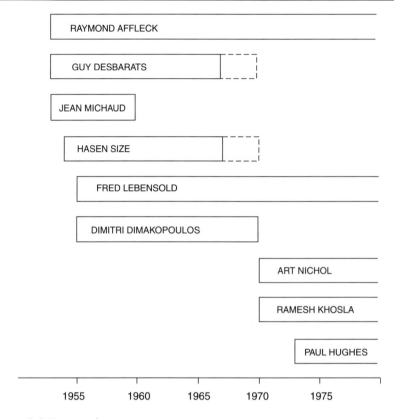

Figure 9.8 Tenure of partners

a strong and collaborative partnership from 1958 to 1967, with only one individual leaving. The partnership was trimmed down in 1967 and formally dissolved in early 1970. A new partnership was established later in 1970, joining the two remaining partners with two former associates. This remained stable to the end of the study period, with the addition of a new partner in 1973.

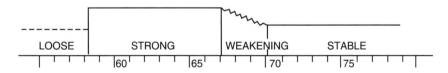

Strategy Diagram 9G Partnership strategies

STAFFING

Intermittent work is not unusual in architecture, where a firm will some-times engage individuals for only a few weeks at a time. But Arcop exhibited especially strong tendencies in this regard, most evident in Figure 9.9, a depiction of turnover ratio, which shows the new staff during a year as a percentage of the total staff. Figure 9.10 shows the total number of staff on the payroll at the end of each year. These last data, when compared with the total volume of work in Figure 9.1, suggest a strategy of matching staff to volume. This, together with

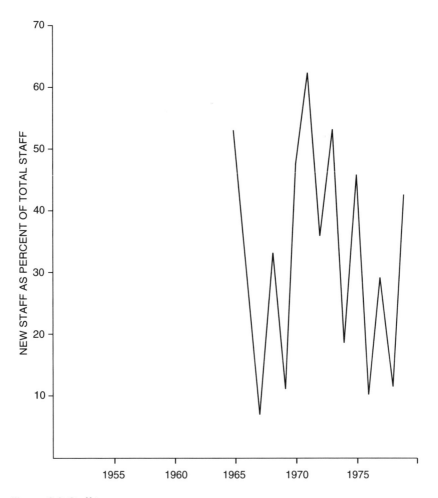

Figure 9.9 Staff turnover

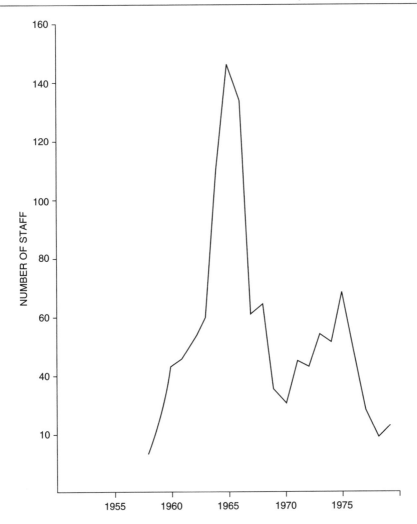

Figure 9.10 Staff total at year end

two growth–decline cycles in staffing strategy, is shown in Strategy Diagram 9H.

OFFICES

While Arcop opened and closed many temporary local offices to facilitate construction work on large jobs, it made only one permanent change. The firm operated exclusively out of Montreal until 1970, when an

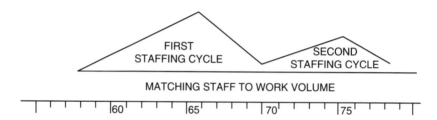

Strategy Diagram 9H Staffing strategies

associate was appointed in Toronto; this became a full-fledged office with its own staff in 1973, with the addition of a new partner. From that point on, each office acquired and handled its own work, although some jobs were shared. Two office strategies are depicted in Strategy Diagram 9I.

AFFILIATION WITH OTHER ARCHITECTS

In addition to using specialized consultants, Arcop often affiliated with other architectural firms to conduct work, either in the form of a loose association or by creating a new legal entity to pursue a joint venture. In almost all of these affiliations, the firm had been primarily responsible for the design phase of the work. In many cases, the affiliated firm was situated close to the construction site and so able to contribute primarily to the construction phase. Such affiliations also enabled Arcop to cope with national barriers or parochial attitudes in pursuing distant work. Figure 9.11 shows the percentage distribution of affiliated and unaffiliated work. Note that this curve is almost a mirror image of that of total volume of work, implying that Arcop turned to affiliations in bad times or, more likely, given slight lags in the curve, turned away from them when it no longer needed them. The strategies are shown in Strategy Diagram 9J.

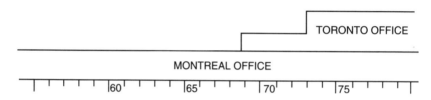

Strategy Diagram 9I Office strategies

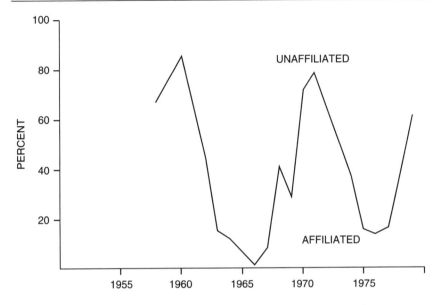

Figure 9.11 Percentage distribution of affiliated and unaffiliated work

MARKETING

Professional firms gain new business largely on the basis of an established reputation. Nevertheless, that can be supported by a variety of marketing efforts, such as the development of personal contacts, doing promotion in the form of brochures, entering competitions, or even doing speculative work at little or no cost to the potential client.

Figure 9.12 shows the competitions Arcop entered and won. The job that created Arcop came about through a competition in 1955. From 1958 to 1961 the company entered seven competitions, winning five of them. There was no more activity until 1967, when two were entered and lost.

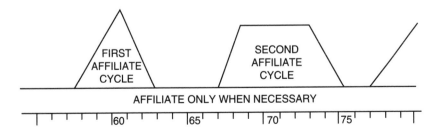

Strategy Diagram 9J Affiliation strategies

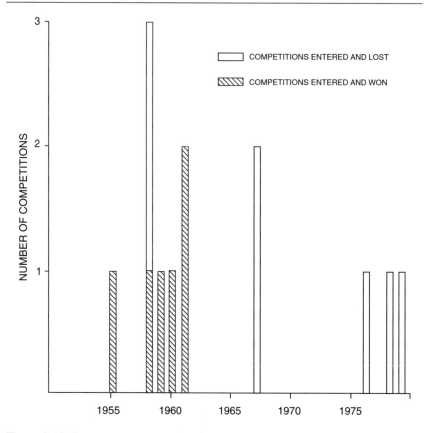

Figure 9.12 Competitions entered and won

Finally in each year 1976, 1978, and 1979 the firm entered and lost a competition.

As for promotions and speculative work, while Arcop never engaged heavily in such activities, its efforts varied significantly. Various marketing strategies, largely based on interview data, are depicted in Strategy Diagram 9K.

STRUCTURE

Archival documents reveal some clear tendencies with regard to the formal internal structure of Arcop. In brief, one tendency was always strong—a project orientation with a good deal of decentralization to individual experts on each job. Staff at all levels generally worked on more

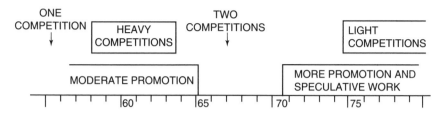

Strategy Diagram 9K Marketing strategies

than one job at a time. Moreover, there were always strong pressures to keep the structure loose and fluid.

But for a time these tendencies were challenged by various efforts to structure the organization more formally. There was an increasing emphasis on grouping staff by function (design, drafting, graphics, specifications, field supervision, and interior design) beginning in 1961, peaking around 1966, and largely phased out by 1970. In parallel to this, an administrative hierarchy was built up between 1962 and 1965. Technical managers, business managers, and a construction manager were appointed. Most significantly, a position of executive director was created in 1965, with the broadest range of management functions. All these positions were systematically eliminated between 1967 and 1970. Finally, formal committees were established in 1964 consisting of partners, associates, and administrators. They dealt with issues of general administration as well as with specific areas of salaries, finances, and procedures. These had also declined by 1970. The strategies pertaining to organizational structure are depicted in Strategy Diagram 9L.

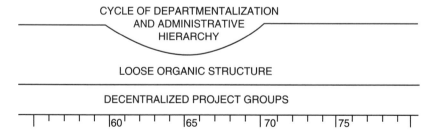

Strategy Diagram 9L Organization strategies

Performance of Arcop

Arcop's performance results are discussed in three categories: billings, net profits, and prizes and awards.

BILLINGS

Figure 9.1 showed the actual annual billings to clients in the year in which they were invoiced. Billings grew sharply from 1958 to 1966, and then declined just as sharply between 1967 and 1970. They rose again less sharply from 1971 to 1975, and then declined sharply in 1976 and 1977.

NET PROFITS

Figure 9.13 presents actual net profits, and Figure 9.14 presents net profit as a percentage of annual billings. (Profits were reported before payments to partners or bonuses to employees.)

The profit curve inexactly mirrors the billing curve, in part because high quality standards often overrode cost controls, with the partners occasionally redoing complete stages of work at the expense of profits. Nevertheless, given the wide fluctuations in billings, profits were rather steady, generally in the 10 to 25 percent range, with the exception of 1958, 1959, 1960, and 1973, when they were unusually high and 1977, the only year in which there was a loss.

PRIZES AND AWARDS

Besides billings and profits, another measure of an architectural firm's performance is the extent to which its buildings receive recognition and commendation from the profession.

Prizes

Competitions invite design submissions for intended buildings, the successful firm usually being awarded the contract for the job. Arcop entered eight competitions during the period 1955–61 (see Marketing) and won six of them. The resulting jobs brought in a total of close to $1 million in billings. The firm subsequently entered two competitions in 1967 and three more during 1976–9, all without success.

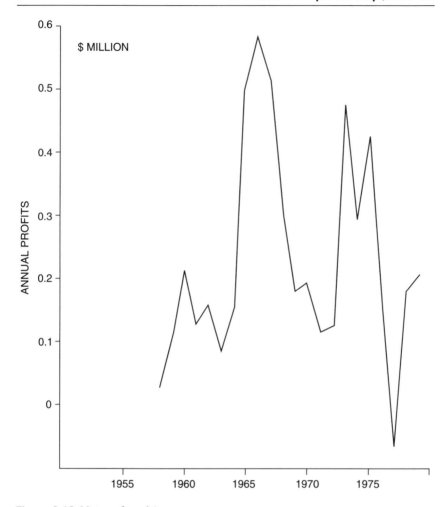

Figure 9.13 Net profits of Arcop

Awards

A different kind of competition involves awards for completed work. Arcop received awards for seven buildings that were completed between 1955 and 1972. In addition, eight of the firm's works reached award semifinals between 1960 and 1966. Arcop won only a single award after 1972, for an overseas job completed in 1977. However, there had been a general reduction in the number of awards given in Canada, particularly since 1975.

Figure 9.14 Net profits as percentage of billings

Arcop's Industry

This section provides some background description of the Canadian architectural industry. Data are drawn primarily from *Canadian Architects' Services* (Barnard Associates 1979) and from publications of Statistics Canada. Where appropriate, comparison is drawn to Arcop activities.

INDUSTRY BILLINGS

Figure 9.15 presents industry billings since 1961. The curve indicates rapid growth throughout, except for moderate decline in the 1970–2 period and slower growth after 1976. It is significant that Arcop's

254

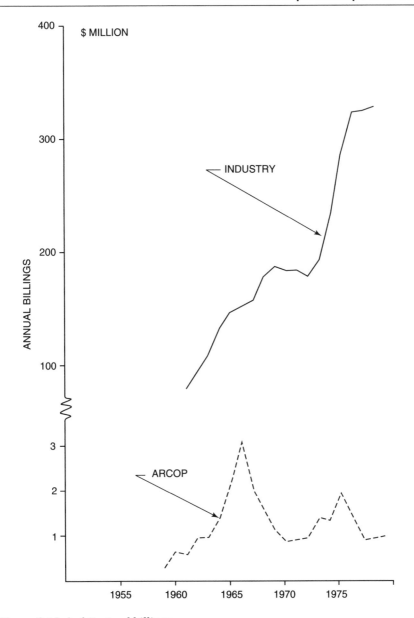

Figure 9.15 Architectural billings

decline in revenues between 1967 and 1970 and during 1976 to 1978 occurred in periods of strong industry growth. The firm's volume also increased slightly in 1971–2, while there was a decline in industry billings.

NUMBER AND SIZE OF FIRMS

The number of Canadian architectural firms increased steadily from the late 1950s and doubled after the late 1960s. In general, architectural firms decreased in size after the late 1960s. By 1977, 88 percent of all firms billed less than $500,000 annually, with half billing less than $100,000. These latter firms usually employed fewer than three people.

TYPES OF JOBS

Since the late 1960s, many firms undertook study and planning work, although design and construction work continued to represent the major activity.

Residential

This work increased steadily, except for a 1967–73 downturn. This work accounted for 13 percent of industry billings in 1961, 20 percent in 1968, and 22 percent in 1977. Arcop was somewhat underrepresented in this category.

Commercial

This work increased consistently, with sharp growth during 1960–6 and 1969–76. Mixed-use and office-building activity turned down between 1966 and 1973, while retail buildings, including hotels, increased. This category of work accounted for 18 percent of industry billings in 1961 and 24 percent in 1976. Arcop was strongly overrepresented here.

Leisure

This work showed consistent slow growth, with more pronounced increases during 1965–7 and 1973–8. Work in this category tended to depend on a few large projects, such as those resulting from Expo 67 and the 1976 Olympics, both in Montreal. This work generally averaged around 5 percent of industry billings, making Arcop strongly overrepresented in this category.

Industrial

This work was less important, although it did account for as much as 10 percent in occasional years. Arcop was perhaps somewhat underrepresented in this category.

256

Institutional

This work showed a rapid increase between 1960 and 1968 and declined consistently after 1968. It was dominated by educational and medical buildings. This work accounted for 48 percent of industry billings in 1961, 51 percent in 1967, and only 24 percent in 1977. Arcop was consistent with industry averages in the late 1960s but underrepresented during the mid and late 1970s .

Governmental

This work was relatively consistent with the strongest growth during 1960–7 and 1973–8 and accounted for 5 percent of industry billings in 1961, 6 percent in 1968, and 10 percent in 1977. On average, Arcop was somewhat overrepresented. Since the late 1960s, the private sector gained in importance in comparison with the public sector. In 1961, 53 percent of industry billings were derived from work from the public sector (largely consisting of governmental leisure and institutional work); in 1977, this figure had declined to 41 percent. Medium-sized firms with annual billings between $250,000 and $500,000 tended to rely more heavily on the public sector. Arcop generally had a greater than average involvement with private-sector clients.

WORK LOCATION

(1) Quebec: This province exhibited strong growth during 1960–5 and 1971–6, accounting for close to 25 percent of industry billings in 1961, 1968, and 1977. As would be expected, Arcop was very strongly overrepresented in Quebec.

(2) Ontario: Work grew from 1960 to 1966 and from 1971 to 1975, accounting for 48 percent of industry billings in 1961, 45 percent in 1968, and 35 percent in 1977. Arcop was erratically involved in Ontario but on average was underrepresented.

(3) Eastern Canada: This area exhibited growth during 1960–6, 1968–70, and 1973–6, accounting for around 5 percent of industry billings in 1961, 1968, and 1977. Arcop participated heavily in each of the growth spurts noted and was generally strongly overrepresented in Eastern Canada.

(4) Western Canada: This region generally exhibited strong growth, particularly in British Columbia between 1958 and 1974 and Alberta during 1960–6 and 1973–8. It accounted for 26 percent of industry

billings in 1961, 28 percent in 1968, and 36 percent in 1977. Arcop was severely underrepresented here.

(5) US and Overseas: In 1977, only 2 percent of industry billings came from outside Canada, and of these, only 9 percent from the US. Most foreign work was being done in the Middle East, Africa, and the Caribbean. Indeed, through 1977, only 8 percent of the Canadian firms had done any work outside Canada. After 1969, Arcop was thus relatively strongly overrepresented in foreign markets.

Periods in the History of Arcop

The next step in the research process was to scan all the above strategy diagrams together to identify major turning points and distinct periods in the history of Arcop. Certain strategies, particularly those related to types and locations of jobs, tended to be of short duration, changing almost continuously. Others, for example, related to size of jobs, partnership, and staffing levels, did suggest larger-term cycles and more permanent changes, particularly around the years 1958, 1967, and 1970. Those were used to infer four periods in the history of Arcop, labeled as follows: 1953–8: Getting Started; 1958–67: Growth and Coping with Growth; 1967–70: Disruption and Decline; 1970–8: Starting Again. Each of these periods is described below.

1953–8: GETTING STARTED—A PERIOD OF ORGANIZING

The origins of Arcop can be traced to 1953, when Ray Affleck, Guy Desbarats, and Jean Michaud pooled their resources to start their own independent architectural practice in a basement office (joined shortly after by Hasen Size). All but Jean had met while teaching architecture on a part-time basis at McGill University.

In these early years, they each obtained and conducted their own work, most of which was in the form of small residential or commercial jobs. Their collaborative effort began when Jean and Ray worked together on the Town of Mount Royal Post Office, and Hasen and Guy worked on the Beaver Lake Pavilion (in a Montreal park).

This work also reflected a shared commitment to innovation and excellence as these were generally regarded as the first modern buildings in Montreal. The Town of Mount Royal Post Office became the first public building to receive a Canadian national award for architecture.

The development of Arcop was encouraged by the many architectural competitions being organized all across the country to support the development of domestic talent. In late 1954 the group joined forces with Fred Lebensold, also from McGill, and one of Fred's students, Dimitri Dimakopoulos, to prepare a submission for a performing arts center in Vancouver. They won it, and the group, now with six architects, had its first large job: the Queen Elizabeth Theater.

The award necessitated a firm partnership agreement. As Fred noted, 'We suddenly realized ... that it wasn't just a competition ... it was a real job. ... We had never done a job of that size before ... never.' It had to be shared among all the partners. It also marked the first work on performing arts buildings, which was to continue on and off for almost twenty years, even though, as Ray described it, 'We did the Vancouver competition not because we were particularly interested in performing arts centers. ... It was just the nature of the competition.'

The partners, however, continued to work more or less on their own, on other small residential and commercial jobs, occasionally splitting work on a job. In 1956, they moved into a two-storey house in Montreal and hired several architects and draftsmen, primarily to assist with the work of the theater. The total staff reached fifteen people by early 1958. An office manager was hired to oversee nontechnical office functions, including billing and record maintenance.

Around this time, the emerging organization was further crystallized as a result of a visit from I.M. Pei and Associates, a large US firm in need of a local group to supervise production of a major commercial complex planned for Montreal. Ray noted 'They were very New York, offices right on Madison Avenue ... asked to see our brochures, c.v.'s ... we did not have any, of course, so we had to put something together.'

Dimitri recalled a key meeting:

They came up to see us in our building. ... We had quickly fixed the office up, put pictures on the walls, we all tried to look proper. ... While we were sitting around the conference table, I.M. Pei leaned back and one of the pictures we had stuck on the wall fell off and landed on his head. ... There was a grim silence for a moment or two, then we all burst out laughing spontaneously. ... It seemed to clinch the job.

Arcop was selected to work with I.M. Pei on the Place Ville Marie complex, which was the first skyscraper in Canada and involved extensive aboveground and underground levels, mostly oriented to commercial and retail activities. Arcop managed the later stages of work, leading to construction, and provided only limited input to the design.

As the Place Ville Marie job developed, the partners decided to expand their partnership to cover all their jobs. They adopted the name 'Arcop', standing for 'architects in copartnership', which emphasized the values of equality and collaboration. The laws governing professional practice, however, required use of the names of the partners, so these were placed in alphabetical order to denote lack of hierarchy.

Despite the egalitarian intentions, the partners discovered that, with so many partners, someone had to take formal charge of the execution of each project, whether or not the work was shared. They also found that clients preferred dealing with a single partner as the primary contact. Hence there was an understanding that one partner would take charge of each job, and this was usually worked out between them on an informal basis.

The group was also learning to work in affiliation with other architectural firms. As a mirror image of its work in Montreal with I.M. Pei, Arcop associated with a firm in Vancouver to supervise the construction work on the Queen Elizabeth Theater.

In summary, the 1953–8 period saw the six partners being drawn into a closer and closer relationship. They banded together informally to enter a competition, and winning it forced them to band together formally. They scrambled to create the appearance of a more-tightly knit group to get the Place Ville Marie job, and getting it knitted them more tightly together in all their work. By 1958, from a group of individuals largely doing their own work, the group had coalesced into a full-fledged partnership with feelings about a strong architectural mission.

1958–67: GROWTH AND COPING WITH GROWTH—A PERIOD OF EXPANSION AND GROWING TENSION

With the partnership firmly established, Arcop experienced a period of dramatic growth and professional achievement. From 1958 to 1961, the firm entered seven competitions and won five of them. The quality of their winning designs was felt to reflect the intense collaboration among the partners. In addition, to solicit other new business, the group engaged in moderate promotion and speculative work through the early part of this period.

In 1958, they moved to a large office in downtown Montreal, and soon after some of the partners began working on the design of an office building to house Arcop's own practice. The overall staff grew from fifteen in 1958 to forty-three at the beginning of 1961, largely as a response to the construction work on Place Ville Marie. The firm was hiring bright young architects and giving them major responsibilities on various jobs. It had also appointed two associates by 1961. With the addition of another performing arts center, Place des Arts in Montreal, the work centered largely in Quebec, at least early in the period (93 percent by 1961).

Most of the collaboration among the partners occurred in the early stages of conceptual design work. Once work got under way, collaboration was usually limited to meetings to review the progress on different jobs. Individual partners generally controlled their own jobs, working closely with their clients.

The partners were also learning to manage bigger jobs. Staff was organized into teams headed by job captains, who were responsible for different sections. Later, project managers were appointed to assume overall charge of jobs, working under a partner. With the increased workload, tensions arose around the participation of one of the partners, who was perceived by some of his colleagues as less involved in the architectural work. He left the partnership in 1960.

The rapid growth also required increased attention to the management of the overall practice. Guy Desbarats tended to assume responsibility for most of the administrative work, assisted by Susan Ellis, the office manager. The partners discovered that they differed fundamentally in their emphasis on formal organization and structure. In particular, Ray preferred a loose structure that would not restrict his work, while Guy favored a clearer and tighter one. Ray commented, 'In the early days, it was a healthy difference.' But it remained an ongoing tension, alongside the selection of partner in-charge on desirable projects. In this and other cases, conflicts were generally sorted out informally among the partners, but underlying stresses remained in the group.

In 1961, Arcop hired a firm of management consultants to consider some of these issues. The consultants concluded that the partners had to decide between design achievement and profitability, since most jobs, excepting Place Ville Marie, were not generating sufficient profits. The partners were also urged to reach a consensus on their preferred size for the firm, on the services to be offered, and on the types of work to be pursued (i.e. to formulate intended strategies). It was also suggested that a senior management person be hired to handle business affairs, and that other roles be established to schedule and plan the work.

Around the same time, the volume grew and became more diverse. With work winding down on Place Ville Marie and Place des Arts in Montreal, new work included another performing arts center and a set of provincial government buildings, both in Prince Edward Island, in Eastern Canada (where work rose close to 25 percent in 1963 and 1964). Other jobs continued in or around Montreal on the Laval Civic Center and on a few educational buildings, mostly for McGill University.

With continued growth, certain suggestions made by the management consultants were gradually implemented. Expertise was built up in the areas of design, drafting, graphics, specifications, field supervision, and interior design. In something of a matrix-management approach, individuals from these functions worked closely with each other on job teams, coordinated by a project manager. Ray described one clear example of the resulting departmentalization: 'We got some young ladies...they had a little corner.... They were not architects; they were specialists in furnishings, colors.... We formed them into a little department.' Other changes included the appointment of a production manager, with responsibility for scheduling and supervising the staff on various jobs, and the hiring of business managers to manage finances. Finally, a construction manager was appointed to assist the technical and field supervision staff with the construction phase of the jobs.

In 1963, the firm—with fifty-two staff members at this point—moved into the office building that some partners had begun to design in 1958. This put the firm into the realty business in a small way, in order to rent the excess space. A modified profit-sharing plan was also introduced for the associates and the senior staff in 1963.

As the mid-1960s approached, the firm was about to experience its greatest spurt of growth, the result of the simultaneous occurrence of several very large jobs. Work on Expo 67, the world fair held in Montreal in conjunction with Canada's centennial of 1967, involved a group of exhibition buildings. The performing arts center stream continued with the National Arts Center in Ottawa and the Arts and Culture Center in St. John's, Newfoundland. Commercial work continued with Place Bonaventure, a combination exhibition hall, office building, shopping concourse, and hotel. Although Ray took this job somewhat reluctantly, it eventually had a major impact on his and Arcop's reputation. Another commercial job consisted of subsequent additions to the ongoing Place Ville Marie complex. As such, the work of the firm began to return to Quebec, which together with Ottawa accounted for over 85 percent of volume by 1966.

As might be expected, Arcop also experienced its most dramatic growth of staff, which increased from 52 in 1963 to a peak of 146 in early 1966. The number of associates also grew, from two in 1963 to six in 1965.

Staff were added to fill in the various functional areas until the end of this period. The interior design department, in particular, began to lobby for a more independent practice. Its members wanted to take steps, including a possible change of location, to solicit independent work. The partners rejected the idea, however, because most viewed the department's role as serving the architectural function.

Administrative demands paralleled the growth in work, with the result that a number of senior office positions, including one to handle public relations, were created. Nevertheless, there was a growing concern among the various administrative managers that the firm was making insufficient profits and even losing money on the big jobs. Ray commented that 'there was a feeling that we were inefficient . . . we should be making more money . . . everything should be going like clockwork.'

Another management consultant was hired in 1964, and this one recommended more standardized accounting techniques and more systematic performance control reports. The partners subsequently asked the other senior staff, mostly associates, to form a management committee to deal with the administration of the firm. This committee was headed by Roger Marshall who, in 1965, was appointed executive director and given extensive powers to manage the daily operations. Under Roger's direction, committees were established to deal with specific management challenges—for example, to create job descriptions and clarify responsibilities, to review job contracts and administer budgets, and to review salaries and recommend employment or dismissal of staff.

Further, two separate subsidiaries were registered in 1966, largely as a result of Guy's initiatives, each employing a different section of the staff to control the operations of the practice, minimize taxes, and give more control to the senior staff, who were appointed directors and executives. These subsidiaries billed the partnership for services rendered.

All these efforts at formalization and control, however, received little support from the other partners, who insisted on being consulted on almost all decisions and would tolerate no changes that infringed on personal control of their jobs, regardless of cost or profit considerations.

While all this was going on, the partners were working increasingly on their own jobs, even during the initial design phase where collaboration had been so productive in the early years. An early indication of breakdown in the collaborative ethic occurred in 1963 when a plaque appeared at the completed Place des Arts building specifically mentioning one partner as the architect. This ran contrary to the agreement that the firm as a whole would be credited with all work. Although the plaque was subsequently removed, the incident was a harbinger of conflicts to come. These showed up particularly in the distribution of the larger jobs. Guy had developed criteria for the appointment of partners-in-charge on new jobs, emphasizing rotation among them, depending on their current workloads, but this did not prevent them from lobbying for prestigious jobs in a manner that undermined the cooperative spirit of the firm.

The declining collaboration among the partners brought increasing polarization among the rest of the staff, as each partner began working more exclusively with certain individuals. In one instance, according to one interviewee, a job was lost because one partner would not release a particular staff member requested by a potential client.

The continuing rapid growth put the unresolved conflicts into sharp perspective. Guy noted of the period, 'the more successful we were, the more tensions we created.' The core conflict revolved around the growth and formalization of the firm. Again, the different orientations were represented particularly by Guy, who pushed for a larger and more tightly organized firm, and Ray, who preferred a smaller and looser practice that would not curb his freedom. The breakdown in collaboration became a breakdown in communication. Dimitri remarked that, 'Guy and Ray found themselves in boxes...with no windows or doors open.'

Eventually, in 1966, the partnership began to disintegrate visibly, although not without some last-ditch efforts to maintain it. The partners attempted to recreate the earlier atmosphere through weekend retreats away from the office, but these were unsuccessful. Reflecting on the period, Guy commented, 'Our spirit had lost its dynamism...because of the individual thrust.' Dimitri recalled, 'There was a feeling of a lost touch.'

In summary, the innovative design work that resulted from the collaboration of the partners produced great success for the firm over the period. But the success eventually drove the partners away from the very collaboration that produced it. This drift eventually forced a choice about the type of organization that could best carry out the basic mission. Fundamentally different views about this choice necessitated the breakup of the partnership.

1967–70: DISRUPTION AND DECLINE—A PERIOD
OF SCALING DOWN

The cracks in the partnership, which became visible in late 1966, continued to widen over this next period, until the partnership was essentially reconstituted in 1970. Though billings in the industry continued to grow through 1969, Arcop's own volume declined rapidly starting in late 1966, as work on Place Bonaventure and the Expo buildings wound down. The major jobs during this period consisted of ongoing work on the National Arts Center in Ottawa and new work on school buildings in suburban Montreal and on a large complex at Dalhousie University in Halifax. The period also witnessed the emergence of study and planning work as a significant complement to the main design and construction work of the firm. A major one of these, La Cité Development, was eventually to introduce new conflict to the firm and, in some sense, to become the final blow to the original partnership. In terms of location, the early part of the period was dominated by Quebec and Ontario, the latter by Eastern Canada.

In spite of this work, combined volume fell far short of that achieved in 1966, and staff numbers fell precipitously, from 136 in 1966 to 61 in 1967 and 30 in 1970. The office was moved in late 1966 from the Arcop-owned building to a downtown location. The vacated building was sold soon after, resulting in the elimination of realty operations by 1967.

Following the overt conflict of 1966, the partnership shrank to three active partners. Guy, who earlier had accepted a half-time teaching position at the University of Montreal, chose to increase his load there in 1967 and reduce his involvement with Arcop. Hasen Size ceased to be a partner in 1967, although he continued to receive some benefits from the practice as part of his settlement.

The emphasis on different services declined sharply during this period as well as several areas other than design and drafting were scaled down or eliminated. By 1968, only one interior designer remained in the practice. There was also a sharp reduction in office staff, while those people who remained assumed multiple roles—for example, the interior designer also handled public relations.

The move away from functional specialization was a result partly of declining work volume and partly of Guy's diminished involvement in the firm. He had strongly backed specialized departments, but the other partners, in particular Ray, felt that work should be solicited for the overall job and not for individual departments. Ray explained: 'Our experience has been that the types of work we get has always been very erratic. Sometimes we get something to do requiring specifications or interiors, sometimes we don't.'

Six of the eight associates left during this period, starting with the departure of Roger Marshall in late 1967. Four new ones were appointed, but one of these had also left the firm by 1970.

They left for many reasons. One was the reluctance of the partners to involve them in the management of the firm. Throughout this period, the different management committees were gradually eliminated, and the two subsidiaries were wound down. In essence, the management structure set up in the previous period was dismantled in this one. Commenting on Roger Marshall's departure, Ray noted: 'It was a terrible disfavor we did to him. . . . In my view, the position never worked at all. . . . I found he was trying to coordinate the uncoordinatable.' In contrast, Guy lamented that Roger's departure 'was really the disintegration of any possibility of setting up a managed firm'.

The associates also left because of the general decline in work volume. Arcop had concentrated on large jobs, 'monuments', often in the public sector and particularly performing arts centers. In the face of the decline of this type of work, the firm found that it did not have a base of private work, particularly in small commercial, industrial, and residential jobs. Guy explained this gap in the following way: 'They were all cut fee jobs. We did not take cut fee jobs. We were very proud. We were very moral in our approaches. It did not bring us more work.'

Finally, associates left in part because of the slim prospects of eventually becoming full partners. The existing partners were reluctant to involve the associates in the design stage of their work (just as they excluded each other). They were also unwilling to consider bringing other design-oriented architects into the partnership, given the tensions they had experienced among themselves.

Meanwhile, the individualistic thrust had developed to the point that the prospect of competitions did not bring about the earlier collaboration. The firm entered two competitions in 1967, the first ones since 1961. However, the three active partners did not get involved, and most of the work was handled by two of the associates. The firm did not win, in Guy's opinion, 'because we did not have our hearts in it'.

The divisions between two of the remaining three partners were eventually widened beyond repair as a result of La Cité, a major study and planning project for an urban apartment complex. Ray recalled his involvement and subsequent withdrawal from the project as follows:

It started as an interesting job...the notion of a great big development in an existing urban fabric. It involved a fair amount of demolition and of pushing people out....That kind of thing I don't think any developer would even try to do today....I attempted for quite a while to involve the citizens in the decision-making...it ended up in quite a clash of values that I found myself very much caught in....I resigned that commission because I was pretty divided in my loyalties, and I couldn't perform, in my opinion, with integrity and commitment, particularly with respect to the client.

Dimitri disagreed strongly with Ray, and recalled his feelings at the time: 'I felt it was our duty to examine the situation properly....I think Ray abandoned the job without examining all the possibilities...it was easier pulling out....' Given this sense of commitment to client and community, Dimitri took over the job as Ray withdrew.

The conflict over the La Cité job was so deep that the only partnership questions that remained were whether Ray or Dimitri would leave, and with whom Fred would align. Dimitri left Arcop to start out on his own, taking with him the La Cité job as well as several staff members who usually worked with him. At around the same time, Guy completed his withdrawal. Ray and Fred decided to continue the Arcop practice.

In summary, the period witnessed a decline in work volume at a rate equivalent to that of growth in the previous period. At the same time, the period also witnessed the disintegration of the original partnership and the dismantling of the organization structure built up in the previous period.

What precipitated the drastic scaling down of operations? Three explanations are possible: that the available work fell off, that the conflicts preoccupied the partners and so deflected the firm from pursuing its basic mission, and that deliberate choices were made to scale down the operations.

Although Canadian billings continued to grow, there was a decline of activity in Quebec; perhaps Arcop was not able to respond quickly enough to find work in other locations. And conflict between individualistic partners who jealously guarded their spheres of influence was certainly a factor. The strongest element, however, seems to have been differences over the type of organization that each of the partners wanted. In other words, we believe that at the root of the conflict was not so much interpersonal relations per se as fundamental differences about Arcop's size, and the threat or opportunity that these posed to what the various partners wished to do. Fred spoke later about the nature of this conflict. 'Once we get institutionalized, organized, categorized, that's when we are dead.... The most important considerations for us were the preservation of our spirit... and the preservation of our quality.'

In other words, despite the elements of decline and breakdown in this period, there was a quality of deliberateness to it as well. The predominant partners, particularly Ray, favored a smaller, looser organization. The shrinkage of the firm was evidently well managed, if the rather stable level of profitability throughout this period (16–26 percent) is any indication. In any event, the firm went through a difficult time between 1966 and 1970 and, at the end of this period, might be characterized as 'sadder but wiser'.

1970–8: STARTING AGAIN—A PERIOD OF MODERATE RENEWAL

In the 1967–70 period, much of the attention and energy of the principal actors was directed inward, at the nature of their relationships, the necessity for administration, and the values to be pursued in their work. The subsequent shift of attention outward, to the realities of operating in an increasingly competitive architectural world, marked the start of the next and final period of the study. The label 'starting again' is used to draw attention to the interruption of what might be called 'soul searching' in favor of 'business searching'. While total billings in the industry grew rapidly again, the number of firms pursuing that volume doubled. Arcop's business swung moderately up and then down during this final period, but the cycle was not accompanied by the marked strategic changes that characterized the previous cycle.

Ray and Fred decided to continue working together after the decision was made to terminate the earlier partnership agreement; they became successors to the Arcop practice. Two of the four associates remaining with the firm, Art Nichol and Ramesh Khosla, were made partners. Art had been the first associate appointed in the firm in 1958, while Ramesh had joined the practice in 1966 and only recently appointed an associate.

Work in the US dominated the early part of this period, reflecting in some part the decline of work in Canada. One of the significant jobs involved the lower levels of the World Trade Center in New York City. This came to the firm on the basis of the reputation it had earned with the recently completed Place Bonaventure. Another major job was the Onondaga County Civic Center in Syracuse, which, although partly governmental, resulted from the firm's history of success with performing arts centers. Work on it was carried out in joint venture with some young architects in Syracuse. In addition, there were some smaller jobs spun off from the work on the World Trade Center in New York, and scaling down of work on the building for Dalhousie University in Halifax. The US work accounted for around 70 percent of the total volume during the early part of this period, in 1971 and 1972.

Study and planning work continued at previous levels of about 25 percent of total volume, but the emphasis shifted to urban development as opposed to single sites. The most significant jobs came, after 1972, in the development of the waterfront in Halifax and the harborfront in Toronto.

Meanwhile, staff levels grew moderately, from thirty people in 1970 to forty-three by early 1973. The number of associates had dropped to two by 1972. The office remained in the same location over the period.

During its renewed growth, the firm moved clearly away from departmentalization of the staff. With the departure in 1971 of the last interior designer, no specialized departments remained. Most of the remaining staff were general-purpose designers and draftsmen. Even when, in 1971, three urban designers were hired in response to the volume in urban planning work, they retained a strong job orientation, working with architects on project teams. Similarly, after the departure of the last manager in 1971, the partners avoided the creation of formal managerial positions, other than those connected with particular jobs (such as project manager). Ray explained the shift: 'Managers tend to be too administratively oriented. They are not close enough to the work.'

At the beginning of the period, there were clearly fewer tensions in the partnership than in the previous period. In addition to the shift to a task orientation, a hierarchy had emerged in the partnership structure. Ray and Fred were viewed as the senior partners, while Art and Ramesh were, in a sense, feeling their way into the partner role. The decline in the ideology of equality was further indicated by Fred's negotiation of first listing of his name in the partnership. The partners also tried to stay clear of organizational issues, which had created such conflicts in earlier years. Within the generally looser management structure, Art Nichols, who had been substantially involved in administrative work even as an associate, assumed many of the management responsibilities. His more junior partnership role helped to ensure that administrative work would not become a major preoccupation of the partnership.

As part of the effort to acquire new business, office operations were established in Toronto. In 1971, an associate was appointed in Toronto, but the arrangement was minimally successful, and terminated in 1973 when Paul Hughes was taken in as a partner to oversee a full-fledged office there which ran relatively independently. Some jobs, however, such as work on the Toronto Harborfront and on the Halifax Waterfront, were shared, creating closer ties between the two offices.

By 1973, several important jobs were developing. These included work on Winnipeg Square and on a proposed Centrum Center in Los Angeles, both resulting from the Place Bonaventure job. Another important job was started on a Holiday Inn in Montreal, stemming in part from the work on the hotel in Place Bonaventure. The firm was also contracted to do renovation work on the Museum of Fine Arts in Montreal. Finally, the office in Toronto contracted significant residential work on an apartment complex in Kitchener, Ontario.

The location of jobs shifted back primarily to Quebec and Ontario, which together accounted for almost 70 percent of work by 1975, reflecting renewed growth in the industry in Canada. The overall focus of the work also began to shift away from the public sector toward the private sector, as public investment began to dry up.

The staff grew, from forty-three people in early 1973 to sixty-eight by late 1975, distributed between the two offices. Similarly, the number of associates in both locations grew, to eleven by 1975. There was an intention again to involve the senior associates in the management of the firm, initiated by Art and Paul. At the end of 1975, another corporate organization was briefly created with involvement of the associates. But these moves did not arouse much interest from the associates, and were never fully implemented.

The partnership, as a whole, had begun to engage more heavily in promotion and speculative work since the reorganization in 1970. This became especially pronounced as the work began to drop off again. In particular, both Paul and Ramesh, the youngest partners were aggressively seeking new work. By the mid-1970s the firm was even seeking work in overseas locations; as Paul explained the moves: 'to go where the action was.'

As a result of these efforts, some new jobs did come into the firm, the largest of these for a complex, Les Terrasses de la Chaudière, in Hull, Quebec. This work was partly commercial, partly governmental. There was substantial work in hotels in some overseas locations, most prominently in the Seychelles Islands. The office in Toronto began work on a large shopping center in Nigeria. The job locations became more dispersed, with substantial volume (almost 16 percent) coming from overseas. Quebec still accounted for at least 40 percent of work volume, but jobs in Ontario declined significantly.

Echoing the events of the mid-1960s, staff levels declined from sixty-eight people in 1975 to nineteen in 1978. The number of associates concurrently declined from eleven to seven. By the end of the period, there was evidence of growing strains in the relations among the partners, and a strong rivalry began to develop between the two senior partners. At first, as a result, Ray and Fred would share work with Art and Ramesh but not with each other. But Art and Ramesh also had difficulties getting along with each other, and the partnership began to polarize. While Art managed to keep himself clear of the growing conflict between Ray and Fred, Ramesh gradually aligned himself more strongly and openly with Ray.

The new conflict came to a head when Arcop, together with another Montreal architectural firm, entered a federally sponsored competition. Art described the events as follows:

It was a great opportunity. There was a great desire for everyone to get involved. However, there were sharp differences in the approaches of Fred and Ray to the job. Things went from bad to worse. Each partner pulled in their favorite staff. It ended up as a competition in the office. Ray's design finally won out, but there was great bitterness created in the process.

The resulting entry lost in the competition. The lingering bitterness in the office was accentuated by a continuing decline in work (and probably vice versa), this time in parallel with a decline in the industry. Therefore, we can more clearly explain this second major drop in work volume by market forces coupled with some interpersonal strife.

Meanwhile Fred began to feel increasingly concerned about the extent of his influence on the nature and direction of the practice. He was also growing concerned about his prospects for attracting work in Quebec, in view of political and economic developments there. His attention turned to Toronto, and he moved there in 1978. Ray Affleck became the only member of the original partnership to remain in Montreal.

Interpreting the Study of Arcop in Conceptual Terms

At this point we wish to move the analysis up to a conceptual level, both to better understand what occurred at Arcop across the decades of the study and to draw some broader conclusions about the process of strategy formation. We begin with a discussion on the cycles of strategic change and conclude that short-term opportunistic cycles, emergent in nature, were nested within a deliberate 'strategic umbrella' which dictated the longer-term periods. Then we shall look at the interplay of the forces of

271

leadership and organization, characterizing Arcop as a 'reluctant organization' that strived to maintain its craft-oriented beliefs in the face of the 'imperatives of administration.'

STRATEGIC CHOICE

The most compelling issues in this study revolved around questions of strategic choice: What did an organization like Arcop really decide about? What aspects of its realized strategy did Arcop control and how?

The distinctions between internal choice, external influence, and result were less than crystal clear in this study. For example, was a new job in Arcop the result of strategic choice (to seek the job in the first place, or at least to accept it), environmental influence (selection by the client), or performance (a sale)? In fact, one can imagine a range of answers, depending on the behavior of the firm. As we struggled with this issue, it became increasingly evident that some important conceptual matters were at stake in its resolution.

Two points quickly became clear. The first was that realized strategy had to be considered as a pattern in a stream of actions, not necessarily decisions (as in our original definition). While architectural jobs certainly gave rise to actions within the organization, it is not clear that they involved specific decisions. (In fact, we came to realize that decision, like the conventional definition of strategy, is rooted in intention; hence, we changed our definition [see Mintzberg and Waters 1990].) The second point, which follows from the first, was that strategies, as consistencies of action, could be determined externally—in other words, the environment could impose a strategy on the organization. Specifically, Arcop's job strategies could have been dictated by the choices made by its clients.

These points opened up our conception of strategy, but they really begged the basic question of strategic choice, which required an analysis to determine which aspects of its activities Arcop really did control, and which it ceded to its environment, and why. That analysis suggested that in some strategy areas, Arcop was highly opportunistic, while in others it was more determined to establish direction for itself. These combined in a subtle, and in somewhat effective way, guided by what we call a 'strategic umbrella', to be described later.

Opportunistic Choices

What stands out strongly about job location and job type strategies in Arcop is the virtual absence of any sustained focus. With the possible exception of Quebec from 1958 to 1967, all the location clusters evident in the charts are clearly of brief duration—short cycles, or just temporary 'blips'. One gets the impression of geographical areas coming and going, almost at random, with no deliberate strategy of geographic location. The firm reacted to the environment opportunistically. (Recall Brian King's definition of emergent strategy cited earlier, when preparation meets opportunism.) Ironically, the one clearly intended geographic strategy— to disperse the work of the firm—had only one specific manifestation—of the establishment of an office in Toronto. But even this limited intended strategy was largely unrealized, since that office closed two years later. Otherwise, Arcop took the work it wanted from wherever it came, so long as it was convenient.

An analysis of Arcop's types of work, probably more important than location, leads to a similar conclusion. Arcop did not seem to favor commercial or leisure or institutional or governmental or residential jobs per se; rather it seemed to cycle almost randomly among all of these. In other words, it sustained focus in no specific markets; it provided its services across a range of them with no apparent consistency. True, the partners did have personal preferences—Ray for mixed-use buildings, Fred for theaters, and so on—so that some personal intentions were present. But these were not organizational, in the sense of being shared by all the partners. Nor were they favored exclusively even by the partners in question, all of whom liked variety in their work. Hence, these intentions were not realized with any consistency.

Thus, Arcop did not pursue specific strategies so much as jobs, from wherever and whomever it could get them. That the jobs happened at times to cluster temporarily may have enabled us to identify broader realized strategies, but that does not necessarily imply intentions on the part of the organization.

Deliberate Strategic Umbrella

In a broader sense however, Arcop sustained focus in design work, which was what the partners liked to do. And, what drove that design work most of the time was the desire to design buildings that were unique, excellent, and visible. Words like exciting, prestigious, unconventional, landmarks, and jewels capture the nature of the buildings Arcop people liked to work on. One competitor described Arcop people as interested in 'opportunities for design'; another expression used by Arcop people themselves was buildings that 'celebrated the spirit of a community', whether a massive commercial complex or a small golf club. In an early promotion brochure, the partners expressed the objective of the firm to 'above all develop the utmost social and artistic values that represent the highest contribution of architecture to our civilization'. These lofty intentions were in good part realized by the work they produced.

Contingent on such work was control of the front-end conceptual design. Only once did the firm surrender such control, when it worked with I.M. Pei Associates on Place Ville Marie. But that experience, rather than breaking the pattern, established it: 'Never again' said the partners of Arcop. These essential characteristics constituted the basic umbrella under which the specific location and job type strategies of Arcop emerged. By 'strategic umbrella' we mean a deliberate set of guidelines within which more specific strategies are allowed to emerge.

Thus Arcop was an organization driven less by specific intentions than by broad values, by normative beliefs. The result was that while Arcop seemed to be opportunistic, intentions did guide what it ended up doing. And these intentions were clearly organizational in nature: while they may not have been defined in terms of explicit plans emanating from a central point, they were shared on a collective basis, internalized in the normative beliefs of the various actors. Thus, while each specific strategy may have been emergent, the overall strategic pattern was deliberate—realized as collectively intended in the form of a strategic umbrella.

Sustaining the Strategic Umbrella

This strategic umbrella can perhaps explain why both markets and locations came and went in short-term cycles. On the one hand, because Arcop was not preoccupied with type of job or location, no pattern was encouraged by specific intentions. On the other hand, there were probably not many design opportunities of the kind that Arcop wanted. So it would appear that the firm had to shift its job types and locations almost continuously in order to maintain its strategic umbrella.

With the exception of the Place Ville Marie job and some small, mundane ones Arcop sometimes took to sustain itself, it never strayed from under its strategic umbrella, although in 1966 it took a crisis to keep it there. When its billings declined, the firm did not compromise its beliefs, but worked instead to sustain them, and so declined.

Staffing strategies seem to reinforce these conclusions. An organization acting in a more deliberate manner would likely have targeted markets, promoted aggressively, and hired staff to meet the demand, and thereafter increased promotion to maintain or enlarge that staff (or at least avoid having to lay people off during downturns). In other words, it would have kept being driven as much by the supply of its own personnel as by the demands of the marketplace. Arcop did none of this. Instead it chose not to manage staffing levels per se, but to allow them to respond to work volume, dictated by market responses. Sustenance of beliefs drove Arcop, not sustenance of organization or even support of staff.

Several elements of Arcop's structure support these conclusions. The firm did engage some of its own specialists, but these were to serve the basic architectural mission, not to help the organization grow, or to broaden the firm's range of services. The story of the interior designers is indicative: the partners would not let them establish an independent unit, which would have constituted a form of diversification that would have encouraged growth (supply-driven).

The surge of formalization in the mid-1960s, the issue that seemed to precipitate the major conflict, tells a similar story. The success in the 1960s necessitated some formalization and elaboration of its structure. But that threatened the strategic umbrella, at least in the eyes of Ray Affleck. So while Guy may have intended to make these changes, he lacked support from his partners, and so could only realize them as ad hoc responses to specific pressures. Thus, while these strategies may have been *personally* deliberate, they were *organizationally* emergent. And when things changed, an organizationally deliberate strategy *was* pursued, namely, to contract and to rid the organization of all vestiges of administrative influence. That strategy can be called organizational because it was shared by those who controlled, or more exactly ended up controlling, the organization.

Subtle Combination of Deliberate and Emergent Strategies

To conclude this discussion, when we compare the findings of this study with the more conventional literature on strategy making, or even with the more conventional organizations we studied, we find much more subtlety in the notions of deliberate and emergent strategy. Whereas the conventional literature and conventional organizations are preoccupied with designing deliberate strategies, here we find an interesting mixture of the two. In particular, umbrella strategy means deliberateness in overall direction without precise specification of pattern, leaving room for emergence in detailed strategies. So while individual actions may appear to have been ad hoc, and individual strategies emergent, the overall pattern among them was not. Broader forces guided them.

Back to Strategic Choice

This subtle combination of deliberate and emergent strategy dictated the choices that Arcop 'chose' to make. And in that respect, this study contains some fascinating messages about strategic choice and about the abdication of decision. Few strategic decisions—by which we mean here specific major commitments to action, whether to set major precedents deliberately or to invest resources for the long term—could be found in Arcop. Yet this did not seem to be an organization that lacked control of its own destiny. Quite the contrary.

The fact is that while Arcop ceded a middle range of choices to its environment—the range that most organizations seem intent to control, namely, about what specific products and services to market and where—this organization retained tight control of choices at either end. At the high end, Arcop defined its own strategic umbrella, to guide the work that it ended up doing. And at the lower end, Arcop maintained tight control over the details of its designs. The choice of doorknobs in Arcop-designed buildings was literally a big issue with some of its people. This can be contrasted with firms whose focus on the middle range forces them to cede control over the broad issues and sometimes even the details too. How many architectural firms, for example, not to mention mass producers, dispense with their early values in their vigorous pursuit of target markets? And how many fall into standard industry recipes (Grinyer and Spender 1979) in their operating details?[2]

Thus, in some sense, Arcop may have ended up in greater control of its destiny than the organization that grows large only to find itself locked into a standard industry template. Arcop's strategies may have been dispensable, but its beliefs were not. It did not need to make decisions or formulate strategies so long as it maintained control of these beliefs. Ultimately, then, this firm may have been less opportunistic than apparent. The message of the Arcop study seems to be that when you are pursuing strategies of design (at least excellent design), you need not design strategies!

ADHOCRACY AND THE RELUCTANT ORGANIZATION

Another theme dominates the story of Arcop: an unrelenting tension between the forces of organization and those of craft. A distinguishing

[2] In what may have been much the same spirit, Konosuke Matsushita said of his leadership in the firm he founded, 'Big things and little things are my job. Middle level arrangements can be delegated.'

characteristic of Arcop is that craft eventually won out. In other words, Arcop did not give in to the imperatives of administration. But it paid a high price for this.

From its inception, Arcop was the 'reluctant' organization—structuring, departmentalizing, and formalizing almost inadvertently, reluctant step after reluctant step, until, faced with crisis, it deliberately reversed the pattern. Arcop may have been in the business of planning for its clients, but it never really accepted planning for itself.

Arcop's original partners had to incorporate—organize, at least officially—to do their first big job; later they had to seem organized to get their next big job; and then they had to introduce hierarchy to satisfy clients that a partner was in charge of each job. Growth required more systems, procedures, and controls just to keep order; if the partners refused to realize it, consultants were there to tell them so (as consultants tend to do).

But some partners sensed an incompatibility between these trends and the kind of craft they wished to practice. Hence, rather than accepting the acceleration of these trends, as do most organizations intent on growing, these partners eventually confronted them, deliberately eliminating most of the administrative component of the organization. Arcop, in fact, so weakened its administrative structure that it becomes fair to ask whether it ended up being an organization at all, or just a group of professionals sharing space.

Arcop as an Organization?

Organization means collective action in the pursuit of a common mission. Arcop was a partnership committed to individual freedom and growth. The partners worked mostly on their own projects, resisting pressures to knit themselves tightly together. Much of the architectural staff, particularly senior people, quickly became used to working under a specific partner. On the other hand, all the partners shared the common mission of doing excellent architectural work that would have an impact on society. Moreover, there was a pool of junior and support staff that generally served the organization as a whole.

An organization is also easily identified. For example, if one out of the many thousands of IBM (International Business Machines Corporation) managers discriminates against a woman or a black, IBM is identified as so doing. In this respect, particularly up to 1966, Arcop was an organization. The very fact that the partners chose to call themselves Arcop, rather than using their own names, was one sign of this. Insisting on putting that label on their buildings, instead of the name of the partner in charge, was another, in form if not substance.

Arcop as Adhocracy

What kind of organization was Arcop? In terminology introduced elsewhere (Mintzberg 1979*b*), Arcop closely resembled *adhocracy:* a project structure staffed by highly trained experts intent on innovating rather than standardizing in their work. Characteristic of an adhocracy, Arcop's structure was highly fluid; the firm never settled down; nothing it did ever became routine. Except for these beliefs, everything was dispensable, and indeed, except for two partners, everything was at some point dispensed with. Perhaps nothing epitomizes adhocracy better than the dramatic swings in Arcop's annual staff turnover (see Figure 9.9).

In fact, one explanation for the continual shifting of locations and job types could be a deliberate effort to sustain adhocracy. As organizations age and grow, the urge to converge, focus, repeat what has worked best, and avoid the fear of the unknown, typically becomes irresistible. Consequently, most organizations move toward a more formalized structure, some form of machine bureaucracy, characterized by sharp divisions of labor and departmentalization, pervasive rules and job descriptions, and emphasis on systems of control and planning.

As it grew, Arcop experienced these pressures too. Ultimately they had to be confronted. But even before this, Arcop appears to have kept these forces at bay by constantly changing, by avoiding concentration, and instead dipping into one market after another. We have no evidence that this strategy of 'keep moving' (clearly a pattern in Arcop's actions) was deliberate. It might have been inadvertent, a consequence of the limited availability in any one market of the kind of work Arcop people wished to do. But that strategy might have been somewhat deliberate too, a conscious (or perhaps subconscious) means to maintain adhocracy in the face of the pressures to formalize. Or perhaps the partners simply had personal needs for continual change and challenge, and consequently discouraged convergence whenever it appeared.

Strategy Making in Adhocracy

This study, as compared with some of our others, seems to highlight some key differences between strategy formation in adhocracy and machine bureaucracy. Machine bureaucracy is a mass producer, adhocracy a developer of prototypes. Hence, in machine bureaucracy central strategists formulate (or more exactly specify) precise intended strategies ('plans') for others to implement; in adhocracy everyone becomes a strategist as his or her specific decisions and actions contribute to the streams from which strategies emerge. Its planning process encourages machine bureaucracy to treat strategies as indispensable. The underlying premise for effectiveness seems to be: if you get your specific strategies straight, nothing else really matters. Adhocracy, in contrast, seems to be based on the premise that if you get your basic beliefs straight, and back them with the right people, nothing else needs to be managed—it will all fall naturally into place. Indeed, strategies may be especially dispensable in adhocracy: as discussed earlier, and as seen so clearly in the study of the National Film Board, it might be that adhocracies *have* to dispense with their strategies periodically—to deliberately destroy focus—in order to sustain their ad hoc, innovative character.

Integration by plan requires tight organization. If you know exactly what you want to do, you must 'get organized' to do it. If, instead, you really wish to innovate—which means you do not know how your work is going to turn out—then organization gets in the way. Indeed, to look at the other side of the relationship, it will only encourage you to start planning.

Efficiency and the system are what matter in machine bureaucracy; administration is paramount. In contrast, the focus of attention in adhocracy is innovation. Thus, while adhocracies like Arcop may build monuments, they have to be careful not to build *themselves* into monuments.

Sustaining Adhocracy

When Arcop was small, the forces for adhocracy were clearly dominant, while those for administration were minor. Craft skill, allegiance to central beliefs, and informal controls of a normative nature could all be maintained. But growth upset the equilibrium. It necessitated more administrative structure, which encouraged formal controls at the expense of normative ones, hierarchy at the expense of commitment, and departmentalization at the expense of flexibility. To be sure, some administration was always necessary to ensure that large jobs were completed with some level of efficiency and to keep the organization from flying apart. But to maintain Arcop's system of beliefs, the impact of these forces eventually had to be limited.

In essence, to maintain excellence in innovative design, key partners felt they could not distance themselves from the details of their work—could not delegate the design of doorknobs, so to speak. Hierarchy and impersonalization were thus seen as a threat to craft excellence. Delegation in the abstract, being 'in charge', supervising others to do things, had to be avoided in favor of doing things themselves. As Dimitri Dimakopoulos put it, 'We had an element that made us successful. The same magic can not be reproduced with the associates.' So the strengthened administration which came with growth eventually had to be confronted and clashes between the commercial and craft orientations became inevitable.

At the center of this confrontation were Guy Desbarats and Ray Affleck. Guy, in particular, felt that the firm could grow without any threat to its basic mission. In fact, he was sure that greater size would contribute to greater excellence in design through diversity of inputs, and that greater scale would provide more opportunities for the firm to pursue its mission. Thus he encouraged the administrative arrangements that would allow the firm to grow.

Ray, on the other hand, exercised his influence in a more implicit manner. He stood for the values and beliefs that had been the roots of Arcop. Ray felt that the orientation of the firm could only be maintained in a small organization, where it was possible to maintain personal contact. In this, he showed little flexibility, and was not easily swayed from his position.

The other partners were thus forced either to swing over to Ray's position or to find a way of getting around him, even it if meant leaving the firm. 'Do what you like', Ray seemed to say, 'but I'm doing X.' And Arcop did X, or, more precisely, those who remained at Arcop did X. In the end, Ray—who never managed Arcop, never held the position of chief executive, never issued the orders—won out. He set the tone. Because he never budged from his position, Arcop never strayed from its beliefs. Arcop, in the final analysis, was Ray. What finally made it an organization—what above all held this mélange of ad hoc projects and temperamental experts together—was this system of beliefs, what we have called the strategic umbrella, and this system was in large part defined and protected by Ray. Such 'implicit leadership'—rooted in norms rather than administration—can be potent indeed, at least in a small organization, where all the members are in personal touch with each other.

A Schizophrenic Organization

When Guy left, he said that Arcop was a schizophrenic organization that wanted grand projects but did not want the organization that went along with them. He was right. After the confrontation, Arcop resolved the problem somewhat by increasing its proportion of smaller jobs and by teaming up on more of the larger ones with other firms that took charge of the construction phase, which required more administration, while it kept front-end design for itself. But Arcop lost a large part of itself in the dismantling process. The organization that emerged in the 1970s was a very different one.

A MESSAGE FOR MONUMENTS

To conclude, the story of Arcop is the story of the reluctant organization, one unwilling to face the fact that it was an organization. This story contains interesting messages about leadership and control, strategies and structures, decisions and choices. It provides insight into what strategic choice and organization itself might mean.

Arcop's story has important implications for today's world of organizations. For here is one that challenged the imperatives of administration and won in its own way, but paid a high price for its victory. Arcop avoided the syndrome of our age—capture by administration—but it consequently destroyed a part of itself in the process. Arcop lost not only its scale but some of its magic too.

Arcop was an organization that created monuments, yet it would not let itself become a monument. It stands in sharp contrast to so many organizations in professional fields such as architecture, management consulting, and law that lose the character of their early successes by institutionalizing them. These are the organizations driven to become monuments at the expense of their own beliefs and talents. Arcop could have been big, but that might have made it bland. It likely could have ensured its survival as an organization, beyond its partners, and sustained its large size, simply by widening its umbrella and deferring more to its administrators. But that might have threatened its integrity. So it chose to ensure that integrity instead.

A MESSAGE FOR SOCIETY

There is a certain sadness to this story, both for Arcop and for society. Arcop survived as a successful organization, on a much smaller scale, perhaps wiser but undoubtedly wearier. It maintained its integrity and decided its own fate, but spent a large part of itself in the process.

Could Arcop have had it both ways—scale as well as integrity? Did it have to choose between craft excellence and commercial success? Some organizations manage not to, at least for a time, because of potent ideologies or highly charismatic leaders. But many of these eventually succumb to the imperatives of administration. And a great many others that do make that choice early on succeed in material terms, but fail in social ones. Size impersonalizes their relationships, dulls their ideology, dampens their commitments, deflects their attention from their central mission. Their normative beliefs give way to formal controls, and administrative forces become ends in themselves.

After Ray Affleck died in 1989, Arcop floundered. The firm brought in a new partner with the needed skills and Arcop continues very successfully to this day, with offices in Montreal, Toronto, Boston, and New Delhi, with major projects in Canada, China, India, and the Middle East.

10

Strategic Management Upside Down
McGill University, 1829–80

Henry Mintzberg and Jan Rose[1]

A number of the fundamental premises of strategic management are put into question in a study that tracks the realized strategies of a prominent university over a century and an half. Amidst continual change in detail, there was remarkable stability in the aggregate, and nothing resembling quantum or revolutionary change in strategy ever occurred. This may be explained in some of the terms most popular in business today: 'empowerment', 'venturing', and especially 'knowledge work'. Thus, while a typical university may seem very different from the typical corporation, its behavior may in fact contain sobering messages for the strategic management of businesses.

Frederick W. Taylor (1911) popularized the term 'one best way' almost a century ago. It remains alive and well in the thinking of strategic management, which has stepped from one 'one best way' to another over the course of its short history: from the strategic planning of the 1960s and 1970s (e.g. Ansoff 1965; Steiner 1979) to the strategic positioning of the 1980s (notably Porter 1980, 1985) to the core competencies of the 1990s (notably Prahalad and Hamel 1990). The fact that all this has worked as prescribed remains an open question; that any of it has worked in the university setting is the subject of this study.

---

[1] Originally published in the *Canadian Journal of Administrative Sciences* (2003: 270–90), with minor revisions in this volume.

There has certainly been a steady stream of calls over the years for universities to engage in strategic management and strategic planning (e.g. Ladd 1970; Hosmer 1978; Lutz 1982; Holdaway and Meekison 1990). Yet seldom have the fundamental differences in strategy been addressed between universities and corporate organizations, for which almost all these prescriptions have been developed.

Consider mission and product-market strategy, the essence of positioning. The mission of the university is research and teaching: to create and to disseminate knowledge. Yet these, especially research, are largely under the control of individual professors (Hardy et al. 1983, 1984). A university of 1,000 professors might be described as pursing 1,000 different research strategies, and many different teaching strategies. Other key strategic issues—for example, the hiring of professors and the rules for tenure—are often determined collectively: not by the careful conception described in the strategic management literature so much as in the give-and-take of complex interactive processes. How, then, do prescriptions about central planning, core (namely common) competencies, and overall competitive analyses apply to universities?

This is not to conclude that universities do not have strategies. In fact, Hardy et al. concluded that universities are inundated with strategies, in the sense of consistent patterns of action: within programs and departments, about pockets of research and approaches to tenure, concerning the construction of buildings and the methods of teaching, etc. We just do not understand the trajectory of such strategies: how they originate, evolve, change, and interrelate in the university setting. This study of a prominent Canadian university across most of its history seeks to address these issues.

McGill University

In his will of 1811, James McGill, a successful fur trader, bequeathed £10,000 to establish a college in his name, on his country estate. After a difficult start, during which the family contested the will, the college began with a medical school in 1829. A century and a half later, McGill University had emerged as an internationally known institution, with a beautiful campus at the foot of Montreal's Mount Royal mountain (a five-minute walk from the center of downtown Montreal), offering an almost full slate of academic degrees to some 20,000 students.

This study tracks the strategies of this institution from 1829 to 1980, in the process addressing some rather unexplored aspects of the strategy-making process. With these dates, we focus on the history—the long trends—and avoid being influenced by what we know best, the recent years that we have lived. After a brief introduction about the sources of data, the university's strategies are described in each of several key areas across the 152-year period, before final conclusions are drawn about strategy making in universities and beyond.

PARTICULAR CHARACTERISTICS OF THIS STUDY

The issue of deliberateness is particularly interesting in the university setting, because of the individual and collective control over so many specific actions. For a strategy to be 'deliberate', not only must the actions have been determined by conscious intentions (namely decisions), but so too must have been the pattern among them. In other words, a series of independent actions that converge on some theme (say the hiring of radical feminists across a number of departments) can be labeled a deliberate strategy only if there was some sort of conscious intention at the outset to establish that pattern. But what may have been deliberate for particular individuals or subgroups may in fact have been emergent for everyone else, including the central management. Can the 'organization' then be said to have pursued a deliberate strategy? (What if the hiring of those radical feminists was promoted by some coalition of a few professors spread across departments. Did the system then exhibit common intention?)

This study proceeded somewhat differently from the others of this book for reasons that will become clear. We first traced action streams and inferred strategies in various areas, as in the other studies. But these did not so evidently fall into distinct periods, meaning that naturally occurring times of comprehensive change were less evident here—an important conclusion in its own right. Certainly there were important events in the history of McGill, such as the appointment of a key principal (McGill's label for president or rector), or the shift to a major new source of funding. But these did not seem to manifest themselves in shifts across a wide range of strategies.

Accordingly, we focus this presentation on particular strategies themselves rather than on periods in the history of the organization. This is followed by broader conclusions that draw conceptual lessons about the entire period of the study.

SOURCES OF INFORMATION

The great advantage of studying a well-known institution over a century and a half is that there is so much interest in its past. We were particularly fortunate to have had access to a two-volume history authored by a distinguished professor of divinity who subsequently assumed senior positions in the university's administration (Frost 1980, 1984). There were, of course, also annual reports, dating back to 1868. Other sources included Academic Calendars, internal telephone books (to identify the introduction of new units), minutes of the Board of Governors and the Senate, organization charts, and student and administration newspapers, as well as interviews.

The disadvantage of extending a study over such a long period of time, of course, is that most of the key players are simply unavailable for interview. Moreover, universities themselves, as we shall see, leave barely any central trace of aspects of their most important activities—notably styles of pedagogy and approaches to research. These tend, as noted, to be carried out on an individual basis, so that the study of a university with dozens of departments and thousands of professors becomes not so much the study of one organization as of a collection of 'loosely coupled' entities (Weick 1976). Hence, with all that we *could* study, certain critical aspects of overall mission were something we could not—at least, not with our methodology and resources. (Chapter 11 makes up for this in a way, by tracking the research strategies of one of McGill's professors.) But, as should become evident, we had our hands full with what was available—not only the available data but also the lessons that could be drawn from them.

In the final analysis, in seeking to extend the study over such a long period of time, we were forced to focus on those areas, which left tangible traces of the actions taken. Listed in the order discussed below, these include:

- Academic offerings, including degrees and certificates, majors and diplomas, research centers and institutes
- Enrollment, by faculty and geographical area, also academic staff levels
- Finances, including funding by source and the resulting surpluses and deficits
- Buildings, including new construction, acquisition, and renovation

• Structure, including principalship, senate, and board of governors membership, and the development of support services and administration

ACADEMIC OFFERING

Figure 10.1 shows various aspects of program activity at the university, organized by the Faculty. 'Faculty' in Canada, aside from reference to the corps of professors, labels major units, or 'schools' as they are called in the US universities, usually comprising several departments. (We shall capitalize the F when using this meaning here.) Medicine was the first Faculty, established in 1829, followed by Arts and Science soon after and then Law, while Management was the last, created in 1968. (The Faculty of Arts and Science was split into two in 1971, 128 years after its creation.)

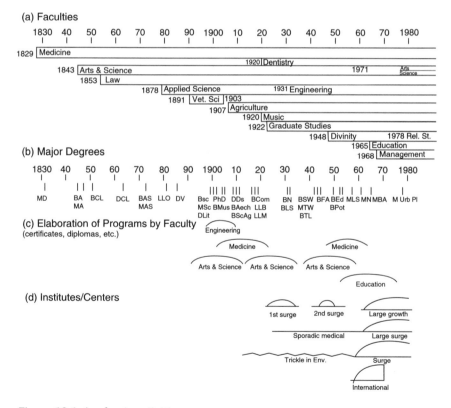

Figure 10.1 Academic activities

Two aspects of this chart are quite remarkable. First, with a single exception (Veterinary Science, which lasted only twelve years, from 1891 to 1903), the university never closed a single Faculty. In other words, nothing that the university started in a serious way over 150 years was ever stopped! At this level of aggregation, the institution remained the sum total of all that it ever did![2]

Second, the introduction of new Faculties is remarkably spread out. Except for three in the years 1920–2 (one, Dentistry, spun off Medicine, and two, Music, always rather small), Faculty introductions spanned rather evenly the entire century and a half. An idea of this spacing can be had by tabulating the years between each successive new faculty: fourteen (Medicine to Arts and Science), ten (to Law), twenty-five (to Applied Science, later renamed Engineering), thirteen (to Veterinary Science), sixteen (to Agriculture), thirteen (to Music), zero (to Dentistry), two (to Graduate Faculty), twenty-six (to Divinity, later renamed Religious Studies), seventeen (to Education), and three (to Management).

Figure 10.1 also records the introduction of major new degree programs, and tells much the same story. (There is about a four-year lag here, as the announcement of the first graduates in the annual report was taken as the most reliable indicator of the introduction of a new program; Graduate Faculty is not shown, since many of these degrees were listed in the Faculties.) Almost all the fifteen decades indicate some activity (the exceptions being the 1850s, 1860s, and 1880s), yet the maximum was only three new degrees in a decade, and that only occurred twice (in the 1900s and 1940s). Six of the decades show two new degrees and four show one. The absence of clustering is rather striking. In fact, when we tabulated graduate degree additions (e.g. an LLM following an LLB), there was even more of a spread.

Only when we considered new certificates, diplomas, and majors by Faculty did some clustering begin to appear, shown as aggregates of the data in Figure 10.1. Some Faculties (e.g. Dentistry and Religious Studies) were only thinly developed, with just a few basic degrees. Others developed extensively, with all kinds of special programs, sometimes across substantial periods of time (notably Medicine and Arts and Science), or else in particular periods (such as Education in the last thirty years of the history).

---

[2] Most recently, a major battle erupted over a proposal to close down the small Faculty of Dentistry. This proposal was finally rejected. It might be added that even Veterinary Science came back in 1940 in the form of a diploma in Veterinary Public Health.

Overall, this activity tends to cluster from the end of the last century into the 1920s, especially in Medicine, Engineering, and (in two clusters) Arts and Science. A second clustering can be seen in the 1940s through 1960s, again in Medicine and Arts and Science, and newly in Education. But note that all this pertains to only four Faculties out of the eleven (leaving aside Veterinary Science and counting Arts and Science as one).

Finally, we tabulated our one clear trace of research activity, the opening of new centers and institutes, where research, largely an individual activity, manifested institutionally—in certain cases, at least. (Centers tended to be created where there was the need for collaborative research and/or for the purchase of expensive equipment.) This, again, is shown symbolically as aggregates of our data.

Perhaps because of its institutional nature, here we see somewhat more clustering, especially in more recent times, with three periods of growth in particular, a first in the 1920s and early 1930s, a second after World War II, and the one large surge beginning in the early 1960s and running till the end of the study period. Only three focal themes could be discerned, one in Medicine (that began sporadically in the late 1920s and developed into a major surge from the mid-1960s), a second related to environmental issues (that began as a trickle toward the end of World War I and also surged in the early 1960s), and a third in the international realm that occurred only during the 1960s.

An effort to identify concentrated periods of attention to any Faculty did not produce anything beyond the fact that some of the professional Faculties figured more prominently in the early years (Medicine and Law) and some in the later ones (Education and Medicine again), while Arts and Science came into and out of attention throughout the history.

ENROLLMENT

Figure 10.2a plots the total student enrollment of the university across its history. The curve does not look particularly remarkable: fairly strong long-term growth with a dip for World War I, somewhat slower growth during the Depression, followed by a major surge after World War II, and then fairly rapid growth near the end.

But when the same figures were plotted, as in Figure 10.2b, on a semilog scale, which highlights comparative rates of growth, a remarkable thing happens: the university seems to have settled on a trend line in the late 1860s (just as Canada became a nation), with about 300 students, and

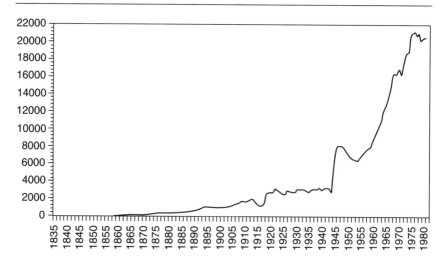

Figure 10.2a Enrollment figures, total

stayed on it for over a century, to the end of the study period, with 20,211 students.

There were all kinds of short-term variations, to be sure, as well as the major blips of the two world wars (when enrollment dipped and later surged, especially after the World War II, when the university initiated special programs to accommodate the returning veterans), and the more noticeable slowed growth of the Depression (itself remarkably steady).

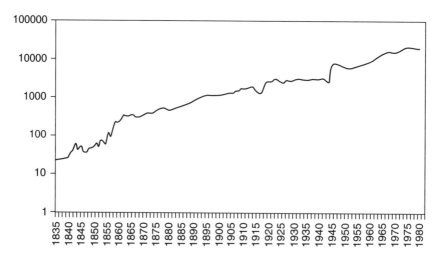

Figure 10.2b Enrollment figures, total (semilog)

But in all cases, the university fell straight back on to its long-term trend line, where it almost precisely remained at the end of the study period in 1980. It is almost as if some larger force was driving this rather fragmented system to attain more or less steady growth for over a century!

Indeed, the university's biggest surge in enrollment ever, from 9,500 students in 1961 to 16,500 in 1969, when considered statistically on the semilog graph, could almost be considered a correction, to get back on the trend line it came off during the Depression thirty years earlier. Might this be explained by the 'baby boom', that itself reflected the Depression followed by the War? With the nature of the university's decision-making process, however, we can hardly talk about a deliberate strategy over such a long period. But we can certainly talk about a realized one, whatever the reasons, of 3.78 percent compounded growth.

When we considered the same figures by Faculty, we seemed to get, not more explanation but less, because the overall highly ordered trend line appears to comprise others of mostly greater variability. Arts and Science, as the largest Faculty, followed a similar trend line but with greater short-term variability around the mean; Medicine appears to have stopped major growth at the turn of the century; Engineering exhibited greater variability until enrollment stabilized after the post-World War II surge; Graduate Faculty grew faster but with greater variability, as did Management, while Law showed slower growth but with higher short-term cyclicity. With the whole university generally growing faster and steadier than its individual Faculties, the conclusion can be drawn that it grew more by adding activities than by expanding existing ones. In other words, McGill grew especially by the *diversification* of its offerings.

Certain Faculties controlled their enrollment very carefully, notably Law and Medicine. In fact, the Quebec Bar controlled numbers in the Law Faculty, for example with a deliberate target for a time of no more than 500 students. In the case of Medicine, the number of beds in the Montreal teaching hospitals was a key factor. Other Faculties, notably Arts and Science, did not limit numbers and accepted any student who met certain criteria. In the case of Engineering, enrollment was partially controlled, especially in times of growth (e.g. before World War I and in the early 1950s), due to equipment restrictions. But when interest waned, enrollment was opened up. Indeed, the university went to great efforts to sustain Engineering when demand dropped, implying a kind of smooth behavior with regard to the total number of students.

Considering the figures overall, Medicine rose first (that is how McGill began its existence), followed by Arts and Science, and then Engineering,

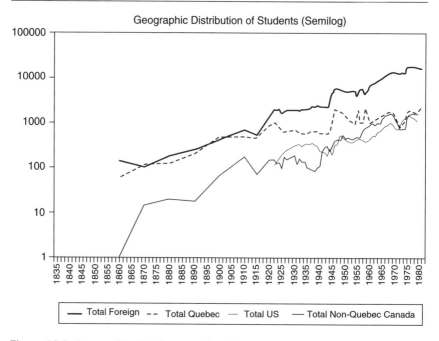

Figure 10.3 Geographic distribution of students

so that just after the turn of the century, the university was a balanced mixture of these three. Then Arts and Science surged ahead, but by the mid-1920s, McGill was a general university with an almost full range of offerings—much as it has remained, although Graduate Faculty enrollment grew rapidly after World War II as research became more prominent.

Considering the geographic breakdown, in Figure 10.3, for most of the study period McGill had a significant population of foreign students. Additionally, before the turn of the century it enrolled as many students from outside Quebec as from within it. Since 1915, however, in waves, it has become an increasingly Quebec-based (and especially Montreal) institution, although foreign enrollments (US and abroad) did grow rapidly after World War II.

Quebec enrollment followed the pattern of total enrollment, more or less, and in fact constituted most of it. The rest of Canada exhibited somewhat wider swings and much slower growth in this century, while growth in US as well as offshore enrollment maintained roughly the same rate as Quebec, but with wider swings. It is interesting that all the lines, save that for Quebec, meet just before the end of the study period.

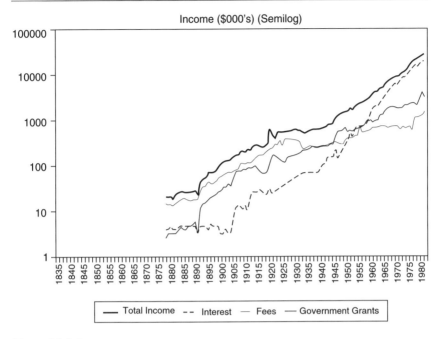

Income ($000's) (Semilog)

Figure 10.4 Income

FINANCES

Figure 10.4 shows the income of McGill University from the 1870s (when reliable data became available) to the end of the study period, broken down by its three main sources. Again, as the plot is on a semilog scale, the steady long-term rise in total income can be seen, which accelerated after World War II.

In some ways, the curve is smoother than the one for enrollment, with the exception of two sharp blips: down and then up late in the last century, and up then down and up again in the 1920s.

The breakdown of this income between student fees, interest (reflecting donations and endowments), and government grants tells an interesting story of the university's history. Rough periods of emphasis can be delineated, identified as much by the crisscrossing trends as by dramatic shifts.

Commensurate with its founding on James McGill's £10,000 grant, not to mention the considerable real estate that accompanied it, McGill was a university supported largely by donations for virtually its first full century: into the new century, interest made up the lion's share of the income. But

293

this belies the history that preceded the data of Figure 10.4, because in its early decades, the university stumbled from one financial crisis to another, through continual bouts of poverty and debt.

It was not until 1837 that the family challenges to the initial grant were exhausted. A first building was then constructed, which ran a factor of three over budget, leaving insufficient funds to pay the professors. After a series of real-estate manipulations, by 1852 the university had to close its doors for one year, firing its entire staff.

What might be called the age of the benefactors began in the early 1860s, shortly after William Dawson, McGill's great principal (and one of its great scholars as well) began his forty-year tenure. Three men in particular supported the university: William Molson of the beer family; and in the 1880s, Sir Donald Smith, who earned his fortune building the Canadian Pacific Railway, and Sir William McDonald of tobacco interests. Major grants from the US Carnegie and Rockefeller Foundations in the 1920s (including a million dollars from the latter for the Medical Faculty in 1920) brought the age of the benefactors to a close, although important benefactors did appear later.

Income from the government was low and relatively steady in most of these years, showing two major increases in the first two decades of this century but still remaining far below the other two sources of income. Fee income rose very sharply near the end of the last century and then began a very steady, if occasionally interrupted, rise. This suggests that, of all the parameters of this study, fee income was among the most stable, and, taking inflation into account, the slowest to increase. By the mid-1930s, for about ten years, fee and interest income were virtually identical, after which the former exceeded the latter in almost all the remaining years.

Government grants increased steadily, and, from the 1940s, at a more rapid rate, bypassing interest income in the 1950s and, after running almost identical with fee income for most of the 1950s, pulling rapidly ahead of it as well. So, by 1960, the year in which McGill took a wrenching decision to accept major and statutory provincial government funding ($5.3 million, compared with grants in the $1.5–2 million range previously), the university slipped closer toward the public sphere. 'Publicly funded' might be a better term than 'public', since McGill has always retained its sizable endowment and the right to add to that, and also its status as a private institution. (In general, universities in Canada are neither as private nor as public as those in the US. Almost all university activity is publicly funded in Canada, yet that allows significant although varying degrees of autonomy.)

Although the perception in the university is that this 1960 decision was a turning point in its history, Figure 10.4 suggests that it was, perhaps, a significant step, in a trend line that went back to the 1930s, albeit this one toward the provincial sphere and away from the federal one. Indeed, the angle of the curve of government grants (i.e. the rate of exponential growth, rather than absolute numbers) from the late 1930s to the mid-1950s matches that after 1962.

BUILDINGS

Our data for the number of buildings—constructed, acquired, and subjected to major alterations—are shown in Figure 10.5. Floor space would have been a more accurate measure of this, if available throughout, but number of buildings does give an indication of activity here.

Until just after the turn of the century, despite the abundance of land owned by the university (twenty-five acres, of which some was sold in 1858–60 to cover debts, includes some of the most expensive real estate in Montreal today), building activity was sporadic, with our records showing a total of ten buildings constructed in seventy-five years, and none acquired or altered.

Then this activity picked up quickly. The first recorded acquisitions, four in all, took place in 1905 and major construction began in 1907, especially for Medicine, but also Engineering and Agriculture, with eleven buildings in that year alone. Thereafter, while single acquisitions took place periodically, construction occurred on a much more regular basis (in particular for Agriculture, Medicine, and Science, as well as for support activities), although, after 1915 not more than one or two buildings were added in a single year. This continued right through the Depression (even with mounting deficits), to the end of World War II, after which, due to the degradation of existing facilities during the war as well as the influx of veteran students, there began the most extensive building activity in the university's history. Fourteen buildings were constructed in 1950 alone, six in 1961, and eight in 1965. (The university grew in size from 1.2 million square feet in 1959 to 5 million in 1971.) This growth slowed somewhat in the 1970s.

Acquisitions, which picked up in the 1940s, also continued to the end of the study period, peaking at six in both 1961 and 1975. Major alteration, which began in 1926, also became more steadily active from the early 1960s to the end of the study period, peaking at seven in 1978.

295

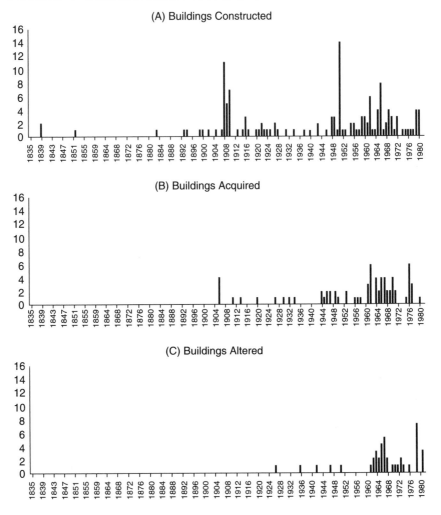

Figure 10.5 Buildings

Structure and Governance

Finally, we consider various aspects of the administrative structure of the university, including the development of its support services, the evolution of its two main governance bodies, and the growth of its administrative staff.

McGill University by the twenty-first century, perhaps typical of large North American universities of its kind, employed almost three other people for every faculty member. In other words, for everyone who actually delivered the basic services (teaching and research), three others supported that activity, either directly (libraries, computing center, etc.) or indirectly (maintenance, payroll, secretarial, student residences, fund-raising, etc.). But this had not always been the case: this kind of mix developed over the course of this century, across academic institutions in general (even if some 'outsourcing' became popular in recent years).

We looked into all the support services existing in the university in 1980 and used old telephone books as well as other sources to find indications of when each had been introduced. This is shown in Table 10.1, under the headings of libraries, residences, administrative control, and indirect support.

This table provides one interesting indication of how the contemporary university has developed. For McGill's first century, aside from the early setting in place of some basic services (purchasing, bursar, auditing, etc.), effort was devoted almost exclusively to the creation of libraries. This began with the opening of the Medical Library in 1829, and proceeded sporadically until near the end of World War I (e.g. the Science Library in 1884, the Law Library in 1892). In a period of ten years, however, from 1917 to 1927, seven new libraries were opened (Architecture, Medicine, Zoology, Ornithology, Chemistry, Chinese Studies, and Information Studies). After that, only one new library appeared (Commerce in 1943), although two were later moved into expanded new facilities (the general library in 1970 and the Commerce Library, renamed Management, in 1976).

Residences did not develop like libraries. The first was opened in 1896 and a second in 1939. Three opened in 1947 alone and, after one in 1962, another four were added in 1965.

Judging from Table 10.1, the contemporary university with its extensive support services is a phenomenon that, ironically, dates from the 1930s, even perhaps the 1920s. The McGill Faculty Club opened in 1924 and its Public Relations Office in 1929. Three major services were added in the 1930s (Placements Bureau in 1933, Investment Advisor in 1934, and Purchasing Agent in 1939). But it was in the 1960s that the real growth of services began, with the Computing Center in 1960, followed by the University Press, Grants Office, Audio-Visual Center, Printing Office, and so on. That growth appears to have been more or less completed by 1970, with only a Director of Development and an Office for Industrial Research added after that (in 1974 and 1976).

Finally, though indirect support developed in the university, administrative control did not, which suggests that universities do not function

Table 10.1 Chronology of major support services

Year	Libraries	Residencies	Administrative control	Indirect Support
1829	Library			Purchasing Stores
1843	Two libraries		Bursar	Registrar Secretary
1849	First librarian			Auditor, Chaplain
1883				Museum
1884, 1892, 1893	Libraries			
1896		Residence		
1903				(Bursar/Secretary/Registrar split)
1909				Power Plant
1917, 1919, 1922, 1923	Libraries			
1924	Library			Faculty Club
1926	Library			Public Relations Office
1927	Library			
1929			Comptroller's Office (created out of Bursar's)	
1933				Placements Bureau
1934				Investment Advisor
1936				(Secretary, Bursar/split)
1939		Residence		Purchasing Agent
1943	Library			
1947		3 residences	Personnel (reorganization of duties between Bursar and Comptroller)	
1951				Bookstore
1960				Computing Center
1962		Residence		University Press
1963				Information Office, Grants Office
1964				Audio-Visual Center
1965		4 residences		Archivist
1966				Printing, French Center
1969				Teaching Resource Center
1970	Expansion of general library		Office of university planning	Publicity Office, Real Estate Office
1974			Management Systems Budget Planning	Development Office
1976	Expansion of Management library			Industrial Research Office

like most other organizations. This activity barely developed at all, let alone in parallel with the burgeoning growth of students, faculty, budgets, and facilities.

Our data shows a Bursar's Office established in 1843, a Comptroller's Office created out of the Bursar's Office in 1929, and the duties between these two clarified in 1947, when a Personnel Office (later relabeled Human Resources) was added. The first office of University Planning was opened in 1970, and Offices of Management Systems and Budget Planning were added in 1974. Even well into the 1990s, the only university-wide units that could be thought of as administrative control, included among dozens and dozens of direct and indirect support services, Accounting, the Comptroller's Office, Internal Audit, and the Vice Principalship for Planning and Resources.[3] All these remained tiny, except for Accounting, whose space in the 1997 telephone book was nonetheless not much more than that for the McGill Research Center for Intelligent Machines. (Music, one of the smallest Faculties, as well as the Fund-Raising Office, each occupied significantly more space!)

As for the direct line management, the university hierarchy has always been very flat, at least in the academic areas (although somewhat more conventional in the support areas), having experienced virtually no significant elaboration over the years. The Faculty of Management, for example, had no intermediate level of supervision between its dean and the sixty-three members of academic staff listed in the 1997 telephone directory. (Its area heads served in support rather than supervisory capacities, and, in fact, these posts were generally filled on temporary, rotating bases.)

Larger Faculties were split into more formal departments, each with a head, but even here similar or in fact larger 'spans of control' have been common (e.g. in the Department of Pediatrics in the Faculty of Medicine in 1997, over a hundred faculty members were listed under a single head, whereas the administrative Accounting Department, in contrast, listed fifty-three people, of whom seven or eight appear to have had managerial titles). There were, of course, what might be called lateral managerial positions, with authority over programs but not over people, as in the post of Associate Dean, Masters Programs, in the Faculty of Management. The elaboration of these positions, as well as those of administrative assistants to aid the deans, appears to have taken place in most Faculties in the 1962–6 period.

---

[3] Most of the larger units, of course, had accounting and budgeting offices.

Between the deans of the various faculties and the principal of the whole university are listed in the 1997 telephone directory six vice principals, one for the Macdonald Campus (mainly Agriculture), two (Academic and Research) for most of the rest of the academic activities, and the others for Administration and Finance, Development and Alumni Relations, and Planning and Resources.

We collected evidence on the changing nature of the university reporting structure, as well as its various organigrams over the years, but those did not produce much information of significance. For the most part, aside from the support services, activity here seems to have consisted of the periodic juggling of reporting relationships between the deans and the vice principals (the deans themselves, of course, pegged to the Faculties, which, as noted, remained remarkably steady once established).

Another aspect of structure is the official governance of the university, particularly the interplay over the years of the largely external Board of Governors and the largely internal Senate. Much can be (and has been) written about these two; in addition, we undertook a study of the size of both as well as a qualitative assessment of their power relationships over time.

Both grew over the years, the Board steadily, especially between 1907 and the early 1920s and after 1960 (to more than forty members at the end of the study period). The Senate, which grew steadily from under twenty members in 1860 to almost seventy by the end of World War I, diminished after the war and again before World War II, to a low of about twenty-five members, before peaking again in the early 1970s at over eighty members.

Qualitatively, in its early years McGill was formally governed by a public body called the 'Royal Institute for the Advancement of Learning', which exerted great influence over it. But by the 1860s power had effectively passed to university's own Board of Governors. The Senate came into formal existence (by that name, at least, and with the beginning of its current powers) in 1935, as the 'highest academic authority in the University'. It participated in the appointment of deans, and could initiate constitutional amendments so long as these were ratified by the Board of Governors. Gradually, as the Board of Governors changed from an all-male, Anglican body early in the last century to include other ethnic and religious groups, women, and eventually, students, the Senate, comprising an increasingly broad mix of people from inside the university, became relatively more influential.

Beyond these two governing bodies, other forms of influence gained in importance, especially that of the Quebec Government, also of the faculty association (not a union as such)—the McGill Association of University Teachers (MAUT)—as well as faculty members themselves, especially in the 1960s. 'Until then, the only significant committees within Faculties consisted of deans and department heads, whose appointments could last for decades [and] Senate as dominated by the deans' (Edward Stansbury, former Vice Principal for Planning, in private correspondence).

And so, over the course of a century, although perhaps accelerated near the end, a rather closed, focused power group had given way to rather dispersed governance, which is consistent with the conclusions we shall now draw about the strategies and the strategy-making process.

Where are the Strategies?

Where is strategy in all this? Or, perhaps more to the point, where is strategy as pattern, whether or not intended, and where are intentions?

Glancing across Figure 10.1, which contains our findings on the central activities of the university, namely its academic offerings as well some indication of its research activity, we see remarkably little patterning (i.e. strategy), emergent let alone deliberate. Faculties came (and rarely went) and degree programs were added from time to time, while less significant certificate and diploma programs did come in clusters, as did research institutes and centers. Not much to say! McGill University grew by diversification to become a more or less fully elaborated university over a century and a half. This may be a strategy of sorts, but hardly different from dozens of other universities.

Yet break any of this down and strategies can be found everywhere. The Faculty of Medicine, for example, enrolled considerable numbers of US students after the Rockefeller Foundation grant in the 1920s, and in the 1960s the new business school became the first in Canada to adopt the theory-oriented approach pioneered at the Carnegie Institute of Technology.

If strategy is pattern, then there certainly was a crystal-clear strategy of growth in total enrollment—3.78 percent annually for over a century. Since it is difficult to imagine a principal of McGill University announcing such a strategy in 1870, we can only conclude that this is about as emergent as a strategy can get!

Emergent, but not likely by chance. This order must have been driven by something. We suggest two explanations.

First is corresponding growth in the university's prime source of students, namely the population of the Island of Montreal. In fact, the area's population grew in exponential fashion, at least from 1861 to 1981, indeed rather more steadily than that of McGill, if somewhat slower, although, like McGill, that growth did slow down during the Depression as well as in the final decade. This suggests that the university enrolled a steadily increasing proportion of the Montreal population, which reflected the growing demand for higher education.

The university attempted to stimulate enrollment from particular groups and particular areas, especially in the later years, and also tried to limit some of the places to particular numbers and even, in some cases, to people of particular strata and ethnic backgrounds. But the university also reacted to the interests, demands, and pressures of the communities that surrounded it.

A second explanation for the steady growth in overall enrollment, as well as more cyclical growth in Faculty enrollment, might be found in Cyert and March's (1963) notion of 'sequential attention to goals': that decisions on growth were subjected to bargaining among the players. For example, one Faculty may have been allowed to grow for a time and then another. Or perhaps champions for growth and consolidation simply came and went in the various Faculties so that, within any given Faculty, these two goals may have been attended to sequentially.

With regard to income, the interesting patterning is in the relative leveling out of fee income and the dramatic growth in government income. Unlike the private universities of the US, McGill went the route of a quasi-public institution, yet managed to maintain a rather large degree of autonomy.

But did McGill *choose* to go that route? As we noted earlier, while its people agonized over accepting the provincial government grant of 1960, which put it somewhat more firmly under the control of Quebec City, the data of Figure 10.4 suggest a trend line that was established back in the 1930s.

The central administration of the university did not have much control over programs. But it did have considerable influence over physical and social structures. Buildings, for example, whether to be constructed, acquired, or altered, require formal decisions. So here we do see some clear patterns: a major surge (read strategy) of construction in the early years of the twentieth century, again after World War II, and significantly in the 1960s, the latter likewise for buildings acquired and altered.

Changes to the social structure, in particular the addition of support services, likewise require formal decisions of a central management. But here we see less patterning, and what there was of it appears to follow outside forces or trends. Library development was widely spread out, while the residences came largely in the heavy growth years of 1947 and 1965. Administrative control units were added only occasionally, while indirect support units came more frequently, particularly in the 1930s and especially the 1960s. But this probably happened in most universities in North America. If 'industry recipes' do, indeed, exist to guide action taking (Spender 1989), the 'industry' of higher education certainly had its share.

Structural reorganizations occurred frequently. But it is not clear that they made much difference to the overall functioning of the university. Throughout, the administrative structure remained thin, which is a characteristic of professional bureaucracy (Mintzberg 1979*b*: 355).

Where are the Strategic Periods?

In the other studies of tracking strategies, it proved rather easy to identify distinct periods in the history of the organization. Often these revolved around crises, as in Volkswagenwerk, followed later by a key 'turnaround' through the redesign of many models; or they appeared as a key in one strategy that drove others, such as a shift to self-service in Steinberg's. Both examples came from rather integrated, centralized organizations, of the 'machine' or 'entrepreneurial' form (Mintzberg 1979*b*). But even in the more 'adhocracy', or project form of organization, no-less dependent on skilled experts than a university (but involving them in much more teamwork), distinct periods were clearly evident, such as in the National Film Board of Canada that experienced cycles of divergence and convergence in the characteristics of the films it made. All this is consistent with the punctuated equilibrium theory of Miller and Friesen (1980, 1984) and Tushman and Romanelli (1985) that long periods of incremental adaptation are interrupted by short bursts of revolutionary realignment. But we saw none of this in the university.

Of course, one can always find periods in the study of any organization: here, for example, up to about 1855, when the university was trying to get on its feet; after 1880, when its development proceeded more quickly; and after 1960, when it accepted that Quebec grant. But were such periods sharp and significant here?

We think not. We have already made our point about the government grant. In fact, while this seems to have been followed by increased activities in support services, construction, and the creation of institutes, changes in what really mattered—the programs offered—really began almost twenty years earlier and ended about ten years later.

Periods can, of course, be defined around key events, or the appointment of new leaders. Such events did occur at McGill—the two World Wars, the Depression, that government grant—but as we have argued, these did not seem to change the course of key strategic parameters, at least not in the long run—and this is a story about the long run.

The appointment of new leaders is how periods are often identified when the histories of institutions are written. But does this reflect the true importance of the leadership, or just the personification of organizational activity, including the attribution of whatever happened to whoever happened to be leading? Might this simply reflect the need to identify periods somehow?

A brief promotional piece issued in 1997, entitled *McGill Facts*, contains a one-page 'History of McGill University' that goes from principal to principal. At one point it reads: 'Taking up office in 1939, Principal Cyril James guided McGill through World War II and the post-war reconstruction period'—as presumably would have any other capable leader! More telling, perhaps, is the following: 'In 1944, seizing the opportunity afforded by the second Quebec Conference, he arranged for the fall convocation to be held at the Citadel in Quebec City so that honorary degrees could be conferred upon US President Franklin Delano Roosevelt and British Prime Minister Winston Churchill.' Significant for the image and status of the university, no doubt, but hardly the stuff of strategic revolution!

The two-volume history of the university by Stanley Frost delineates most of its chapters by periods. It is instructive to look at these. Some cover brief periods—'A Time of Intermission: 1848–1852', 'A Time of Reconstruction: 1852–1855'. A number are identified with particular leaders (four on the years of John William Dawson alone, principal from 1855 to 1892), two chapters span the war period, and several focus on particular disciplines.

While there is no doubt that events occurred and leaders led (or failed to lead), the story told by the facts alone seems to convey another message. It is not that McGill University did not change. Quite the contrary, McGill University changed continuously over the century and a half. That is the key to understanding all this. It never stopped changing. But it never changed in quantum leaps.

This may not be a fashionable conclusion in these times of so-called 'hypercompetition', 'turbulence', 'turnaround', 'renewal', etc. But then again, institutions that last centuries are not very fashionable these days either, even if they do remain rock solid.

Our perspective in this study is, of course, long term. Zoom in more closely, and events do seem the key, for example the impact of the two World Wars on enrollment, most evident in Figure 10.2a. Enormous scrambling had to take place to adapt. But the sobering conclusions of the long-term perspective, too often and too easily overlooked, deserve serious attention too, across the entire field of organization theory no less than across this one organization.

Who are the Strategists?

Most of the literature of strategic management as well as the popular press has a convenient answer to this question: the chief. 'In four years [Chief Executive] Gestner has added more than \$40 billion to IBM's share value', claimed *Fortune* magazine on April 14, 1997 (Morris 1997: 70). But the facts are not so easily ignored in this study. Something had been going on in this institution beyond the formal leadership, namely a rather complex social system, at least by the standards of most of the literature of strategic management.

Hardy et al. (1983, 1984) have presented a model that outlines the elements of this. Shown in Figure 10.6, these include the professors at the operating base, the managers at the hierarchical apex, and a complex system of collective choice in between, involving both. All this is surrounded by an 'environment' of many influencers with all sorts of varied interests.

Our conclusions, above about strategies and periods, can perhaps best be understood by considering the university as a structure of 'professional bureaucracy' (as described in Mintzberg 1979b). Here highly trained experts carry out work that is complex but rather stable, established through professional training. This enables the operating work to be 'pigeonholed', i.e. divided up, with each professional able to work on his or her part relatively free of the need for mutual adjustment with colleagues. Thus, a surgeon and an anaesthetist can coordinate in an operating room with virtually no oral communication.

Loose Coupling

Perhaps no organization fits this model better than the university. This is 'loose coupling' with a vengeance: just consider the independence of

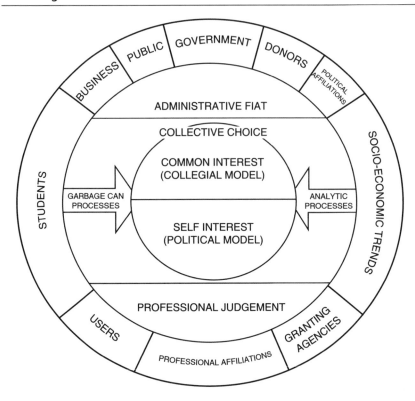

Figure 10.6 Three levels of decision making in the university (from Hardy et al., 1983, 1984)

departments, of programs, of teaching and of research (even from each other), of courses, and of the professionals themselves as individuals (who often work at home).

Lutz (1982) has pointed out, reasonably, that there are pockets of tight as well as loose coupling in universities, and that loose coupling cannot necessarily be relied upon prescriptively. But, descriptively at least, loose coupling does abound in these institutions.

Look for the research strategy of a university and, as noted earlier, you must look at all the professors, each of whom pursues his or her own. There may be some patterning across units, even some across the whole system (the level of quality from one university to another, for example). But this is usually minimal compared with the variations. One need only compare this with the research conducted in a pharmaceutical company, which, despite some variation, can be driven by a rather well-defined agenda (meaning intended strategy). Teaching, the other aspect of the core mission is not much different. So strategies are abundant in universities, as are strategists; they just cannot be found by observers who subscribe to the conventional tenets of strategic management.

Individual Venturing

Professionals are able to pursue their own strategies in professional bureaucracies for one of two reasons. Either their work has little impact on the work of others, e.g. in a research project that can be carried out individually, or if it does, the project has been approved in a collective process, after it has been 'championed' by an individual professional and then debated and found acceptable. The strategic management process in the university thus begins to look like the venturing process described by Burgelman (1983a) and others, in which the individual initiatives of champions give rise to a collection of rather independent products or services (as in a company such as 3M).

Collective Sphere

There remain, however, other areas where the system must act in a more 'collective' fashion—staffing decisions, for example, or the provision of library and computer support services. Here coupling has to be tighter. Some of these decisions are subjected to the complex machinations at the collective level, where professors and managers decide and debate (all too often in that order). Here, as shown in Figure10.6, the common interest of collegiality meets the self-interests of politics. All universities presumably combine the two, although in the most effective way, as McGill appears to have been (and remains), the unifying force of collegiality—including deep-seated beliefs in the institution itself—at least to hold its own.

The battles at this collective level can range from the rather analytical through the intensely political to the hopelessly anarchical. Langley (1990, 1991) has described analysis in the professional bureaucracy as a kind of 'shootout' between opposing forces, in order to persuade more neutral parties, who care less but vote more, while Cohen, March, and Olsen (1972; also March and Olsen 1976), describe the university as a kind of 'organized anarchy', a 'garbage can' of almost randomized behaviors. The problem with this latter view, however, is that it is difficult to partial out processes that are truly anarchic from those that merely look anarchic to observers. In other words, to what extent does the 'garbage can' represent the unexplained variance?

Yet this collective process, cumbersome as it may be (one of the authors had to seek the approval of eleven different committees within the university for a new masters program), serves the purposes of testing ideas, fitting them into the system, ensuring their adequate support, and dampening overly enthusiastic ones (as well, unfortunately, as ones that are improperly understood, politically threatening, or sometimes just novel).

And the Central Management?

In all this, some discretion does remain with the central management especially where there is the need to invest significant amounts of money or other services. In the particular cases of teaching and research, central managers would seem to influence (rather than control) these indirectly, through their ability to allocate certain funds (e.g. endowments), and to control the approval of staffing slots. Otherwise, it would seem more effective for them to try to manage the processes by which strategies emerge rather than the actual content of these strategies—for example, by influencing the structure of the collective process, by making appointments to key committees, and by encouraging (or discouraging) the champions of individual initiatives. Thus, when asked what were the major issues facing him in his job at the time, one vice principal Academic at McGill, considered highly effective, said 'in my opinion, staff relations and staffing policy', then 'working conditions', and 'salary policy'. No mention of mission (teaching and research): imagine such a statement from a corresponding executive of a corporation!

Dramatic change—turnaround, renewal, restructuring, and all the rest—would thus hardly seem to be the appropriate focus for the effective leader of a university. But the other side of the coin is that those leaders who can influence process in a significant way—by making strong appointments, establishing key procedures, and creating cultures of quality—can have a significant long-term impact on the institution, probably far longer than most corporate managers. McGill, for example, had Dawson, whose influence may still be felt more than a century after he departed—although it did take him more than a third of a century to make that impact! It might be hypothesized then that behind every great university lies a great leader, indeed one whose tenure can be measured in decades (which, given today's turnover rates, may also mean one who served long ago).

Our findings suggest, in any event, that it takes a great deal of energy and a long period of time to move a system such as a university. But once moved, the momentum of that thrust can last for many years.

Bifurcated Strategic Management

Put all this together and universities seem to end up with a bifurcated system of strategic management. One (let us call it System I, for individual) concerns a mission that is diffused throughout its operations, with a great many people responsible for micro actions that make up macro directions. The other (let us call it System C, for collective) is more aggregated and sometimes more centralized and more integrated, influential mostly in its indirect impact. Each system has its own strategies, its own strategists, its own style of strategy making, its own periods, and its own logic. One is spread out to many differentiated pockets, the other is concentrated yet opaque, a level of aggregation laid over all those other aggregates.

Our study has focused on the latter, simply because we chose to study the university as a whole. Comprehensive study of the former—of professors and programs and departments—would have taken resources many times what we expended in our study (although the following chapter considers the strategy of one such professor). If a university were a set of activities held together by common parking lots, as it has been described with some semblance of truth, then we would have had to study dozens of organizations. But there is benefit too in studying the university as a single entity, not the least as a way to open up perspectives in the field of strategic management.

What about the 'Environment'?

One actor has been absent in the conclusions so far, in our opinion the most influential of all: the 'environment'. All the discussion, debate, conflict, and analysis, etc. appears to reflect, accelerate, or decelerate changes imposed on the university from the outside. If any message comes through our data, it is about how much internal behavior was determined by external conditions. Universities are organizations that respond continuously to these conditions precisely because there are so many internal actors capable of independent response.

To understand this, System I has to be seen as a myriad of activities—programs, projects, etc.—that mirror certain needs in society: a medical program to train physicians, a research study to understand economic cycles, and so on. Ultimately, almost every activity reflects some sort of external need, brought to life by one or more internal members of a faculty. In effect, a 'champion' promotes a new activity in his or her university, which, when accepted, becomes either a temporary project (as in much research) or an ongoing activity (as in much of the teaching). Often, related activities have already been taking place at other universities, which responded earlier to the same need. Of course, each activity had to start somewhere, and so there are pioneers among universities too, or at least among their faculty members, to whom status accordingly accrues.

The internal system of collective choice acts to dampen these initiatives, by trying to ensure that a proposal is feasible, fundable, and reasonable. Sometimes a consensus of enthusiasm forms quickly around an exciting new proposal, perhaps encouraged by a management that wishes to have its institution seen to be on the 'cutting edge'. But more commonly, the collective process slows everything down until sufficient support can be generated.

In System C, where the whole institution must respond in an integrated fashion, as in McGill's response to the returning veterans after World War I, the central management can play a more active role. But again, to be proactive here usually means to respond quickly to the needs of the environment, not to get the environment to respond to the initiatives of the organization. If you look inside these enrollment decisions, you will find the environment at least as influential as the organization: the university 'accepts' the student, to be sure, but the student also selects the university.

Either way, then, strategy in the university setting is generally responsive to the environment, whether led, lagged, or, perhaps most common, mirrored. In this regard, our study of McGill University is closest to that of the US strategy in Vietnam, and farthest from that of Volkswagenwerk (even if the chapter on these two together highlighted similarities). Universities are certainly not governments, but with regard to their reactiveness, they do resemble them. This can be contrasted with businesses, which can be both more proactive and yet better insulated from the environment. Mass production in particular often requires the sealing off of the technical core, to use Thompson's (1967) memorable phrase.

In a world so obsessed with the proactive management of 'change', this may seem rather old fashioned. (Indeed, universities have historically been rather weak at marketing, which is intended to promote the organization in its environment. And now that they have discovered marketing, in some cases with a vengeance, it seems rather antithetical to their very essence.) But perhaps it is the 'new fashioned' behaviors that need to be questioned, since the citizens of a democratic society should expect their organizations to serve them, and not vice versa. In a society of

310

increasingly aggressive organizations, on every front, universities continue to offer another perspective.

WHAT CONSTITUTES THIS 'ENVIRONMENT'?

Much of organization theory treats the 'environment' as some great amorphous mass that is somehow 'dynamic' or 'complex', let alone 'turbulent' or 'hyperturbulent'. But the history of this university suggests that most of this 'environment' is rather lumpy.

Professional Control

First among these lumps has to be one force opaque to this study: all sorts of peer affiliations—in the form of professional networks, activities in other universities, research granting agencies, accreditation bodies, and so on. What appears within the university to be individual autonomy usually amounts to professional control: professors respond to their not so 'invisible' colleges of peers around the world. And so, the ostensibly independent organizations in which they work are in fact rather conformist institutions. McGill is a university remarkably like many others—better in some spheres, worse in others, reflective of its own particular context and culture to be sure, but hardly dramatically different from, say, the University of Toronto or Oxford or l'Université d'Aix-Marseilles. That is why professors can so easily come and go, carrying on their research and slipping into existing courses (by catalog number at least).

Hence Spender's (1989) term 'industry recipe', coined for business, might in fact apply best to universities. This suggests, too, that many of the premises of strategic management might apply worst to universities: the search for market position, for example, or first-mover advantage, inimitability, and so on. Universities certainly compete with one another. But more certainly, they copy each other, and cooperate happily in so doing. (While business people may try to maximize profits in some sense, or at least claim to, academics try to maximize ego: a new idea is successful, not because it is patented and protected, but if it is diffused and imitated.)

We might conclude that the most popular strategy in the university is the provision of some widely accepted service in its own particular geographic niche. Mintzberg, Ahlstrand, and Lampel (1998: 109) call this strategy 'local producer', and suggest that it may be the most common one of all, found from the corner grocery store to the national post office. Of course, business seems to be moving in the direction of increasing cooperation too, even with competitors. But that only leads us back to the claim that the seemingly unusual form of strategic management in the university may be becoming more usual in conventional organizations.

Outside Funders

A second key set of lumps of the university's environment are the funders, whether the state in the case of a public university or the donors in the case of the private ones (or both in the case of McGill). But while they may seem highly influential, particularly in their ability to demand side payments, our story suggests that these are not really key forces in their own right so much as manifestations of broader outside forces, as well as inside ones. Donors often give money, in response to needs defined by people in the university, which in turn reflect needs in society. Indeed, the Government of Quebec sought to control the new university programs by setting up a reviewing body comprising representatives of the various universities themselves. And McGill's greatest capitulation, to accept that increase in Quebec government funding, came about in part because of its own instrumental role in encouraging government funding of Canadian universities in the first place.

Users

The users of the system, notably the students, are another key group. Yet how are these to be characterized? As customers, in the popular parlance of today? There is certainly an important element of this, for better as well as for worse. Yet these 'customers' must apply and then be accepted, only to be tested and found adequate for release, unless they are found inadequate and so discharged in humiliation. Perhaps, then, the students are better described as suppliers, or even as the raw material on which the system works. Or perhaps the categories are the problem. The students are people—individuals in a particular setting called the university.

Social Forces

Behind all these actors, and actions, is perhaps the most important part of the environment: social forces. For it is to these that the system ultimately responds. And here we believe the findings of this study are most interesting.

The social forces in the environment drove the behavior of McGill University: demographic trends, economic shifts, and changing tastes and preferences, as well as wars, technological breakthroughs, and other dramatic events. One could say that a university is in the business of responding to such forces—of creating and disseminating conceptual knowledge about what is happening in society. As a result, change is business as usual for the university; that is why perhaps we saw no significant *strategic* change. At the micro level, everything in the university is always changing.

Consider so dramatic and pervasive a technology as the computer. Its presence appears in course content, in a computing center that offers a key support service, and in all sorts of applications in pedagogy, budgeting, processing of research data, etc. But can it be argued that the university is a different place today as a result of the computer, or even that it pursues radically different strategies (even if it does have a School of Computer Science as a new pigeonhole for the new technology). Contrast this with the impact of the computer on the operations of banks and airlines.

Or consider a rather dramatic social event, the student revolts of 1968, which impacted McGill much as they did many other campuses: students were appointed to all sorts of committees, some attitudes were opened up and others were closed down, but not much else changed.

MAINTAINING BALANCE

Sometimes McGill University responded quickly to some event (as in the postwar enrollments), other times it moved slowly (perhaps because of temporary fund limitations). But most remarkable is the way it seemed to balance all the pressures, to keep the whole system in a kind of extraordinary equilibrium. Events whose impact could not be balanced in the short run, such as the postwar arrival of the veterans, were eventually balanced in the long run. The university seems then to be the ultimate homeostatic system, eventually dampening the effects of all influences. In effect, lumpy as the environment may intrinsically be, after the university gets through with it, it looks awfully even!

Consider how some important change in the environment is handled in the university. First someone has to champion some manifestation of it within the system, and that seems often to be the solitary professor. Then, unless this is an issue of great crisis or else one outside of the central mission, it must be negotiated through the system of collective choice, which usually has a dampening effect on it. In effect, the organization takes its cues from the environment and then marches at its own pace (if not to its own tune), and not necessarily directed by its own conductor. The strong chief executive facilitates the change process; the ineffective one drowns in it.

313

For almost every force experienced in this system, somewhere can be expected a counterforce: conservative economists in opposition to radical sociologists, promoters of growth challenged by conservers of the status quo, humanists opposed to technologists, friends of the donors facing enemies of the rich, etc. And because power in this system is so diffuse, and about as transparent as an organization can get (and still be called an organization), almost every single one of these internal views can find supporters in the environment, so that internal political battles easily spill into the community. No wonder McGill University rarely got rid of anything (as in the battle over closing the Faculty of Dentistry, vigorously defended by its alumni). Activities did disappear, but more by dying natural deaths than by having been killed.

Why Such Strategic Stability?

What explains the remarkable strategic stability of this organization— the long-term trend lines, the entrenchment of established activities, the steady additions of new ones, the dampening effects of sudden external changes? Is this just a great big bowl of jelly that absorbs everything that comes its way, embracing discontinuities alongside trends to continue at its own steady pace?

Had we tracked components of the university, for example particular courses, or research projects, we would likely have found many changes and even dramatic shifts (as we do, and did, in Chapter 11). Yet our study of aggregations of these revealed nothing dramatic. Apparently the changes did not cluster at any one time, either because they happened not to or else because they were not allowed to.

Perhaps there is some truth in both explanations. The general university, in its range of offerings, mirrors many facets of society. These days we may be inundated with claims about change in society, renewal, turbulence, and so on, but the fact is that some things are always changing in society while many others remain rather stable. We notice what happens to be changing at the time (now, for example, information technology), but not what is not changing (such as automobiles and jet aircraft, which continue to use technologies established, respectively, almost a century and a half century earlier). So perhaps universities change as societies really do change (in order to mirror them): a few things here, a few things there.

That certainly seems to have been the pattern for McGill. One by one, the Faculties established themselves—first Medicine, then Arts and

Science, much later Management, etc. Each grew its own programs, achieved steady state, and later perhaps experienced a resurgence by elaborating some new program (often at the graduate-degree level). Some of these developments took place within programs and Faculties, while others occurred through the addition (or 'diversification') of programs and Faculties. Indeed, most of the academic infrastructure of McGill, like most other universities presumably, was in place long ago. (At least 63 percent of the students graduating in 1980 received degrees that were in place before 1900!)

Moreover, the forces of collective choice may moderate the pressures for change by allowing only a certain amount of change through at a time. After all, each committee meeting has a limited agenda, and, as noted above, for every force (including that for change) there tends to arise a counterforce. As a result, when there is much change, the counterforces for stability likely increase. A great deal of change all at once may be perceived by many people as chaotic and destabilizing; hardly any change, in contrast, may provoke too much political friction over limited resources. Some kind of balance allows for progress without disruption.

Not that anyone consciously manages such a process, at least not if this study is any indication. Each specific change may be managed, indeed very carefully, by its own champion. But the overall pattern of change seems to be guided by larger forces, some kind of invisible political hand, if you like. The system thus exhibits the characteristics of homeostasis: it maintains a dynamic balance among its various components and with its environment, by correcting any excessive swings in any direction (Katz and Kahn 1966).

So fragmentation and loose coupling prevail here, with change that is necessarily piecemeal, not quantum and revolutionary. It is difficult to change the collective mind of such an organization because it has hardly any collective mind. Each individual mind looks out to a different set of affiliations, many of these resistant to dramatic change. Indeed, a prime driver of dramatic change, market failure, that is so evident in other studies of strategic management, figures hardly at all in this one. Veterinary Science may have come and gone, but it had hardly any noticeable impact on the system.

Thus, while strategic revolution may be unlikely in universities, steady incremental change seems to be endemic—microevolutions that add up to macroevolutions. In a sense, universities change like transformers. They sit rock solid, in one place for decades, never seeming to move at all. But that belies the steady humming inside, a state of constant vibration.

315

Put differently, while nothing much ever seems to change overall, in detail things are changing all the time. There may still be a Faculty of Medicine at McGill, as there was almost two centuries ago, but probably not a single course in this Faculty today is the same as it was five years earlier. Of course, all sorts of specific activities do remain stable for a time (overall program designs, particular research projects, etc.) but some things are always changing and all things are sometimes changing.

Rethinking Strategic Management

It is customary, almost ritualistic, to conclude a study like this with a call for more research, to broaden the sample, and so on. While we agree with such sentiments in principle, and even in particular here, we prefer to end on a different note.

Universities are generic institutions. They are so alike, seemingly so common in their behaviors and activities, that we wonder if the history of McGill University is not, in some sense, the history of all universities, or, if you like, with increasing accuracy, the history of all western universities, all (general) North American universities, all (general) Canadian universities. Sometimes a sample of one can reveal a great deal about a phenomenon, as in a psychologist's study of the development of his or her own child or the physicist who split a single atom.

Can any of these conclusions inform strategic management in business? Universities seem so different from corporations, as has been noted in a few places. Yet delve into the 'knowledge work' of corporations—the research laboratories, the design studios, etc.—and you find similarities, with corresponding implications for strategies there. Indeed delve into the many rather loosely coupled corporations, such as the 3Ms and the Hewlett Packards, and you will likely find that a number of the conclusions here have application there: porous boundaries that let environmental forces in every which way; this accompanied by considerable venturing so that strategists and fragmented strategies might be found anywhere; an enormous number of micro changes with relatively little quantum change, and so on.

To the extent that this describes their strategic behavior, much that has been written about strategic management, with its focus on planning and analysis, the chief executives as 'architect' of strategy, and the management of change as driven from the 'top', becomes questionable. Certainly all the hype about turnaround and revolution, etc. needs to be reconsidered in such contexts. Perhaps these companies change best from the inside out, at their own pace, rather than from the 'top-down', frenetically.

Universities are commonly among the oldest organizations of our societies. One study 'identified only sixty-six organizations or institutions that have been in continuous existence in Europe since the Reformation of the sixteenth century'—sixty-two of them were universities! (in Neilson and Gaffield 1986: xiii). Yet universities can also be seen as among the most contemporary organizations of our societies, certainly if one compares the currently popular writings about empowerment, knowledge workers, and venturing with the nature of leadership, collective decision making, and championing in today's universities. Moreover, universities exhibit a sensible kind of stability in a world of often senseless change. And so they may well be beacons for a more reasonable future for our organizations. Perhaps the proper response to all the hype about change and turnaround and turbulence is not more dramatic intervention but more respect for institution.

As at 2007, McGill University continues its existence—in this professors opinion, with much the same spirit it has long had.

11

The Illusive Strategy

Strategies of a Strategy Researcher, 1967–91

Henry Mintzberg[1]

Chapter 10 described how the formation of strategies in a university differed markedly from that in all the other studies reported in this book. In particular, there was remarkably little overall patterning with respect to the central missions of the organization, namely teaching and research. This chapter investigates these activities with regard to a professor in that university, who happens to be the author of this book. It tracks his publications and in lesser detail teaching activities over twenty-five years of his career. The evidence shows how different his strategic behavior has been from that of his overall institution, yet how fully consistent it has been with the conclusions drawn about that institution.

This chapter is excerpted from an autobiography that I was asked to write, in reference to my academic work. Around the same time I received a call from a colleague, Charles Hampden-Turner, at the London Business School, to arrange a faculty seminar about my work. I was to get back to him on the title. When I did not, he left a message that it would be called 'The Illusive Strategy'. Perfect, I thought, I would speak on that. It was an inspired suggestion.

Strategy formation has been my most sustained topic (as will be seen in the data): it was the subject of my first article, my greatest number of articles, and my steadiest stream of articles. While this work revolved

---

[1] Excerpted from a paper originally published in *Management Laureates: A Collection of Biographical Essays*, Vol. II (S. Bedeian, ed., JAI Press, 1993; http://www.henrymintzberg.com/pdf/25years.PDF).

around the definitions of strategy as *realized* in addition to *intended*, and *emergent* in addition to *deliberate*, my own realized strategies have, if anything, tended to be rather deliberate, at least in the earlier years. At the talk in London, I wished to review my work at that time, which involved a rather wide-ranging collection of papers and projects. Because the patterns among them may not have been clear to the audience, I thought it would be interesting to use the talk to search them out, to infer my own strategies. Hence the appropriateness of the suggested title there, and my use of it here.

Data on Research and Teaching

Consistent with the other studies, this one relied especially on the most tangible and reliable data available, in particular publications, as well as, to a lesser extent, teaching activities. These are described in turn.

PUBLICATIONS

All the publications (excluding letters, short newspaper articles, etc.), academic or not, were categorized in three ways. First, they were tabulated as to whether they were empirical (deriving directly from the author's own research, interpreting this rather narrowly to mean articles rooted in empirical study rather than drawing from it), substantially conceptual, or orientated to management practitioners (intended to make findings and concepts available to them). Second, they were categorized into subject matter, such as strategy making, managerial work, organization (including structural and power issues), management in general (including a few publications on research and on the field of policy), analysis and/or intuition, and decision-making. And third, coauthorship was recorded. The histograms for all these are shown in Figure 11.1 (books are shown as shaded; obviously each was the equivalent work of many articles).

The first article, 'The Science of Strategy Making', was published as a doctoral student in 1967, and with the exception of 1969, the second year as a professor, articles were published every year since, from a single article in five of the twenty-five years of the study, to six articles and two books in 1983.

Probably the most consistent substream is the empirical, almost regularly one per year, interspersed by some empty years and a few years with two publications. But the conceptual stream is far fuller, with more

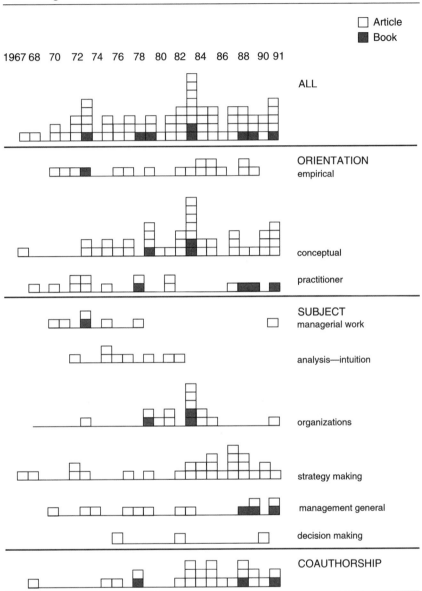

Figure 11.1 Publications

than double the number of publications and sometimes quite frequent in a single year (e.g. 1983, with the two books and five of these articles). Partly this reflects a propensity to conceptualize, but also the fact that conceptual articles, especially when spun off books, were easier to

320

do than empirical ones, and so could be more numerous. Practitioner publications represented a thinner stream, more sporadic, but indicating a personal commitment from the early years to try to reach both audiences.

In terms of content, it could be concluded from the data that there was a passing from one focus to another, initially on managerial work in the early 1970s, then over to analysis and its relationship with intuition from the mid-1970s, then to a heavy concentration on organizational issues (especially structure, power, and forms of organizations) from 1979 to 1984, and then to a stronger and more sustained focus on strategy making through the rest of the 1980s, with a rise at the end of the study period in the management–general category, representing especially two editions of a textbook and one summary book for practitioners.[2]

Three articles on decision making are shown, well spread out, the heaviest concentration of work being for the first one, which was published in 1976, although the work was done in 1973 (indicating the need to take into account what can be long lead times in publishing research).

The management–general category shows a thin trickle from early on to 1983, representing some of the practitioner articles as well as ones on research and on the field of policy in general.

Finally, while strategy making clearly peaks as by far the heaviest concentration of articles through most of the 1980s, this theme was returned to throughout the study period.[3]

The histogram on coauthorship indicates solo writing for most of the early years, some joint work in the mid-1970s, and then considerable and sustained coauthorship after Jim Waters joined the McGill faculty in 1976 and later with Frances Westley and a number of others, increasing in the later years.

TEACHING

Figure 11.2 plots all the teaching activity.[4] As can be seen, there were not a great variety of courses taught, given the number of years.

[2] Footnotes that specify each of these publications, as well as a listing of all the articles used in this analysis, can be found at the end of the original publication (http://www. henrymintzberg.com/pdf/25years.PDF). See also 'Books' and 'Articles' on that site for a full listing of publications.

[3] The first article, as a doctoral student in 1967, opened with a comparison of two approaches to strategy making, Darwinian and Biblical, that anticipated the later distinguishing of emergent from deliberate strategy.

[4] The data here were not so readily accessible, so there may have been some inaccuracies, which should not have affected the overall patterns. The year recorded refers to the beginning

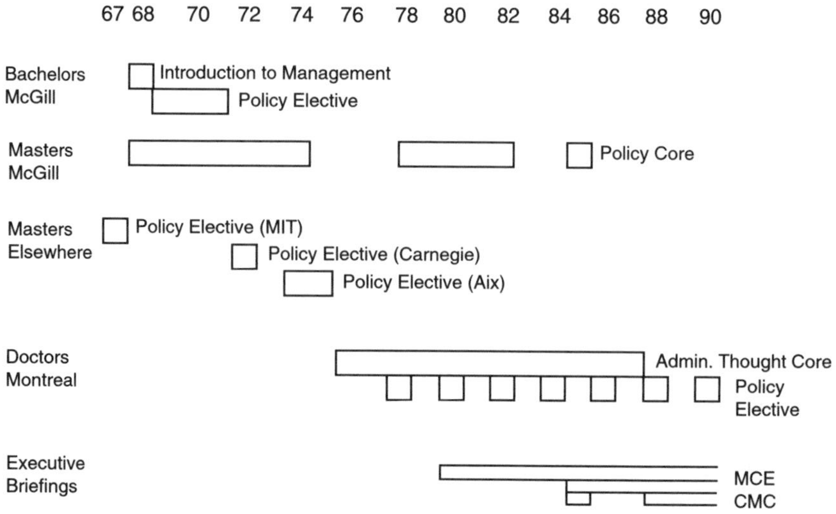

Figure 11.2 Teaching

The mainstay was mostly the MBA policy course (the author having been hired at McGill in 1968 to take over the full-year core course that had fallen into disarray). In general, one or two sections of it were taught in almost all the years at McGill until near the end of the study period, aside from a sabbatical and leaves (to France from 1974 to 1976, and Switzerland in the winter of 1983), as well as three-and-a-half years running the doctoral program in the late 1970s. (Figure 11.3 tabulates appointments, sabbaticals, and visits, etc.) A similar master's elective course was taught as a doctoral student at MIT in the 1960s, and again as a visiting professor at Carnegie Mellon in the Spring of 1973, and again on the sabbatical followed by a year's leave of absence in Aix-en-Provence, France, in 1974–6.

Some undergraduate courses were also taught in the years at McGill (an introduction to management in the first year of teaching and a strategy elective in the next three).

MBA teaching ended in 1986, with negotiation out of it on reduced salary, to concentrate on research, writing, and doctoral training (and to manifest the beliefs expressed in *Managers not MBAs* [Mintzberg 2004]).

Doctoral activity began with the creation in 1976 of a joint program among the four Montreal universities. The author played a major role in

of the academic year: for example, the Carnegie course shown in 1972 was actually taught in the spring of 1973.

322

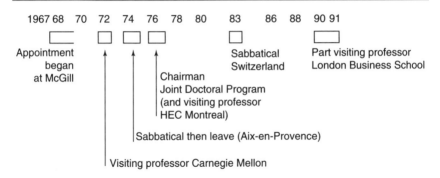

Figure 11.3 Appointments

its design and championing, and upon return from Aix-en-Provence in 1976, was asked to run it, which he did for three-and-a-half years. Teaching included the introductory course required of all doctoral students, called 'Fundamentals of Administrative Thought', as well as a policy elective every second year, more or less, beginning in 1976 and continuing till the end of the study period.

Finally, the chart shows a stream of 'executive briefings' beginning in 1980: a two-day public program for managers held in Europe that drew much of the author's work together. It was offered at first once and later twice a year, a third added in Canada from 1988 onwards.

These data suggest (to the author at least) a clear pedagogical focus in the work. In fact, one central course always served to integrate much of the thinking and activity, and stimulated and directed much of the writing. In the earliest years, it was the McGill MBA core policy course. After the return from France that focus shifted to doctoral teaching, particularly the administrative thought course. And in the later years, the two-day briefings emerged as the focal course. As shall be discussed later, the *push* of theory gradually gave way to the *pull* of issues.

Phases Over Time

Other 'hard data', to come later, perhaps tell the story of the periods best. These are the diagrams used in the publications over the years. When they were considered as part of this exercise, a surprising result (again to the author) emerged: they clustered into three clearly distinct groups.

All these findings suggest that this career unfolded in three fairly distinct phases. In fact, the commencement of all three can be identified

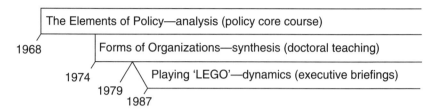

Figure 11.4 Phases

with rather tangible events, although the second and third phases took some time to manifest themselves fully. It was not so much that one phase ended when another began, but rather that the second and then the third phases added to the first as mind-set shifted over time (hence use of the word 'phase', not period). As we travel through life, we do not so much replace baggage as add to the baggage we already carry. In the following sections, the three phases labeled in Figure 11.4 are discussed.

RECTANGLE PHASES, THE ELEMENTS OF POLICY: ANALYSIS (FROM 1968)

I returned to Montreal in 1968 with not only a doctoral thesis but also an outline for a book, to be called 'The Theory of Management Policy'. I set out to write it, chapter-by-chapter, week-by-week, the first time I taught the McGill MBA Policy Course. By 1991, twenty-five years later, I was still writing it.

The dominant textbooks at the time, out of Harvard and containing mostly cases, were either devoid of conceptual material or else soft-peddled bits of it. Policy, or general management, was, as a result, absent from the new theory-based schools of business. I set out to change that, but misjudged the task! Based on an outline I had first developed in 1978 (see Figure 11.5), I opened files on each chapter, to collect notes and relevant articles. Folders soon became boxes, and the boxes began to overflow and multiply. The intended strategy was well formulated; implementation became the problem.

As I wrote the chapters, I began to bind them together to hand out as a kind of text in the MBA policy course. Over the years, some of these eleven chapters appeared as articles, or multiple articles, while others (on managerial work, structure, power, and strategy) eventually emerged as books in their own right.

Policy as a Field of Management Theory

   Ch. 1. Introduction: The Study of Management Policy
   Ch. 2. An Underlying Theory for Management Policy

The Policy Elements

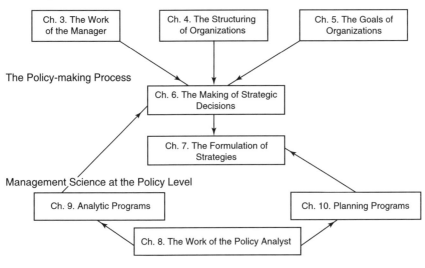

The Policy-making Process

Management Science at the Policy Level

Management Policy Tomorrow

   Ch. 11. The Future of Management Policy

Figure 11.5 Outline of 'Theory of Management Policy', *c.*1973

Hence much of this first phase, up to 1974, was devoted to writing that 'book' as well as to pursuing research that fitted in with its chapters—notably on strategic decision-making and strategy formation. An initial publication in the *Proceedings of the Academy of Management* annual meeting of 1972 outlined a project to be undertaken on strategy making, researched in term of patterns in streams of decisions.

Most of the publications of this period were likewise related to these chapters, two on strategy making and several on managerial work, including a first book based on the thesis (*The Nature of Managerial Work*, 1973), and various articles spun off it. Miscellaneous publications of this period included two for Canadian practitioners, one of them in a government journal that came out of a consulting assignment, and two monographs for the US National Association of Accountants and the Canadian Society of Industrial Accountants, about the use of normative models and about

325

why managers did not use accounting information the way accountants, at least, thought they should.

Aside from this focus on the textbook, looking back on that phase, I see myself as a rather conventional academic. My world was neatly compartmentalized into organizations conveniently chopped into various elements and processes, which served as the focus of my pedagogical activity, writing, and research. Despite some rumblings about upcoming attention to emergent strategies and managerial intuition, in retrospect the work at that point seemed most decidedly deliberate and analytical. One need only look back on those nicely sequenced sets of rectangles in Figures 11.5 and 11.6, typical of almost all the diagrams of this phase.

BLOB PHASE, FORMS OF ORGANIZATIONS: SYNTHESIS (FROM 1974)

Leaving for a sabbatical to Aix-en-Provence in the fall of 1974 proved to be a turning point, or at least coincided with one; both personal (opening up to the splendor of southern France) and professional.

Before leaving, I read all the collected literature in the boxes on the structuring chapter, and set out to develop a detailed outline to take along. The problem was to find an integrating framework. Pradhip Khandwalla, who joined the McGill Faculty of Management in 1971, found in his doctoral thesis that organizational effectiveness depended less on doing any particular thing (such as planning, or decentralizing power), than on doing several things in interrelated ways (such as centralizing power while staying small and remaining informal). We came to call these 'configurations'. So the problem of the outline came to be solved by synthesizing the literature of organizational structuring around several distinct configurations, or 'ideal types', of organizations.

By the time of departure for Aix in September 1974, I carried a 200-page outline of the 'chapter', so specific that by December I was able to complete the first draft of what was to become a 512-page book, *The Structuring of Organizations* (Mintzberg 1979*b*).

The first parts of the book laid out various 'design parameters' (such as unit grouping and liaison divisions), followed by findings on how these were influenced by various 'contingency factors' (such as the size of the organization and the complexity of its environment). Combing all this led to five basic configurations of organizations, labeled simple structure, machine bureaucracy, professional bureaucracy, diversified form, and adhocracy. Everything seemed to fall naturally into place in terms

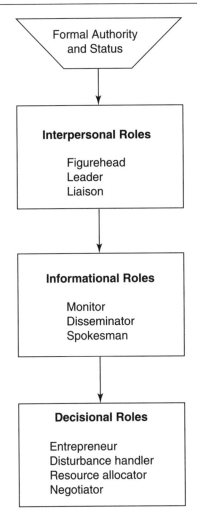

Figure 11.6 The manager's working roles

Source: *The Nature of Managerial Work* (Mintzberg 1973*b*, p. 59).

of these five forms. To depict all this, I developed a basic diagram that was used in various ways. It became the book's logo of sorts, as illustrated in Figure 11.7.

The next 'chapter', on goals and power, took much more time. (I failed to do a detailed outline.) It made use of the same notion of configuration, and finally appeared as *Power In and Around Organizations* (Mintzberg 1983*a*), exactly 700-page long. The original 'textbook' was becoming a series of books. Also, whereas its original outline cut up the world of

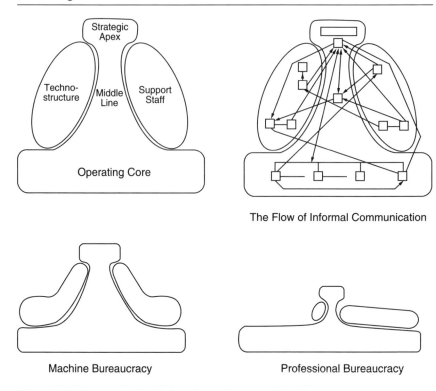

Figure 11.7 Structuring book logo in various manifestations

Source: *The Structure of Organizations: A Synthesis of the Research* (Mintzberg 1979b).

organizations into categories such as structure, power, and strategy, the writing of it changed my perception into combinations of these in the form of whole organizations. The field of organizational theory needed to distinguish its 'species' no less than the field of biology.

Before the departure for France, we had developed a proposal for a McGill doctoral program in management. When the other Montreal schools got word of it, given the need for approval at the level of the provincial government and the concern that McGill's program might preempt others, they produced proposals of their own. The government committee decided that the four Montreal business schools should get together and develop a joint doctoral program. So we sat down and did that, and my return from France was greeted with a request that I run the new program, which I did for three-and-a-half years. Suddenly, the management of an adhocracy made up of four professional bureaucracies came to life in my life.

This was supplemented by my teaching in the program, especially the course in administrative thought. While coming back to the MBA policy course upon my return from France, my pedagogical focus shifted, from young aspiring managers to older aspiring researchers. A number of ideas developed in the administrative thought course, particularly concerning the role of intuition in management, especially as published in a review of Herbert Simon's (1977) book *New Science of Management Decision* (Mintzberg 1977, see also 1976). This too became an important turning point, as discussed below.

Configurations had entered my mind, but the elements of the original textbook outline remained in my writing. In fact, by far my most concerted effort after returning from France was the research project on strategy making. With a sizable research grant from the Social Science and Humanities Research Council of Canada, we began to track the strategies of organizations over time, as reported in this book.

Much of this work was done with a new colleague at McGill, Jim Waters, while doctoral students in the joint program carried out a number of these studies. The configuration notion was not lost, but gradually began to appear in how we saw the strategy-making process in different contexts (e.g. entrepreneurial, what was earlier called simple structure, in Steinberg's, adhocracy in the NFB, again as reported in this book, and carried further in Chapter 12).

Other articles published during this second phase spun off the books of structuring and power, including some on social issues (e.g. 'Who Should Control the Corporation?' [Mintzberg 1984]). One lengthy publication, entitled 'Beyond Implementation: An Analysis of the Resistance to Policy Analysis' (Mintzberg 1979*a*), related to the intended Chapter 8 of the original textbook, and there were in 1978 two articles on research methodology. Also two articles appeared in the *Harvard Business Review*, 'The Manager's Job: Folklore and Fact' (Mintzberg 1975), which summarized the conclusions of the thesis for a practitioner audience, and 'Planning on the Left Side and Managing the Right' (1976), which related some findings about the brain's two hemispheres (Ornstein 1972) to some thoughts about the nature of managing.

Both changed the course of my career. The former brought my work to a wide audience for the first time—I was told it evoked the largest immediate demand for reprints that the *Review* had experienced to that time—while the latter had its effect on me personally.

Ornstein's book seemed to explain much of what I had observed in my research: that managers seemed to 'know' in two very different ways; that managerial work was characterized by 'calculated chaos'; that what seemed to matter most in strategic decision-making (such as diagnosis and design) remained a great mystery. 'Planning on the Left Side and Managing on the Right' was written rather quickly, and sent to the *Harvard Business Review*, which accepted it. Then a copy was sent to Herbert Simon, professor at Carnegie Mellon. He replied soon after, commenting, 'I believe the left–right distinction is important, but not (*a*) that Ornstein has described it correctly, or (*b*) that it has anything to do with the distinction between planning and managing or conscious–unconscious.' Simon referred to it as 'the latest of a long series of fads'.[5] A day or two later, as I recall, the *Harvard Business Review* wrote that they needed the final draft immediately.

Herbert Simon was to me not just the most eminent management theorist of our time but one with no close equal. He had been devoting the latter part of his career to issues of human cognition, in the psychology laboratory. Did Simon know something I did not? Or was there some kind of block in his thinking? After brief agonizing, I decided on the latter. My right hemisphere, my own intuition, won this debate, and my career took a turning point. Coming from the side of analysis, it had arrived at the knife-edge of intuition, and by this decision went over to the other side.

I broke with the long-dominating rationalist view of management, represented especially in the work of Simon himself, who later came to define intuition as 'analyses frozen into habit' (Simon 1987). I later came to compare a 'cerebral' view of management with an 'insightful' one.

So this second phase was a time of loosening up and of opening up, a shifting from the rather analytic toward intuitive, with more attention to synthesis. If my realized strategy could not strictly be labeled emergent, it had certainly become less formally deliberate. Perhaps it could be called an umbrella strategy, guided by the notion of configuration, with that old textbook outline still infusing my thinking, perhaps most tellingly by the rectangles that had become those blobs in Figure 11.7.

[5] This and our subsequent correspondence were reprinted with Simon's permission (in Mintzberg 1989: 58–61).

CIRCLE PHASE, PLAYING 'LEGO': DYNAMICS (1979–87)

In 1978, a student in our doctoral program, Alain Noël, asked me a question that was to change my thinking a second time: 'Do you mean to play jigsaw puzzle or LEGO with the elements of organizations?'

The answer at that point seemed to be jigsaw puzzles—*The Structuring of Organizations* put the elements of structure together in five predetermined ways, the power book in some more. But the question led to much more thinking about 'LEGO', and the collecting of examples of organizations that did not fit into one or other of the configurations so much as combined elements of several. This was the beginning of the third phase, shown in Figure 11.4 as a diagonal line from 1979, when that question was posed, to when I began work on a serious answer (published as 'Forces and Forms in Effective Organizations' [in Mintzberg 1989]). This did not dismiss the five forms so much as consider them as five forces by which to build different kinds of organizations. The skeleton of this idea is shown in Figure 11.8.

In 1980, I was invited to do a two-day 'top management briefing' for the Management Center Europe (MCE). This led to doing such briefings on a

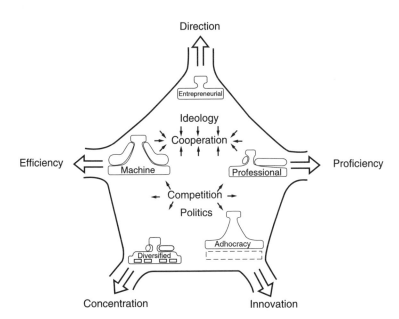

Figure 11.8 Skeleton of the forces framework

regular basis. The teaching focus thus shifted toward practicing managers, and how the concepts that I had been developing in my research and writing could be of use to them. In other words, this took me another step from the push of concepts, so common in the business school, to the pull of issues.

In 1985, I served as the faculty representative on a university-wide committee concerned with budgeting problems. I suggested that the university could eliminate its deficit if it paid professors for what they really did, for example less if they stopped doing research. It soon occurred to me that I could apply this to myself. I was becoming increasingly disillusioned with conventional management education (see Mintzberg 1989, chapter 5): it no longer made sense to me, socially or economically, to continue the pretense of creating managers in a classroom. The MCE courses made clear to me that management education should be reserved for people who know how organizations work, whose experience is deep and tacit, and whose place in the classroom is determined by their accomplishments, not their aspirations.

So I proposed to the dean at McGill that I stop teaching the MBA policy course, go on reduced load and salary, and concentrate on writing, research, and the supervision and teaching of doctoral students. I also began new research to revisit managerial work, by spending a day with various managers to get a better sense of the varieties of ways in which management is practiced.

I explain all this before discussing the publications of the third phase because the order of presentation reflects the phase itself. This is what drove my work in these years.

As befits more pull and closer connection to practice, my writings became more disparate: hence the 'illusive strategy'. The study of strategy formation at the National Film Board of Canada indicated that the absence of clearly focused strategy for a time does not necessarily mean a lack of success; it can be quite the opposite. Perhaps that applied to me too in this phase; certainly my own behavior was shifting from that of a professional bureaucrat to more of an adhocrat.

Two applied books appeared in this phase. *Mintzberg on Management* (1989)—I preferred the subtitle, *Inside our Strange World of Organization*—drew together various published articles as well as a few new ones for practitioners. (It became, in a sense, the closest to that originally intended textbook, but not with that outline.) And the second was a real textbook (with James Brian Quinn), entitled *The Strategy Process*. It comprised the cases he wrote, or chose, and the readings I mostly chose, or had already written.[6]

On the more scholarly side in this phase, many of the publications in the late 1980s brought to fruition work of the previous phase, especially the studies of strategy formation (reported in this book), followed by an article entitled 'Crafting Strategy' (Mintzberg 1987*a*) to draw out the broad conclusions. Work also began during another sabbatical, in 1984 in the Swiss Jura, on the originally intended chapter 7, about strategy making. The outline divided that 'chapter' into two books, the first called *Strategy Formation: Schools of Thought*, intended to review the literature, and the second, *Strategy Formation: Towards a General Theory*, to extend the configuration notion to strategy stages across the evolution of organizations.

The first volume appeared in a preliminary form as half of someone else's book (Mintzberg 1990). [Later, this became a book in itself, coauthored with Bruce Alhstrand and Joseph Lampel, called *Strategy Safari* (1998), while one of its chapters, on the 'planning school', also appeared as a book in its own right, called *The Rise and Fall of Strategic Planning* (Mintzberg 1994). And now, in 2007, that proposed second volume finally appears here, after a fashion, in Chapter 12.] Related publications appeared on the nature of strategy, strategic vision, strategic positions, decision-making (once again), and cycles of organizational change (see Figure 11.9).

One characteristic of this third phase, already suggested, was a greater willingness to go with ideas as they came up, much as did the National Film Board of Canada in its periods of divergence. This resulted in a number of 'one-off' papers and articles, mostly coauthored, for example on customizing strategies, strategies for financial services, and managing design.

Two major activities of this phase included revisiting work done in the first phase. The return to observing managers at work has already been mentioned. This included a restatement of my original model of managerial roles, this time in the form of concentric cycles, related to information roles (communicating, controlling), people roles (leading, linking), and action roles (doing, dealing), as shown in Figure 11.10.

Finally, there were two publications on broader social issues. 'Training Managers, Not MBAs' explained my dissatisfaction with conventional

---

[6] There was an interesting irony here. Finally, given the chance to do a real policy textbook after so many years of struggling with one, indeed with most of the chapters already written and some awaiting publication, I ended up doing something different.

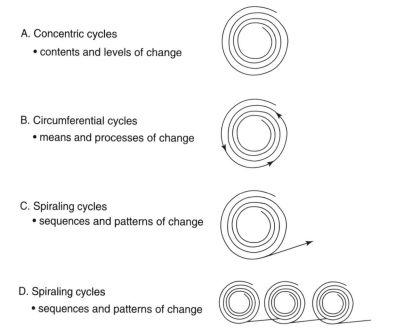

A. Concentric cycles
  • contents and levels of change

B. Circumferential cycles
  • means and processes of change

C. Spiraling cycles
  • sequences and patterns of change

D. Spiraling cycles
  • sequences and patterns of change

Figure 11.9 Cycles of organizational change (from Mintzberg and Westley 1992: 41)

management education, while 'Society Has Become Unmanageable as a Result of Management' (both in Mintzberg 1989) expressed my concerns about the prevailing practices of management. 'Learning in (and from) Eastern Europe' (Mintzberg 1992) described the need for grassroots learning rather than formal planning in times of difficult social change, while suggesting that it was not capitalism that had 'triumphed' in the West so much as balance among the private, public, and social sectors. [This will become my next focus of activity, in the form of an 'electronic pamphlet' entitled 'Getting Beyond Smith and Marx: Toward a Balanced Society', a rough version of which was drafted about ten years ago.]

So where is that illusive strategy? Not so illusive, unless one insists on the kind of intended strategy that drove my earliest work. As my activities have grown more varied, I believe that the overall thrust has become more integrated, coming together around the themes that have been struggling to get out in these past twenty-five years: working to achieve more effective and humane organizations. Gradually I have come closer to organizations while always maintaining my distance from them, in order to consider their impact more broadly, while probing into their specifics.

A Model of Managerial Work

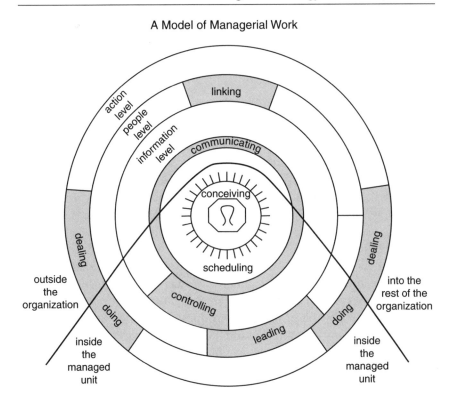

Figure 11.10 Framework for describing managerial work

Source: Adapted from Mintzberg, 1994*b*.

Overall, I have been searching for their deceptive effectiveness, first through study of their elements, subsequently combined to understand their forms, these then surpassed to reveal their dynamics, all the while concerned with the dark recesses of intuition hidden amidst the brilliance of their formal analysis. Cycling has characterized my own behavior as well as the theory I have developed, as I have come to see organizations in increasingly dynamic terms. One need only look at the circling and cycling diagrams of this third phase, illustrated in Figures 11.9 and 11.10, even in a sense, 11.8!

A Conceptual Interpretation

We turn now to a conceptual interpretation of this study, in terms of the questions posed about strategy and strategy formation in each of the preceding studies, but here with what appears to be different answers—or perhaps not.

ORGANIZATION?

This study, of course, differs from all the others in one notable respect: there was no organization here, or at least the organization was in the background, McGill University as a professional bureaucracy that enabled its professors to act rather autonomously.

But there were other aspects of organization here too. As in Steinberg's and Canadian Lady, the individual could develop a strategy more or less as he or she wished, since working in a professional organization is a bit like being the leader in an entrepreneurial organization. There was also some evidence here of the momentum found in the machine organizations as well as others, such as the NFB, as strategic baggage was carried forward. So perhaps some aspect of bureaucratic momentum is embedded in our personal beings no less than in our formal organizations.

As time went on, the professional in question opened up increasingly to his environment—that 'real world' academics like to talk about, if not interact with. And so he took on characteristics of an adhocrat. This study of an individual, ostensibly rather independent of the forces of organization, thus provides traces of all four forms of organization that have been seen in this book: entrepreneurial, professional, machine, and adhocracy.

LEADERSHIP? ENVIRONMENT?

Leadership was obviously absent in this study, at least in any conventional sense, because the subject under study had no one to lead but himself. Others could, of course, have chosen to follow—either his concepts or his initiatives. But that was up to them.

But there was still the interplay of leadership with the environment. Did the individual, in his research, publications, and teaching, lead or follow it? The most obvious answer is that because most of his conceptual work was descriptive rather than prescriptive—in other words, designed to learn about the world and convey that learning, rather than to propose changes—he followed the environment. He took his cue from what it conveyed to him.

But that implies a rather simple view of descriptive research: that the researcher tells it as it is. More accurately, he or she tells it as it looks through the lens chosen and where that lens is aimed. So there is an interesting interplay between leadership and environment here, back and forth, with each influencing the other (or at least trying to), much as strategy formation was described in the professional organization itself in Chapter 10. The same can be said of teaching too. The professor has to teach not only what the students of the subject are expected to know (e.g. in a strategy course, Porter's view of the process as analytical and deliberate), but also what he or she believes they ought to know (e.g. that emergent strategies are equally important).

LOTS OF EMERGENCE IN THOSE DELIBERATE STRATEGIES

This story itself was mostly one of deliberate strategies, certainly in the early years. The individual in question may have promoted the notion of emergent strategy, and challenged strategic planning, but the thrust of his early work was driven by very clear intentions—the outline of that original textbook—which continued to influence some of his work to the end of the study period.

To be true to him, I should point out that this was not inconsistent with how he saw and described planning: not to create strategy, but to program the strategies that have been created in other ways (in his case the original outline did not come out of any planning process: he learned his way into it over time). But this study certainly suggests a prevalence of deliberate strategies.

But not entirely. As time went on, there were clearly emergent aspects, to the point that the label 'umbrella strategy' was used: a deliberate strategic perspective under which could emerge a variety of strategic positions. Indeed, by the last phase, of that 'illusive strategy', even patterning (realized strategy) was not entirely clear. Much like the NFB, there was somewhat of a drift to diversity: the individual allowed himself to be led somewhat by issues he perceived in the environment. As noted earlier, the professional bureaucrat was becoming more of an adhocrat.

PHASES, NOT PERIODS

Interesting in this regard, as already noted, is how a person, like an organization, can accumulate conceptual baggage over time, so that the old strategies are not replaced by new ones so much as supplemented by them.

At McGill University, we did not find distinct periods, unlike all the other studies. But here, for a professor in that university, we did find such periods. Except they have been labeled phases rather than periods, because of that baggage carrying over from one to the next. Also, while there was a rather sharp turning point between the first two phases, there was more of a phasing in between the second and the third. Still, the phases were distinct, most evidently so in the changing nature of those diagrams.

This individual has always been predisposed to using diagrams in his work. (Perhaps this can be explained by his long-forgotten training in mechanical engineering, never practiced.) But he was never consciously aware of how the forms of those diagrams changed over time until he undertook this systematic study of his own behavior. Like an organization that can be surprised to be shown the patterns that appear in a study of its own history (such as McGill's student population growing by a compounded rate of 3.78 percent over more than a century), this individual was likewise surprised by seeing all those rectangles followed all those blobs (which he was, of course, aware of doing, but not compared with what came before and after), followed by all those circles and cycling [and, at the time of this writing in 2007, many triangles]. That is one great benefit of systematic research, a message that has finally been driven home to this systematic researcher!

INSIDE THE LONE STRATEGIST'S MIND

This leads us inside the strategist's mind. He had to study himself to find this out, and also become more aware of turning points in his career. Here, as in Canadian Lady, we see the impact of the occasional but critical event or decision on subsequent strategies. Of course, in this study it has been convenient, once again, not only to be able to identify one clear strategist, but also to have that strategist available for the brainstorming (even if he did it by himself).

Perhaps the most interesting aspect of the last two studies considered together, McGill University and one of its professors, is how the behavior of the individuals who make up an organization, assuming that the subject of this study is typical of his colleagues, can be so opposite of the collective behavior of that organization. McGill had no distinct periods, no clear turning points, few deliberate strategies, and so on. In the university, there are so many individual minds that perhaps the collective mind hardly gets a chance!

Such are the wonderful anomalies of studying strategy all over the 'real world'—even that of professors and universities!

Henry Mintzberg has continued to publish on management, organizations, analysis and intuition, decision-making, social issues, and even strategy. His latest book, *Tracking Strategies... Toward a General Theory*, has been published in 2007 by the Oxford University Press.

12

Toward a General Theory of Strategy Formation

Evident in these eleven studies have been both marked differences and striking similarities in how strategies form in organizations. This final chapter seeks to carry both toward a general theory of strategy formation.

The first part of this chapter considers the most evident differences. The organizations studied, and the strategy processes they used, seemed to fall roughly into four distinct groupings, or 'configurations': a visionary process in the entrepreneurial-type organizations, a planning process in the machine-type organizations, a learning process in the adhocracy-type organizations, and a venturing process in the professional-type organizations. Of course, there were all kinds of behaviors in all eleven situations. Even the most decentralized adhocracy, for example, can be guided by a central vision, while even the most machine-like organization can experience venturing, however clandestine. But some kind of a convergence, as above, around these four configurations was rather marked.

The second part of this chapter looks beyond different types to common stages: how these strategic processes of visioning, planning, learning, and venturing order themselves over time as organizations are created, developed, mature, and may subsequently be 'turned around'. This second section, we shall see, does not necessarily contradict the first, because the configurations can order themselves in stages too; for example, organizations tend to be founded with visioning in the entrepreneurial form, under strong leadership, no matter where they end up.

340

Configurations of Organization and Process

Chapter 1 introduced four basic definitions of strategy:

- Plans for the future (intended strategy)
- Patterns out of the past (realized strategy)
- Positions on the ground (generally concerning products and markets)
- Perspectives in the abstract ('theory of the business' in Peter Drucker's words)

Combining these in pairs, as was done in the matrix shown in Chapter 1 and reproduced here as Figure 12.1, suggests four basic processes of strategy formation:

- Strategic Planning: deliberate plans about tangible positions
- Strategic Visioning: deliberate plan as a broad perspective
- Strategic Venturing: emergent patterns manifested as tangible positions
- Strategic Learning: emergent patterns that result in a broad perspective

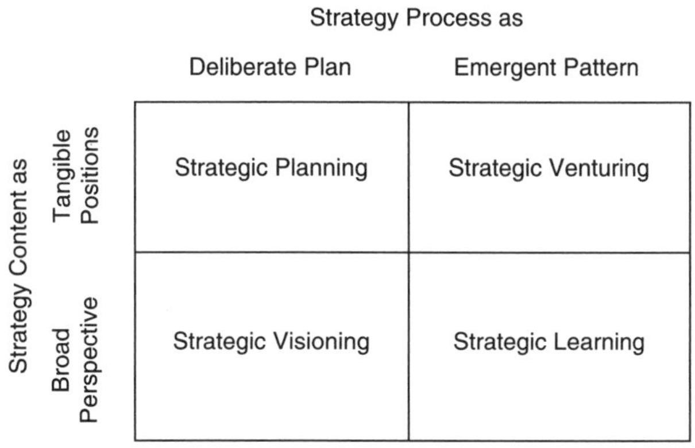

Figure 12.1 Four processes of strategy formation

THE FOUR ORGANIZATIONS MAPPED ON TO THE FOUR PROCESSES

These four processes were rather evident in the various studies reported in this book. And so too were the four basic forms of organizations

Internal Power

		Centralized	Decentralized
External Environment	Stable	Machine Organization	Professional Organization
	Dynamic	Entrepreneurial Organization	Adhocracy Organization

Figure 12.2 Four basic forms of organizations

developed in *The Structuring of Organizations* (Mintzberg 1979, 1983c, the labels used here are from 1989: part II). These are depicted in the matrix of Figure 12.2, and are described as follows:

- *Entrepreneurial Organization*: controlled personally by a single leader (or sometimes a small, tight team); generally found in startups, small organizations, and turnarounds, which often require firm leadership, and in environments that are competitive, or dynamic in other ways

- *Machine Organization*: produces mass, standardized products or services with rather unskilled labor, subject to many technocratic controls; generally but not necessarily large and usually mature; found in rather stable environments

- *Adhocracy Organization*: organized around teams of experts working on projects to produce novel outputs, generally in highly dynamic settings

- *Professional Organization*: dependent on highly skilled workers who work rather autonomously, subject to professional norms; mostly provides standardized services in stable settings

The relationships between the four processes of strategy formation and these four forms of organization seemed to be rather strong in this research, as we shall see in discussing each of the studies.

US Strategy in Vietnam

The context of US strategy in Vietnam was significantly machine bureaucratic, particularly with respect to a military that was fighting a foreign and largely guerrilla war, although the State Department could also be described as a professional organization, and the White House at times as an entrepreneurial one. The favored process of strategy formation was clearly planning, especially in seeking to implement in Vietnam the strategies that were formulated in Washington. This was carried to its penultimate form in Secretary of Defense Robert McNamara's Planning, Programming, Budgeting System (PPBS). The realities on the ground, however, sometimes demanded rather more of an emergent process, although little of what happened can be described as strategic learning, let alone venturing. There was vision at some stages—most clearly that of the 'Domino Effect'—which proved to have been flawed.

Volkswagenwerk

Here was a classic machine organization—a mass producer with a vengeance. And most of the history was about the programming of existing strategic positions and perspective through formal planning. The exceptions to this were the original startup of the 1930s, the re-startup in 1948, and the turnaround in the 1970s, all of which can be described as strategic visioning in the entrepreneurial form.

Steinberg's

This was the archetypical entrepreneurial firm, with the founder still at its helm, firmly in charge, at the end of the study period, sixty years later. The dominant process of strategy formation was visioning, as the leader elaborated, adapted, and occasionally renewed his vision. Yet toward the end, in an organization grown large and diversified, beyond his sphere of personal knowledge, it became somewhat machine bureaucratic in structure, as the leader's visioning gave way somewhat to more formal planning.

National Film Board of Canada

As much as Volkswagenwerk was the classic machine, the NFB was the classic adhocracy, with teams of filmmakers producing their novel outputs. Here, in fact, we see a great deal of strategic venturing, with some of that leading to strategic learning, as the organization converged periodically on one theme vision or another, before going off on a new cycle of eclectic venturing.

Canadian Lady

Remaining relatively small throughout the study, and always tightly managed by members of the founding family (even after it was sold to a large conglomerate), Canadian Lady was another entrepreneurial organization.

It was classically influenced by strategic visioning, as became especially evident when one of its chief executives described how he renewed its strategy in response to market forces.

Air Canada

Here, again, was classic machine bureaucracy, in the business of providing standardized services on a mass basis. And as noted in the study, Air Canada during the study period was an obsessive planner, but not a particularly novel strategist.

Sherbrooke Record

This was a study of entrepreneurship, given the small size of this organization and the ease with which its owners could exercise control. One of them, however, chose not to do so, but rather let it drift, with little attention to strategy, as position or perspective. An intermediate sought to exercise that control, but lacked the necessary resources, and so failed to affect a turnaround. The next arrived with the necessary resources as well as a clear vision, and drove that turnaround, for better and for worse.

Arcop

Here we come back to adhocracy, in the form of a creative, would-be collegial company of architects carrying out one novel design project after another. Again, we saw a good deal of venturing, which periodically fed a process of strategic learning. Behind the scenes, however, was an entrepreneur of sorts—one of the founders who was the driving force, even if not the formally designated chief executive. From him came the vision that always set the organization's course.

Dominion Textile

Here was another large, machine-like mass producer, inclined to strategic planning. Over its long history, this company experienced significant external changes, especially in the form of competitive processes in the later years, which at one point gave rise to entrepreneurial leadership to affect turnaround.

McGill University

This was certainly the classic professional organization, with a highly trained corps of professors who pursued their own interpretation of the organization's mission, namely teaching and researching. And so venturing abounded, some of it strategic in the sense of adding to or changing the mission, through the elaboration of personal or departmental positions and perspectives. Overall, there was little collective strategic planning, almost no collective strategic learning, and only the broadest of strategic vision (that hardly changed in over a century). No clear period of overall change could be discerned in the long study period. The study of one of its professors illustrated this role of venturing, alongside that of personal strategic visioning and individual strategic learning.

So the mapping of the four approaches to strategy formation on to the four forms of organization seems to work rather well, with two modifications: the existence of strategic venturing alongside strategic learning in the adhocracy organization, and the appearance of strategic visioning in any form of organization when a forceful leader has to take charge, which in a sense reverts it—however temporarily—to the entrepreneurial form.

We can now consider the characteristics of each configuration of strategy formation, as indicated by these studies.

STRATEGIC VISIONING IN THE ENTREPRENEURIAL ORGANIZATION

Leadership in the Lead, for Better and for Worse

In this configuration, leadership dominates the strategy process, for better and for worse. The rest of the organization, in contrast, tends to be malleable and responsive to that leader. And while the environment here can be demanding and perhaps competitive, what appears to characterize this configuration is the capacity of the leader to confront it: first by stepping back to see what needs to be done, and then by going forward into a certain void to take action, as was most evident in the case of Larry Nadler at Canadian Lady.

Startup, Turnaround, and Small Size

Such entrepreneurship was most evident in these studies under three conditions: startup, turnaround, and small size.

Almost all the organizations started life in its entrepreneurial form, the one evident exception being McGill University, which lacked strong founding leadership and so struggled for years before it got going. This sort of leadership was evident in pretty much all the other organizations studied, even the NFB adhocracy, which quickly became an adhocracy but was nevertheless firmly directed in its first six years by its founding leader. Likewise, Air Canada, a classic machine bureaucracy, was strongly guided in its formative years, not by its own chief executive so much as by the minister of government who championed its creation.

Entrepreneurship was also prevalent in turnaround, and not only in the organizations that were already entrepreneurial, namely Canadian Lady, the *Sherbrooke Record*, and Steinberg's. Volkswagenwerk and Dominion Textile, both machine-like organizations, reverted to the entrepreneurial form in order to bring about major needed changes. In other words, they consolidated powers around single forceful leaders, who could effect these changes. It could also be argued that President Kennedy was an entrepreneur of sorts when, in the early 1960s, he chose to single out Vietnam as the place to confront communism in Asia.

Small size is the third condition that favors the entrepreneurial form, because in the small organization forceful leadership is often the easiest way to coordinate activities. This was most evident in the *Sherbrooke Record*, which never grew large, and was therefore always responsive to its leadership, even when it was passive. Arcop too, never grew really large, and despite the adhocracy nature of its work, when push came to shove, it deferred to its true leader even though he was not its official chief executive.

The Steinberg's study, as noted, bore evidence that when an organization grows large under its founder, despite strong pressures to become machine-like, it can retain much of its entrepreneurial character. At least this seems to apply to retailing, where, as noted, a single leader can retain entrepreneurial control because 200 stores can amount to one store repeated 200 times.

Of course, the focus on the single individual is what makes the entrepreneurial organization especially vulnerable. One heart attack, or a leader unwilling or unable to exercise responsibility, can quickly undermine the whole organization. This was evident at the *Sherbrooke Record*.

Strategic Visioning, Deliberately Emergent

Strategies as plans, patterns, positions, and perspectives can be found in any organization. But what seems to characterize the entrepreneurial organization is perspective—strategy as a clear and sometimes novel vision—and therefore the strategy process as especially one of visioning.

Strategic vision can be described as deliberately emergent, in the sense that while the vision, as eventually worked out, sets direction rather deliberately, it also does so flexibly, serving as a kind of umbrella under which specific strategic positions can emerge. So general visions, unlike specific plans, tend to provide considerable scope for strategic venturing and learning, as was evident in a Steinberg's that could engage in all kinds of experiments, such as its no-frills discounting of the 1970s. Compare this with Air Canada's foray into a half-hearted shuttle service between Montreal and Toronto.

Steady Adaptation with Rare Strategic Shifts

The very fact that there can be steady adaptation of strategic positions under the strategic umbrella means that the umbrella itself, the strategic vision (perspective), need not change very often. Indeed it was a remarkable feature of the entrepreneurial organizations how rarely their strategic perspectives changed: perhaps three times in sixty years at Steinberg's, two in thirty-seven years at Canadian Lady, once in thirty years at the *Sherbrooke Record*.

Dedicated entrepreneurs seem to find their strategic perspectives and stay with them, concentrating their attention on bringing them to fruition through true continuous improvement. No flavor of the month for these people, rather visions that remain stable over long periods of time. (If you believe this has changed in these times of so much hype about change, consider IKEA.)

Of course, it is their general nature, unlike specific plans, that makes these visions sustainable: the organization can do a great deal of adapting under that umbrella. What especially distinguishes the great entrepreneurs, such as a Sam Steinberg, is their ability to choose such visions. Even at Volkswagenwerk, so machine-like, the great visions came from the two entrepreneurial leaders, Nordhoff, who took the reins after the war (in what amounted to a startup condition), and Leiding, who turned the company around in the late 1970s and then promptly got fired. The first vision lasted almost twenty years. Indeed one large part of it, Porsche's original idea about the 'people's car', came ten years earlier, while it might be argued that shades of the second vision continue to this very day, almost forty years later. (Take a look at the Beetle, Golf, and Passat.)

Not that the entrepreneurs cannot change their own visions: we saw that strength in Sam Steinberg—as long as he understood the business.

When he did not, when he expanded beyond his knowledge base, he was incapable of coming up with a strategy.

The Entrepreneurial Issue: How to Get into the Mind of the Strategist?

It may be useful to identify one major issue of strategy formation for each of the configurations, and summarize briefly how it has been exposed in this research.

In the entrepreneurial configuration, with the focus on the single leader, the issue might be: What happens in the mind of the strategist? Or, what is strategic thinking anyway?

The question applies directly here, in the case of the single strategist. It also has a broader application, namely the mind of the collective strategist, i.e. when people interact to come up with a collective vision. This we shall discuss under the adhocracy configuration.

The study of a Sam Steinberg, or better still a Larry Nadler at Canadian Lady, because he was able to brainstorm with us, proved most helpful in addressing this question.

At Steinberg's, in tracking its diversification into other forms of retailing (see Figure 3.6), we had clear evidence of how an organization learns its way into a strategic perspective under entrepreneurial leadership, as one move evoked another. And at Canadian Lady, we had the unfreezing–changing–refreezing model applied with Larry Nadler, also the discovery that one or two critical incidents can lead to a eureka-type flash, and thus consolidate a good deal of learning into the kernel of a new strategic perspective.

The trick, of course, as discussed in the Steinberg's study, is to distinguish the discontinuities in the environment that matter from the great many that require no major adjustment. But the very fact that one leader dominates the entrepreneurial organization means that if he or she can see it, the rest of the organization can usually be convinced to respond to it. Unlike the machine organization that often seeks to control its environment, the entrepreneurial organization, especially its leader, tends to be attuned to changes in the environment and can be more responsive to them.

It might be noted that the adhocracy organization is likewise so attuned, since there is a strong connection between the environment and the organization's ever-changing projects. But collecting all that response into some coherent perspective is its problem, unlike the entrepreneurial organization, where one person can act. This, by the way, is true of the professional organization, where, in a sense, each professional can be an entrepreneur unto him or herself.

STRATEGIC PLANNING IN THE MACHINE ORGANIZATION

Organization takes the Lead

In these stable mass-production or mass-service organizations, which are usually large, the organization tends to dominate, with its need for stability and order, while leadership follows, in the sense of catering to the organization's need for order. Even the environment can be obedient, if the organization has chosen its place well, as such organizations are inclined to do, or else has gained enough power to impose its will on the environment.

Above all, the machine organization tends to resist external changes in order to maintain its standardized processes and steady output. These 'machines' are after all built for production, not change. And so their strategies are built into the designs.

When the outside pressures build up, however, the leadership will try to encourage some response. But if this proves insufficient, or the organization fails to respond adequately, as is common, there may be no choice but to revert to the entrepreneurial form (as discussed earlier).

Focus on Deliberate Strategic Planning

Accordingly, the strategic process in the machine organization tends hardly to be strategic at all, but one of programming the strategic vision that has been built into the structure.

This tends to be called 'Strategic Planning', since it takes place on a regular basis in a formalized way, ostensibly looking ahead five years or so, updated with annual budgets, schedules, and operating plans, etc. While the vision may remain fixed, or else obscure, there can be attention to new strategic positions, in the form of new products and markets within the overall strategic perspective—as discussed in Chapter 1, a new Egg McMuffin or two, but rarely a McDuckling a l'orange.

With the machine organization's emphasis on standardization, however, even this level of strategy tends to be 'generic', as rather formalized positions, often in conformity with those of competitors, rather than novel forays into the marketplace. The machine organization tends to take its strategies off the shelf, so to speak, often to be applied in its own geographic niche.

Decades of Stability Interrupted by Bursts of Change

The description of the soldier's lot—months of boredom interrupted by moments of terror—applies more or less to the machine organization. As noted, it prefers stability, or perhaps more accurately, continual fine-tuning of its business model. And so it does what it can to maintain that, tending to put off serious change until a crisis occurs. And then it is not the existing organization that changes so much as the form of organization: the machine form reverts to the entrepreneurial form, suspending its standards and procedures so that a strong leader can take charge and force the needed changes. A new strategic perspective is developed, the organization is 'turned around' to accept it, and then it can settle back into its machine form.

Volkswagenwerk

The clearest example of all this is Volkswagenwerk, which kept modifying its famous 'Beetle' until the market made it clear that the company would have to undertake serious change.

So it did, but in a disorganized fashion, 'groping' and 'grafting' for a time until a new strong leader appeared to consolidate those efforts into a new strategic perspective. Even here, in a company so large and formalized, the new strategy emerged out of the learning of the dispersed groping and grafting. Then the company settled down with its new direction: back to the fine-tuning. So much so, in fact, that the new entrepreneurial leader was forced out. He had done his job; his kind of leadership was no longer acceptable to a majority of the board.

Vietnam

The US strategy in Vietnam mostly followed a similar pattern of stability interrupted by periodic change, except that here the major shifts took place more frequently, almost like an adhocracy cycling in and out of focus (to be discussed later). That was because the 'environment', notably the 'competition', namely the enemy, was very aggressive.

An early leader (Kennedy) was certainly proactive, but unfortunately so because this created the quagmire that a later, weaker leader (Johnson) could not escape, as the bureaucratic momentum built up.

The interplay of deliberate with emergent strategies was especially interesting here, especially due to the bureaucratic momentum and drift: emergent strategies that come to be formalized as deliberate, intended strategies that once realized became unexpectedly emergent, and intended strategies that were, destructively, overrealized.

Air Canada

Many factors, as noted, drove Air Canada into a highly machine bureaucratic form of organization: its size, its heavy investment in equipment, the inherently mass-programmed nature of its services, and a necessary obsession with safety. All this, together with an overriding need for the formal planning of its operations and investments, encouraged conservatism in its strategy formation process, which appeared largely incremental and resistant to major change, even to strategic thinking.

Even its founding entrepreneurship was of a restricted kind, as noted, largely outside its own boundaries, in the person of the government minister who championed its creation. And subsequently, in the four decades of this study period, there was no entrepreneurial intervention for turnaround.

Strategies, as a consequence, were not only highly deliberate, but often deliberately imposed: by the initial champion and later by the norms of the industry to which the organization faithfully subscribed. Air Canada slotted into its role as Canada's flag carrier, much as did so many other airlines around the world, each operating in its own geographical niche. Some of its strategies, as noted, even became deliberate to the point of being implicit, as the organization focused so concertedly on fine-tuning its business model (as in the example of planning in terms of 'thin' southern routes, as if this thinness was a given).

Dominion Textile

This organization came out somewhere between Air Canada and Volkswagenwerk. Like both, it was a large, established mass producer, the dominant player in its geographic niche. So it was drawn strongly to the machine form.

But more like Volkswagenwerk, it had to face tough competition at times, and so was forced to react, also reverting to entrepreneurship to change its strategic perspective. Thus we saw considerable stability interrupted by the occasional need for significant change, sometimes of an emergent nature (e.g. when those 'sideshows' moved to center stage).

In this study, we saw most clearly the power of the dominant company in an important industry to drive, or at least influence, the political agenda of its government. Solidly behind this was its leadership, much of the time protecting the organization from external changes.

The Machine Issue: How to Notice the Need for Change Amidst all that Fine-tuning?

As was evident in all these studies, but especially those of Air Canada and Vietnam, the focus on strategic planning as programming can render the management insensitive to important changes taking place in the environment. After years spent concentrated on fine-tuning the machine, how are people to perceive big changes that sneak up in little ways— for example, the Volkswagen Beetle gradually losing its appeal? Strategic thinking seems to atrophy when there are so many people tinkering with so many details.

It appears that only when the environment hits the management over the head with some event, a kind of dramatic manifestation of some long-developing trend, such as the Tet offensive in Vietnam, does the management of many a machine organization seem to respond.

Of course, entrepreneurial organizations face such changes too, while the management fine-tunes in its own way. But its own way makes all the difference. For here, systems of a formalized nature do not tend to get in between the leadership and the operations. The entrepreneurial leader is inclined to be hands on, personally immersed in the details, as were Sam Steinberg and Larry Nadler. And that is where changes in the environment make themselves known—in the tangible events on the ground, not the aggregate statistics in the offices. So the leader, at least when he or she cares, can respond rather quickly, as we saw in these entre-preneurial organizations. A management instead absorbed—mesmerized might be a better word—by strategic planning and business analyses, etc., to keep the machine running smoothly, can be far less receptive to these messages.

STRATEGIC LEARNING IN THE ADHOCRACY ORGANIZATION

From two rather centralized forms of organization, even if rather dif-ferently so, we turn now to a third form: adhocracy, which is highly decentralized. Here a great deal of influence rests with teams of experts who work on novel projects in a dynamic setting—for example, films in the National Film Board of Canada or architectural projects in Arcop.

The Prevalence of Emergent Strategies

As pointed out in Chapter 1, and has been somewhat evident in the discussion earlier, most strategies have emergent as well as deliberate elements. But with teams of experts working on projects to create novel outputs, we should expect the emergent aspect of the strategies that do form, to be especially prevalent; in other words, for them to grow out of spontaneous convergence, as single projects set precedents that create patterns. Put differently, the adhocracy organization is most inclined to *learn* its way into new strategies, as positions and perspectives. We saw this in the NFB's first feature film that led a stream of such films, as well as in Arcop's first design of an arts center that led to many more such projects.[1]

Cycling In and Out of Focus

In both adhocracies of this research, these patterns—that spontaneous convergence of a strategic perspective, came and went. Both organizations repeatedly focused for a time, and then diverged, to provide wider scope for their creative talents, whether in response to external forces or merely to the fashionable preferences of their experts. Indeed, even in the periods of convergence there was always some divergence at the margins: projects that did not fit into the patterns, or patterns in strategic positions that did not fit with the dominant strategic perspective position (e.g. experimental films in the NFB).

So alongside the strategic learning was always a good deal of strategic venturing, some that helped to establish new patterns, some that broke existing patterns, and others that simply went their own way.

Unlike the entrepreneurial and machine configurations, however, here we found shorter periods of convergence, or focus on strategy, and longer periods of divergence, or functioning without a clear strategic perspective. Not only were the adhocracies apparently able to tolerate times without clear strategic orientations, but also they seemed to thrive on them. As noted, some of the NFB's best films were produced during periods out of focus.

So while clear strategic positions seem to be indispensable in machine organizations, and compelling strategic visions likewise in entrepreneurial organizations, that seems not necessarily to be the case in adhocracy organizations. Indeed, these organizations seem to have to dispense with their overall strategic perspective periodically, and deliberately, in order to sustain their adhocracy status.

One final note of interest: US strategy in Vietnam seemed in a way also to cycle in and out of focus. Could there have been an adhocracy aspect

---

[1] It should be noted that the establishment of such patterns does not undermine subsequent creativity. This simply continues under the umbrella of the new strategy perspective (i.e. no two NFB feature films were ever alike).

to it too? In two respects, perhaps yes. The military tends to be orga-nized, classically, as machine bureaucracy. But faced with an opponent organized for guerrilla warfare—in other words, in small, flexible, hit-and-run units, which can be described as quintessential adhocracy—it may have to respond somewhat in kind. And second, US strategy in Vietnam was as much a political as a military endeavor. So while the politicians were directing a massive military bureaucracy in Asia, in Washington they were also producing their own streams of ad hoc political and diplomatic decisions. To do this, they themselves had to be organized in adhocractic ways.

Environment Taking the Lead

Adhocracies are fundamentally opportunistic, in the sense that they tend to respond quickly and directly to their environments. That is what project work is all about: each and every output is a response to some specific external need. The same can hardly be said about tomatoes in a supermarket or automobiles coming off an assembly line.

Conventional business is often described as opportunistic. But the very nature of mass production and mass service means that strategies are settled upon, clear and deliberate, even if they originally emerged, in order to drive rather standardized operations. So the organization does not respond to the environment, at least not continuously, so much as it tries to figure out the environment and then proceed in the hope that it has guessed more or less correctly for a considerable period of time. As the chief executive of Canadian Lady expressed it so clearly, once he had his new vision, it was time to put their heads down and proceed at full steam. So too with Volkswagenwerk, once it had that new strategic perspective, and even with the US government in Vietnam during those periods of stability in strategy.

The adhocracy, in contrast, only hopes that each particular project proves right, as it moves from one to the next. Indeed, even the projects themselves are flexible: each is a problem-solving exercise, the object of which is to get things right by the end, not the beginning. If it guessed wrong, it simply adapts. Indeed, that is where much of the creativity comes in, as in the NFB going with its first feature because a meant-to-be shorter film ran long. So it is the adhocracies that are truly opportunistic; they have the most porous boundaries of all the organization forms.

Indeed, they can be too responsive to the environment and too impul-sive. We saw examples of these organizations going with what was fashionable at the time, even if inappropriate, as when the NFB leaped into its early series for television.

Leadership is the least important force here—is less of a force than in the entrepreneurial and machine organizations and less influential than the environment as a force, as well as the organization, wherein these projects are carried out, rather independently of the leadership.

This is not to say that leadership should be counted out in adhocracy. It can be an important force in any organization, as was demonstrated by how long the founder's vision continued to influence the NFB—to the end of the study period almost four decades later—and how influential Ray Affleck was whenever he cared to exercise his power at Arcop.

As for organization, this can be counted out even less, at least in the form of the experts who made up these two organizations. They may have acted opportunistically, often in their own interests and according to their own tastes as teams. So internal forces, beyond formal leadership, were also highly influential.

Hence the functioning of adhocracy really comes down mainly to the interplay between organization and environment. The teams seek to impose their preferences on the environment, but to be successful they must remain very attuned to the needs of that environment. This was true to such a degree at Arcop that in our report we questioned whether the projects were chosen by the organization, or by its customers. We might conclude that the experts of the adhocracy take their lead from the environment, and then seek to fashion their responses to it.

Conventional machine organizations, especially large, established ones such as Air Canada and Dominion Textile, seem to exercise great control over their environments. But their sheer size and deliberate strategies can in fact lock them into rigid positions in that environment, notably in the marketplace. Compare this with the rather casual flexibility of the adhocracy, and then ask yourself where proactive free will really resides.

The Adhocracy Issue: How to Read the Organization's Mind?

The issue discussed for the entrepreneurial organization was how to get into the strategist's mind. In the adhocracy configuration, strategy formation is largely a collective process, with many people acting on behalf of the organization. And so adhocracy affords us the opportunity to delve into the collective mind. How do we read that?

This is obviously not a simple question, and we are certainly not going to answer it here, if anyone will ever do so anywhere. But our studies provide some clues, especially concerning the comings and goings of rather emergent strategies, unintended order, 'where preparation meets opportunism' (King 2006).

We have seen examples of how single precedents create patterns that constitute strategies. We have also seen how many individuals, by choosing to diverge from these patterns, can lead the organization into a period of creative divergence. And we have seen all this happening without the intervention of any formal leadership—unless you take the precedent-setters to be the leaders (it is not sure that they so take themselves!).

Can we even talk about the collective mind of an organization? No less, perhaps, than we can talk about the culture of a society. From a cognitive as well as a social point of view, the two phenomena may be quite similar. After all, strategy as a collective process is certainly rooted in the culture of an organizational community. And culture itself is rooted in the collective behavior of some community.

What our two studies of adhocracy make clear is that the highly decentralized organization can sometimes move in a remarkably organized manner, even if that was not planned or directed. Do we thus have the wisdom of crowds in organizations (Surowiecki 2004)?

And if this can be so evident in adhocracy, can it not appear, if more subtly, in other forms of organization? We saw shades of this in the US strategy in Vietnam, which was influenced, in the final analysis, by a large swing in public opinion, and perhaps in Volkswagenwerk too, when its new strategy converged out of the groping and grafting toward new models. Did leadership in these two cases 'decide' on the new strategies, or did it follow the wishes of the collective mind? As Isaac Bashevis Singer puts it, 'We have to believe in free will; we've got no choice.'

STRATEGIC VENTURING IN THE PROFESSIONAL ORGANIZATION

Reduce the team of adhocracy to the individual, couple many of these individuals together even more loosely than the different teams of an adhocracy, reduce the need for novelty, and you end up with the professional organization. Here, a group of individuals pursue their own professional interests under the banner of a common organization.

I write this book, for example, in the process contributing to the central mission of my university, namely the creation and dissemination of knowledge. But aside from having studied a number of Montreal-based organizations, I could have been doing this anywhere—it has little to do with McGill University in Montreal per se. Few of my colleagues even know I am doing it, including the central managers of the university. Sometimes, of course, we professionals work on our ventures with colleagues—in fact, for most of the studies of this book. But many of these colleagues were not even at McGill University.

McGill has in fact contributed to this effort enormously, but indirectly, by providing support: it pays my salary, offers me all kinds of administrative backup, and for me most important of all, has created an atmosphere, a culture that makes it a very comfortable and effective place for me to work.

So we end up in the professional organization with a great deal of venturing but hardly any of the collective learning found in adhocracies. People learn here in their own way, or at least with the help of their colleagues, who are as likely to be in other professional organizations, as in their own departments. The real organization might thus be the professional association: for me the Academy of Management, or the Strategic Management Society, where I have had opportunities over the years to present and discuss my ideas with colleagues from all over the world. The professionals thus *constitute* their own professional organization, but they do not *consolidate* it.

Rare Periods of Overall Change?

The prime manifestation of all this, at least as indicated by the study of McGill University, is the absence of clear periods of change. If changes are happening constantly, but independently, all over the place, then does there have to be much overall change? The answer, of course, has to be yes when the environment speaks to various parts of the organization with one voice. At McGill University, it hardly ever did—remarkably, even after the ravages of war and depression, except to adjust back on course.

So to understand strategy formation in the professional organization, you have to go where most of the strategies form: to the individual professionals, and behind them, to the professional associations that set their standards of practice.

We found that adhocracies tend to mirror changes in society. But they seem to do so selectively, at certain cutting edges of innovation: a new film here, a new building design there. Professional organizations mirror social changes too, but in a broader and more pervasive way: for example, knowledge creation and dissemination across a wide range of social and technical phenomena in the university, or many aspects of acute treatment in the general hospital.

So it should not be surprising to find that such organizations change as societies change. For example, as the population of Canada and Quebec grew rather steadily for over a century, so did the enrollment at McGill University. And where there was particular change in certain pockets of that society—in practices of health-care and styles of English literature and theories of management—then there were parallel changes in the pockets of the university that concerned themselves with these phenomena.

This suggests that the boundaries of the professional organization are even more porous than those of the adhocracy, with the professionals connected personally every which way—with clients, with community groups, with professional colleagues around the world, and with the professional associations that set and maintain the standards.

We have, as noted earlier, all the hype these days about turbulence and hyper-competition, etc. Everything is supposed to be changing all the time. That seems to be true of the professional organizations, but in a totally different way: lots of things are always changing around them, but the organizations themselves seem hardly to change at all, at least if McGill is typical. Perhaps that is no less true of society itself! (More on this later.) Both march merrily along, hardly immune to change, just treating it as business as usual, in many spots in particular but nowhere in general.

Deliberate Strategies if not Deliberate Strategy

As a consequence, we could not find much overall deliberate strategy at McGill, nor much central strategy at all, for that matter, at least concerning the overall mission: research and teaching, the creation and dissemination of knowledge. Yet the study of just one of its professors suggested that the university hardly lacked for strategies, even deliberate strategies. Multiply this one professor by a thousand and you get the idea.

If the issue in adhocracy is to read the collective mind, maybe the equivalent in the professional organization is to recognize that there is no collective mind, only a great many individual minds (which can, of course, be read like the entrepreneurial leader's mind).

Of course, all this overstates, even if it does suggest some central tendencies not found in the other configurations. For one thing, there exists an intermediate level in universities, comprising schools and departments, etc. (not studied) that may fall somewhere between professional individuality and collective behavior. Here there can be collective strategy (e.g. in the degree program offered by a department, or a research project conducted by a team). But these do not add up to collective strategies, or overall periods of strategy and change, for the whole organization.

Indeed, an interesting aspect of the professional organization is that, just that as the whole organization is divided into departments (schools in universities, clinical services in hospitals, etc.) which are given considerable autonomy over their own programs, so too are these programs divided into activities, such as courses in the university, medical interventions in the hospital, over which individual professionals are given considerable autonomy. A major problem in these organizations, as a consequence, is that when the need for flexible coordination arises between these various departments, programs, and activities, it is rarely forthcoming in any spontaneous way.

Another aspect of central tendencies in these organizations is what might be called overall 'style', for example, an emphasis on the fields of technology in an MIT or on practical learning in a US state college. Can we call these styles strategic perspectives? They seem to be so, until we realize that they tend to be permanent, built into their institutions, sometimes for centuries, and so hardly patterns of choice. Perhaps we should call them meta-perspectives, or just plain cultures, and recognize that strategies are about how these styles are manifested, in the operating reality, as all the micro positions and more specific perspectives that appear all over the organization.

There are, of course, spheres where strategy does have to be common for the whole professional organization, but they tend to concern support activities more than mission itself. At McGill, for example, funding was an important central issue where strategies did change over time. But even here, the changes tended to be more gradual than sudden. Even what seemed like the best example of sudden change—accepting a large provincial grant for the first time—turned out, upon investigation, to be the continuation of an established trend: one could see it coming. Is this typical of the professional organization? Obviously, the answer will require studies of more such organizations.

Individual Leaders Taking the Lead, in Response to their own Environment

Who is the strategist in the professional organization? Mostly it is the individual professional; that is, all kinds of individual professionals all over the place, like cats each after their own prey, and not to be herded together.

So if overall leadership with regard to strategy formation tends to be weak here—never entirely weak, just relatively so the other configurations, particularly the entrepreneurial and machine compared wish—the overall organization is even weaker, although the components of that organization can be very strong if we can talk about an organization at all, compared with a group of loosely coupled individuals.

But do not count out the environment, for the same reason as in adhocracy—what matters here is the interplay between the individual and that part of the environment to which he or she responds, together with immediate colleagues. In the university, for example, that is the local teaching hospitals for certain professors of medicine, the latest novels for certain professors of English, etc. So the environment of the professional organization cannot be conceived as one homogenous entity, as in the market for cars in an automobile company, or the market for food in a supermarket chain (however segmented each may be). It is more like a collection of lumps.

This relationship of professionals with their environments seems to resemble that of adhocracy teams with their environments: interaction back and forth, with the professional sometimes seeking to lead it and always prepared to respond to it, if not to follow it. But professional work tends to be far more standardized than project work in adhocracy, which is about innovation. There may be innovation in some of the research of universities (although far from all; most researchers do what Kuhn [1970] has called 'normal science', namely working obediently to solve little puzzles within an established paradigm). And there is far less innovation in the teaching. And when you move to other professional work, such as medicine or accounting, the degree of standardization is even more pronounced. (Anyone for a creative surgeon?)

So, reminiscent of the machine organization, the professional settles down with his or her strategy for a time. Venturing for most is at best an occasional thing. In the university, for example, developing a new teaching program or undertaking a new research project can establish rather standard behaviors for years, even decades (as was true for the research project reported in this book). In adhocracy, in contrast, creative venturing is continuous and advanced with each new project.

The Professional Organization Issue: What is Strategic Management Anyway?

Add up all the above and you end up with what might be called a homeostatic organization—one in a dynamic equilibrium, with many small changes adding up to little big change, like a transformer vibrating in one place. No wonder that such a high proportion of the organizations that last for centuries are universities. Why change the organization when it is just a collection of mirrors reflecting the many changes in society?

And that puts into question all the conventional notions of 'Strategic Management' (as discussed in the conclusion to the McGill study): Should strategies be formulated in order to be implemented? Has the role of the planner been overrated? Is Strategic Planning the answer to concerns about strategic thinking, or just an oxymoron? Might explicit, deliberate strategies get in the way of strategic venturing? Does strategy get lost when the chief executive views him or herself as the 'architect' of strategy? Is 'turnaround' the necessary answer to the long-term survival of an organization?

What comes out of the McGill study is that the strategy formation process can be far more devolved and nuanced than the Strategic Management literature suggests. But is this just a quirky institution, with no relevance for more conventional organizations?

Not if one reads other literature, about how organizations are changing: toward more knowledge work, more 'empowered' workers, more venturing and decentralized championing, and, with the rise of all kinds of alliances and joint ventures, more porous boundaries. Perhaps it is Strategic Management, as conventionally and commonly practiced, that will ultimately prove quirky. Perhaps it is also time to recognize that there are not two 'conventional' kinds of organizations—the entrepreneurial and the machine—but four, including the professional and the adhocracy. The thinking in conventional business has driven the thinking in other spheres for long enough; it is about time that these other spheres SWOTed back.

Table 12.1 summarizes our findings about these four configurations.

Stages of Strategy Formation

Outlined above were four distinct categories, of strategies, processes, organizations, and conditions, called configurations. But there were also indications that these can overlap, and infiltrate each other, for example when a machine organization changes by reverting to the entrepreneurial form, or when pockets of adhocracy infiltrate a professional organization (as in research teams).

Here we shift from the categories to the overlaps, by considering the findings of these studies in a different way: as stages in the life cycles of organizations, as they appear, develop, falter, and are renewed. This, we

Table 12.1 Configurations of organization form and strategy formation process

	Entrepreneurial Organization	Machine Organization	Adhocracy Organization	Professional Organization
Studies	Steinberg's, Canadian Lady, *Sherbrooke Record*	Vietnam, Volks-wagenwerk, Air Canada, Dominion Textile	NFB, Arcop	McGill, Mintzberg
Conditions	Startup, Turnaround, Often small organization, Dynamic environment	Mass production and service, Mature organization, Stable environment	Innovation, High technology, Dynamic environment	Skilled workers, Stable environment
Power vested in	The leadership	The system	The project teams	Each professional
Integration	Strongly coupled by direct suspension	Tightly integrated by formal design	Loosely coupled	Decoupled
Favored strategy process	Personal Visioning	Planned Programming	Collective Learning (and Venturing)	Individual Venturing
Strategies	Umbrella perspective, Flexible positions (emergent within deliberate)	Entrenched perspective Firm positions (deliberate)	Emergent positions and perspectives	Portfolio of individual positions (deliberate and emergent)
Pattern of change	Steady progress with periodic shifts	Long stability interrupted by occasional revolution	Cycling in and out of focus	Frequent shifts of positions within overall stability
Environment, leadership, organization	Leadership takes the lead	Organization takes the lead	Environment takes the lead	Professionals in the organization take the lead
Key strategic issue	Mind of the strategist?	Recognizing need to change?	Collective mind?	Strategic Management in question?

shall see, takes us closer to an overall model of the strategy formation process.

THE ART, CRAFT, AND SCIENCE OF THE STRATEGY PROCESS

Figure 12.3 shows a triangle based on three main approaches to human endeavor: art, which is about creative insights, and is rooted in the imagination, usually of an individual; craft, which is about practical learning,

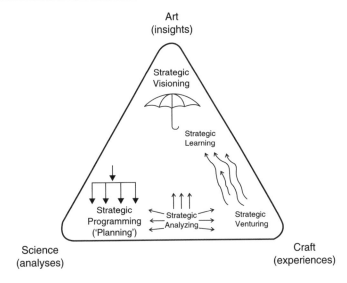

Figure 12.3 Strategy process as art, craft, science

and is rooted in experience, often shared by many people; and science, which is about systematic evidence, and is rooted in analysis, often carried out by specialized experts.

Inside the triangle are located the various strategy formation processes that have been discussed in this chapter: Strategic Visioning, by virtue of its creative nature, even its very label, closest to art; Strategic Venturing and Strategic Learning, by virtue of building on tangible experience, closest to craft (but learning approaching art in its results); and Strategic Programming ('Planning'), by virtue of its systematic nature, closest to science. Added is Strategic Analyzing, in the form of SWOT (strengths, weaknesses, opportunities, and threats) and competitive analyses, etc., close to science but feeding its results toward all three corners of the triangle. Considering all these in terms of how organizations develop over time, and so take on different forms, leads us to a life cycle model of organizations—in the stages of initiation, development, and renewal. Each is discussed in turn.

INITIATION

How do organizations get started, and where do their initial strategies come from? Clearly, and most of our studies bear evidence of this, they commonly begin with entrepreneurship of one kind or another, as well as some form of strategic vision, typically from a strong leader who creates the organization in the first place. Steinberg's was the most evident example of this, but close behind was the NFB, with its first leader, and even Air Canada, with the government minister behind it. Only McGill, with a very hesitant beginning, was an exception.

(A) Starting with the Founder's Vision

But where do these leaders' visions come from? Most evidentially, they are learned personally, though experimentation in one form or another, namely by venturing. So what ends up as art begins as a craft. The vision—the strategic perspective—emerges, even if it can later appear to be so deliberate.

This learning can happen before the organization is founded—indeed, the vision can be the basis of its founding. We saw this in Porsche's concept of the people's car, that led to the establishment of Volkswagenwerk, also in Grierson's beliefs about documentary filmmaking, developed though his experiences in Scotland, and brought to Canada for the founding of the NFB.

(B) Learning that Vision along the Way

But the vision can also develop in an emergent fashion, within the new organization, as the founding leader learns from his or her experience there. Sam Steinberg started at a very young age in his mother's store; he imbibed her beliefs about customer service, and learned about buying fruit and vegetables, etc. But the rest, about running a supermarket chain, he had to learn along the way. Even at Volkswagenwerk, which really got started as a commercial enterprise in 1948, Nordof inherited Porsche's notion of the people's car, but not much else. The rest he had to learn as he went along.[2]

(C) Importing that Vision

Sometimes, however, the founder does not create the vision but imports it, fully developed, from some other organization. Canadian Lady was the clearest example of this, starting off as the Canadian 'licensee' of an existing US undergarment operation. The firm was the 'local producer', if you like, with an imported strategy applied in its particular geographic niche.

---

[2] IKEA is an even more interesting case: Ingvar Kamprad began by selling pens; apparently took over a decade to develop the company's interesting business model.

DEVELOPMENT

The second stage, once the organization has been established, is development. As we have seen, organizations can develop in sheer size (the US effort in Vietnam), or else in their capabilities (Arcop), although some develop hardly at all (the *Sherbrooke Record*).

Limited Growth

The *Sherbrooke Record* remained rather small and limited to its geographic niche. There are a great many other organizations that do so too, although not included in this research: the corner grocery store, for example, or the gourmet restaurant. The latter, of course, tends to develop in its capabilities, as did Arcop. Arcop grew, but then consolidated, more than once, partly in response to market forces, but also to maintain its design capabilities and adhocratic nature. So the firm kept learning, unlike the *Sherbrooke Record*, perhaps, which simply continued to operate as an entrepreneurial organization in its niche.

Entrepreneurial Growth

Other organizations in this research grew, some retaining their entrepreneurial character for long periods of time. Most notable was Steinberg's. It grew in waves for six decades under its founding entrepreneur, attaining large size that put increasing pressure on him. He retained control because, as noted, in retailing many stores can constitute one store repeated many times (also because no one else ever gained control of the voting shares). Only when the company moved into other spheres of retailing—another province, other kinds of cultures—did his control become problematic.

Canadian Lady, too, retained its entrepreneurial character throughout. Partly it did not grow so large, and partly its industry too required the flexibility of entrepreneurial leadership.

Programming the Vision

But with development, many organizations need to change form. The evidence of this research suggests they do so in one of two ways.

Some, predisposed to mass production or the mass distribution of services, as they grow large are drawn to the machine form of organization and the planning and analyzing processes of strategy formation. They formalize their processes, both operating and strategic, by programming their initial vision into tangible market positions and specific operating plans.

Air Canada was the most evident example of this, but hardly the only one: Volkswagenwerk and Dominion Textile were the others. Even, or should we conclude especially, US strategy in Vietnam can be described in this way, particularly when Robert McNamara, as secretary of defense, applied his PPBS system, which turned out to be a lot more about *p*rogramming and *b*udgeting than about *p*lanning in any *s*trategic sense.

The programming of strategy, as discussed especially in the case of Air Canada, can inhibit strategic thinking and so lock the organization into an established strategic vision. It can, in fact, push that vision into the background, as attentions turn to the details of programming, budgeting, and fine-tuning, etc. As a consequence, the organization can drift away from the needs of its markets, until awoken by some kind of shock, as we saw in the case of Volkswagenwerk.

Venturing within the Vision

Other organizations, not predisposed to mass production or the mass distribution of services, but rather to expert teamwork in the adhocracy form, develop under their initial vision in a different way: they engage in strategic venturing, pursuing specific initiatives under the vision's guiding umbrella.

This was particularly the case for the NFB, which initially, and to some extent always, functioned under Grierson's vision of making quality documentary films. Arcop, too, focused on novel quality throughout the period of study.

Programming as well as Venturing under the Vision?

Can an organization do both: formally program its vision and informally venture within it? Of course it can. In fact, it is difficult to imagine any organization that does not.

The NFB had budgets, even 'strategic plans' (that were largely ignored, except to satisfy the requirements of the government controlling agency), while Air Canada had a venture in Rapidair, and Volkswagenwerk certainly did its share of venturing in its period of groping and grafting. Even Steinberg's and Canadian Lady, while still formally under entrepreneurial control, did their share of planning in their mature years. Every organization needs some directed order as well as some creative learning, which is another way of saying that all effective social endeavors require a combination of science, art, and craft.

But just as clearly, the organizations of this research demonstrated a tendency to favor one over the other: venturing and periodically learning in the NFB, planning and analyzing in Air Canada, etc.

Just Plain Venturing

The one professional organization in this study provides evidence that an organization can function quite well without much of a founding vision other than importing a general orientation from like organizations elsewhere. (To call a general-purpose university that emphasizes research a strategic vision seems to be a bit of a stretch.) They develop as all kinds of venturing occur all over the place, without necessarily any collective learning. Strategies abound, but these are the strategies of individuals, or small subunits. People do their own thing, as the saying goes, albeit in well-articulated professional niches. So the umbrellas under which they work tend to be professional, not organizational.

Strategic Analyzing that Feeds Planning, Learning, Visioning, and Venturing

Organizations of all forms, as they develop, can engage in a good deal of Strategic Analyzing too. We might expect the greatest amount of this in machine organizations, especially within their planning and programming processes, where analysis helps the central managers make their decisions, or else justify the decisions already made, to boards and bankers, etc. We might, in contrast, expect less analyzing in entrepreneurial organizations, where the leaders are inclined to follow their own gut instincts, also because the organizations tend to be smaller and younger, or else in difficulty, and thus have less data to analyze, and less time as well as staff, to do the analyses. Still there is some role for Strategic Analyzing even here, if only to convince the bankers, etc.

In professional organizations, which are so decentralized, we might expect little Strategic Analyzing. But Hardy et al. (1983) argue the opposite, at least in the university setting. They conclude that such organizations tend to be inundated with analyses, used as weapons by the professionals who compete with each other for financial support for their individual or departmental ventures. Every champion comes to the meetings armed with analyses to justify his or her activity and to shoot down those of colleagues' competing for the same resources. The same is likely to be the case in adhocracies, where power is also divided among the experts, here working in project teams.

RENEWAL

The study of organizations over much of their history is bound to reveal a third stage in their lives, namely crisis and renewal. Certainly we found a good deal of this in our research. All but two of the organizations studied experienced this (although in the NFB, it tended to be renewal without crisis). The exceptions were Air Canada (that came later!) and McGill (we are still waiting!).

But this stage was not frequent: one of the interesting findings of this research is that in most cases we needed to track strategies across very long periods of time, many decades, to find truly significant changes. The organizations studied tended to get themselves into a secure niche and remain there largely unchanged for decades: McGill University for over a century and a half, Air Canada over the forty-year study period, others, such as the *Sherbrooke Record*, Volkswagenwerk, and Steinberg's, for decades before external forces drove major changes. The only clear exceptions to this, with renewal more frequent, were the NFB and partly Arcop, likely because their renewals were opportunistic, and influenced by cultural fashion, and US strategy in Vietnam, as noted because of the intense political and military pressures (also opportunistic when Kennedy voluntarily chose this as the place to confront Asian communism).

Strategic Renewal in these 'Times of Great Change'
Of course, this conclusion comes from research with cutoff dates some years ago. Is it, then, an artifact of earlier times? Can such a conclusion be taken seriously in this age of touted 'hyper-competition' and unrelenting change, etc.? Yes, indeed.

Are these times really so different? Do we really live amidst such change? Are we even good judges of that change, or will history be the judge?

Looking back on a century of two world wars and a great depression, it is difficult to accept the hype about change since 1945. Certainly there have been significant technological advances, most notably in information technology. But is this more significant than the introduction of the automobile a century ago, or the railroad before that?

And while information technology has certainly had great influence on some industries, especially the ones it created, what about other industries? The automobile we drive today uses the same fundamental technology as the Model T (a four-cycle internal combustion engine); the clothes we wear are much like those of our parents, even our grandparents. (Why must I wear a tie to give a speech?)

Did you stop and think as you got dressed this morning why, if we live in times of such great change, are we still buttoning buttons? If not, then maybe you should stop and think about the fact that we only notice what *is* changing, and most things are not. Then you can stop and think about whether the strategic change in most of the organizations and industries you know is truly change of perspective, or just a lot of shifting of positions? Indeed, how much of it is really cosmetic, promoted as great new strategies?

Change for the Sake of Change

And where change does seem to be truly significant, ask yourself if the changes rendered were necessary and well conceived, or for their own sake, perhaps to satisfy the ego of a new chief executive intent on putting his or her stamp on the organization. Recall Kennedy in Vietnam. Engaging the US forces directly was certainly a change in perspective. He was looking for a place to confront Asian communism, to stand up to the 'Domino Theory'—if one country falls, they will all fall—and Vietnam was it. (Better than China.)

How many of today's great strategic changes in business or governments rest on the same questionable foundations? In business, we see the great mergers: AOL-Time Warner, Vivendi, Hewlett Packard with Compaq. The record is not good. Contrast this with some of the most successful companies today that, to use Peters and Waterman's expression of 1982, have stuck to their strategic knitting for decades: Toyota in automobiles, IKEA in furniture, McKinsey in consulting. Indeed, when did the institutions behind so much of the hype about change—the business schools—last change their own strategic perspective? (The answer is the 1950s, according to my assessment in *Managers not MBAs* [Mintzberg 2004: 21–67].)

For the renewals that did take place in the organizations studied, there was evidence of several patterns, as follows:

Bringing New Vision to an Entrepreneurial Organization

For an organization under threat, usually because it has lost touch with a changing environment or has drifted away from a successful vision, the simplest solution is to 'turn it around' through a new vision imposed by a strong leadership. We found this in organizations that were already entrepreneurial, as well as in machine organizations that reverted to the entrepreneurial form for change. The first is discussed here, the second in the next section.

Because entrepreneurs, at least if engaged and informed, tend to be attuned to external changes, they can often make the internal necessary changes themselves. We saw this most clearly in Steinberg's, in the 1930s and again the 1960s, as well as in Canadian Lady with its adoption of a new technology for a particular market segment.

But other times, because the leader in the entrepreneurial organization lacks the imagination, capacity, resources, or just plain will to act, he or she becomes the problem, and has to be replaced somehow if the organization is to change, as in the *Sherbrooke Record*, where one leader lacked the will to act and the next one lacked the resources needed to do so. Only when new leadership came in from the outside was the organization saved from its problems. Even a Sam Steinberg became a problem when his company needed new strategies in the spheres that were outside his personal knowledge (supermarket operations in Ontario, discount retailing in Quebec).

The source of these new visions, whether from the existing leader or a new one, varied. The Black group arrived in the *Sherbrooke Record* with its strategic vision; Sam Steinberg imported his in the 1930s from the US self-service practice, and returned to parts of that vision in the 1960s, while Larry Nadler, in contrast, developed his own new vision for Canadian Lady.

In all these cases, while there was certainly external threat, the leaders were proactive: we can say that they oversolved their problems, turning them into opportunities that proved highly successful.

Of course, what eased the making of these changes was the nature of this configuration: the leadership was in firm control while the organization was pliable. So as long as the vision was good, the change proved successful. Even Larry Nadler, whose renewal strategy met resistance, was able to circumvent it relatively easily by setting up a parallel organization. He was, after all, the one who called the shots.

Turning Around the Machine Organization in Temporary Entrepreneurial Form

Renewal required something quite different in the machine organizations, because their bureaucratic momentum made it more difficult, both to achieve a new vision, and to carry it to fruition.

For example, during some critical periods in Volkswagenwerk and Vietnam, the leadership hesitated, causing some costly drifting before there was finally a response. Even then, the response at first tended to be disjointed, more groping than visionary. The organization needed to learn, but initially proved maladroit at doing so. The likely reason was that the leadership in these large machine organizations was distant from the tangible reality; unlike the entrepreneurs just discussed, they were removed from the operations. As a consequence, Volkswagenwerk, for example, required some very expensive learning—new automobile models being introduced every which way—before the company finally settled down on a new vision. This came thanks to a new entrepreneurial leader who saw the new perspective and drove it into the organization.

Kennedy, as noted earlier, was a proactive entrepreneur of sorts too, coming into office with considerable personal power and choosing to bring a new strategic perspective to the US strategy in Vietnam. Unfortunately, however, he was not heading up an entrepreneurial organization, but a massive bureaucracy, really several of them, especially in the Pentagon. And it, as well as he, faced an enormously difficult situation that they did not seem to understand well. And so Kennedy willingly led the country into what ultimately proved disastrous. Johnson's reactiveness got the blame, but Kennedy's proactiveness created the problem.

More Frequent Collective Renewal in Adhocracy

Most interesting was how the adhocracies renewed themselves, and not always when under threat.

They changed collectively, as their various projects converged on new kinds of strategic themes, which became the strategic perspective. People in the organization learned through their shared experiences. Or else these projects went off in various ways, to create a new period of diversity. Sometimes the experts were drawn to some new trend or technology, sometimes they just felt like doing something new.

In the NFB, for example, television appeared: Why not do that? Eventually this proved problematic, at least in how it was done (as regular series), so the filmmakers backed off, redirecting their efforts within television as well as to other spheres. Or someone made a first feature film: 'Hey, I can do that too.' So there was some convergence around a new theme. Arcop, for its part, won a competition for an arts center, and did well: Why not go after more such work?

Track such efforts over time and you find a rather different pattern of change in these two adhocracy organizations compared with the others.

They did not commit to any particular strategic perspective for decades, let alone try to hang on to one for dear life. They did focus, but for shorter periods of time, and then moved on. The nature of their project work meant that they could change rather quickly and easily—each team had to consider what to do next as soon as its project ended, and so the whole organization could change as soon as many of these projects ended.

Overall, as a result, we saw in these organizations not occasional quantum change but rather regular cycling in and out of strategic focus. Sometimes the organizations converged on a vision through collective learning and other times they ventured all over the place. Yet the latter proved not to be problematic at all as noted in the NFB study, some of its most successful years were ones out of focus.

Thus we can describe adhocracy as the most flexible of the four forms, even more so than the entrepreneurial organization. The latter may benefit from the capacity of one leader to act, but that person still has to move the whole organization himself or herself.

Renewing Merrily and Disconnectedly in the Professional Organization

The study of McGill University revealed another pattern of change. If there was no clear vision, then there was evidently no need to change it! So there was no need for leader-driven or even collective strategic renewal. Indeed, how can we even distinguish here between the three stages of initiation, development, and renewal? The university had no clear entrepreneurial leader at its initiation, and likely developed as it always functioned: with its professors and departments doing their work rather autonomously. Change could vary from one part of the organization to another—a course in radiology, for example, or research on current politics, changing rather frequently—while a course in Greek history or a research project on strategy formation could remain consistent for decades.

Can we call this kind of change strategic? Sure, as soon as we get past the idea that strategy can only be common and collective, dictated or at least articulated by a central management. If strategy is about product–market positions, even perspectives, in the professional organization these can be found all over the place. Cumulatively, they add up to the organization's strategies.

And this suggests that strategic change can happen rather easily in the professional organization. Each professional can be an entrepreneur of sorts, except without much of an organization to worry about. So any professional who wants to initiate some new venture has a good chance to do so, subject to one small and one big constraint. The small one is that the professional has to get the approval of colleagues, who may, as noted earlier, challenge it, leading to all sorts of strategic analyses, pros and cons, not to mention politics. But assuming the professional can find the necessary resources, he or she can usually proceed subject to that bigger constraint: it must be acceptable to the professional associations, and colleagues elsewhere, that set the standards. If a pharmacology professor, for example, wants to focus a course on Bhutanese herbal medicines, he or she might get censured. That is why I concluded that it is the adhocracy, and not the professional organization, that is the most flexible of the four forms—it is much more tolerant of innovation.

Renewing Each Form in its Own Way

To summarize, Figure 12.4 shows our four forms of organization in the triangle of art, craft, and science, to indicate how each renews itself. Three remain in place to change, more or less, and the fourth reverts to another form to change itself.

The entrepreneurial organization is shown in the corner of art, with its emphasis on the insights and vision of its leader. It stays in place to change; that is, it retains its dependence on strong leadership, whether the existing leader or a new one. Either way, the new vision comes out

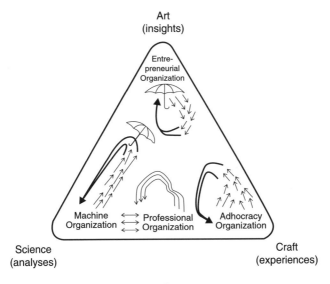

Figure 12.4 Renewal in the four forms of organizations

of a process of connected personal learning, which means it tends also toward craft, even if it remains rather firmly anchored in art.

The professional organization can be found between craft and science, since professionals combine personal experiences with formalized training, 'evidence-based' is the term used in medicine—combined with experienced-based. And here the organization remains for renewal, since this is not a separate activity but business as usual. But because this renewal is based on personal learning, and can involve some personal visioning, the individual may be drawn toward craft and art, science too in the strategic analyses involved with such changes.

The machine organization has to stay firmly rooted in the corner of science, since its whole existence depends on planning, programming, analyzing, etc. But there it cannot renew itself, which such organizations generally have to do from time to time as changes in the environment build up. So the machine organization needs to rely on another form by which to change, which we have found to be the entrepreneurial one, so as to be 'turned around' by a strong new leader who can suspend the planning and programming and standards, etc. To achieve this, the organization, as in the case of Volkswagenwerk, may have to go through a difficult process of learning (toward craft), unless the new leader has been able to import the new vision directly. But once that new vision is in place, the organization must revert to the machine form quickly, to resume its mass production of goods and services, which may mean replacing the leader again, as happened in Volkswagenwerk.

This, of course, assumes that the new vision maintains the organization in mass production. It may, instead, move it to more individualized professional service, as when a company upgrades the capability of its staff—say a bank that moves from tellers to financial advisors—in which case it shifts toward the professional form. Or it can move into customized production, as when a clothing company shifts from the production of standardized garments to short runs of designer clothes. We did not encounter either of these cases in this research, either because of the nature of the sample chosen or because such changes are less common. Machines are, after all, built for particular purposes.

Finally the adhocracy form is anchored in the corner of craft, where its venturing takes place based on experience. Much of its renewal takes place here as well, based as it is on collective learning, but there are also tendencies toward art in the emergence of collective vision.

Crafting Strategy

The formation of strategy, as suggested in the research reported in this book, is largely about the interplay of craft and art: experience and insight, learning and visioning. In other words, it tends to run along the right side of the triangle.

In the left corner is science, which certainly feeds into the process through various forms of analysis, and feeds out of it and through programming to operationalize strategies that have become deliberate. But we cannot say that this *is* the process. Strategic Planning, so called, based on the use of formal analysis to create strategy, has, in the words of one prominent critic of its use in the form of PPBS in government, 'failed everywhere and at all times' (Wildavsky 1974: 205). That is because, while planning is about analysis, strategy is about synthesis. And analysis cannot produce synthesis. (This is discussed at length in my book *The Rise and Fall of Strategic Planning* [Mintzberg 1994].)

So the heart of the strategy formation process can be found in learning from tangible experiences and visioning from creative insights. It lies, if you like, in the answer to those two issues discussed in the entrepreneurial and adhocracy configurations: how to get into the mind of the strategist, and how to read the mind of the organization.

Understanding art, let alone intervening to make people better artists, or managers better visionaries, is no easy matter. In a sense, this is wrapped up in the person. If research on the two hemispheres of the brain is to be believed (Ornstein 1972; see also Mintzberg 1976), much of the art is hidden in the brain's mute right hemisphere, which seems to deal with spatial matters. And so, if you lack the art in your organization, and need it, you had better find it, in the person of an artist. (Look around: some forgotten or marginalized strategic artist is probably waiting in your organization right now.)

So the real hope for changing strategic behavior lies in the lower right-hand corner of our triangle, in the place labeled craft. Here is where experience can be used to make tangible improvements, so long as the strategy process can be weaned from its emphasis on analysis. That has certainly been one strong message in the findings reported throughout this book.

Analysis is a kind of magnet that can draw people in, especially those oriented to craft, since the artists are more inclined to stand firm. We have no shortage of that happening in organizations today, with so much attention to systems, procedures, standards, etc., under the influence of all that planning, analyzing, and, measuring. Every organization needs some of this, but many organizations need less of it, especially when it comes to strategy formation. In its place, they need more of that forgotten or ignored element called craft. The science is all too clear, as are the results of it: it is time for the craft. So let me end this book with a statement about crafting strategy at times reiterating some key points made earlier.[3]

The Soul of the Craftsman

Imagine someone *planning* strategy. What likely springs to mind is an image of orderly thinking—a senior manager, or a group of them, sitting in an office formulating courses of action that everyone will implement, on schedule. The keyword is reason: rational control, the systematic analysis of competitors and markets, organizational strengths and weaknesses, and the combination of these analyses into clear, explicit, full-blown strategies.

Now imagine someone *crafting* strategy. A wholly different image appears, as different from planning as craft is from mechanization. Craft evokes traditional skill, dedication, and perfection through the mastery of detail. What springs to mind is not so much thinking and reason as involvement, a feeling of intimacy and harmony with the materials at hand, developed through long experience and commitment. Formulation and implementation merge into a fluid process of learning through which creative strategies evolve.

My thesis is simple: the crafting image better captures the process by which effective strategies come to be. The planning image, long so popular in the literature, distorts this process and thereby misguides organizations that embrace it unreservedly. With this in mind, let us consider the manager's role in crafting strategy.

Crafting Action with Thought

Does the strategist, should the strategist, sit on a pedestal dictating brilliant strategies for everyone else to implement? While recognizing the importance of thinking ahead and especially of the need for creative vision in this pedantic world, we need another view of the strategist—as a pattern recognizer, a learner if you will—who manages a process in which strategies can emerge as well as be deliberately conceived. We also need

[3] What follows comes largely from a *Harvard Business Review* article by this title (Mintzberg 1987).

376

to redefine that strategist, from that someone into the collective entity made up of the many actors whose interplay speaks an organization's mind. This strategist *finds* strategies no less than creates them, often in patterns that form inadvertently in an organization's behavior.

What, then, does it mean to craft strategy? Let us return to the words associated with craft: dedication, experience, involvement with the material, the personal touch, mastery of detail, a sense of harmony and integration. Managers who craft strategy are involved, responsive to their materials; they learn about their organizations and industries through personal touch. They are also attuned to experience, recognizing that while individual vision may be important, other factors must also help to determine strategy.

Managing Stability

Managing strategy is mostly about managing stability, not change. Indeed most of the time, senior managers should not be formulating strategy at all; they should be getting on with making their organizations as effective as possible in pursuing the strategies they already have. Like distinguished craftsmen, organizations become distinguished when they master the operating details.

To manage strategy, then, at least in the first instance, is not so much to promote change as to know *when* to do so. Advocates of strategic planning often urge managers to plan for perpetual instability in the environment (e.g. by rolling over five-year plans annually). But this obsession with change is dysfunctional. Organizations that reassess their strategies continuously are like individuals who reassess their jobs or their marriages continuously—in both cases, they can drive themselves crazy, or else reduce themselves to inaction.

At work, the potter sits before a lump of clay on the wheel. Her mind is on the clay, but she is also aware of sitting between her past experiences and her future prospects. She knows exactly what has and has not worked for her in the past, and has an intimate knowledge of her work, her capabilities, her markets. As a craftsman, she senses rather than analyzes these things; her knowledge is 'tacit'. All this is working in her mind as her hands are working the clay. The product that emerges on the wheel is likely to be in the tradition of her past work, but it may also break away and take her in a new direction too.

In this metaphor, managers are craftsmen and strategy is their clay. Like the potter, they sit between a past of organization capabilities and a future of market opportunities. And if they are truly craftsmen, they bring to their work an equally intimate knowledge of the materials at hand. That is the essence of crafting strategy.

Detecting Discontinuities

Environments do not change on any regular or orderly basis. And they seldom undergo continuous dramatic change, claims about 'hyper-competition' and 'turbulence' notwithstanding. Much of the time, change is minor and even temporary, requiring no strategic response. Once in a while, however, there is a truly significant discontinuity or, even less often, a gestalt shift in the environment, where everything important seems to change at once. But these events, while critical, are also easy to recognize.

The real challenge in crafting strategy lies in detecting the subtle and developing discontinuities that may eventually undermine the organization, or provide it with a special opportunity. And for this, there is no technique, no program, just sharp minds in touch with the situation. Unfortunately, this form of strategic thinking tends to atrophy during the long periods of stability that most organizations experience. So the trick is to manage for long within a given strategic orientation yet be able to pick out the occasional discontinuity that really matters.

Knowing the Business

Sam Steinberg was the epitome of the entrepreneur, a man intimately involved with all the details of his business, who spent Saturday mornings visiting his stores. He boasted about his knowledge of his business, his merchandise, costs, selling, customers: 'I knew everything, and I passed on all my knowledge . . . Our competitors couldn't touch us.'

Note the kind of knowledge involved: not intellectual knowledge, not analytical reports or abstracted facts and figures (although these can certainly help), but personal knowledge, intimate understanding, equivalent to the craftsman's feel for the clay. Facts are available to anyone; this kind of knowledge is not. Wisdom is the word that captures it best. But wisdom gets lost in the bureaucracies we build for ourselves.

Craftsmen have to train themselves to pick up things other people miss. The same holds true for strategists. It is those with a kind of peripheral vision who are best able to detect and take advantage of events as they unfold.

Dealing with Patterns

Key to managing strategy is the ability to detect emerging patterns and help them take shape. The job of the strategist, therefore, is not just to preconceive specific strategies, but also to recognize the emergence of patterns and intervene when appropriate.

Like weeds that appear unexpectedly in a garden, some emergent strategies may need to be uprooted immediately. But management cannot be too quick to cut off the unexpected, for today's anomaly can become tomorrow's vision. Thus some patterns are worth watching until their effects have more clearly manifested themselves. Then those that prove useful can be made deliberate, and be incorporated into the formal strategy, even if that means shifting the strategic umbrella to cover them.

To manage in this context, then, is to create the climate within which a wide variety of strategies can grow. In more complex organizations, this may mean building flexible structures, hiring creative people, defining broad umbrella strategies, and watching for the patterns that emerge beneath them.

Reconciling Change with Continuity

Finally, managers need to keep in mind the biblical claim that there is a time to sow and a time to reap. Some new patterns must be held in check until the organization is ready for strategic renewal. Managers who are obsessed with either change or continuity are bound to do harm. All managers have to sense when to exploit an established crop of strategies, and when to encourage new strains to replace them.

While strategy is a word usually associated with the future, its link to the past is no less central. As Kierkegaard has observed, life is lived forward but understood backward. Managers may have to live strategy into the future, but they must also understand strategies evolved from the past. Like potters at the wheel, they need to make sense of the past if they hope to manage the future. Only by coming to understand the patterns that form in the behavior of their own organization do they learn about their capabilities and potential. Thus crafting strategy, like managing craft, requires a natural synthesis of the future, the present, and the past.

STEPS IN RESEARCH ON STRATEGY FORMATION

This document was developed with Jim Waters in 1979 to guide the people working on our research, or using our approach to do their own. It was updated more or less as presented here in 1982.

Stage 1: Basic Data (Traces)

1.1 Gain overview of the organization and its industry.

1.2 Make a rough pass at delineating the key strategy areas (e.g. for a magazine—content, format, administration), as well as aspects of the environment, and of performance, to guide the search for data.

1.3 Collect data ('traces') to develop chronologies of decisions and actions, trends and events, and results. (Sources, in-house and published, can include any recorded traces: annual reports, catalogs, files, personal records [many people keep all kinds of obscure data], plans [that contain historical data], organization publications, stock reports [e.g. Dunn and Bradstreet], deeds, etc.) It is usually best to begin with a systematic (even if incomplete) source of information, such as the annual reports. These get the work started and provide an overview; as you gain familiarity with the organization and its employees, you can begin to dig for more obscure data.

Note—At this stage, the search is for tangible traces, *not* perceptions. Note also that it has been found useful to jot down *any* ideas (relationships, hypotheses, concepts, etc.) that come up, for later conceptual analysis (Stage 4). Do not discard any thoughts at this stage; you never know what will prove invaluable later.

1.4 Also collect all available reports and analyses of significant decisions and issues (e.g. books, organization reports, consultants' reports, news analyses, and articles). These should be scanned for decisions and events and otherwise held for Stage 3 analysis.

1.5 Conduct interviews, but at this stage only to fill in gaps of data on decisions and actions (that cannot be found in documents, e.g. on past advertising campaigns or structural changes). It is important that lists of questions for these interviews and those in Step 3.1, on interpretations, be developed throughout Step 1.3 as gaps appear and issues arise. These first interviews will often be held with specialized old-timers who know the history of specific strategy areas intimately.

1.6 List chronologically (a) the decisions and actions by strategy area (the list of these having been reworked frequently during Steps 1.3 and 1.4, and finalized just before this step), (b) the environmental events and trends, and (c) the results.

1.7 Also plot across the whole period of the study (on a common abscissa, if possible) everything plotable, especially related to the key strategy and result areas (e.g. introduction of new products, construction of new facilities, sales, capital invested, consumer price index, number of competitors). These are invaluable for later analysis—the more the better.

OUTPUT DOCUMENTATION

1: Chronological listing of (a) decisions and actions by strategy area, (b) results, events, and trends. See Exhibit A.1.

2: Graphs, graphs, and more graphs.

Stage 2: Determination of Strategy Patterns

2.1 For each strategy area, infer from its chronology and related graphs the basic strategies (patterns in action streams) over the entire period of study (as well as intermediate times of flux, of strategy evolving, of no strategy—no decisions made, or no consistency in the ones made, etc.) and label each.

2.2 Depict by strategy area, on a common timescale, each of these strategies (and intermediate periods) in some way that will aid visual perception (e.g. showing a strategy of expansion as an expanding trapezoid; see Exhibit A.2). Also do the same thing for environmental patterns where possible. Finally, show also with an arrow *major* one-time decisions, actions, and events that should be considered but fit into no pattern (e.g. the change of a chief executive, the move to a new headquarters, an important competitor action). It is imperative that up to this point the focus be entirely on each strategy area as a separate entity. No thought should be given to the interrelationships of strategies in different areas or the delineation of overall periods. That will be done inductively, in the next step, based on the outputs of this one.

2.3 Attach all these diagrams together on a long sheet of paper in some logical order on the common timescale. Then, in scanning vertically for concurrent changes in a number of important strategies, delineate overall periods for the whole study and label them on the sheet. Periods may be ones of

US DECISIONS & ACTIONS	1965	EXTERNAL EVENTS
At Johns Hopkins, Johnson stresses willingness to negotiate and suggests 1 billion aid program for SE Asia.	4/7	
	4/8	USSR proposes Cambodian neutrality conference.
	4/11	NVN officials denounce Johnson offer.
	4/12	Gordon Walker unsuccessful in UK attempts to meet officials in Hanoi and Peiking.
US urges Hanoi to consider plea of 17 nonaligned nations.	4/14	
Secretary Rusk–Cambodia parley.	4/23	
More troops arrive.	5/3	
	5/3	Cambodia breaks diplomatic relations with US.
Johnson requests 700 million supplemental appropriation.	5/4	
House approves request 408 to 7.	5/5	
SEATO condemns Comm. aggression in SVN.	5/5	
Senate passes appropriation 88 to 3.	5/6	
More troops activated.	5/7	
	5/12	Red China calls for preparation for war (atomic).

Exhibit A.1 Example of a chronology record

continuity (no major changes in patterns), of global change (most strategies changing), of piecemeal, or incremental change, of flux, etc. These labels are guides; it is best to invent your own that best describe the period in question. (*It is in the very labeling of strategies and periods that the conceptual interpretations form.*) This step should probably be done in a meeting with other members of the team.

OUTPUT DOCUMENTATION

3: One giant sheet depicting the strategies by area on a common timescale, also showing the overall periods of the study. See Exhibit A.2.

Stage 3: Analysis of Each Major Period

3.1 Investigate intensively each period of the strategy, including the forces that shaped it, the underlying causes of changes in strategy, and the nature of

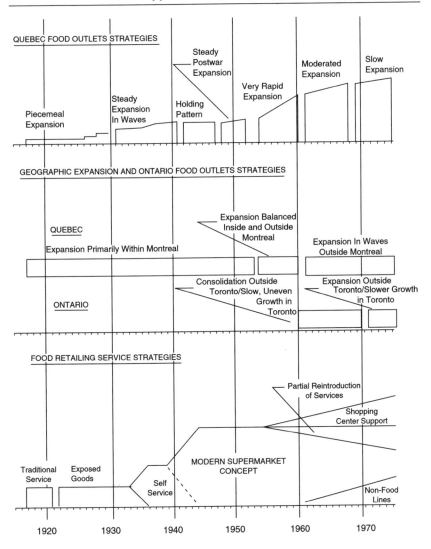

Exhibit A.2 Example of strategies depicted

the interrelationships among the different strategies (e.g. which led and lagged). This is based on (a) study of background information (records, news analyses, consulting reports, etc.; see Step 1.4), and (b) interviews with knowledgeable people inside the organization (executives and secretaries, long-term employees, etc.) as well as outside (retired employees, people who know the industry and the organization, etc.). This

383

investigation, in addition to probing causes in an open-ended way, should also consider for each period the 'Dimensions' listed at the end of this appendix.

3.2 Systematic theoretical analysis then takes place of each period of change in the strategy, guided by the dimensions and the list of questions that follow.

OUTPUT DOCUMENTATION

4: A descriptive report, covering each distinct period of the study, including discussion of major decisions, actions, and strategies; the events, trends, forces, etc. that influenced them; and the results, that explore how and why all this happened. This also includes the graphs of earlier documentation, exhibits, etc.

5: A theoretical interpretation of the strategies and strategy formation process for each of the periods.

QUESTIONS FOR EACH PERIOD OF CHANGE IN STRATEGY IN STAGE 3

1. How were the different strategies interrelated—in hierarchical fashion, around a dominant element, in some gestalt configuration, grafted onto an existing gestalt, new disjointed pieces, etc.? When and why did peripheral strategies become central ones?

2. What were the characteristics of each strategy (e.g. expand, diversify, retrench, copy, lead, monopolize) and its attributes (e.g. conservative, hedge, defensive, bold, flexible).

3. What form did the strategy take (public, explicit, implicit, or not consciously recognized)? Was there inconsistency between the intended and realized strategies? Why?

4. What appear to be the key characteristics on which the strategy was based (strength, threat or pressure, opportunity, climate, managerial personality, etc.)? What was the 'key strategic' (or success) factor of the period? The critical strengths or distinctive competencies? (How did the organization know or find out?) What degrees of freedom ('strategic windows') were available to the organization?

5. What evoked or influenced any changes in strategy? What was the relationship between the change and external events and trends? Did forces develop slowly, or was there a single stimulus, or both? (Possible stimuli: competition, depleted or newly available sources of supply, unused resources, economic conditions, new coalition, new management, technological breakthrough, changing client taste, failure of old strategy, pressure groups, natural occurrence, unfulfilled aspirations, threat of resource loss, innovative ideas, etc.)

6. In general, what brought on the new period? (Needs in last period? Release of major constraint? Everything just lining up? Gestalt shift in the environment? Foundation finally ready? Emergent pattern perceived?)

7. How were the strategic choices made—single individual, debate, bargaining? What role did formal analysis play? What alternative proposals were considered and who generated them?

8. What factors of timing, delay, and interruption entered into the process?

9. Can the change be described as incremental, piecemeal, or global (or some combination)?

10. Can strategy-making behavior be described as reactive or proactive (entrepreneurial, bold, or transforming)? Where can it be placed along a continuum of opportunity–problem–crisis, and why?

11. Was strategy made explicitly, a priori (intended), which determined subsequent actions, or were decisions, or actions, made one by one which evolved into an emergent strategy? Could decisions in fact be identified, or only actions?

Stage 4: Theory Building

4.1 Four or five people of the research team read the report carefully and then sit down for marathon brainstorming session(s) to interpret the findings in conceptual terms—to extract/invent hypotheses, conceptual insights, etc. on the strategy-formation process in this study—using the second set of questions that follow as a guide. This is the time to pull out the hundreds of notes you have made throughout the study.

a) Review periods by strategies, pasted on the wall

b) Characterize each period—main characteristics

what's going on

central themes

overriding forces

find key words—label each period

c) Diagram for each period—what drove it: what was the external stimuli

leading/lagging strategies

d) Analysis of whole study show the whole study *symbolically,* labeling each period as well as the *overall pattern.* See Exhibit A.3.

OUTPUT DOCUMENTATION

6: Theoretical report on the study (i.e. ideas written down from the brainstorming sessions), including overall diagram.

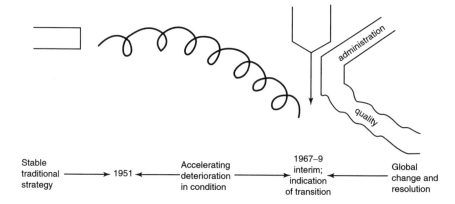

Exhibit A.3 Example of a study shown symbolically

7: Normative report: ideas on what the conclusions suggest about how to improve the strategy-formation process.

QUESTIONS CONCERNING THE WHOLE STUDY OF STRATEGY FORMULATION IN STEP 4

(For group discussion and hypothesis generation)

1. Under what conditions do organizations follow certain *patterns* in the development of their strategies (e.g. life cycle, series of random bumps, steady development, growth/consolidation cycles)?

2. How do organizations *balance change with stability*? When do they change everything for a time and then consolidate (global)? When do they change one thing at a time, holding all else constant (piecemeal), and when do they change in incremental fashion? How are periods of change, continuity, flux, limbo, etc. sequenced, and why?

3. How do organizations *interrelate their strategies*? When are gestalt (integrated, unique) strategies made? When are elements grafted onto an integrated strategy? When are strategies disjointed? What is the role of planning and analysis, leadership, and bargaining, in interrelating strategies? What is the role of dominant elements, shared goals, mutual adjustment, managerial vision?

4. What factors of *timing and delay* enter into the process of strategy formation? How do interruptions affect strategy formation? What is the effect of hedging? Of ignoring intelligence information?

5. How does *environmental change pattern* itself, and affect strategic change?

6. What is *'environment'* anyway? What do 'complex', 'dynamic', 'hostile', 'diverse', etc. mean? How do organizations deal with this?

7. What are the relative influences of *environmental, organizational,* and *leadership* forces? Which of the following factors appear to most strongly influence strategy making: competitor/opponent moves, external change agents, resource availability (depleted, available), unused (slack) resources, economic conditions, change in coalition, new management, desire to innovate, new aspirations, technological breakthrough, changing client tastes, failure of old strategy, natural occurrences, organization age and size, environmental stability and homogeneity, ownership and control, type of industry and technology, other factors?

8. When (and how) is strategy made *deliberately* and when (and how) does it evolve as a convergence of actions (*emergent*)? What is the interplay between these two? Why do strategies take on specific forms (explicit, implicit, not perceived)?

9. When is an organization proactive and when reactive, and why? What do *entrepreneurial* and *adaptive* mean in these contexts?

10. What is *planning* anyway?

11. What influence *do past actions and strategies* have on subsequent ones? What kind of actions set precedents and what kind reinforce them? Does strategy formation follow an 'exponential smoothing' theory, in which the more recent and more significant (and more successful) an action, the greater its influence on strategy? Or a 'sunk cost' theory, in which past commitments determine present strategies? Does strategy formation follow a 'simple model' theory, in which strategy-makers continue to use old, simple models until they fail them? Or a 'slack resources' theory, in which strategies reflect the excess or lack of key resources? Or a 'key event' theory, in which each significant change in strategy is signaled by a key event? What other theories can explain the evolution of strategies?

12. What is the relationship between the process of strategy formation and (a) structural *configurations* (entrepreneurial, machine, professional, adhocracy), (b) power configurations and types of internal and external power coalitions (dominated, divided, passive, or personalized, bureaucratic, ideological, professional, politicized), and (c) managerial roles and styles? Do structural and power configurations, and more encompassing ones, hold up?

13. What do the terms *determinism* and *free will* mean in the context of this study?

Dimension

INDUSTRY FACTORS

- product and line services—describe each
- diversity

- rate of change (e.g. % change per year)
- complexity of knowledge base of industry
- stability of industry (nature of supply and demand: periodicity, predictability, rate of product obsolescence)
- stage of industry—birth, growth, maturity, decline, revival

COMPETITION FACTORS

- industry concentration
- organization's position in industry (e.g. market share)
- nature of price, product, and marketing competition

Other sources of complexity and dynamism in environment

AGE AND SIZE OF ORGANIZATION

- Age of organization (and characteristics of founding period)
- sales (or budget)
- number of employees
- number of executives

PHYSICAL ASSETS OF ORGANIZATION

- facilities (describe each, including location)
- type of equipment

TECHNICAL SYSTEM AT ORGANIZATION

- unit (custom), mass, continuous process, diverse
- extent to which requires expertise—in development, in operation
- extent to which regulates work of operators
- extent to which automated
- rate of change (e.g. % of equipment changed per year)

FINANCIAL STATUS OF ORGANIZATION

- balance sheet, income statements, other performance data
- data/equity figures (and sources)
- liquidity
- value added (labor, nonlabor)
- proportion fixed/variable costs

ORGANIGRAPH (PHYSICAL CONFIGURATION OF THE ORGANIZATION):

- macro—map of overall facilities
- micro—plan of operating facilities and central administration

Organigram, or list of departments

List of key operator groups; for each:[1]

- period, type, and location (in-house or out) of training necessary for job (i.e. extent skilled or professional)
- extent tasks specified by rules, procedures, standards, work orders, job descriptions (i.e. formalized)
- extent outputs predetermined or standardized
- extent tasks routine
- extent work solitary or in groups
- extent work guided directly by first-line supervisors
- size of work units (i.e. span of control of first-line supervisors)

STRUCTURAL FACTORS

Number of levels in hierarchy

- Bases of grouping at each level in hierarchy
- Breadth of hierarchy (i.e. tall/flat; unit size or span of control at levels up hierarchy)
- Use of at specific levels
  - action planning systems (e.g. production scheduling, capital budgeting, manpower planning, strategic planning)
  - performance control systems (e.g. MBO, MIS, variance reporting, responsibility centers, flash reports, financial reporting; in general, extent to which goals are standardized)
  - liaison devices: standing committees and task forces (by level and line vs. staff membership); liaison and integrating managers (e.g. brand managers, project managers); matrix structure (at what level?)
  - For five parts of organization (operating core, middle line, strategic apex, technostructure, support staff): clarity of each, size of each

Ownership

- owned outright (by individual, family, parent organization)
- closely held
- widely held
- member owned
- non-ownd (e.g. trust, foundation, NGO)

Formal governance

- size and membership of board (owners, managers, bankers, lawyers, etc.)
- rules in control of, service to, organization

---

[1] The following was developed to help identify the organization in terms of the structural configuration (of machine bureaucracy, adhocracy, etc., as in Mintzberg 1979).

MAJOR INFLUENCERS

- list of influential groups, their size and relative influence (including organizational dependency)
- owners
- suppliers, customers, partners, competitors
- unions and professional associations
- communities, special interest groups, and governments and government agencies
- their major external means of influence: i.e. incidence of government legislation, pressure campaigns, social norms, direct controls (e.g. imposition of budgets, approval of decisions)

LEADERSHIP

- description of senior management group, personalities, values, interrelationships
- period of tenure and experience in industry and organization

FORMAL AND INFORMAL INFLUENCE OF INTERNAL GROUPS

- in strategic and other decision-making
- to initiate, to advise, to execute, to block, displace or conflict
- influence of culture—of technology and sagas, of natural identification with organizational goals, and of identification through socialization and indoctrination, of missionary goals
- influence of system goals—of growth and survival, control of the organization's environment
- managerial style factors (craft, artistic, analytic, etc.)

Bibliography

Andrews, K. R. (1980). *The Concept of Corporate Strategy*, rev. edn. Homewood, IL: Irwin.

Ansoff, H. I. (1965). *Corporate Strategy*. New York: McGraw-Hill.

Austin, B. (1983). 'Chronology of the Textile Manufacturing Industries of Canada 1883–1983 [Special Centennial Issue]', *The Canadian Textile Journal*, 100(6): 117–58.

——— (1985). 'Life Cycles and Strategy of a Canadian Company, Dominion Textile: 1873–1983', Unpublished doctoral dissertation. Concordia University, Montreal.

——— (1992). 'Structural Adaptation in a Family Firm, Hamilton Cotton/Hamilton Group 1832–1991', in P. Baskerville (ed.), *Canadian Papers in Business History*, Vol. 2. Victoria, BC: University of Victoria Press, pp. 24–45.

——— (1993). 'Structuring Organizational Capabilities' in E. Perkins (ed.), *Essays in Economic and Business History*, Vol. 11. Los Angeles, CA: University of Southern California, pp. 231–46.

——— and Mintzberg, H. (1996). 'Mirroring Canadian Industrial Policy: Strategy Formation at Dominion Textile from 1873 to 1990', *Canadian Journal of Administrative Sciences*, 13(1): 46–64.

Barnard, C. (1938). *The Functions of the Executive*. Cambridge, MA: Harvard University Press.

Barnard Associates, P. (1979). *Canadian Architects' Services*. Federal Department of Industry, Trade, and Commerce. Toronto, Canada: The Associates.

Bennis, W. G. and Slater, P. L. (1964). *The Temporary Society*. New York: Harper & Row.

Bliss, M. (1987). *Northern Experience*. Toronto, Canada: McClelland & Stewart.

Boston Consulting Group. (1972). *Perspectives on Experience*. Boston, MA: The Boston Consulting Group.

——— (1975). *Strategy Alternatives for the British Motorcycle Industry: A Report Prepared for the Secretary of State for Industry*. London: HM Stationery Office.

Bourgeois, J. L. III and Lindblom, C. E. (1963). *A Strategy of Decision*. New York: Free Press.

Bowman, E. H. (1976). 'Strategy and the Weather', *Sloan Management Review*, Winter: 49–58.

Braybrooke, D. and Lindblom, C. E. (1963). *A Strategy of Decision*. New York: Free Press.

Brunet, J. P., Mintzberg, H., and Waters, J. A. (1986). 'Does Planning Impede Strategic Thinking? Tracking the Strategies of Air Canada from 1939 to 1976', in R. B. Lamb (ed.), *Advances in Strategic Management*, Vol. 4. Englewood Cliffs, NJ: Prentice-Hall.

Burgelman, R. A. (1983*a*). 'A Process Model of Internal Corporate Venturing in the Diversified Major Firm', *Administrative Science Quarterly*, 28: 223–44.

—— (1983*b*). 'Corporate Entrepreneurship and Strategic Management: Insights from a Process Study', *Management Science*, 29: 1349–64.

—— (1984). 'On the Interplay of Process and Content in Internal Corporate Ventures: Action and Cognition in Strategy Making', in J. A. Pearce II and R. B. Robinson Jr. (eds.), *Academy of Management Proceedings*. Mississippi: Academy of Management, pp. 2–6.

Burns, T. and Stalker, G. M. (1966). *The Management of Innovation*, 2nd edn. London: Tavistock.

Caldwell, G. (1974). *A Demographic Profile of the English-Speaking Population of Quebec: 1921–1971*. Quebec, Canada: International Center for Research on Bilingualism.

Chandler, A. D. (1962*)*. *Strategy and Structure*. Cambridge, MA: MIT Press.

Chandler, M. K. and Sayles, L. R. (1971). *Managing Large Systems*. New York: Harper & Row.

Cohen, M. D., March, J. G., and Olsen, J. P. (1972). 'A Garbage Can Model of Organizational Choice', *Administrative Science Quarterly*, 17(1): 1–25.

Cole, A. H. (1959). *Business Enterprise in a Social Setting*. Cambridge, MA: Harvard University Press.

Collins, O. and Moore, D. G. (1970). *The Organization Makers*. New York: Appleton-Century-Crofts.

Cyert, R. M. and March, J. G. (1963). *A Behavioral Theory of the Firm*. Englewood Cliffs, NJ: Prentice-Hall.

Davidson, J. D. (1981). 'Four Vice Presidents, Four Directors, and a Partridge in a Pear Tree', *Interfaces*, 11(1): 59–61.

Dill, W. R. (1979). 'Commentary', in D. E. Schendel and C. W. Hofer (eds.), *Strategic Management*. Boston, MA: Little, Brown, pp. 47–51.

Drucker, P. F. (1970). 'Entrepreneurship in the Business Enterprise', *Journal of Business Policy*, 1(1): 3–12.

Fayol, H. (1949, first published in 1916). *General and Industrial Management*. London: Sir Isaac Pitman & Sons.

Feld, M. O. (1959). 'Information and Authority: The Structure of Military Organization', *American Sociological Review*, 24: 15–22.

Filley, A. C., House, R. J., and Kerr, S. (1976). *Managerial Process and Organizational Behavior*. Glenview, IL: Scott, Foresman.

Frost, S. B. (1980). *McGill University: For the Advancement of Learning*, Vol. I: *1801–1895*. Kingston and Montreal, Canada: McGill-Queen's University Press.

—— (1984). *McGill University: For the Advancement of Learning*, Vol. II: *1895–1971*. Kingston and Montreal, Canada: McGill-Queen's University Press.

Galbraith, J. K. (1967). *The New Industrial State*. Boston, MA: Houghton Mifflin.

Galbraith, J. R. (1973). *Designing Complex Organizations*. Reading, MA: Addison-Wesley.

—— (1983). 'Strategy and Organization Planning', *Human Resource Management*, 22: 63–77.

Gray, C. W. (1973). *Movies for the People: The Story of the NFB's Unique Distribution System*. Montreal, Canada: Information and Promotion Division, National Film Board of Canada.

Grinyer, P. H. and Spender, J. C. (1979). *Turnaround—Managerial Recipes for Strategic Success*. London: Associated Business Press.

Hadamard, J. (1949). *Psychology of Invention in the Mathematical Field*. Princeton, NJ: Princeton University Press.

Hafsi, T. (1981). 'The Strategic Decision-Making Process in State-Owned Entrepreneurs', DBA thesis. Boston, MA: Harvard Graduate School of Business Administration.

Halberstam, D. (1972). *The Best and the Brightest*. London: Random House.

Hardy, C., Langley, A., Mintzberg, H., and Rose, J. (1983). 'Strategy Formation in the University Setting', *The Review of Higher Education*, 6: 407–33.

—— —— —— —— (1984). 'Strategy Formation in the University Setting', in J. Bess (ed.), *College and University Organization*. New York: New York University Press.

Hardy, F. (1979). *John Grierson: A Documentary Biography*. London: Faber & Faber.

Hedberg, B. (1974). 'Growth Stagnation as a Managerial Discontinuity (Reprint Series)', *International Institute of Management*, Berlin I: 41–74.

Henderson, B. (1979). *On Corporate Strategy*. Cambridge, MA: ABT Books.

Holdaway, E. A. and Meekison, J. P. (1990). 'Strategic Planning at a Canadian University', *Long Range Planning*, 23(4): 104–13.

Hosmer, L. T. (1978). *Academic Strategy*. Ann Arbor, MI: University of Michigan Press.

James, C. R. (1968). 'The National Film Board of Canada: Its Task of Communication', Unpublished Ph.D. dissertation. Columbus, OH: Ohio State University.

Jones, D. B. (1976). 'The National Film Board of Canada: The Development of its Documentary Achievement', Unpublished Ph.D. dissertation. Palo Alto, CA: Stanford University.

Katz, K. and Kahn, R. L. (1966). *The Social Psychology of Organizations*. New York: Wiley.

Kiesler, S. and Sproul, L. (1982). 'Managerial Response to Changing Environments: Perspectives and Problem Sensing from Social Cognition', *Administrative Science Quarterly*, 37: 548–70.

King, B. L. (2006). 'The Venture Capitalist as Strategist: Planning, Opportunism and Deliberate Emergence', Paper presented to the Crafts of Strategy Colloquium organized by Long Range Planning. Toulouse, France, May 22.

Kuhn, T. S. (1970). *The Structure of Scientific Revolutions*, 2nd edn. Chicago, IL: University of Chicago Press.

Ladd, D. R. (1970). *Change in Educational Policy*. New York: McGraw-Hill.

Langley, A. (1990). 'Patterns in the Use of Formal Analyses in Strategic Decisions', *Organizational Studies*, 11(7): 17–45.

—— (1991). 'Formal Analyses and Strategic Decision Making', *Omega*, 19(213): 79–99.

Lawrence, P. R. and Lorsch, J. W. (1967). *Organization and Environment*. Homewood, IL: Irwin.

Lewin, K. (1951). *Field Theory in Social Science*. New York: Harper & Row.

Lindblom, C. E. (1959). 'The Science of "Muddling Through"', *Public Administration Review*, 19: 79–88.

—— (1963). *The Intelligence of Democracy: Decision Making Through Mutual Adjustment*. New York: Free Press.

—— (1968). *The Policy-Making Process*. Englewood Cliffs, NJ: Prentice-Hall.

Lutz, F. W. (1982). 'Tightening up Loose Coupling in Organizations of Higher Education', *Administrative Science Quarterly*, 27: 653–99.

McInnes, G. (1974). 'One Man's Documentary', Unpublished manuscript history by former employee, National Film Board of Canada.

McKay, M. (1965). 'History of the National Film Board of Canada', Unpublished manuscript by former employee, National Film Board of Canada.

Mahon, R. (1984). *The Politics of Industrial Restructuring*. Toronto, Canada: University of Toronto Press.

March, J. G. and Olsen, J. P. (1976). *Ambiguity and Choice*. Bergen, Norway: Universitetsforlaget.

Massey Commission (Vincent Massey, Chairman). (1951). *Report of the Royal Commission on National Development in the Arts, Letters, and Sciences, 1949–1951 ('The Massey Report')*. Ottawa, Canada: Edmond Cloutier.

Miles, R. E. and Snow, C. C. (1978). *Organizational Strategy, Structure and Process*. New York: McGraw-Hill.

Miller, D. and Friesen, P. (1978). 'Archetypes of Strategy Formation', *Management Science*, 24(9): 921–33.

—— —— (1980). 'Momentum and Revolution in Organizational Adaptation', *Academy of Management Journal*, 23: 591–614.

—— —— (1984). *Organizations: A Quantum View*. Englewood Cliffs, NJ: Prentice-Hall.

—— and Mintzberg, H. (1983). 'The Case for Configuration,' in G. Morgan (ed.), *Beyond Method: Strategies for Social Research*. Beverly Hills, CA: Sage, pp. 57–73.

Mintzberg, H. (1967). 'The Science of Strategy-Making', *Industrial* (now *Sloan*) *Management Review*, 8(2): 71–81.

—— (1972). 'Research on Strategy-making', in *Proceedings of Division of Business Policy and Planning*. Academy of Management National Meeting.

—— (1973*a*). 'Strategy Making in Three Modes', *California Management Review*, 16(2): 44–53.

—— (1973*b*). *The Nature of Managerial Work*. New York: Harper & Row. (Reissued by Prentice-Hall, 1983.)

—— (1975). 'The Manager's Job: Folklore and Fact', *Harvard Business Review*, 53(4): 49–61

—— (1976). 'Planning on the Left Side and Managing on the Right', *Harvard Business Review*, 54(4): 49–58.

—— (1977). 'Review of the "New Science of Management Decision" by Herbert Simon', *Administrative Science Quarterly*, 22(2): 342–51.

—— (1978*a*). 'Beyond Implementation: An Analysis of the Resistance to Policy Analysis', in K. B. Haley (ed.), *Operational Research*. Amsterdam, The Netherlands: North-Holland.

—— (1978*b*). 'Patterns in Strategy Formation', *Management Science*, 24(9): 934–48.

—— (1979*a*). 'Beyond Implementation: An Analysis of the Resistance to Policy Analysis' (Proceedings of the 1978 IFORS Conference), in K. Haley (ed.), *Operational Research'78*. Amsterdam, The Netherlands: North-Holland.

—— (1979*b*). *The Structuring of Organizations*. Englewood Cliffs, NJ: Prentice-Hall.

—— (1981). 'What is Planning Anyway?', *Strategic Management Journal*, 2: 319–24.

—— (1982). 'A Note on that Dirty Word "Efficiency"', *Interfaces*, 12(5): 101–5.

—— (1983*a*). *Power In and Around Organizations*. New York: Prentice-Hall.

—— (1983*b*). 'The Mind of the Strategist(s)', in S. Srivasta (ed.), *Functioning of the Executive Mind*. San Francisco, CA: Jossey-Bass.

—— (1983*c*). *Structure in Fires*. Englwood cliffs, NJ: Prentice-Hall.

—— (1984). 'Who Should Control the Corporation?' *California Management Review*, 27(1): 90–116.

—— (1987*a*). 'Crafting Strategy', *Harvard Business Review*, 65(4): 66–75.

—— (1987*b*). 'Five P's for Strategy', *California Management Review*, 30(1): 11–24.

—— (1989). *Mintzberg on Management*. New York: Free Press.

—— (1990). 'Strategy Formation: Schools of Thought', in J. Frederickson (ed.), *Perspectives on Strategic Management*. New York: HarperCollins, pp. 105–235.

—— (1992). 'Learning In (and From) Eastern Europe', *Scandinavian Journal of Management*, (8)4: 335–8.

—— (1994*a*). *The Revise and Fall of Strategic Planning*. New York: Free Press.

—— (1994*b*). 'Rounding out the Manager's Job', *Sloan Management Review*, 36(1): 11–25.

—— (2004). *Managers not MBAs*. San Francisco, CA: Berrett-Koehler.

—— Ahlstrand, B., and Lampel, J. (1998). *Strategy Safari*. New York: Free Press.

—— Brunet, J., and Waters, J. A. (1986). 'Does Planning Impede Strategic Thinking? Tracking the Strategies of Air Canada from 1937 to 1976', in R. Lamb and

P. Shrivastava (eds.), *Advances in Strategic Management*, Vol. 4. Greenwich, CT: JAI Press, pp. 3–41.

Mintzberg, H. and McHugh, A. (1985). 'Strategy Formation in an Adhocracy', *Administrative Science Quarterly*, 30: 160–97.

—— Otis, S., Shamsie, J., and Waters, J. A. (1987). 'Strategy of Design: A Study of "Architects in Co-partnership"', in J. Grant (ed.), *Strategic Management Frontiers*. Greenwich, CT: JAI Press, pp. 1–33.

—— Raisinghani, D., and Theorêt, A. (1976). 'The Structure of "Unstructured" Decision Processes', *Administrative Sciences Quarterly*, 21: 246–75.

—— and Rose, J. (2003). 'Strategic Management Upside Down: Tracking Strategies at McGill University from 1829 to 1980', *Canadian Journal of Administrative Sciences*, 20(4): 270–90.

—— Taylor, W. D., and Waters, J. A. (1984). 'Tracking Strategies in the Birthplace of Canadian Tycoons', *Canadian Journal of Administrative Sciences*, 1(1): 1–28.

—— and Waters, J. A. (1982). 'Tracking Strategy in an Entrepreneurial Firm', *Academy of Management Journal*, 25(3): 465–99.

—— —— (1984). 'Researching the Formation of Strategies: The History of Canadian Lady, 1939–1976', in R. Lamb (ed.), *Competitive Strategic Management*. Englewood Cliffs, NJ: Prentice-Hall.

—— —— (1985). 'Of Strategies, Deliberate and Emergent', *Strategic Management Journal*, 6(3): 257–72.

—— —— (1990). 'Does Decision Get in the Way', *Organization Studies*, 11(1): 1–6.

—— and Westley, F. (1992). 'Cycles of Organizational Change', *Strategic Management Journal*, 13: 39–59.

Morris, B. (1997). 'Big Blue', *Fortune*, April 14: 68–81.

Newman, W. H., Summer, C. E., and Warren, E. K. (1972). *The Process of Management: Concepts, Behavior, and Practice*, 3rd edn. Englewood Cliffs, NJ: Prentice-Hall.

Neilsen, W. A. W. and Gaffield, C. (eds.) (1986). *Universities in Crises: A Medieval Institution in the Twenty-first Century*. Montreal, Canada: The Institute for Research on Public Policy.

Noël, A. (1989). 'Strategic Cores and Magnificent Obsessions: Discovering Strategy Formation, through daily activities of CEGS', *Strategic Management Journal*, 10, SI pp. 33–49).

Ornstein, R. E. (1972). *The Psychology of Consciousness*. San Francisco, CA: Freeman.

Pascale, R. T. (1984). 'Perspectives on Strategy: The Real Story behind Honda's Success', *California Management Review*, 26(3): 47–72.

Perrow, C. (1970). *Organizational Analysis: A Sociological Review*. Belmont, CA: Wadsworth.

Peters, T. J. (1980). 'A Style for All Seasons', *Executive*, Special Issue on Leadership. Ithaca, NY: Cornell University Press, pp. 12–16, Summer.

Peters, T. and Waterman, R. H. (1982). *In Search of Excellence*. New York: HarperCollins.

Porter, M. E. (1980). *Competitive Strategy: Techniques for Analyzing Industries and Competitors*. New York: Free Press.

—— (1985). *Competitive Advantage: Creating and Sustaining Superior Performance*. New York: Free Press.

Prahalad, C. K. and Bettis, R. A. (1986). 'The Dominant Logic: A New Linkage Between Diversity and Performance', *Strategic Management Journal*, 7: 485–501.

—— and Hamel, G. (1990). 'The Core Competence of the Corporation', *Harvard Business Review*, 68(3): 79–91.

Quinn, J. B. (1980). *Strategies for Change: Logical Incrementalism*. Homewood, IL: Irwin.

Rumelt, R. P. (1974). *Strategy, Structure, and Economic Performance*. Cambridge, MA: Division of Research, Graduate School of Business Administration, Harvard University.

Sabourin, V. (1992). 'Strategic Groups and Technological Change: A Comparative Analysis of the Textile and Steel Industries', Unpublished Ph.D. dissertation, McGill University, Montreal.

Salutin, R. (1978). 'The NFB Red Scare', *Weekend Magazine* (Montreal), September 23: 17–20.

Scott, B. R. (1973). 'The Industrial State: Old Myths and New Realities', *Harvard Business Review*, 51(2): 133–48.

Selznick, P. (1957). *Leadership in Administration*. New York: Harper & Row.

Sexty, R. W. (1980). 'Autonomy Strategies of Government Owned Business Corporations in Canada', *Strategic Management Journal*, 1: 371–84.

Siggins, M. (1979). *Bassett*. Toronto, Canada: J. Lorimer.

Simon, H. (1957). *Models of Man*. New York: Wiley.

—— (1977). *New Science of Management Decision*. Englewood Cliffs, NJ: Prentice-Hall.

—— (1987). 'Making Management Decisions: The Role of Intuition and Emotion', *The Academy of Management Executive*, 1(1): 57–64

—— and Newell, A. (1972). *Human Problem Solving*. Englewood Cliffs, NJ: Prentice-Hall.

Spender, J. C. (1989). *Industry Recipes*. Oxford, UK: Basil Blackwell.

Starbuck, W. H. and Hedberg, B. L. T. (1977). 'Saving an Organization from a Stagnating Environment', in H. B. Thorelli (ed.), *Strategy and Structure Performance*. Bloomington, IN: Indiana University Press, pp. 249–58.

Statistics Canada (1979). *Office of Architects: 1977*. Ottawa, Canada: Department of Industry, Trade, and Commerce.

Steiner, G. A. (1969). *Top Management Planning*. New York: Macmillan.

—— (1979). *Strategic Planning: What Every Manager Must Know*. New York: Free Press.

Stinchcombe, A. L. (1963). 'Social Structure and Organizations', in J. G. March (ed.), *Handbook of Organizations*. Chicago, IL: Rand McNally.

Surowiecki, J. (2004). *The Wisdom of Crowds*. New York: Doubleday.

Taylor, F. W. (1947, first published in 1911). *Scientific Management*. New York: Harper & Row.

Taylor, W. D. (1983). 'Strategic Adaptation in Low Growth Environments', Ph.D. dissertation. Montreal, Canada: École des Hautes Études Commerciales.

Thompson, J. D. (1967). *Organizations in Action*. New York: McGraw-Hill.

Tilles, S. (1963). 'How to Evaluate Corporate Strategy', *Harvard Business Review,* 41: 111–21, July–August.

Toffler, A. (1970). *Future Shock*. New York: Bantam Books.

Tushman, M. and Romanelli, E. (1985). 'Organizational Evolution: A Metamorphosis Model of Convergence and Reorientation', in L. Cummings and B. Staw (eds.), *Research in Organizational Behavior*. Greenwich, CT: JAI Press.

Wallas, G. (1926). *The Art of Thought*. New York: Harcourt, Brace and World.

Weber, M. (1958). *From Max Weber: Essays in Sociology*, H. H. Gerth and C. Wright Mills (trans. and eds.). New York: Oxford University Press.

Weick, K. E. (1976). 'Educational Organizations as Loosely Coupled Systems', *Administrative Science Quarterly*, 21(1): 1–19.

—— (1979). *Social Psychology of Organizing*, rev. edn. Reading, MA: Addison-Wesley.

Wildavsky, A. (1973). 'If Planning is Everything, Maybe It's Nothing', *Policy Sciences*, 4: 127–53.

Woodward, J. (1965). *Industrial Organization: Theory and Practice*. London: Oxford University Press.

Index